Twayne's History of American Childhood Series

Series Editors
Joseph M. Hawes, Memphis State University
N. Ray Hiner, University of Kansas

From Virtue to Character

American Childhood, 1775–1850

From Virtue to Character

American Childhood, 1775–1850

Jacqueline S. Reinier

Twayne Publishers
An Imprint of Simon & Schuster Macmillan
New York
Prentice Hall International
London • New Delhi • Singapore • Sydney • Toronto

34984148
DLC

12-20-96

From Virtue to Character: American Childhood, 1775–1850
Jacqueline S. Reinier

Twayne Publishers
An Imprint of Simon & Schuster Macmillan
1633 Broadway
New York, New York 10019

Library of Congress Cataloging-in-Publication Data

Reinier, Jacqueline S.
  From virtue to character : American childhood, 1775–1850 /
Jacqueline S. Reinier.
    p.   cm. — (Twayne's history of American childhood series)
  Includes bibliographical references and index.
  ISBN 0-8057-4102-X (cloth)
  1. Children—United States—History.   2. Child rearing—United
States—History.   I. Title.   II. Series.
HQ792.U5R37 1996
305.23'0973—dc20   96-25091
                                                    CIP

The paper used in this publication meets the minimum requirements of American National Standard for Information Sciences—Permanence of Paper for Printed Library Materials. ANSI Z3948-1984. ∞™

10 9 8 7 6 5 4 3 2 1   (hc)

Printed in the United States of America

For Nettie, January 31, 1905–December 24, 1994

Contents

Introduction

As nations break from autocratic rule and democracy is championed around the world, it is useful to explore the hopes and dreams, fears and unexpected consequences of the early American republic. Populations still seek values of liberty, government by consent, and peaceful change, still struggling with the issue of how the human personality can be fitted to achieve such goals. As Anglo-Americans addressed these concerns in the eighteenth century, political developments and thought were closely linked to speculation about the family. In a general revolt against tyranny and patriarchy, philosophers, physicians, journalists, and printers championed and publicized the affectionate nuclear family, based on warmly tender, voluntary ties. Marriage founded on loving consent came to be seen as a kind of school for citizenship, and the malleable child shaped by affectionate parents and educators material for the virtuous, autonomous adult. As these ideas were folded into the ideology of the early American republic, the staggering notion that one could mold the human personality in a desired direction generated optimism that a truly new affectionate and voluntary society could emerge.

Because child-rearing concepts that culminated in middle-class domestic ideology by 1850 were rooted in this eighteenth-century Anglo-American anti-patriarchal tradition, this book begins with a discussion of various authors and their views. Literature of advice on correct behavior can be traced to Italian Renaissance manuals such as Baldassare Castiglione's *Book of the Courtier,* delineating a courtly ideal that was emulated by members of English royal and aristocratic circles by the early seventeenth century. Although historian Richard L. Bushman emphasizes the courtly antecedents of this tradition, which he has labeled "gentility,"[1] these behavioral ideals were interpreted to the urban bourgeoisie and gentry by Whigs supportive of England's Glorious Revolution, which sought to limit monarchical and patriarchal rule. Familial ideals that resonated in the American colonies were those articulated by John Locke in his influential manual, *Some Thoughts Concerning Education,* and elaborated on by Joseph Addison in his widely admired *The Spectator* papers. As Lockean advice was mitigated by treatises of the Scottish Enlightenment and popularized in children's books, sentimental novels, and medical manuals, it generated a cluster of thought that I prefer to label "enlightened child-rearing."

These ideas resonated in eighteenth-century America because social change that challenged patriarchy—rule of the family by the father and the body politic by the monarch—was already under way. As American revolutionaries repudiated monarchical rule, the anti-patriarchal tradition was incorporated into republicanism—another Renaissance tradition of "civic humanism," which sought stability for a fledgling republic in the virtue of citizens, capable of exercising sovereignty and enduring vicissitudes of fortune through moral restraint.[2] In post-Revolutionary decades, as printers, physicians, clergymen, and educators sought to shape colonial regional cultures into a national polity, they turned to enlightened child-rearing to implement republican goals. If virtue was essential for citizenship, they argued, then enlightened methods and materials could be utilized to mold children they perceived as malleable into future citizens and citizens' wives.

Yet republicanism was not the only cultural theme competing for dominance in post-Revolutionary America. Ferment and war unleashed forces of turbulent and chaotic democracy, raising the aspirations of ordinary people. Surges of religious populism instigated by evangelical preachers empowered the young and lowly to challenge established clerical authority and seek salvation for themselves.[3] Passions for buying and selling evident before the Revolution increased greatly, accelerating the demand for local and imported consumer items that would fuel the development of capitalism. Optimistic parents welcomed large numbers of children, and the high birthrate created a nation in which about half the population was under age 16. Post-Revolutionary republicans who sought to channel this dynamic, democratizing, young society feared for social cohesion. How could affectionate union be achieved and stability ensured when allegiance to a common monarch was repudiated and external restraints removed?

Americans had long experience with the voluntary principle; since the seventeenth-century Dissenting congregations, distant from ecclesiastical authority, had gathered not only to worship but also to conduct their own affairs. Grounding authority in the Bible and gathering in voluntary association, already they had learned to impose a fragile social order on their rapidly changing world. When clergymen imbued with Revolutionary zeal mobilized Americans for war through denominational networks and vocabularies, previous religious experience seemed to exemplify republican principles. As they joined forces to separate church and state, rationalists as well as revivalists viewed religion as the proper source of social harmony and public virtue.[4] Thus, in the 1780s and 1790s when patriots sought to stabilize the new republic, they adapted European thought to this American experience, blending enlightened child-rearing with Protestant belief. Seeking to create an affectionate union, they allocated to wives and mothers of the anti-patriarchal family the task of molding minds, morals, and manners in a republican society.

As the nineteenth century progressed, capitalism transformed the Northeast, families migrated west, and plantation slavery spread throughout the South. Concepts of child-rearing rooted in Anglo-American antecedents continued to evolve. In the formative 1820s Americans struggling to define a national identity began to produce their own child-rearing materials. Retaining a fervent faith in the malleable child, they reworked post-Revolutionary adaptations of enlightened child-rearing to suit a transforming economy and expanding nation. Still seeking to impose voluntary order on the aspiring individuals of a dynamic and democratizing society, a new generation shifted the focus on republican virtue—the necessity for citizens to submit private interest to the public good—to the industrious activity tempered by disciplined self-restraint appropriate for an economy of developing capitalism—what the nineteenth century called "character." Physicians adapting European enlightened medical advice advocated rearing children with new, indirect controls. Managers of the American Sunday School Union blended evangelical emphasis on individual conversion with enlightened child-rearing methods, seeking to instill internalized restraint across the nation. Softening evangelical themes with older behavioral ideals, authors democratized gentility, defining respectability for the new middle class. Character formation became the task of institutions, as children attended new public schools. In burgeoning urban centers philanthropic individuals sought to reform character in children they considered neglected by their parents. By 1850, national faith in forming character so permeated the middle class that some advocated the removal of malleable children from the family by the state for their own and the public good.

Ironically, adult efforts to form and to control yielded unexpected consequences as they touched the lives of real children. Although enlightened medical advice probably produced improved methods of physical management for upper- and middle-class children, it also accomplished an "American Revolution" in medicine that advocated treating children's diseases with dangerous and frequently fatal depleting measures. As focus on the individual child increased, mortality rates did not decline, devastating parents who had abandoned the older comforts of stoic or religious resignation. Improved economic conditions for some children proved costly to others. As capitalism created a new middle class, material comfort and education reached larger numbers of children in the Northeast and later in the Northwest. Yet, to meet increased consumer demand, rural and poor urban children were drawn into outwork performed at home or repetitive labor in large manufacturing units. As slavery spread through the South and a professional slave trade developed, enslaved children were viewed as a commodity, providing needed income to pay for education and provide an inheritance for privileged white children. Although national evangelical culture and concepts of character reached the South, most Southerners repudiated Northern commercial values. As late as 1850, lessons Southerners taught their children reiterated eighteenth-century child-rearing concepts, extolling men and women of the Revolution for love of country and heroic bravery.

Child-rearing patterns, reflecting adult attitudes and behavior, deeply reveal the values of a culture. Amid fast-moving events of the early republic, adults from various regions hoped through children to implement their differing visions of a new American society. Yet, actual change in child-rearing patterns occurs only very slowly, as each adult retains memories of his or her own childhood on various levels of consciousness. Continuities with old countries and old ways persist, as each individual recalls how he or she was raised, perhaps in a more stable, orderly world. Experience with my own two children has convinced me that adults do not control development of children; they hope and try, yet what the child becomes reflects who that child is and what that child hopes for and wants to be. I have searched, then, sometimes in vain, for historical sources that reveal the perceptions and experiences of early American children themselves from birth through age 15. Sometimes the only record left by a child who died young is a surprising scrawl across a parent's letter. Some children recorded in journals and copybooks their valiant efforts to perform as adults expected; others were profoundly preoccupied with their own pursuits. But in the letters and diaries that still exist, their voices resonate through time with honest and startling clarity.

Acknowledgments

The author who compiles a book-length manuscript accumulates many debts. Years ago, when I began studying childhood in the early republic for my doctoral dissertation at the University of California, Berkeley, I was fortunate to receive the advice and support of Professors Winthrop D. Jordan and Henry F. May. As I conducted that early research in Philadelphia, I received special help from Librarian Caroline Morris at the Pennsylvania Hospital. Howell J. Heaney and Robert D. Newkirk in the Rare Books Room at Philadelphia's Free Library alerted me to penciled annotations by the Committee of Publications in some of the books published by the American Sunday School Union. This research was financed by a pre-doctoral fellowship from the National Institute of Mental Health, later supplemented by a summer stipend from the National Endowment for the Humanities.

Almost twenty years later I was encouraged to expand that early research by the very able field editors of the Twayne American Childhood Series, Joseph M. Hawes of Memphis State University, and N. Ray Hiner of the University of Kansas. Their comments on the manuscript as it has evolved, as well as those of Gail Murray of Rhodes College in Memphis, have been very helpful. At this stage of the project I also benefited from stimulating discussions of the San Francisco Bay Area Seminar on Early American History and Culture. Members of that seminar—Dee Andrews, Steven Deyle, and Michael Mullin—read and commented on various chapters. Glenna Matthews generously read the entire manuscript. As the manuscript evolved into a book, I have appreciated the help of Ann Davidson, editor at Twayne, and Andrew Libby, the generous and meticulous production editor.

As I was completing this manuscript, I was saddened by the death of my mother, Nettie Steadry Reusser, on Christmas Eve, 1994. Much of her life was consumed by thoughtful and selfless child-rearing, and it seemed appropriate to dedicate the book to her. Yet it also should be dedicated to my own children and their spouses—Jill Reinier and Michael Bael, and Jason Reinier and Catherine Girardeau—and to Sam Meblin who shares with me the pleasures and frustrations of everyday life. My appreciation for and understanding of early childhood recently has been enriched by the joyful birth of my first grandchild, Nataniel Joseph Bael, on February 17, 1996.

Berkeley, California, 1996.

1

Enlightened Child-Rearing

The Anti-patriarchal Family and the Malleable Child

> To inform the Mind, and govern the Actions of their yet ignorant Nonage, till Reason shall take its place, and ease them of that Trouble. . .
>
> —John Locke, 1690

Throughout the eighteenth century, Anglo-American attitudes toward the family and the child underwent gradual change. Historian Lawrence Stone has labeled this change the rise of "affective individualism," referring to withdrawal of the nuclear family from kin and community, increasingly affectionate domestic relationships, companionate and perhaps more sensual marriage, and a new appreciation of childhood as a distinct stage of life.[1] Challenge to rule of the family by the father, the development of warmly tender domestic ties, and even some "coddling" of young children by their parents, were evident in the American colonies by the 1760s. These tendencies in familial patterns can be linked to demographic change, shift in landholding and inheritance patterns, the growth of a commercial economy, and American religious practices, as we shall see in the following chapter. Nevertheless, part of a wider Anglo-American cultural shift, these patterns also were influenced by the British literary materials that inundated the colonies as the eighteenth century progressed.

Richard L. Bushman has traced colonial receptivity after 1690 to what he calls "gentility," reflected in a refinement of architectural style and material culture and an increasing civility of manners. These behavioral ideals can be traced to the Italian Renaissance and manuals such as Baldassare Castiglione's *Book of the Courtier,* delineating personal and social behavior that was emulated in England by the 1620s at the court of Charles I. As these personal and social ideals influenced the English aristocracy, they were diffused to the gentry and urban bourgeoisie as well as to colonial ruling elites. England's commercial prosperity expanded colonial markets in the eighteenth century, and demand for consumer items that indicated social merit spread to the American "middling ranks"—farmers and artisans—with ties to urban centers.[2] Although Bushman stresses the courtly antecedents of genteel behavioral ideals, it is important to point out that these ideals were interpreted in materials American colonials read by British Whigs who supported England's Glorious Revolution of 1688, which sought to limit absolute monarchy and patriarchal power.

For Anglo-Americans, changing views of the family were one component of a more general revolt against tyranny and patriarchy and were closely linked to political developments and thought.[3] During the debates that accompanied the American Revolution, all points of view would be voiced in terms of the family analogy, as loyalists lambasted disobedient children and patriots identified the affectionate anti-patriarchal family with their rejection of monarchy and commitment to republican government. Anti-patriarchal views and the emphasis of Enlightenment thought on the malleable child— the belief that the human personality could be molded by environmental influences—would be folded into concepts of republicanism, which stressed the necessity of virtue, meaning moral restraint exercised by sovereign citizens able to subordinate personal interest to the public good. In post-Revolutionary decades, American printers, physicians, clergymen, and educators would draw on these ideas as they attempted to create a genuinely republican society; plasticity of the human personality would provide the hope of shaping American children into future citizens and citizens' wives.

The thinker who most influenced eighteenth-century Anglo-American attitudes toward childhood was physician and philosopher John Locke. Even before the Glorious Revolution of 1688 Locke had refuted Sir Robert Filmer's *Patriarcha,* which argued that divinely endowed royal authority was analogous to that of the patriarchal father, and just as children were born subject to paternal power, human beings were born subject to political rule. In the manuscript that would later be published as *Two Treatises of Government,* Locke attacked the patriarchal analogy by proposing that a king is not the "father" of his people but that government is founded on social contract, when, in the state of nature, men consent to form a government to protect their property and provide justice in disputes. Consequently, when a leader usurps the authority given him, the people have the right and even duty to rebel, dissolving that tyrannical government and forming a new one.[4]

As Locke challenged Filmer's analogy between government and the patriarchal family, he also contributed to a new model of family relationships. Power over children is not paternal but parental, he argued in *Two Treatises of Government*; the power from begetting children is shared by the father with the mother. A husband's power over his wife is conjugal and not political; it extends only to family matters, not to those pertaining to the wife alone. Wives are subject to their husbands only because of custom and contract, not because of divine or natural law. The power of parents over children is only to preserve them and to provide for them, "To inform the Mind, and govern the Actions of their yet ignorant Nonage, till Reason shall take its place, and ease them of that Trouble . . ." Children should be subject to parents only until their rational capacity develops, when they become able to govern themselves through the natural law of their divinely endowed reason.[5]

By 1690, after the successful Glorious Revolution, Locke was able to publish not only his *Two Treatises of Government* but also his *Essay Concerning Human Understanding*. In addition, he worked up the letters he had exchanged with his cousin Mary Clarke and her husband Edward concerning the rearing of their eldest son into a book that provided child-rearing methods appropriate to the anti-patriarchal family and political system based on consent—*Some Thoughts Concerning Education,* published in 1693.[6] The child-rearing goal that Locke sought in his manual of advice was the development of the rational, autonomous adult. He had argued in his *Essay* that the mind receives knowledge through sense impressions, which are ordered by the innate organizing power of reason. Human rationality, however, is frail and easily waylaid by demands of the body—appetite, passion, or disease. The task of the parent is to build in the child the strong body and habits of mind that allow the fragile capacity for reason to develop.

To build the strong constitution, Locke urged parents to avoid indulging their children and to inure them to physical hardships, advising "gentlemen to use their children as the honest farmers and substantial yeomen do theirs." Loose clothing, fresh air, and exercise would "harden" children of both sexes; the cold bath and deliberately leaky shoes would teach them not to rely on bodily comfort. Although hours of sleep and habits of elimination should be regular, plain and simple meals on an irregular schedule would avoid dependence on routine. If disease occurred, the physician Locke advised that medicines should be simple and used with caution, for diet and the healing powers of nature could achieve the cure. The parent who sought to create the rational adult should prepare the child's constitution according to the following rules: "Plenty of open air, exercise and sleep; plain diet, no wine or strong drink and very little or no physic; not too warm and straight clothing; especially the head and feet kept cold, and the feet often used to cold water and exposed to wet."[7]

"As the strength of the body lies chiefly in being able to endure hardships," Locke continued, "so does that of the mind." For "the great principle and foundation of all virtue and worth, is placed in this, that a man is able to deny himself his own desires, cross his own inclinations, and purely follow what reason directs as best, though the appetite lean the other way." Not only could strong appetite deflect rational choice, but Locke believed that human beings, who naturally desire liberty, tend toward excess of that trait, dominion over others. Parents could train children in strict obedience to parental authority, even in the first year of life. If the very young child clearly wants something, the parent should make a point of denying it, repeatedly staging a little behavioral lesson until the child develops habits of denial of appetite and of curbing his wish to dominate over others. "It seems plain to me," Locke explained, "that the Principle of all Virtue and Excellency lies in a Power of denying ourselves the Satisfaction of our own Desires, where Reason does not authorize them. This power is to be got and improv'd by Custom, made easy and familiar by an early Practice."[8]

Once habitual self-denial and obedience were firmly established, parents could gradually relax their authority. Locke's desire to remove the individual from dependence upon sensual pleasure and pain led him to formulate his notion of appropriate rewards and punishments. Because he believed that the growing child would be motivated to industry through his natural love of liberty, Locke disapproved of corporeal blows and restraints. Instead, he advocated psychological manipulation of love and fear in the form of states of "esteem" and "disgrace," essentially the bestowal and withdrawal of parental approval and affection. For example, in a "state of reputation," a child "will necessarily be belov'd and cherish'd by every Body, and have all good Things as a Consequence of it," while for a child in a state of "neglect and contempt" as a result of a punishment, "the want of whatever might satisfy or delight him will follow." The child seeking parental praise and worldly reputation would be motivated to industrious activity, yet excesses of liberty would be restrained through fear of parental disapproval or shame. With this firm foundation in habitual self-restraint and motivation through desire for reputation, as the child grew into the reasonable youth, he could be granted increasing independence, while the parent assumed the important new role of "friend."[9]

As Locke interpreted and transmitted behavioral ideals in his discussion of the education of a young gentleman, he stressed the cultivation of Virtue, Wisdom, Good Breeding, and Learning, in that order of importance. Rather than instruct in classical learning through rote memorization, he argued that lessons should exercise powers of observation and reflection. As an empiricist, Locke based his precepts on observation of the individual children he knew. Rather than encouraging the child to behave like a little adult, he preferred to observe him as he was and to tailor his plan of education to the child's individual nature. A child could be taught through observation of concrete objects in the domestic environment. In order that he not be discour-

aged, learning should be pleasant; it could even be camouflaged as play. Soon
after he learned to talk, the child could be taught to read with the aid of simple playthings. When he was ready, he could be given "some easy pleasant
Book, suited to his Capacity . . . wherein the Entertainment that he finds
might draw him on, and reward his Pains in Reading, and yet not such as
should fill his Head with perfectly useless Trumpery, or lay the Principles of
Vice and Folly."[10]

Even in the late seventeenth century, friends of the bachelor philosopher
who were parents considered Locke's emphasis on hardening a child and
denial of appetite severe.[11] Nevertheless, by the time of Locke's death in
1704, his advice was beginning to be applied and popularized. His emphasis
on observing the child, developing his rational capacity, and relaxing parental
authority as he grew would create new methods and standards for the education of boys.

Although Locke emphasized good breeding and the use of plain language,
the individual who set standards of eloquence and taste emulated by Anglo-
Americans throughout the eighteenth and into the nineteenth centuries was
another political Whig, Joseph Addison. In his immensely popular *The Spectator* papers, first published in 1711, Addison not only delineated personal
and social behavioral ideals but also disseminated Lockean child-rearing
advice, which he applied to the education of girls.[12]

As a literary man and admirer of the Latin poets, Addison extolled a
Roman concept of citizenship; his tragedy, *Cato,* which would provide a
model of republican restraint for George Washington and the revolutionary
generation, was essentially an appeal for virtue in public life. Yet Addison's
talent for eloquent conversation shone most brilliantly in his private circle of
the literary and political Kit-Kat Club. In 1709 his "renowned" style began to
be recognized in his anonymous contributions to *The Tatler,* a one-page daily
paper circulated by his friend Richard Steele. Although Steele's sheet was
designed to entertain fashionable London, its ulterior motive was the reformation of bawdy Restoration manners, and Addison's contributions struck a
chord with England's rapidly emerging bourgeoisie. After *The Tatler*'s
demise, Addison began on March 1, 1711, to publish his own daily sheet, the
immensely popular and influential *The Spectator.*[13]

As the paper progressed, about one-fourth of its articles were addressed
to women, an intention Addison made clear when he announced his desire to
bring philosophy "out of Closets and Libraries, Schools and Colleges, to
dwell in Clubs and Assemblies, at Tea-Tables, and in Coffee-Houses." By the
early eighteenth century, tea equipage of Chinese, Japanese, or later Dutch
porcelain appeared in fashionable homes, and Addison hoped that topics in
his paper would be discussed at the tea table. "I shall take it for the greatest
Glory of my Work," he wrote, "if among reasonable Women this Paper may
furnish *Tea-Table Talk.* In order to it, I shall treat on Matters which relate to

Females." "I would therefore in a very particular Manner recommend these my Speculations to all well regulated Families, that set apart an Hour in every Morning for Tea and Bread and Butter," he continued, "and would earnestly advise them for their Good to order this Paper to be punctually served up, and to be looked on as a Part of the Tea Equipage."[14]

Addison admired Milton's *Paradise Lost* and endeavored to increase the poem's popularity.[15] A new model for his female readers would be Milton's portrayal of Eve, whose transgression was no longer that of the temptress but merely gullibility and whose virtues were "Innocence and Virgin Modesty." In fact, in a passage Addison quoted in his June 12, 1711, paper, it was Eve's virtue and chastity that made her irresistible to Adam:

> Yet Innocence and Virgin Modesty,
> Her virtue and the conscience of her worth,
> That would be woo'd, and not unsought be won,
> Not obvious, not obtrusive, but retir'd,
> The more desirable, or to say all,
> Nature her self, though pure of sinful thought,
> Wrought in her so, that fleeing me, she fled;
> I follow'd her, she what was Honour knew,
> And with obsequious Majesty approv'd
> My pleaded reason. To the Nuptial Bowr
> I led her blushing like the Morn_ _.[16]

Addison, then, not only viewed females as capable of reason and virtue but considered that capacity, enhanced by chastity, the very source of their attractiveness to men.

Issues of *The Spectator* addressed to women and girls warned against attention to "Ornaments of Dress" and coquettish behavior and advocated cultivation of reason, virtue, and gentle wit. A favorite story compared the sisters Laetitia and Daphne; the former was beautiful but vain and insolent, the latter, less beautiful but reasonable and good-humoured. Daphne won the suitor,[17] a turn of events that, according to later issues, became the subject of much tea-table conversation. The daily paper also popularized the new concept of the affectionate anti-patriarchal family. Repeatedly, Addison advocated companionate marriage and domestic happiness. Here the positive model was Aurelia, who, "tho' a Woman of Great Quality, delights in the Privacy of a country Life; and passes away a great deal of her Time in her Walks and Gardens. Her husband, who is her Bosom Friend, and Companion in her Solitudes, has been in Love with her ever since he knew her." This ideal domestic couple "both abound with good Sense, consummate Virtue, and a mutual Esteem; and are a perpetual Entertainment to one another. Their Family is under so regular an Oeconomy, in its Hours of Devotion and Repast, Employment and Diversion, that it looks like a little Commonwealth within itself . . ." Addison contrasted Aurelia with Fulvia, who, considering housewifery beneath a woman of quality and longing to be out in the world, "grows Contemptible by being Conspicuous."[18]

The Spectator thus contributed to idealization of domestic life and privatization of the nuclear family. Women of reasonable good humor, virtue, sense, and wit could shine at the tea table but not in the world. In this era of intense partisan zeal on the part of Whigs and Tories, Addison was adamant that women should not engage in political discourse. Of "all those little Spots and Blemishes that are apt to rise among the Charms which Nature has poured out to them," he wrote, ". . . [t]he Spot which I would here endeavour to clear them of, is that Party-Rage which of late Years is very much crept in their Conversation." "[T]here is nothing so bad for the face as Party-Zeal." Women should "distinguish themselves as tender Mothers and faithful Wives, rather than as furious Partizans," for "[f]emale Virtues are of a Domestick turn. The Family is the proper Province for Private Women to shine in."[19]

Women who excelled in private, however, were to be literate, a point made clear in *The Spectator*'s discussion of female education. "The general Mistake among us in the education of our children, is, that in our Daughters we take Care of Persons and neglect their Minds; in our Sons, we are so intent upon adorning their Minds, that we wholly neglect their Bodies." Like Locke, Addison believed that the sound body was necessary grounding for the reasonable mind, and he declared, "The true Art in this Case is, To make the Mind and Body improve together."[20]

The impact of *The Spectator* on Anglo-American culture in the eighteenth and nineteenth centuries cannot be overemphasized. Read aloud in coffeehouses and homes, the paper spread from London and Westminster to provincial towns and villages. At its demise in 1712, it had already been compiled into a collected volume and was admired throughout Europe and reprinted in the colonies. *The Spectator* popularized Lockean thought; many Anglo-Americans who did not read *Two Treatises of Government* learned "a tea-table version of the doctrine of John Locke" through the issue praising the British Constitution. "A fashion of writing had been established," and throughout the eighteenth century imitations appeared on *The Spectator* model.[21] Compilations of issues addressed to women were produced for the new female reading public. Anna Laetitia Aikin Barbauld, an author of children's literature in the 1770s and 1780s who compiled one of these volumes of selected issues for girls, commented:

> When those were young who are now old, no books were so popular, particularly with the female sex. They were the favorite volumes in a young lady's library; and probably the very first that, after the Bible, she would have thought of purchasing . . . From the papers of Addison we imbibed our first relish for wit; from his criticisms we formed our first standard of taste; and from his delineations we drew our first ideas of manners.[22]

Thinkers of the Scottish Enlightenment added to Lockean sensational psychology and effort to develop the rational capacity of the child an emphasis on affectionate familial and social ties and the democratic concept of the moral sense. In his *Inquiry Into the Original of Our Ideas of Beauty and Virtue,* published in 1725, Francis Hutcheson, a Scottish Presbyterian physician at the University of Glasgow, combined Locke's insights in the *Essay Concerning Human Understanding* with an analysis of Addisonian taste. Dissatisfied with the Lockean implication that virtuous action results from self-interest calculated by reason, Hutcheson sought to account for spontaneous responses of the human heart. In addition to the five external senses receiving the impressions through which simple ideas are formed—sight, hearing, touch, taste, and smell—he postulated two internal senses or perceptions: a sense of beauty and a sense of virtue, or the moral sense.[23]

Before Hutcheson tackled the moral sense, he painstakingly described the sense of beauty. Human beings receive pleasure, he argued, by recognizing uniformity amidst variety, whether in mathematics, architecture, poetry, gardens that imitate nature, or the relation of parts to the whole in a well designed mechanism. Even very little children, he had observed, can be seen admiring "regular figures in little diversions" in arrangements of pebbles. This spontaneous reaction, which is only blunted or made complex by reason and education, he argued, has been placed in mankind by the benevolent Deity, for what human beings perceive as beautiful is the harmony of the great machine of the Newtonian universe itself.[24]

Similar to the internal sense of beauty, Hutcheson continued, is the pleasure individuals receive from witnessing acts of disinterested benevolence. This pleasure from virtue could not arise from self-interest because human beings experience it even when advantage to themselves is not at stake. Antecedent to custom or education, this highest impulse of humankind can be observed most purely in the uneducated: in children, women, and the lower classes. The democratic implications in Hutcheson's thought become clear in his moral calculus, through which he worked out formulas to determine the amount of virtue or benevolence in a particular action. Because M (the moment of good) = B (the benevolence of the act) × A (the ability of the actor), a small action by a person of small ability is as virtuous as a great action by a person of great ability. Thus, Hutcheson allows a democratic hero or heroine; not only the statesman, general, or prince, but any human being, is capable of heroism or virtue. Because the moral sense is universal, citizens of all nations of the world possess it; immoral behavior by societies can be attributed to errors in reason, not to inferior moral capacity. It is this internal sense of virtue that leads human beings to perform disinterested acts of benevolence to promote the public good, and, according to the moral calculus, true virtue is that which brings the greatest good to the greatest number, contributing through good to a part to the good of the whole.[25]

Hutcheson's notion of the moral sense mitigated Lockean sensational psychology with important implications for rearing children. Because the moral sense is universal and antecedent, its operation can be observed in children "upon hearing the Storys with which they are commonly entertain'd as soon as they understand Language." Children "always passionately interest themselves on that side which *Kindness* and *Humanity* are found," he observed,

> and detest the *Cruel,* the *Covetous,* the *Selfish* or the *Treacherous.* How strongly do we see their Passions of *Joy, Sorrow, Love* and *Indignation* mov'd by these *moral Representations,* even tho there has been no pains taken to give them Ideas of a *Deity,* of Laws, of a future State, or of the more intricate Tendency of the *universal Good* to that of each *Individual*!

Consequently, Hutcheson rejected disciplining children through Lockean states of esteem and disgrace. Seeking reputation or avoiding shame, he argued, flows from self-interest and should not be used to motivate children to virtuous behavior. Children are naturally compassionate and will respond to the plight of others because of the pleasure they feel in doing so. A parent needs only to strengthen the moral sense with "*Cultivation.*" If a child is overcome by interest or self-love, such obstacles should be removed, and the moral sense will reassert itself. "NATURE itself," he insisted, "will incline us to Benevolence."[26]

In the 1740s these enlightened Lockean and Scottish views on child-rearing and the anti-patriarchal family were popularized by physicians and printers. Eighteenth-century British physicians, who considered themselves *medicin philosophes,* elaborated on Locke's emphasis on the strong constitution as the foundation of the rational mind. Concerned about high rates of infant and child mortality, they sought to instruct a wider audience on proper physical management of children. Dr. William Cadogan published his *Essay upon Nursing and Management of Children* in London in 1747. Convinced that mortality could be reduced through "reasonable and more natural" methods of child management, he sought to eliminate the "mystery and magic" of care by female nurses, by placing infants and young children under the care of enlightened male professionals. "In my opinion," he wrote,

> this business has been too long fatally left to the Management of Women, who cannot be supposed to have proper Knowledge to fit them for such a Task, notwithstanding they look upon it to be their own province. What I mean is a Philosophical Knowledge of nature, to be acquir'd only by learned Observation and Experience, and which therefore the Unlearned must be uncapable of.[27]

Cadogan's suggestions were plain and simple. Infants are hardy and strong by nature, he insisted; it is indulgence by adults that makes them weak. "Children in general are overcloath'd and over-fed and fed and cloath'd improperly. To this cause I impute almost all their Diseases." Dress for the infant should be cool and loose; a little flannel waistcoat without sleeves, an attached petticoat, a light and flimsy gown, and only one cap was surely an adequate costume. The physician objected to the "Swaddling-cloaths, Swathes, Bandages, Stays, and Contrivances" traditionally used in Europe. The infant body can support itself, he claimed; bandages and stays are not needed to mold and form it but probably contribute to the physical deformity apparent throughout English society.[28]

Proper feeding of infants was considered even more essential than proper clothing to the reduction of mortality. Cadogan insisted that every mother nurse her own child unless her "Fountains" were "greatly disturbed or tainted" or she suffered from hysterical complaints. Nothing was to be fed to the infant prior to the coming in of the mother's milk. "The general Practice of cramming a Dab of Butter or Sugar down its throat, a little Oil, Panada, Caudle, or some such unwholesome Mess" he considered definitely harmful. Mother's milk would be enough food for the first three months. After that, more substantial meals of good light bread soaked in warm water or cow's milk, or light broths with bread or rice, could be given to the child two or three times a day. At six months the meals could become more substantial and at 12 months the child could gradually be weaned. If the mother absolutely could not nurse, her substitute should be a clean, healthy country wet nurse, between 20 and 30 years of age, only two or three months beyond her own lying-in and able to support two infants with her milk.

Cadogan went on to recommend a simple, natural regimen for children up to three years of age. Diet should remain plain and simple: light bread with butter, any kind of mellow fruit, roots of all sorts, produce from the kitchen garden, and a little flesh meat when teeth appeared. Teething he considered neither a fatal nor even a dangerous stage of development. Disorders for children between the ages of one and three were more likely due to "acid corruption of their food" and could be corrected by diet and a mild purge. Young children were to be encouraged to use their limbs freely, to stand and to walk when they seemed so inclined, and to use both hands with equal skill. Clear speech was to be encouraged by "speaking plain distinct Words" to them "instead of the Namby Pamby Stile." "I think," declared the enlightened physician, "they cannot be made reasonable Creatures too soon."[29]

While Cadogan's advice was essentially Lockean, Dr. William Buchan's *Domestic Medicine,* first published in Edinburgh in 1769, reflected the views of the Scottish Enlightenment. Dr. Buchan was also outraged by what he considered the unnecessary mortality of children, "that almost one-half of the human species perish in infancy by improper management or neglect." Through his experience in Foundling Hospitals, he, too, was convinced that infant death was not a natural evil and could be avoided. "Whenever I had it in my power to place the children under the care of proper nurses, to instruct these nurses in their duty, and to be satisfied that they perform it, very few of them died," he wrote, but when "the children were left to the sole care of mercenary nurses, without any person to instruct or superintend them, scarce any of them lived."[30] Dr. Buchan hoped to combat infant and child mortality through the instruction of gentlemen. Yet he believed that mothers could and should be educated to rear their children properly. Because he attributed the evils of traditional child care to the advice of hired nurses, Buchan assigned to enlightened mothers the tasks of surveillance of daily regimen and protection of the child from abuses by lower-class servants.

Buchan's recommendations for child care were similar to Cadogan's "reasonable and natural" regimen. Mothers were admonished to nurse their newborns. After the third or fourth month, a light diet of solid foods could be introduced gradually. The child was to be dressed in loose clothing, and all artificial stays and contrivances to support the body were to be avoided. Buchan believed that disease could be prevented through a regimen that emphasized cleanliness, fresh air, and exercise. Young children were to be carried about and allowed to use their limbs freely. Talking to them and pointing out objects would encourage mental alertness. Both boys and girls were to run about in the open air. Following Locke's advice, Buchan advocated "hardening" a child; to promote circulation he recommended the cold bath and washing the child's hands and feet daily in cold water.[31]

When disease occurred, Buchan, like Locke, advised parents to confine treatment of the child to diet and regimen, relying on the healing powers of nature to achieve the cure. He warned, "I think the administration of medicines always doubtful and often dangerous and would much rather teach men how to avoid the necessity of using them, than how they should be used." Because he believed that most infant disorders were the result of improper feeding, he recommended treatment with gentle evacuations—vomits or purges. A cooling regimen—cleanliness, light diet, and loose clothing—would not only comfort the infant but would also reduce the heat of bodily fluids that contributed to the state of disease. Dr. Buchan did view teething as a dangerous stage, recommending that a "drain" be kept open on the body throughout the teething period—perhaps a leech behind each ear or a small "pitch plaster" between the shoulders. Yet he did not recommend bloodletting in the treatment of children's diseases. Bleeding "in young children ought always to be sparingly performed," he warned; "it is an evacuation which they bear the worst of any." "There is now hardly one fever," he insisted, "where the lancet is necessary."[32]

While the advice of Locke the physician was popularized and expanded by medical men, printers elaborated on his educational plan. Sons of farmers and artisans, these entrepreneurial printers sought to supply material for the developing market created by the growth of literacy in the eighteenth century. Earlier readers had owned only a small number of books, such as the

Bible and religious commentary, which were read over and over as guides to life. By the mid-eighteenth century, however, literate individuals began to seek in books and periodicals information and entertainment, exhibiting a "craving for novelty" and developing the habit of more "extensive" and "general" reading. Subscription lists reveal that many new readers were of the professional and merchant middle class, often wives and daughters who had some leisure and could spend time reading. Yet in provincial and colonial cities artisans and workingmen also visited circulating libraries, and even those unable to pay for books could develop new habits and a new taste for reading popular works.[33]

The printer who created a new genre of children's literature was John Newbery, a farmer's son who moved to London and, under his sign of the Bible and the Sun in St. Paul's Churchyard, produced his first *Little Pretty Pocket-book* in 1744.[34] In the two prefaces to this first of his children's books, Newbery revealed the sources from which he drew. His preface for children consisted of two letters to Little Master Tommy and Pretty Miss Polly from Jack the Giant-Killer, a folk hero familiar to any child or adult who had learned traditional English legends, ballads, and tales from popular eighteenth-century chapbooks. And the preface addressed "to the Parents, Guardians, and Nurses in Great Britain and Ireland" essentially paraphrased John Locke's child-rearing advice in *Some Thoughts Concerning Education*.[35]

The Newbery books were designed to please children with their small size and bright wallpaper covers. They viewed childhood as a distinct stage of life and made learning pleasant, using "pretty" language and camouflaging instruction with play—balls and pincushions, games, riddles, and jests. To protect the waxlike mind of the unformed child, Newbery relied on censorship. Traditional folk figures like Jack the Giant-Killer or Tom Thumb appeared not in the context of the original tales but to introduce stories of moral instruction in which good children were rewarded with esteem and disobedient children punished with disgrace. Newbery's books were permeated by entrepreneurial values; children who engaged in diligent and dutiful behavior earned social status and material success. The poor but good boy would become a great man "with horses and coaches a-plenty," possessing a large fortune and perhaps a political office. The poor but good girl would be esteemed in her neighborhood for her benevolence; eventually she would marry a "kind, indulgent, and affectionate husband" who was sure to be elected Lord Mayor. Both of them could count on riding in a coach and six. Naughty children, who were more obstinate than truly wicked, would not rise in the world and would miss the chance to ride in a fine coach.[36]

The London printer advocated the benefits of trade and promoted his own products within the texts of his stories. For example, Goody Two Shoes' father dies because he is not treated with Dr. James' Fever Powder, which just happened to be sold at the sign of the Bible and the Sun. Good children like little Peter Pippin would beg their parents to reward them with presents of the little books sold by their "good friend in St. Paul's Churchyard." In the story of Mrs. Williams and her plum cake, the middle-class woman gives a rather pointed lesson to a gentleman's son on the worth of honest trade. Cutting a savory plum cake in wedges, she points out that all its good ingredients—sugar, spice, even the plums—came from trade. Then she tells the young aristocrat, "A Man of Fortune, my dear, does harm, for he who lives an idle life, Lives like the Drone in the Bee-Hive by the Labour of others." At this point the hungry little gentleman has no choice but to cry, "Trade and Plum Cake forever, Huzza."[37]

While Newbery popularized Lockean child-rearing advice, Samuel Richardson, also a printer, described for Anglo-Americans norms and values of the affectionate anti-patriarchal family. Although he was an established London printer in the 1720s and 1730s, it was not until the 1740s that Richardson began to produce the sequences of fictional letters that became the first sentimental novels. Expansion of literacy, especially among women and girls, created a demand for model letters to educate unskilled writers. Richardson responded in 1740 with a sequence of letters from a servant to her father, asking the parent's advice on how to respond to the seductive advances of her master's son, published as *Pamela, or Virtue Rewarded*. Pamela, who eventually reforms and marries her unsuccessful seducer, is the new democratic heroine. According to Francis Hutcheson's moral calculus, her virtue is great, even though she is middle-class and female, because it is proportionate to her ability and issues from her moral sense. Not unlike Milton's Eve, her virtue and protected chastity make her immensely attractive, and Richardson's "novel" became an immediate success not only in Britain, but also on the Continent and in the colonies.

The success of *Pamela* spurred Richardson to a much larger and more conscious effort: the seven volumes he began to publish in 1747 as *Clarissa, Or the History of a Young Lady*.[38] The story of virtuous Clarissa, also told through letters, explores tension between old and new family patterns. Richardson's view of child-rearing was essentially Lockean; the Harlowe family, both father and eldest son significantly named James (the name of the English king dethroned by the Glorious Revolution), err through adherence to patriarchy in refusing to allow Clarissa liberty in marriage choice. A rising family, the Harlowes are concerned with augmenting their fortune, and Clarissa has upset the patriarchal transfer of land by inheriting an estate directly from her grandfather. She is also literate, a young woman of sense, wit, and Addisonian taste, which arouses suspicion and some resentment among her male relatives. Possessing Hutchesonian moral sense, she trusts her own responses of approval or aversion and refuses to marry a man she cannot love. When her father and elder brother press their selection, Clarissa's more sympathetic mother is unable to help her: she has lost her power by submitting too often to her arbitrary husband simply to keep family peace.

The outcome of tyrannical patriarchy, the sacrifice of Clarissa's liberty and happiness to the avarice of her family, is tragic. She is forced to flee with her complicated aristocratic suitor, Lovelace, of whom she does not approve because of his licentious reputation. For his part, while Lovelace's sexual desire is inflamed by Clarissa's chastity and virtue, he also loves the intrigue of her escape in an increasingly mercantile society that allows little outlet for his aristocratic values and skills. He will not, however, be reformed by the heroine's virtue; after placing her in a brothel, Lovelace drugs and rapes Clarissa. When, bereft of the opportunity for an affectionate marriage, she accepts the inevitability of her death, Lovelace also dies, finally recognizing that his mortal wound in a duel is just punishment.[39] The Harlowes have made a serious mistake. By mid-eighteenth century, the novel proclaims, fathers and elder brothers who press the claims of patriarchy are wrong; sons and even daughters who reach the age of reason should be granted liberty. Marriage, the grounding of the commonwealth of the affectionate family, can be founded only on consent.

The last of these European manuals of child-rearing advice that would influence post-Revolutionary Americans was Jean-Jacques Rousseau's *Emile,* first published in 1762. Working from a French context, Rousseau expanded enlightened themes of the affectionate family and malleable child, relating them even more specifically to preparation for citizenship. Believing that "[e]verything is good as it leaves the hands of the Author of things" and "degenerates in the hands of man," Rousseau sought to rear the "natural" child who would become the compassionate adult, affectionate husband and father, and responsible citizen. His plan for infancy and early childhood was similar to the "reasonable and natural" regimen advocated by enlightened physicians.[40] Like Dr. Buchan, he emphasized the role of the mother, who played a crucial role as first caretaker of the innocent unformed child. Ideally, the mother would be aided and supervised by the father, although for Rousseau's pupil, Emile, this role would be played by a tutor.

To rear the natural child, Rousseau advocated maternal nursing, loose clothing, fresh air, cleanliness, and physical liberty. Like Locke, he suggested "hardening" the child with the cold bath, even accustoming him to unpleasant masks and the firing of guns that he not be fearful later in life. But he did not recommend Lockean early discipline or denial of the child's legitimate desires. Children cry because of need, he argued, and needs should be met promptly. Tears that become orders can be discouraged simply by not paying attention to them. Although he did not believe in the moral sense, Rousseau argued that children do possess an innate sense of justice. Thus, they should not be resisted by another will but only by things, because the natural, democratic man accepts limits not from other people, but only from necessity.[41]

Rousseau believed that the growing child should be allowed to run about freely, engaged in self-motivated industrious activity. Because it can always be cut short by death, childhood should be recognized as a distinct and innocent stage of life and should be fully experienced and enjoyed. Emile is not restrained but allowed full exploration of his environment. Yet, to ensure that the child is limited only by things, this environment is strictly controlled and even manipulated by the tutor. For example, to teach Emile the concept of property, Rousseau returned to the Lockean theory that one owns that for which one has mixed his labor with fruits of the earth. Emile and his tutor plant beans and "with transports of joy" "see them sprout." But one day the child, who has learned to love his beans, comes to the garden to find them gone, surreptitiously pulled out by the tutor. Emile is devastated, pained by injustice, and the gardener is summoned. The indignant gardener complains that he had planted melons for the child to enjoy, which Emile destroyed by planting his beans. The child's grief is distracted by distress at not eating the melons, and he is able to make a contract with the gardener. For a corner of the garden to cultivate beans, he promises not to disturb the gardener's work and to share with him half of his produce. Emile has learned the concept of property and made his first social contract, but by manipulating the lesson, the tutor has deceived the innocent child and caused him emotional distress.[42]

In his pleasant but controlled environment Emile is not bothered with things he does not need to know, like conventional lessons. In fact, he learns to read only because he wishes to know the contents of pleasant invitations that the manipulative tutor has arranged to be sent but Emile has missed because he cannot read. But the child engages in almost continuous physical exercise to build a strong constitution, and he learns to sharpen his senses, the foundation of his knowledge, by solving problems and using tools. During this stage his only book is *Robinson Crusoe,* as Emile, too, figures out how he would provide for his physical needs on an isolated island. When he is 12, however, Emile's isolation ends and he begins to learn about social exchange and money by learning a trade. As an apprentice to the village carpenter a few days a week, he can learn work ("an indispensable duty for a social man") and experience the learning by doing, harmony of body and mind, and sense of accomplishment that characterized the educational experience of the eighteenth-century artisan.[43]

At 15 Emile enters puberty and, in addition to experiencing the *amour de soi* or self-preservation he felt as a child, begins to experience *amour propre,* through which he compares himself to others as he seeks to become lovable. At this point, the teenager, who possesses conscience or an instinctive love of good, still needs to learn compassion. If he enters the world of those richer or more fortunate than he, his budding *amour propre* will only be excited to envy. But if he witnesses the plight of the miserable, he will feel not only pity but satisfaction that he does not share their plight. Thus, Emile is shown selected scenes of human misery, learning a common democratic humanity through suffering. Compassion, although learned through self-love rather than a moral sense, is Rousseau's version of Hutchesonian disinterested benevolence, through which the youth, who has previously sought only to meet his own needs, begins to become a social creature.

Also at this age, Emile's new feelings make him capable of friendship, and he begins to feel gratitude toward his tutor, whom he now views as his friend. This new friendship, however, does not bring a Lockean relaxation of authority, for Emile's environment continues to be controlled and manipulated by the tutor. He can now study history—Thucydides and Plutarch—for as he reads about the great of the past and his *amour propre* invites comparison with himself, he will feel not envy but only pity for the historical torments and self-delusion of his fellow men. And he can be given LaFontaine's *Fables*, to learn from someone else's troubles lessons too dangerous for him to experience himself. By coming to know the passions without experiencing them, Emile is gradually being prepared to live in the world.[44]

As Emile matures, Rousseau begins to address a basic issue for democratic society: if Robert Filmer in *Patriarcha* is incorrect and human beings are not born subject to political rule, what will induce them to participate in civil society? For Rousseau, the sex drive is dangerous for men, but if correctly manipulated, this strongest of passions can motivate them to seek appropriate mates and form families that will be the basis of the state. Therefore, as Emile approaches the age of 20, the tutor begins the delicate task of forming him into a moral being and future citizen. The youth is allowed to choose his own religion, but the tutor explains that only natural religion, understood through sense impressions and human reason, is appropriate to his previous education. The tutor also tells his pupil the story of his education, and in a burst of gratitude for his tutor's devotion, Emile promises to place himself voluntarily under his preceptor's guidance and discipline. This is the moment to tell the young man about women, and with his tutor's guidance Emile forms an imaginary vision of his beautiful and virtuous idealized mate, "Sophie." It is safe now for Emile to enter polite society in search of Sophie; other women, who cannot match his vision, will not be snares for him. And, as the ardent lover, he is ready to learn the arts—literature, theater, and poetry—and to cultivate Addisonian taste.[45]

Although the Sophie Emile finds has not been raised to be his wife, she has already been selected by the tutor as a young woman of virtue and appropriate education. Rousseau believed that women are not and should not be equal to men, but he did view marriage as a reciprocal relationship, emphasizing the harmony of parts in the Newtonian whole. Sophie's function is to bear and help rear children. But she must also be virtuous, because her chastity and fidelity, as well as her beauty and character, will inflame Emile's imagination, idealizing his sexual desire into love. This sentiment (and the certainty of fatherhood) will keep him at her side through their children's long childhood, creating the affectionate commonwealth of the family, the essential foundation of the state.

Sophie, then, has been educated differently from Emile to fulfill her particular role. Although Emile has not been raised to be concerned with reputation, Sophie has, because female virtue rests on the good opinion of others. Although Emile has not been restrained as a child, Sophie has, for women, who will live lives of constraint, need to learn early to submit not only to necessity but also to the wills of others. While Emile chooses his religion through reason, Sophie accepts hers on authority. Sophie has also been taught to develop her charms, because her future depends on her ability to please men.

Nevertheless, Sophie, too, is a natural child, allowed physical liberty; loose, comfortable clothing; and participation in public dances and ceremonial occasions. Raised by her mother, her closest friend, she has been trained in cleanliness and housewifery. She has been taught needlework and accomplishments—drawing, singing, playing the harpsichord—some reading and writing, a little arithmetic, and Addisonian taste. Rousseau granted females reason and conscience but thought both should be trained for the practical duties of wife and mother. As he put it, "Sophie has a mind that is agreeable without being brilliant, and solid without being profound." Yet, although she will obey her husband, she will not be passive in marriage. Through her previous chastity, her charm, and her modesty—her ability to retain power over the granting of her person and her favors—she will be able to influence and sometimes even govern her husband.[46]

Sophie is allowed to choose her spouse ("since loving or not loving is not within our control") with only a veto power reserved by her parents. But neither Sophie nor Emile really chooses, because their meeting has been carefully arranged by the governing adults. For three months Emile visits his beloved, and the young couple experiences supervised transports of romantic bliss. But again the tutor designs a lesson; one morning he awakens Emile's receptivity to instruction by announcing that Sophie is dead. The moment has come to teach the young man virtue—the ability to rule passion and master himself—in order that upon his eventual marriage he can become a citizen. While Locke had taught the very young child denial of appetite and obedience to parental authority through little lessons, Rousseau saved that instruction for the young adult, who will learn to conquer passion only after it has been aroused.

Sophie, of course, is not dead, but Emile must leave her temporarily in order to travel and study government. Only by conquering himself—by learning to detach himself from his passions—can the natural man learn to submit to the moral necessity of law, and as a citizen, sacrifice his self-interest to the public good. Sophie will spend the two-year separation reading Joseph Addison's *The Spectator* to learn "the duties of decent women" necessary for a citizen's wife. When Emile returns from his travels to take up the life of husband, father, farmer, and citizen, Emile and Sophie are joyously reunited, and at their wedding receive one last piece of advice from the ubiquitous tutor. Now that their idealized love has entered reality, only by respecting the other's desires and individuality can they keep that love alive and maintain the companionate marriage and affectionate family so necessary to the well-being of the state.[47]

Throughout the eighteenth century this cluster of thought, which can be labeled "enlightened child-rearing," reached colonial readers. Historians have argued that Locke's *Some Thoughts Concerning Education* was a more influential document in the colonies than *Two Treatises of Government*. David Lundberg and Henry May found Locke's educational advice in 25 percent of colonial libraries representing the time period 1700 to 1776.[48] Jay Fliegelman believes that Locke's *Thoughts,* reprinted 19 times in America before 1761, "served in its various popularized forms as perhaps the most significant text of the Anglo-American Enlightenment."[49] Joseph Addison's *The Spectator,* reprinted as separate issues or compiled in volumes of selections, as well as a plethora of imitations, introduced boys and girls to "the elegancies of knowledge" throughout the eighteenth and into the nineteenth centuries.[50] Linked to the "consumer revolution" of the increasingly wealthy British empire, *The Spectator* probably did follow the path of the tea table into colonial homes. Historians of material culture have demonstrated the acquisition of tea equipage—circular tripod tea tables, porcelain or china teapots, handleless cups and saucers, silver spoons and sugar tongs, and "slop" bowls for used tea leaves—by "the prosperous and governing classes" in the early 1700s and even by farming and artisan families by 1775.[51] Performance of the tea ceremony by a mother or daughter, sometimes at breakfast but usually at supper around five o'clock, indicated colonial pretensions to gentility and Addisonian taste.

Francis Hutcheson's *Inquiry Into the Original of Our Ideas of Beauty and Virtue* was the seminal work of the Scottish Enlightenment, which, as Garry Wills has pointed out, was perhaps even more congenial to Americans than Lockean thought.[52] The advice of enlightened physicians (William Cadogan, William Buchan, and others) was available in the American colonies by the 1770s. Samuel Richardson's *Clarissa* was an Anglo-American "best-seller," and after 1772 it was pirated and abridged by American printers. In the last quarter of the century printers in Boston, Philadelphia, and New York began to pirate the Newbery books, the first in a new juvenile literature designed to amuse as well as instruct children. And, by the 1790s, Americans began to produce their own child-rearing manuals, some based on their reading of Rousseau's *Emile.*[53]

Texts of enlightened child-rearing were linked to increasing Anglicization of colonial life, as by the 1760s, well-to-do Americans increasingly adopted

English norms and values as they sought to impose refinement of manners and accoutrements of gentility on their rough and distant periphery of the British empire. Rituals of dress, behavior, and manners served to distinguish the genteel from the common for those who wished to maintain hierarchy in a rapidly expanding society in which lines of distinction were not clear. Material objects—houses, furnishings, costumes, and coaches—as well as individual presentation could indicate those of merit belonging to the "better sort." Yet by the 1770s even the "middling ranks" composed of prosperous farmers and artisans were acquiring the imported cloth, books, clocks, and tea equipage that indicated some pretension to gentility. Colonial passion for English consumer goods would lead to the effort to pressure Parliament through economic boycotts in the growing conflict with Great Britain.[54]

Yet these texts of enlightened child-rearing also contained crucial elements of an evolving republican political ideology. American patriots toppling statues of George III would reject rule by a patriarchal monarch. The anti-patriarchal family would become the basic unit of the new republican society. Affectionate and voluntary marriage would be seen as a kind of school for citizenship, analogous to social and political ties based on consent. If the human personality could truly be formed by environmental influences, then children of those families could provide the stability and affectionate union necessary for that republic to survive. In post-Revolutionary decades, as American printers, physicians, clergymen, and educators sought to transform colonial regional cultures into a genuinely republican society, this was the cluster of thought to which they turned. Perhaps methods and materials of enlightened child-rearing adapted to the circumstances of the new republic could be utilized to shape ordinary American children into virtuous and disciplined citizens and citizens' wives.

2

Rearing the Republican Child

American Childhood and Revolutionary Republicanism

> *It remains yet to establish and perfect our new forms of government, and to prepare the principles, morals, and manners of our citizens for these forms of government after they are established and brought to perfection.*
>
> Benjamin Rush, 1786

Throughout the eighteenth century, as texts of European child-rearing advice reached American readers, the precepts they contained resonated differently according to colonial regional cultures. In the seventeenth and eighteenth centuries emigrants from various localities in Great Britain, western Europe, and west Africa transmitted distinctive values and folkways to the areas they settled. By the 1770s in each of these regions— New England, the coastal South, the middle colonies, and backcountry— while continuities persisted, change that affected the family was also under way. Increasing commercialization, pressures on land created by a burgeoning population, unprecedented movement of people, and fervent pietism had already begun to produce more contractual relationships; loss of parental control; and affectionate, voluntary ties.

The American colonies, however, were still hierarchical and patriarchal. Regional cultures joined in loyalty to the British monarch; colonials continued to believe that order rested on the vertical ranking of individuals, that inferiors should defer to superiors, and that the model for civic authority was the patriarchal father. Only repudiation of the king, intellectual debate and religious enthusiasm surrounding the Revolution, and actual experience of war would fully challenge these deeply held assumptions.[1] After the successful conclusion of the war, a generation of patriots struggled to create a national polity and to restructure colonial regional cultures into a republican one. Concepts of virtue articulated before the war became explicitly linked to citizenship. Hoping to shape the human personality into the sovereign unit of a truly voluntary political system, adults focused on the child in an unprecedented way. Perhaps the malleable child of enlightened thought could be molded into the virtuous, autonomous citizen. As European texts of enlightened child-rearing became increasingly available on the American market, printers, physicians, clergymen, and educators rushed to adapt them to their new republican situation.

Yet Revolutionary arguments and war raised the aspirations of ordinary people, releasing democratizing forces that could not be contained. Farmers and artisans, even laborers and apprentices, sought to engage in political activity. Buying and selling, demand for consumer items, increased greatly. Surges of popular religion empowered the young and lowly to rely on private judgment and seek salvation for themselves. Optimistic parents produced large numbers of children until half the population was under age 16. As patriarchal authority was challenged and the old hierarchical order crumbled, even patriots feared the loss of cohesive social bonds. Although Revolutionary leaders espoused varying degrees of enlightened thought, most Americans had been mobilized to war through religious networks and vocabularies. Dissenting congregations had long experience in gathering in voluntary association, and clergymen throughout the colonies supported the Revolution. Although church and state were separated, rationalists as well as revivalists viewed religion as the source of social harmony and public virtue.[2] Thus, as citizens sought to stabilize their new republic and build a cultural identity that would transcend regions, printers and authors adapted European materials to American experience, blending enlightened child-rearing precepts with inherited values and religious beliefs.

Historian David Hackett Fischer has argued that by 1775 four regional cultures—New England, the Tidewater South, the Delaware Valley, and the Backcountry—reflecting origins of separate waves of immigration from Great Britain were fully established in colonial America. Inhabitants of different regions spoke distinct dialects of the English language and followed different folkways as they established farms and communities, worshiped, formed families, and raised children.[3] All of these regions experienced the impact of burgeoning growth through high birthrates or unprecedented immigration. All had been affected by economic vicissitudes that accompanied American participation in imperial wars. In each region, change that affected the family was already under way. Yet children absorbed different values and beliefs as they grew up within the folkways of a distinctive culture. Cultural leaders interpreted European child-rearing materials in different ways to exemplify and advocate varying definitions of virtue.

Puritans emigrating from counties of eastern England in the 1630s had brought to Massachusetts and Connecticut their version of Calvinist theology, their desire for Congregational church governance, and their concept of the covenanted family. Believing in the natural depravity of the newborn child, who inherited original sin, parents sought to "break the will" or destroy the spirit of autonomy of the very young child as soon as evidence of it appeared. Fathers as well as mothers participated in child-rearing, instructing children through example and exhortation, yet relying on corporal punishment when necessitated by recalcitrant or disobedient behavior. As children grew, parents selected an appropriate "calling," "putting out" their teenage children with other families to receive instruction and perhaps ease tension in crowded households.[4] In the seventeenth century patriarchal fathers with ample lands at their disposal had been successful in settling their sons around them and selecting marriage partners for their daughters, perhaps exerting more control over grown children than would have been the case had they stayed in England.[5]

By 1775, however, as high birthrates and relatively low mortality produced families with as many as seven or eight surviving children, increased pressure on eastern lands forced New England fathers to grant increasing independence to their children. As farms in eastern inland towns were divided into smaller parcels over generations, fathers, no longer able to settle their grown sons around them, had no choice but to watch or assist them as they went off to form new farms and towns on northern or western lands, or migrated to urban centers. In his study of Andover, Massachusetts, Philip Greven found that less than half of the town's young men coming of age after mid-century chose or were able to stay there. What distinguished this generation from earlier ones was that fathers expected to let go of the economic bonds that tied their children to them.[6] These same fathers were losing control over the marriage choices of their daughters, especially, as Robert Gross has shown in his study of Concord, Massachusetts, when confronted with the fact of an existing pregnancy, an increasing possibility as the eighteenth century progressed.[7] As the skewed sex ratios of an immigrant population— many more men than women—balanced out with natural increase, husbands and wives were closer to one another in age. Perhaps the Andover couples, who after mid-century differed in age by only about two years, enjoyed a more "companionate" marriage.[8]

New England Puritan thought was reworked in the eighteenth century by the Rev. Jonathan Edwards of Massachusetts in ways that anticipated nineteenth-century religious trends. Edwards was well acquainted with British enlightened child-rearing advice; early in life he had read the *The Spectator* and such compilations, probably belonging to his mother, as the 1714 *Ladies' Library,* which contained excerpts from Locke's *Thoughts Concerning Education.* Norman Fiering has demonstrated that the New England intellectuals who taught Edwards were familiar with British and Continental thought. In addition, after instigating the remarkable revival of religion in Northampton in the late 1730s and witnessing with growing concern the Great Awakening of the 1740s, Edwards read widely in British moral philosophy, including Francis Hutcheson's *Inquiry.* Nevertheless, Edwards rejected Hutcheson's democratic notion of the moral sense, reserving an inner affective sense only for the regenerate few. Edwards's God was not a reasonable parent but an absolute, monarchical power; human beings, born in original sin, were destined for hell unless infused with God's grace. True virtue could only be "infused" virtue, acquired when divine intervention altered habit or inclination of the heart. Character resulted not from acts of rational will but from internal disposition, which could be changed only through the total transformation that human beings experienced as conversion.[9]

As a parent, Edwards resorted to Lockean methods of early discipline. He sought to develop the rational capacity of his children. Yet, the goal of his child-rearing method was to curb early signs of willfulness or depravity and accustom his children to obedience to God in order to prepare them for the possibility of conversion. According to Edwards's follower, the Rev. Samuel Hopkins:

> He took special care to begin his government of them [his children] in season. When they first discovered any considerable degree of will and stubbornness, he would attend to them till he had thoroughly subdued them and brought them to submit. And such prudent thorough discipline, exercised with the greatest calmness, and commonly without striking a blow, being repeated once or twice, was generally sufficient for that child: and effectually established his parental authority and produced a cheerful obedience ever after.

This minister and father also sought to direct his children "in the right way." "He instructed, exhorted each alone in his study," quizzing them on the *Assembly's Shorter Catechism,* "asking them questions on each answer and explaining it to them," and praying with them alone and as a family.[10]

Sarah Pierrepont Edwards, who worked to render "every thing in the family agreeable and pleasant," became a model of the affectionate wife and mother. Their followers observed and admired the Edwards's marriage and "the perfect harmony and mutual love and esteem, that subsisted between them." Of Sarah, they reported:

> She had an excellent way of governing her children; she knew how to make them regard and obey her cheerfully, without loud angry words, much less heavy blows.

She seldom punished them; and in speaking to them, used gentle and pleasant words. If any correction was necessary, she did not administer it in a passion; and when she had occasion to reprove and rebuke, she would do it in few words, without warmth and noise, and with all calmness and gentleness of mind.

Although Sarah Edwards appealed to the reason of her children, "that they might not only know her inclination and will, but at the same time be convinced of the reasonableness of it," she also used early discipline to prepare her children for conversion. "She regularly prayed with her children, from a very early period . . . with great earnestness and importunity." "[I]t was her rule to resist the exhibition of temper or disobedience in the child, however young, until its will was brought into submission to the will of its parents: wisely reflecting, that until a child will obey his parents, he can never be brought to obey God."[11]

Younger sons of gentry families from the south of England who emigrated to Virginia and Maryland in the third quarter of the seventeenth century brought to America the values, manners, and behavior of the courtier, worked out in the Renaissance by guidebooks such as Baldassare Castiglione's *The Book of the Courtier* or introduced in England by such manuals as William Caxton's *Book of Curtesye or Lytyll John,* published at the beginning of printing in the English language in 1477.[12] Although high mortality and unstable family life led to rough equality in the Chesapeake in the seventeenth century, by the 1740s, planters holding wealth in land and slaves were able to establish a self-conscious ruling class as they solidified domestic patriarchy, began to build stately dwellings, and enjoyed enough leisure to fulfill their pretension to gentility.[13] This generation, which included such individuals as William Byrd II of Westover, presided over their families and slaves with unchallenged authority. Nevertheless, by 1775 Daniel Blake Smith found evidence of "a strikingly affectionate family environment" among the Chesapeake gentry, in which "children became the centerpiece of family attention."[14]

In her analysis of children's portraits, Karin Calvert observed small changes in the dress and presentation of Chesapeake gentry children, indicating a view of childhood as a distinct stage of life, as early as the 1750s. In John Wollaston's painting, circa 1757, of 10-year-old Mann Page and his sister Elizabeth in Virginia, Mann, although dressed in frock coat, waistcoat, and knee breeches, does not look exactly like a small version of an adult. His hair is pulled loosely behind his head and tied with a black ribbon, and he carries a pet or toy bird tied to a string. His younger sister, although still dressed like a grown woman in low-cut and full-skirted gown, also has a toy, the doll on her lap (see figure 1).[15] By the third quarter of the eighteenth century Chesapeake gentry mothers, aided by prosperity and slave labor, were able to devote their attention more exclusively to child-rearing. Visitors observed that not only mothers but also fathers indulged their very young children,

Figure 1. *Mann Page and His Sister Elizabeth.* John Wollaston; Virginia, c. 1757. By mid-eighteenth century some Virginia gentry were beginning to view childhood as a distinct stage of life. Although the Page children wear clothing patterned on that of adults, their hair is loosely tied and Mann holds a toy or pet bird and Elizabeth a doll. *Courtesy of the Virginia Historical Society, Richmond.*

showering them with affection, delighting in their antics, and encouraging signs of autonomy. As Tidewater lands were taken up, fathers were forced to recognize the autonomy of grown children, settling sons on western plantations and allowing the marriage choices of daughters.[16]

    Although Chesapeake gentry parents did not break the wills of their children and even encouraged autonomy, the pretension to gentility that increasingly defined their status required that children yield to rituals and restraints signifying their place in the social hierarchy. David Hackett Fischer has pointed out the importance of dancing, the social ritual that became a form of discipline for Virginia children, who learned to execute gracefully and with great propriety the complex steps of minuets and country dances. Children also learned rules of genteel conduct from such eighteenth-century books of courtesy as the many adaptations of Lord Chesterfield's letters to his illegitimate son Philip, first published in London in 1774. Editions of Chesterfield's letters published in America, often compiled by an Anglican clergyman, excluded the original racy, pleasure-oriented instructions and provided tips on genteel carriage, cleanliness of person and dress, and elegance of conversation. A boy was taught table manners, how to propose a toast, and to treat superiors with respect and inferiors with grace.[17]

In 1746, when he was 14, George Washington copied 110 such "Rules of Civility & Decent Behavior in Company and Conversation" in his copybook, consciously acquiring the disciplined self-restraint he later demonstrated in his Revolutionary leadership. Washington's rules focused on respect for others and correct behavior in a social hierarchy. "Let thy ceremonies in courtesy be proper to the dignity of his place with who thou converses," he copied, "for it is absurd to act the same with a clown and a prince." Other commands taught bodily restraint; for example, "Shift not yourself in the sight of others nor gnaw your nails," or "Shake not the head, feet, or legs; roll not the eyes; lift not one eyebrow higher than the other; wry not the mouth; and bedew no man's face with your spittle by approaching too near him when you speak." Youth was instructed to defer to age and maintain a pleasant but grave demeanor.[18]

Although these particular rules were based on French maxims of courtly behavior, the young Washington also learned self-restraint and genteel taste from the Whig Joseph Addison's influential *The Spectator*. Addison was a monarchist who, after the period of intense party zeal in 1709 and 1710, sought to promote national patriotism and virtue in public life. Nevertheless, middle-class Britons and colonials identified him with the Roman concept of citizenship he explored in his 1713 tragedy *Cato*,[19] which Washington read in the company of his neighbor Sally Fairfax. "Turn up thy eyes to Cato!" Addison wrote:

> There mayst thou see to what a godlike height
> The Roman virtues lift up mortal man.
> While good, and just, and anxious for his friends,
> He's still severely bent against himself.

Washington was so taken with the stoic virtue in public life exemplified by *Cato* that he later ordered the play performed for his officers at Valley Forge. Still later he would include quotations from Addison's tragedy in his presidential papers.[20]

Nevertheless, the privileged position of the Chesapeake gentry depended on wealth in land and slaves. Importation of 54,000 Africans from 1700 to 1740 allowed planters in Virginia and Maryland the leisure to develop their distinctive regional lifestyle.[21] As Lockean emphasis on environmental influences trickled into colonial libraries, only a few perceptive Virginians, among them Thomas Jefferson, recognized the ill effects of slavery not only on the children reared as slaves but also on the children of slave owners.

Educated in the ethics of the Scottish Enlightenment by Dr. William Small at the College of William and Mary in the 1760s, Jefferson came to believe in Francis Hutcheson's concept of a universal moral sense.[22] In 1781, when he composed his *Notes on Virginia,* he acknowledged that thefts by slaves "must be ascribed to their situation, and not to any depravity of the moral sense." He also feared that white children growing up in a slave society would not learn, as Locke advised, to curb their tendency to wish to dominate over others. "There must doubtless be an unhappy influence on the manners of our people produced by the existence of slavery among us," he wrote:

> The whole commerce between master and slave is a perpetual exercise of the most boisterous passions, the most unremitting despotism on the one part, and degrading submissions on the other. Our children see this, and learn to imitate it; for man is an imitative animal. This quality is the germ of all education in him. From his cradle to his grave he is learning to do what he sees others do . . . The parent storms, the child looks on, catches the lineaments of wrath, puts on the same airs in the circle of smaller slaves, gives a loose to the worst of passions, and thus nursed, educated, and daily exercised in tyranny, cannot but be stamped by it with odious peculiarities. The man must be a prodigy who can retain his manners and morals undepraved by such circumstances.[23]

Like Jefferson himself, Virginians would be trapped by the institution of slavery, as their efforts to instill genteel restraint in their children were undermined not only by their own indulgence but also by plantation life.[24]

In the 1680s Quakers emigrated from northwestern England and Wales to the Delaware Valley, bringing to William Penn's colony their gentle and distinctive child-rearing methods. As early as the 1650s, founder of the Society of Friends, George Fox, with his convert Margaret Fell of Swarthmore Hall, had sought through "holy conversation" with kin and neighbors to quiet the false, prideful self and let God's word speak from within. Fox redefined marriage as if original sin had not occurred; women were spiritually equal to men and, as mothers, were instrumental in creating the loving family atmosphere that nurtured children. If parents had either attained or were working toward perfection, their sexual relationship contained no taint and their children would be born innocent. The tendency to sin would not develop until the child actually sinned at the age when he or she could distinguish right from wrong. In order for innocent children to develop as they hoped, Pennsylvania Quaker parents sought to shelter them from sinful influences. The Quaker family became a controlled environment in which the child's will was subject to that of the parent. But Quaker authority was nurturing and sought to buttress autonomy; parents appealed to reason in their children and taught them subordination less to individuals than to a community of values.[25]

In many ways, Quaker child-rearing methods resembled those advocated in Rousseau's *Emile.* The child was allowed to unfold organically within the controlled environment, and marriage choice initiated by grown children was carefully supervised by adults. Young people attracted to one another needed not only the permission of their parents but also the approval of both men's and women's monthly meetings. After announcing their intentions, bride and groom were interviewed separately by investigating committees. When each appeared once more before his or her respective meeting, the match could be warned off if considered unsuitable, or if approved, could take place. Barry Levy has argued that the availability of rich and ample land in Pennsylvania allowed Quaker fathers to acquire in order to uphold familial and communal values. In the 1690s sons in rural Chester County and the Welsh Tract could be allotted 300- or 400-acre farms, a limestone house, and livestock; as many as three-quarters of the children of the first generation married within the meeting. By 1750, however, rapid growth and commercial activity in Pennsylvania made discipline harder to maintain. Only the well-to-do could settle their children near them, and almost half the children from middling and poor families married outside the faith.[26]

Although British Quakers dominated Pennsylvania, William Penn's policies of religious freedom and tolerant naturalization had attracted a variety of ethnic groups, and the colony was characterized by cultural and religious diversity from its founding. From 1717 to 1775 immigrants from British borderlands (northern Ireland, Scotland, and the north of England), many of whom were Presbyterian, averaged more than 5,000 a year. Some stayed in their entrance port of Philadelphia, but others migrated to western Pennsylvania and by the 1730s began to make their way along the Great Wagon Road to the southern backcountry. Rhineland and Palatinate Germans (both Catholic and Protestant), who immigrated in the same years, followed a similar path.[27]

As the eighteenth century progressed, Philadelphia, a busy seaport at the center of a rich farming area, was increasingly influenced by the fluctuations of a world market economy. In the first half of the century commercial prosperity had allowed the merchant to accumulate a modest fortune, the artisan to make a decent competence, and the laborer or immigrant to move off the bottom. By the 1760s, however, the economic boom that accompanied the Seven Years War and the depression that followed it contributed to economic inequality. As high prices consumed real wages, artisans found their position precarious, and the numbers of the poor swelled. Social stratification became increasingly evident, and inhabitants tended to divide families into "the better sort," "the middling ranks," and "the poor."[28]

Nevertheless, European enlightened ideas resonated clearly in cosmopolitan Philadelphia, and inhabitants continued to believe that economic opportunity existed in their city. No one more than Benjamin Franklin symbolized the honored place of artisans who, through industrious labor and the acquisition of literacy and skills, could become property owners and leading citizens.

When Franklin began to write his *Autobiography* in 1771, he demonstrated how an enterprising artisan could acquire virtue through improved habit. As a teenage apprentice in the 1720s, he had taught himself to write plain prose by copying *The Spectator*. He had also taught himself arithmetic and had read Locke's *Essay Concerning Human Understanding*. In 1784, when he completed the account of his life, Franklin explained how he had worked on each virtue (industry, temperance, frugality) one at a time, marking his lapses in a book ruled with red ink until its practice became habitual and he could progress to the next one. The motto in his red-ruled book was from Addison's *Cato*:

> If there's a power above us
> (And that there is, all nature cries aloud
> Thro' all her works), He must delight in virtue;
> And that which he delights in must be happy.

A Lockean who trusted sense impressions, Franklin was not sure that he had acquired the *"reality"* of virtue, although he was content that he had mastered the *"appearance"* of it.[29]

Immigration from British borderlands brought not only backcountry hunters and yeomen but also intellectuals to America. Dr. John Witherspoon, who arrived from Scotland to become president of the New Side Presbyterian College of New Jersey in 1768, introduced students to the ethics texts of Francis Hutcheson.[30] In *Letters on Education* Witherspoon also stressed the acquisition of virtue through habit, drawing on post-Lockean associationist psychology. Habitual behavior could be established so early in life, he argued, "that even memory itself should not be able to reach back to its beginning." "Habits in general may be very early formed in children. An association of ideas is, as it were, the parent of habit."

Witherspoon recommended Lockean lessons in obedience to parental authority when the child was as young as eight or nine months. As soon as children "begin to shew their inclination by desire or aversion," he advised, "let single instances be chosen now and then (not too frequently) to contradict them." If the child has something in his hand that he is inclined to or delights him, "let the parent take it from him" and not give it back. "This experiment frequently repeated," Witherspoon advised, "will in a little time so perfectly habituate the child to yield to the parent whenever he interposes, that he will make no opposition." As children grew, Witherspoon recommended that parents retain authority as magistrates should over citizens, "always cool and reasonable in their conduct, prudent and cautious in their conversation."

Witherspoon's child-rearing advice blended genteel virtue acquired by Washington with Jonathan Edwards's insistence that true virtue was infused only by God's grace. He sought a nurturing family atmosphere in which children would "be formed to politeness, as well as to virtue." Yet the goal of his child-rearing methods was "the glory of God in the eternal happiness and salvation of children." Children were to be taught "a deep conviction that unless we are reconciled to God we shall without doubt perish everlastingly." "While the body is tender, to bring the mind to submission, to train up a child in the nurture and admonition of the Lord," he insisted, "I know is not impossible."[31]

By 1775 concepts of the affectionate, anti-patriarchal family and malleable child had penetrated each of these regional cultures. Pressure on eastern lands through high birthrates, increasing commercialization of colonial economies, unprecedented movement of people, and varying religious beliefs and practices had already influenced family change. As regions joined in common opposition to policies of the parent country, Anglo-American anxiety about changing familial relationships provided one lens through which to view the imperial crisis. England became the tyrannical or indulgent parent, and America, the abused or unruly child. As colonials wrestled with the issue of separating from the mother country and patriarchal monarch, for many it made common sense when Thomas Paine argued in January 1776, if "Britain is the parent country . . . [t]hen the more shame upon her conduct. Even brutes do not devour their young, nor savages make war upon their families." If ties of affection break, "[e]verything that is right or natural pleads for separation, and the weeping voice of nature cries, 'TIS TIME TO PART." "The infant state of the Colonies . . . so far from being against, is an argument in favor of independence," for "[y]outh is the seed time of good habits, as well in nations as individuals."[32]

In every region a generation of children in families of every nuance of political persuasion experienced the wrenching ferment of the American Revolution. In 1770, 10-year-old Anna Winslow, the daughter of a Massachusetts soldier who became Commissary-General of the British forces in Nova Scotia, and thus a Tory, was sent to Boston to live with her childless aunt and to attend school. Anna exhibited a love of fashion that Boston patriots condemned as courtly luxury; she wrote in her diary in 1771 of her yellow coat, black bib and apron, "pompedore" shoes, cap with blue ribbons, and "very handsome loket in the shape of a hart." She also wore a "HEDDUS roll" made of a red cow tail, horsehair, and "a little human hair of yellow hue," which with her own hair smoothed over it made an elegant headdress, although she did admit "It makes my head itch, & ach, & burn like anything Mamma." But Anna's pleasures would be disrupted by war. When British forces left Boston in 1776, her father fled to England never to see her again— left with her mother in rural Massachusetts, Anna died from consumption in 1779.[33]

Many American children suffered greatly from dysentery and other diseases made epidemic by the movement of troops. In June of 1775, Abigail

and eight-year-old John Quincy Adams watched the Battle of Bunker Hill
from a promontory near their Braintree home. By September of that year
dysentery swept the Boston area, and Abigail, her mother, and three-year-old
Tommy Adams fell ill. "The desolation of War is not so distressing as the
Havock made by the pestilence," Abigail wrote to John. "Some poor parents
are mourning the loss of 3, 4, and 5 children, and some families are wholy
striped of every Member." When her mother succumbed to the disease a few
days later, Abigail lamented, "Have pitty upon me, have pitty upon me o!
thou my beloved for the Hand of God presseth me soar."[34]

In September of 1777, when the Philadelphia merchant Henry Drinker
was arrested and imprisoned with other prominent Quakers for refusing to
take a loyalty oath supporting the Revolution, his wife Elizabeth recorded
that six-year-old Henry Jr. was "very low" with "fluxey stools." As Washington's army retreated and the British approached Philadelphia, Drinker stayed
by her son's bedside, watching from the window the "number of waggons,
Drays, and other Carriages which past." Not until the occupying army
entered Philadelphia in October was little Henry able to walk alone and come
downstairs; the life of the family would be further disrupted in December
when British officer Crammond, accompanied by servants, Hessians, horses,
cows, and turkeys, commandeered their front parlor.[35]

During the Revolution American adults drummed a variety of messages
into their children. Martha Laurens of Charleston, South Carolina, who at
the age of 11 had lost her mother in 1770, was trapped in Europe by the Revolution. Her father, Henry Laurens, a president of the Continental Congress,
would be charged with high treason and held in the Tower of London after
Charleston fell to the British. In 1776 he feared that war and his political
position would demolish the family's genteel lifestyle supported by their rice
plantations and the slave trade. "[P]repare yourself for a reverse of fortune,"
he urged his only daughter. "Prepare for the trial of earning your daily bread
by daily labour . . . [I]t would rejoice me to hear . . . that you earned as much
every day by your needle, as would pay your daily expenses." "God knows
through what scenes you are to pass. If, instead of affluence . . . servitude is to
be your portion, qualify yourself for an upper place. Fear not servitude;
encounter it if it shall be necessary, with a spirit becoming a woman of an
honest and pious heart."[36]

Stephen Allen of New York learned republican principles from the
city's artisans. In 1775 his uncle ("a true Whig, a friend to the rights of man
and the liberties of America") took the seven-year-old fatherless boy to
political meetings and to see the Liberty pole, tapering upward 50 feet to
the Liberty cap at the top. His uncle, who subscribed to periodical literature, "appeared much delighted with the political writings of Thomas
Paine" and in 1776 insisted that his young nephew read *The American Crisis* aloud. Fifty years later Allen recalled:

[A]lthough I barely knew how to read at that early age, much less to comprehend what I read, I nevertheless received some benefit from the operation, for the explanations with which he would accompany my reading of particular passages, which forcibly struck his own mind, had a tendency to impress them upon mine, and of inspiring me with a feeling of reverence for those engaged in the cause of their country, which has never left me to this day . . .

Allen remembered when the British frigates the *Rose* and the *Phoenix* entered the port of New York, and women and children were frightened "most unmercifully," and when he saw his older brother John for the last time marching down Warren Street with the militia. When he and other boys gathering nuts and berries on Long Island were held overnight by British soldiers, he "stood gazing at their red coats and finely polished guns and bayonets." He also recalled hungry American prisoners in the "Sugar-Houses" calling out to him when he went with his aunt to take them soup. As the occupation of New York dragged on, Stephen and his brother William were apprenticed to a Tory sail-maker, but Stephen's "predilections in favor of the cause in which my Country was engaged . . . had in fact increased" with the years, and the teenage boy and his brother knew they were "rebels."[37]

The wrenching experiences and powerful memories of the American Revolution transcended regional differences. Children and adults who experienced the war would remember it as the defining event of their lives. Social hierarchy was challenged by the new revolutionary creed that human beings were free and equal to each other. The Anglo-American cultural shift toward the anti-patriarchal family that had occurred gradually over the eighteenth century was accelerated and suddenly seemed justified by republican arguments. Patriarchal authority was further undermined as personal independence and individual autonomy became desirable goals. Revolutionary ideology and the experience of war released democratizing forces as ordinary people with raised aspirations learned to rely on their own judgment. Farmers and artisans, and even laborers and apprentices who served in militias, sought to engage in political activity. Passions for buying and selling evident before the Revolution were unleashed. Surges of popular religion empowered the young and lowly to challenge established clerical authority and choose salvation for themselves. The high birthrate produced a potentially unruly population in which half of the individuals were under age 16.

In the 1780s and 1790s a generation of Americans who had come of age during the Revolution struggled to create a national polity from colonial regional cultures. They also hoped to transform their society into a republican one in which sovereign individuals joined in purely voluntary ties. Lessons from earlier republics in the Renaissance and Anglo-American tradition of "civic humanism" demonstrated the fragility of republican governments—their propensity to decay, the necessity for individuals to subordinate private interest to the public good in order for a republic to survive. As sovereignty shifted from King-in-Parliament to the people, varying definitions of virtue focused on the moral restraint that would be essential in each individual citizen. To many in the new republic, the swirl of activity by ordinary people seemed alarming. If hierarchical bonds no longer held individuals together, what would provide the social cement? What could contain unruly, unsociable behavior when external restraint was removed? How could citizens be virtuous when individuals seemed determined to pursue their own self-interested goals?

Struggling to respond to such concerns, some Americans focused on devising forms of government—revising democratic state constitutions or centralizing authority and checking power in a stronger national government. Others turned to cultural concerns. Perhaps cohesion could be created in a pluralistic nation through allegiance to a common culture.[38] Perhaps the human personality could be shaped and the moral restraint essential for citizenship could be instilled in children while they were still malleable. Printers, physicians, clergymen, and educators rushed to adapt European enlightened child-rearing materials to perceived needs of their American political environment. Seeking stability for the young republic, they mitigated the educational plans of Locke or Rousseau with the emphasis of the Scottish Enlightenment on affectionate sociability.

They also drew on the unique American religious experience. Since the seventeenth century, Dissenting congregations, distant from ecclesiastical authority, had gathered not only to worship but also to conduct their own affairs. Grounding authority in the Bible, they had learned to impose a fragile voluntary social order on a rapidly changing environment. When congregations splintered under the impact of the Great Awakening, many viewed political issues in essentially religious terms. As clergymen imbued with Revolutionary zeal mobilized Americans for acts of war through denominational networks and vocabularies, for many, their own religious experience exemplified republican principles. Rationalists as well as evangelicals attributed the success of their rebellion to God's providential plan. Although church and state would be separated, Americans of varying persuasions viewed religion as the proper source of social harmony and public virtue.[39] Thus, seeking stability for their new republic, post-Revolutionary printers and educators adapted European thought to this American experience. On various levels of consciousness, they incorporated denominational vocabulary and content into enlightened child-rearing sources, blending them with inherited values and religious beliefs.

During the intellectual debate that accompanied the Revolution, wide variety and competition in printing flourished. After the war, individual printers, responding to consumer demand and the opportunities of the market economy, pirated British literary materials. Republishing books without crediting their sources, they freely made changes they deemed appropriate for the local environment. Isaiah Thomas in Worcester, Massachusetts, William Spotswood in Philadelphia, and Hugh Gaine in New York almost simultaneously selected John Newbery's children's literature for reprinting. Each tailored the books to the new republican situation, freely changing names and places. London became New York or Philadelphia, and the Lord Mayor's gilt coach became the "Gouvernour's." American printers retained the Lockean child-rearing precepts and entrepreneurial values of the original books, but they supplemented the enlightened advice with their own additions of inherited religious content.

For example, when the Philadelphia (probably Presbyterian) firm of Young, Stewart and M'Culloch pirated Newbery's *History of Little King Pippin* in 1786, they added divine intervention to the story. Peter Pippin is the usual Newbery poor boy whose dutiful behavior is rewarded with esteem when his fellows elect him "King of the Good Boys." Naughty George Graceless, however, is punished not by Lockean disgrace but by death. And when at the last moment Harry Harmless remembers his prayers, God intervenes to protect him. Although wild animals devour the four naughty boys who forget their prayers, the animals lick Harry's face, and a little white horse trots up to take him home.[40]

By 1788 child-rearing methods based on those of Locke and Rousseau were disseminated in American urban centers through a new "realistic" children's literature. Mrs. Barbauld's *Lessons for Children* were introduced in Philadelphia by Benjamin Franklin Bache, whose grandfather had known the author in England. Anna Laetitia Aikin Barbauld attempted in her children's books to re-create the education she had received in English Dissenting academies, based on Lockean precepts of observation through sense impressions and reflection encouraged through conversation.[41] In *Lessons for Children from Two to Four Years Old,* designed for her adopted son Charles, the two-year-old is taught elementary reading, arithmetic, and science through the observation of concrete objects in the domestic environment. In *Lessons for Children of Four Years Old,* through affectionate conversation with his mother, Charles is encouraged to develop his rational capacities of discrimination and organization and is taught to make comparisons.[42] In *Lessons for Children from Four to Five Years Old,* five-year-old Charles is ready for moral instruction through stories "about good boys and naughty boys . . . for you know what it is to be good now."[43]

Barbauld's little lessons became immensely popular among American printers, but they, too, were blended with regional religious beliefs. For example, when the Philadelphia Quaker firm of Johnson and Justice put out their *New England Primer, Much Improved* in 1792, they mingled little scientific lessons with religious instruction. The child is told that the world does not stand on a great turtle "But is balanced on its own cen-tre, and goes round the sun, the o-pen space, once e-ve-ry year." Yet the primer still reminded children as it had since the seventeenth century that "Xer-xes the great did die, / And so must you and I."[44] *The Child's Instructor,* written in 1793 by Quaker schoolmaster John Ely, continued such incongruous mingling—or mangling. Ely's interpretation of Locke reflected the Quaker practice of the gentle nurturing of the seed of the divine within each child:

> As the mind of child is like soft wax, which will take the least stamp you put on it, so let it be your care who teach, to make the stamp good, that the wax be not hurt.

To make learning pleasant, Ely borrowed Newbery's "pretty" language and associated lessons with games that urban children played—"hide a whoop," whip the top, jump the rope, and marbles. He pirated Barbauld's scientific lessons without changing them, but he also quoted Scripture, told Bible stories, emphasized the importance of church attendance, and told his young readers, "God sees you all the time." And to suit his book for the new republic, he urged children to emulate such worthy models as George Washington and Benjamin Franklin.[45]

Rousseau's child-rearing precepts were popularized by the English author Thomas Day, whose *History of Sandford and Merton* was published in America in 1788. Day's identification with Rousseau was reinforced by his friend, Richard Lovell Edgeworth, who encouraged him to expand Barbauld's conversational method for older children. His book describes the reeducation of a young aristocrat, Tommy Merton, who is taught to emulate the virtues of the "natural" child, Harry Sandford, the yeoman's son. The local curate Mr. Barlow is the tutor who manipulates Tommy's environment to create little lessons in order to break the bad habits Tommy has learned from his fashionable mother and an early childhood corrupted by the institution of slavery in Jamaica. For example, when Tommy refuses to work, he is not allowed to share the cherries that others have picked. He feels not only hunger but later shame when kind Harry is willing to share his portion. The lesson is reinforced by a reading comparing the industry of ants with the frivolity of flies.[46] Thomas Day sought to correct the social ills of England in the 1780s through moral reformation of the individual child. In America this "natural" child, taught the dignity of honest work, would become the republican citizen.

The short patriotic account of the life of George Washington was America's contribution to enlightened children's literature. A typical biography of Washington, written while the president was still alive, presented its subject as the archetype of the good boy, whose "unvarying habits of regularity, temperance, and industry," acquired early, make him great. In the Revolution he demonstrates his ability to control his passion and persevere in the face of great difficulty, yielding his strong individual will to the greater goal of independence. His stoic virtue wins him the Lockean reward, the esteem of his countrymen.[47] American blending of enlightenment and classical literature with religion is evident in the companion piece to this life of the hero, the tale of the bad boy Judas Iscariot. In a complicated story, the traitor Judas kills his father and marries his mother in addition to betraying Christ. In despair, he can only hang himself in utter public disgrace as "all his bowels gushed out" and the entire world can view his inner treachery. Unregulated by acquired habits, his life is a grand whirl of disorder, and his punishment is not only ignominious death but public revelation of his corrupt inner being, in which the contents of his bowels are somehow linked to the evil in his treacherous heart.[48]

Americans who adapted enlightened child-rearing to their new republican situation emphasized the environment created by the affectionate, anti-patriarchal family. In 1790 Enos Hitchcock, a Congregational clergyman from Providence, Rhode Island, who had served as army chaplain at Ticonderoga and Saratoga, published *Memoirs of the Bloomsgrove Family*. Inspired by the ratification of the Constitution and the commencement of the new Federal government, Hitchcock composed his work as a series of letters to Martha Washington, explaining to her that "systems of education written in Europe, are too local to be transferred to America." "[I]t is now time to become independent in our maxims, principles of education, dress, and manners, as we are in our laws and government." Hitchcock modeled his advice on *Emile*; however, the Bloomsgroves, in raising their children, would follow "Rousseau's maxim, but not his method." In a republic, work is both necessary and proper, the clergyman argued; parents would not have the leisure to have their children always in their sight. Instead of manipulating the environment, these busy American parents would have to seize the moment to instill lessons.[49]

During the first stage of childhood, the first seven years, Rozella and Osander are raised by their mother, and Mrs. Bloomsgrove implements an educational plan based on "Mr. Locke's" advice. She breast-feeds her children herself and builds the strong body essential to the sound mind through "cleanliness, air and exercise," "plainness and simplicity in food and drink," and hardening with "temperate" clothing and the cold bath. Young children, whose knowledge is gained through perception, during the period when "the little plant of reason is now in embryo," must be protected from such harmful sense impressions as stories of ghosts and wonders still told by lower-class servants. Yet Hitchcock abandoned Lockean lessons of early obedience in favor of Rousseau's maxim that children learn to submit only to necessity. Mrs. B., who teaches her children "self-command" by example, allows Rozella to burn her hand on a candle and Osander to cut his finger with a knife, and each learns through experience the effect of rashness. And like Rousseau, she teaches property rights in the garden; when Rozella, falling on Osander's hoe, breaks his vine, and he pulls up her tulip in anger, Mamma seizes the moment to arrange a social contract and convince each to replace the destroyed plants with new ones.[50]

Although previously Mr. Bloomsgrove, an enterprising American merchant, only applauded the actions of his wife, during the next seven years the father will participate "in bringing forward the fruit to perfection, the early buds of which she had so tenderly cherished." Although Mamma has treated both sexes alike, by age seven gender differences are emphasized; Osander learns Latin and Greek, and 13-year-old Fanny comes to live with the family as an example to Rozella. During this period, by inventing their own amusements and making their own toys, both children develop "habits of activity and industry" and a "relish" for labor appropriate for republican children. Osander digs in his garden and makes his own bow and arrows, marbles, ball, top, and sled—toys he continues "to use without being cloyed, or wishing for others, because he was first employed in making and then in using them." Rozella does not dig but pulls weeds and sweeps in her garden; she dresses and undresses her doll, as she "nurses, instructs, and corrects" it, "never tired of this business because it gives her exercise." For both children industrious activity is its own reward, and the virtue of industry is reinforced in the evening through stories told by Papa.[51]

Hitchcock feared that Locke's emphasis on rational individual autonomy would make children "selfish and covetous" and preferred Scottish notions of affectionate benevolence for moral education. During the first stage of childhood, the Bloomsgroves had nurtured evidence of the benevolence that flowed from self-love in their children; "[t]he little plant had been nourished with great care, was constantly cherished by exercise, and supported by their own examples." During the second stage, benevolent habits are developed through repeated acts fortified by stories, again with virtue itself its own reward. According to the plan of the Scottish author Lord Kaimes, each child is given a small sum for charity, which, encouraging competition, is doubled for the child who distributes it most judiciously. To develop the habit of fidelity, the Bloomsgroves place confidence in their children; Osander is trusted with small sums and Rozella with the key to Mamma's closet. To cultivate habitual sympathy, the children care for animals; Rozella has a bird and squirrel, Osander a pet dog. Because the children learn early to obey and admire their parents, punishment is rarely necessary; most faults can be corrected through shame or a few moments of reflection in solitude. Only for cases of extreme obstinacy would Hitchcock resort to corporal punishment.[52]

The third stage of childhood begins at puberty when Rozella is 13 and Osander 15. "Now is the season for the cultivation of both head and heart in our young pupils"; the daughter is "trained in the line of her sex," and the son "in the higher branches of learning." Although Locke advised that children be tutored at home, Hitchcock insisted that American youth could be instructed in schools. In the new republic Mr. B. and his neighbors join to hire a teacher and build a schoolhouse, "where all concerned might have an equal advantage." Rozella, along with neighborhood girls, learns "writing, arithmetic, geography, grammar and the belles lettres" at this district school. Because Osander has discovered that he dislikes memorizing Latin and Greek, he is allowed to pursue the more practical studies toward which his nature is inclined, with study of the classics only an interlude.[53]

At this point Mrs. B. seeks to inspire Rozella to love occupations "proper for her sex." While Osander will pursue an entrepreneurial business career, Rozella will find fulfillment as mistress of a family. In a "republican country" a husband's industry can gain an estate, but a wife's economy will preserve it. Thus, by the age of 12, Rozella can cook and inspect the house, aiding her mother as a favor. She has also been trained in modesty, delicacy, and protection of her reputation, because, as Rousseau suggested, it is by these means that she will be able to charm her husband. Mrs. B.'s good example for her daughter is reinforced by reading. Although Richardson's *Clarissa* is "the most finished model of female excellence which has ever been offered for their imitation," Hitchcock feared that girls might miss the moral point while reading love scenes, and preferred "those periodical pieces where the powers of wit, fancy, and judgment, have united in exposing vice and folly, such as *The Spectator*."[54]

Although Rousseau deferred religious instruction until Emile was in his teens, the Bloomsgroves have nurtured their children in a rational Christianity. Mrs. B. has represented religion to the children in a pleasant light, teaching them "to look up to God as their heavenly father and friend." Mr. B. has attempted to stamp on the children's minds "an impression of a benevolent Deity . . . the great principle which binds together universal intelligence, and leads all rational beings up to the common source." The family has observed the Sabbath and attended meeting; for Hitchcock "[a] well regulated house of public worship is a school of refinement and good manners, as well as of instruction and devotion." Thus, at 20 and 22, Rozella is pious, cheerful and good, and Osander views God as his friend. In a few years both will be married, as Mr. B. launches Osander in his career and Rozella realizes the end for which she has been trained, to be "a useful and agreeable companion in the matrimonial state."[55]

Charles Willson Peale of Philadelphia was also inspired by Rousseau, although he found Democratic-Republican implications rather than Federalist ones. Interrupting his artisan career, which evolved from apprenticeship with a saddler to metalworking and watch-repair to painting, Peale crossed the Delaware with Washington and wintered at Valley Forge with the Philadelphia militia. Member of the "Furious Whigs" and friend of Thomas Paine, he supported Pennsylvania's democratic constitution and won a seat in its controversial unicameral legislature. Although he withdrew from politics, in the 1780s and 1790s Peale attempted to provide visual embodiments of republican ideals. In the gallery attached to his Philadelphia home he displayed his portraits of Revolutionary heros who exemplified virtue, and on patriotic occasions he built gigantic illuminated transparencies with feminine symbols personifying justice, peace, or "the genius of America." In the "open book of nature" of his natural history museum, Peale arranged examples of "the animal, vegetable, and mineral kingdoms" according to the Linnaean system in order to create a visual school of science, reason, and morality, which he hoped would provide the "virtuous education" necessary to maintain "republican government" and "the liberties of the people."[56]

Referring to "that great Philosopher, the friend of Children," Peale attempted to rear his 11 children according to a rough approximation of Rousseau's plan. Both boys and girls (all named for artists or heroes) participated in their affectionate father's industrious activity, learning to paint; use tools; and prepare birds, reptiles, fish, and insects for exhibition. Peale had rebelled against his own harsh treatment as an apprentice and punished his children only through shame. When Rembrandt threw an object and accidentally broke a kitten's back, his father nursed it back to health, believing that the crippled animal would serve as a reminder of the effect of hasty temper. Peale's effort to arrange a lesson to cure Raphaelle of his dislike of baker's bread was thwarted, however, when the family nurse secretly slipped the hungry boy cakes. In 1794 when the family, along with its bald eagle in a wire cage and female elk (tethered in the State House yard), moved with its museum into the new hall of the American Philosophical Society, a relative remembered their household as "a brilliant confusion of paints, brushes, and tools, strange birds and beasts, alive as well as dead, strange plants and flowers and strange machinery," where "[t]here was always some great business afoot" and "unruly children or grandchildren to enliven the unruly scene."[57]

Charles Willson Peale's legacy, however, was largely visual, and his paintings of affectionate domestic scenes best express his vibrant and romantically enlightened view of childhood. His portrait The Peale Family, begun in the early 1770s and finished in 1808, depicts happy informality and warm affection, with adults resting their hands on each other's shoulders and holding on their laps cuddly children with short haircuts dressed in soft muslin frocks (see figure 2). Rachel Weeping, also begun in the early 1770s, is a poignant and realistic portrayal of Peale's first wife's grief at the death of her infant daughter from smallpox, who, pale-faced, chin bound, and arms tied down with satin ribbons, lies formally dressed for burial in a lace cap and linen dress (see figure 3). The Staircase Group of 1795 shows real boys—Raphaelle and Titian Ramsay I, with rumpled hair and pensive looks above their frock coats and breeches—mounting a staircase, which is cleverly painted and placed in a real doorway with a step at the bottom to convince the viewer that the boys actually exist (see figure 4).[58]

Figure 2. *The Peale Family.* Charles Willson Peale; Annapolis and Philadelphia, c. 1770–1773 and 1808. Peale's portrait of his own family depicts happy informality and warm affection, with adults resting their hands on each other's shoulders and holding on their laps cuddly children with short haircuts dressed in soft muslin frocks. *Collection of the New York Historical Society.*

Other educators of Peale's generation were more ambivalent about democratic forces unleashed by the Revolution. Noah Webster of Connecticut, whose father mortgaged the family farm in order that he could attend Yale, found himself perilously independent in 1778 when his father gave him an eight-dollar bill in Continental currency and said, "Take this; you must now seek your living; I can do no more for you." "In this state of anxiety" Webster identified with the Revolutionary cause, and at the end of the war "formed the design of composing elementary books for the instruction of children."[59] In the introduction to the *Grammatical Institute,* which became his famous "Speller," the American schoolmaster threw "his mite into the common treasure of patriotic exertions" and sought cultural independence for the new nation:

> Europe is grown old in folly, corruption and tyranny—in that country laws are perverted, manners are licentious, literature is declining and human nature debased. For America in her infancy to adopt the present maxims of the old world would be to stamp the wrinkles of decrepit age upon the bloom of youth and to plant the seeds of decay in a vigourous constitution.

Yet Webster, who would become a Federalist and later experience conversion to evangelical Congregationalism, was alarmed by the disorder and

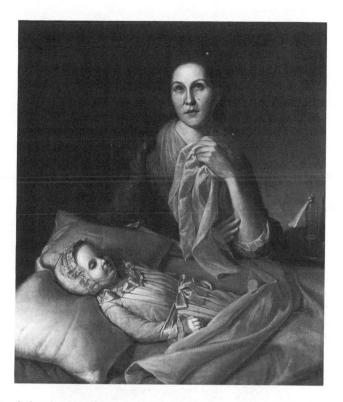

Figure 3. *Rachel Weeping.* Charles Willson Peale; Annapolis and Philadelphia, 1772 and probably 1776. Peale depicts his first wife, Rachel Brewer Peale, weeping over the body of their infant daughter Margaret, who died from smallpox in 1772. The figure of Rachel and table with medicines were added later to illustrate the futile attempt of the parents to save their child. *Philadelphia Museum of Art: Given by the Barra Foundation, Inc.*

regional divisions of the new nation and sought to create standards of pronunciation and spelling for a uniform national language. Through verses, examples, and stories, he wove into his textbook both the emphasis on industrious habits—"I-dle-ness will bring thee to pov-er-ty; but by in-dus-try and pru-dence thou shalt be filled with bread"—and the internalized restraints—"No man may put off the law of God, / My joy is in his law all the day"—of his native New England heritage.[60]

Benjamin Rush of Philadelphia was also concerned with creating a cohesive national culture, which he sought to achieve through the affectionate family and educational experiments. Rush had been converted to republican principles while a medical student at the University of Edinburgh; when he first "heard the authority of Kings called in question," he later recorded,

Figure 4. *The Staircase Group.* Charles Willson Peale; Philadelphia, 1795. This portrait of Raphaelle and Titian Ramsay Peale I depicts real boys with rumpled hair and pensive looks above their frock coats and breeches. Peale enhanced the realism of the painting by displaying it in a doorway with a wooden step at the bottom. *Philadelphia Museum of Art: The George W. Elkins Collection.*

"[t]his great and active truth became a ferment in my mind. I now suspected error in everything I had been taught, or believed, and as far as I was able began to try the foundations of my opinions upon many other subjects."[61] During the Revolution Rush was originally allied with radicals who supported Pennsylvania's democratic constitution. But as he served in Congress—although he welcomed popular sovereignty—he began to distrust what he observed of popular rule. By the 1780s, in both state and national arenas he not only worked to establish the bicameral legislature and strong executive in "forms of government" but also pondered how "the principles, morals, and manners of our citizens" might be molded in order to create a virtuous and affectionate republican society.[62]

Rush explored the interconnection between republican principles and enlightened child-rearing in a paper he wrote in 1784 entitled *Thoughts upon the Mode of Education Proper in a Republic*. Assuming that habits of good health and reasonable and moral behavior could be molded in the malleable child through manipulation of sense impressions and early associations, Rush argued that republican citizens could be formed in "nurseries of wise and good men" in which "our modes of teaching" were adapted "to the peculiar form of our government." Yet, influenced by both his education in Scotland and his experience in pluralistic Pennsylvania, Rush feared that social ties based only on rational choice would not be binding. The American republic would have to become a union of affection, in which the emotional "*prejudice*" of patriotism was reinforced in children through their early associations. Young Americans educated in their own country, "who have trodden the paths of science together, or have joined in the same sports, whether of swimming, skating, fishing, or hunting," would form bonds of "mutual benevolence." "Our schools of learning," argued Rush, "by producing one general and uniform system of education, will render the mass of the people more homogeneous and thereby fit them more easily for uniform and peaceable government."[63]

Although Rush advocated industrious activity, he feared that industry without restraint would threaten tenuous social bonds. "Let our pupil be taught that he does not belong to himself, but that he is public property," he argued. "He must be taught to amass wealth, but it must be only to increase his power of contributing to the state." One way to instill the self-restraint essential to republican virtue would be grounding education in Christianity. "Without religion," he argued, "there can be no virtue, and without virtue, there can be no liberty, and liberty is the object and life of all republican governments." Like many Americans, having identified civic humanism with Christian eschatology, Rush believed that Christianity taught republican principles. "A Christian," he maintained, "cannot fail of being a republican"; and, in a republic, the Bible should be the primary textbook.[64]

Internalized restraint could also be instilled in children through early discipline by parents and schools. Espousing the concept of the moral sense, Rush thought that absolute obedience to authority would not only protect the health of children and allow their capacity for reason to develop, but, by removing disorder of body and mind, would free them to act morally. Republican children, Rush insisted, should "have never known or felt their own wills till they were one and twenty years of age." Habitual obedience learned in childhood would create the adult citizen capable of submitting personal inclination to the rule of law, and private interest to the public good. "It is plain," Rush concluded, "that I consider it as possible to convert men into republican machines. This must be done if we expect them to perform their parts properly in the great machine of the government of the state." A republican government was founded upon sovereign units of individual wills, but these wills "must be fitted to each other by means of education before they can be made to produce regularity and unison in government." Although his model was Newtonian, Rush's hopes were millennial: "From the combined and reciprocal influence of religion, liberty, and learning upon the morals, manners, and knowledge of individuals, of these upon government, and government upon individuals," he mused, "it is impossible to measure the degrees of happiness and perfection to which mankind may be raised."[65]

While Rush sought to prepare boys to participate in republican forms of government, he planned for girls to fulfill the second part of his twofold program; when they inevitably became wives and mothers, their task would be to mold the minds, morals, and manners of the new republic. When in 1787 Rush addressed the students of John Poor's Young Ladies Academy in Philadelphia, he argued that female education "should be accommodated to the state of society, manners, and government of the country in which it is conducted." He believed that American girls would marry early and, while their citizen-husbands engaged in public pursuits, find themselves "stewards and guardians of their husband's property" and principal instructors of their children. Thus, they "should be qualified . . . by a peculiar and suitable education, to concur in instructing their sons in the principles of liberty and government." Future wives and mothers of citizens should be taught a practical curriculum: grammar and accounting, some geography and history, and even a little natural philosophy. Training in vocal music might "soothe the cares of domestic life," while instruction in dancing "promotes health and renders the figure and motions of the body easy and agreeable." Most important, education for republican girls should also be grounded in "regular instruction in the Christian religion." Not only was the "female breast" the "natural soil of Christianity," but a woman "taught to believe its doctrines and obey its precepts" would develop a self-restraint similar to that of her husband and sons.[66]

Rush advocated for girls the same strict discipline he insisted upon for boys; they, too, must obey absolutely the authority of parent or schoolmaster. The girl who learned habitual obedience as a child could be subsumed within her family as an adult, able to submit personal inclination to the demands of domestic life. Although engagement in useful benevolence was the only activity Rush approved of for women outside the family, within the domestic circle their potential sphere of influence was endless. Educated and virtuous republican women could temper the behavior of suitors: "our young men would then be restrained from vice by the terror of being banished from their company." They would reward in private the endeavors of their citizen-husbands: "and the patriot—the hero—and the legislator would find the sweetest reward of their toils in the approbation and applause of their wives." As mothers, they would mold malleable children into citizens: "for it has been remarked that there have been few great or good men who have not been blessed with wise and prudent mothers." Yet their ultimate task would be insuring the success of the republican experiment and even ushering in the millennium, "that at least, one spot of the earth may be reserved as a monument of the effects of good education, in order to show in some degree what our species was before the fall and what it shall be after its restoration."[67]

Thus, in post-Revolutionary decades Americans of varying religious denominations and political persuasions adapted enlightened child-rearing to their new republican circumstances. Gradually, they began the process of forming colonial regions into a national republican culture. As this culture coalesced, hope for the new republic focused on the malleable child in an altogether unprecedented way. Varying concepts of virtue fused into concern with instilling the moral restraint essential for citizenship. The affectionate anti-patriarchal family became the environment in which virtue could be inculcated, delineating a new role for wives and mothers. Affectionate ties could be forged, social cohesion achieved, and moral restraint reinforced in uniform, perhaps even public, schools. Moral restraint internalized through inherited religious belief could serve republican goals in a new instrumental way. As the eighteenth century slipped into the nineteenth, American adults would seek to shape and control the development of children. But as their plans reached the lives of real children, these children would be affected in ways printers, physicians, clergymen, and educators of the Revolutionary generation could barely anticipate.

3

Physical Management of Children

Child Health and Mortality, the Evolving Maternal Role, and the "American Revolution" in Medicine

Let your tenderness, then, render you tremblingly alive to every appearance of danger.

Mary Palmer Tyler, "the maternal physician," 1811

Hence the lancet is oftener required than the stimulating draught; and hence, too, the reason why the European physician, whose circle of observation may have been confined to disease of an opposite character, hears with astonishment of the depleting system of the United States and especially of Philadelphia.

Dr. James Mease, 1811

In the early American republic, the primary caretaker for the first seven years of a child's life was usually the mother. The educational theorist Benjamin Rush assigned to American women a role that Linda Kerber has labeled "republican motherhood"—the responsibility to instill civic virtue in children in the first years of life. American women would not be citizens, but they would play a crucial quasi-political role in stabilizing the new republic.[1] Yet even Rush saw women first as wives and then as mothers.[2] And letters and diaries left by women who experienced the Revolution seldom refer to political implications of their maternal duties. These mothers were deeply concerned with the religious education of their children. In the colonial period women had outnumbered men as church members and had assumed the task of reinforcing religious values within the family.[3] They were also profoundly, even desperately, absorbed with issues of child health. As they cared for their children, upper-class literate women throughout the early republic read enlightened medical advice and anxiously attempted to follow its precepts.

Early in the nineteenth century, Americans began to produce their own medical manuals. Not unlike printers and educators, authors of these works adapted European enlightened thought to American experience. Sharpening the definitions of maternal duty, they contributed to the demarcation of the maternal role, which would be elaborated as the century progressed. In 1811, Mary Palmer Tyler of Vermont, who called herself "the maternal physician," combined the enlightened advice she read with her own observations and practices, only implicitly linking her child-rearing to republican ideology. By the 1820s, as capitalism transformed the northeastern economy, Americans sought cultural independence and a national identity. When Philadelphian Dr. William Potts Dewees published his *Treatise on the Physical and Medical Treatment of Children* in 1825, he reiterated precepts of enlightened child-rearing. Yet he also prescribed for the new commercial middle class a sentimental definition of maternal duty and management of children with new, indirect controls. And he disseminated across the nation the "American Revolution" in medicine, worked out in post-Revolutionary decades by physician and educator Benjamin Rush.

The "American Revolution" in medicine revealed an ironic, darker side of optimistic republican efforts to mold and control. In the 1790s, as physicians struggled to gain control over health and loss of life, they evolved and defended a therapy of vigorous intervention, including "copious" blood-letting and violent purging. As democratizing forces continued to generate attacks on established authority, encourage the movement of people, and stimulate entrepreneurial activity, by the early nineteenth century this active medical therapy seemed well suited to the aspiring, disorderly, and young population of the United States. When Dr. William Potts Dewees applied the "heroic" practice to the treatment of children in 1825, the tragic and unexpected consequences of that approach had already been evident for a generation. As the nineteenth century progressed, methods of physical management of children may have improved in upper- and middle-class homes. Mortality of infants and children, however, remained high, particularly among the poor, who lived in crowded conditions. Affectionate parents, increasingly valuing each child's individuality, were forced to confront the harsh reality of child death.

As they expressed their thoughts in letters and diaries, early republican mothers and grandmothers were profoundly absorbed in rearing children; yet they rarely referred to political implications of their task. Literate upper-class mothers did read enlightened child-rearing advice and consciously attempted to follow its precepts. Yet even wives and daughters of patriots could be deeply ambivalent, resentful and melancholy when left alone, instructing their children more forcefully in religious than civic values. Abigail Adams, the quintessential "republican mother," did persuade seven-year-old John Quincy to read "Rollin's ancient History" aloud to her in 1774 while her husband served in the Continental Congress. Relying on post-Lockean associationist psychology, she hoped that Johnny's "desire to oblige" would transfer the affection he felt for her to classical examples of virtue. Yet, as Edith Gelles has pointed out, Adams missed her son like a "Limb lopt of[f]" when she reluctantly allowed the 11-year-old to accompany his father to Europe in 1778. Although she advised Johnny to "Improve your understanding for acquiring usefull knowledge and virtue, such as will render you an ornament to society, an Honour to your Country, and a Blessing to your parents," she also admonished him to "Adhere to those religious Sentiments and principals which were early instilled into your mind," and rather harshly concluded her letter, "I had much rather you should have found your Grave in the ocean you have crossd, or any untimely death crop you in your Infant years, rather than see you an immoral profligate or a Graceless child."[4]

Martha Laurens Ramsay of Charleston, South Carolina, daughter of one patriot and wife of another, "studied with deep interest most of the esteemed practical treatises on education, both in French and English" in the 1780s and 1790s. Although she read Rousseau, her "decided preference" was for "the writings of Mr. Locke and Dr. Witherspoon." This mother would follow enlightened precepts in rearing the 8 surviving of her 11 children, but, deeply convinced of her own sinfulness since her conversion at the age of 14, she also "early taught" them "their miserable and corrupted state by nature: that they were born into a world of sin and misery—surrounded with temptations—and without the possibility of salvation, but by the grace of God." When she sent David Jr. off to Princeton in 1810, Ramsay reminded him to "give dignity to the Carolinian name," but urged more forcefully: "Be not ashamed of religion; read your Bible diligently; it will not only make you wise unto salvation, but you will find in it excellent direction for your conduct in the affairs of this life."[5]

Margaret Izard Manigault, daughter of a patriot who became one of South Carolina's first United States Senators, found Charleston "extremely dull—The ladies lying in, & the Gentlemen setting out," when her husband Gabriel left her with two small children to attend the state legislature in Columbia in 1792. Having already lost two of four infants, this 24-year-old mother, again pregnant, could not contain her passion and her melancholy.

"At these moments I am anxious, weary, restless beyond description," she wrote her citizen-husband. "It is leading this melancholy, solitary, moping kind of life, which I have never been accustomed to, which I hate." In a jealous outburst, Manigault threatened, "I wish I could amuse myself, instead of sitting moping all alone as I do. For I'm told that there are ways & means of diverting oneself a little in this Town!" To which her husband replied: "You are certainly right in thinking that it is wrong to sacrifice our happiness to our patriotism. How very often have I thought so since I left you."[6]

Well-to-do mothers and grandmothers in cosmopolitan Philadelphia had ready access to materials on enlightened child-rearing. Elizabeth Drinker, wife of a wealthy Quaker merchant, bought, and then read and recorded her opinion of, each child-rearing manual and new model of children's literature almost as soon as it appeared in local bookstores.[7] Less confident mothers of a younger generation, such as Sally Logan Fisher or Nancy Shippen Livingston, learned Lockean advice from neighbors and friends and carefully copied in journals or commonplace books enlightened child-rearing maxims they learned from reading.[8] Yet Quaker women did not link these maxims to republican ideology. Both Drinker and Fisher had suffered persecution by radical patriots when their husbands were imprisoned for their refusal to sign loyalty oaths during the war; both had experienced economic distress when their parlor and dining-room furniture, mirrors, and tableware were seized by patriots as fines.[9] Patriotic persecution caused the neutral Quakers to become more concerned about protecting their children in a rapidly changing urban environment that no long offered asylum to members of their faith. Quaker men repeatedly visited the women's meeting, exhorting mothers to take their maternal role seriously, speaking "beautifully & very forcibly to the Wives & Mothers present pointing out to them their several Duties & the great benefit that arose to Society if they performed them."[10]

These women had been born into colonial ruling elites, but most mothers of the early republic lived on farms or in villages. When the midwife Martha Ballard moved to Hallowell in northern Massachusetts (which would later become Maine), 100 families, many still living in log houses, were spread along 10 miles of the Kennebec River. There Ballard engaged in the domestic production, economy of barter and local exchange, and neighborly service characteristic of colonial New England. According to historian Laurel Thatcher Ulrich, in post-Revolutionary decades Ballard was more a colonial goodwife than a republican mother: "Her life had been altered by the Revolution, but her identity was unrelated to the rituals of republicanism . . . Her values had been formed in an older world, in which a woman's worth was measured by her service to God and her neighbors rather than to a nebulous and distant state."[11]

In the 1790s, Daniel Drake grew up in Mayslick, Kentucky, where his barely literate mother exhibited the deferential attitudes of a hierarchical society and kept house first in "a covered pen built for sheep" and then in a log cabin fitted into a side hill with a pen beneath it to protect the sheep from "both wolves and weather" in the winter.[12] Although he lived on the western fringe of settlement, Drake's experience was not unusual in the early republic. In analyzing records kept by the assessors of the 1798 federal Direct Tax on households, Jack Larkin discovered that more than 40 percent of American homes were valued at $100 or less. Many families of artisans and small farmers lived in one- to three-room one-story wooden dwellings. Archaeological investigation has revealed the tiny 14- by 17-feet structures that housed one or two families in the poor "Snowtown" neighborhood in Providence, Rhode Island. Many slaveholders throughout the South still lived in the kind of small earthfast vernacular wooden dwellings that Southerners built throughout the colonial period, while slaves grew up in one-room unpartitioned cabins that were 12- to 15-feet or 10-feet-square. Only one white American family in 10 owned a home valued at more than $700, such as a substantial two-story farmhouse with six or seven rooms. And only one family in 100 could live in the elite Federal style—a gracious and well-furnished home in the countryside with double chimneys and a central hallway leading to four well-proportioned rooms on each of two stories, or an elegant three-story row or detached house in a city.[13]

These American dwellings, large and small, overflowed with children in post-Revolutionary decades. From the 1790s to 1830, the median age of Americans was approximately 16. Household size in 1790 ranged from an average of 5.7 in the area that became Maine to 9.5 in South Carolina and 9.1 in Maryland, where plantations with large numbers of slaves skewed the figure upward. Yet these snapshot figures do not accurately reveal family size. Most women, married by their early 20s in the North and late teens in portions of the South, if marriage was not interrupted by death, bore children in 24- to 30-month intervals until they experienced menopause in their late forties. In these "stair-step" families, mothers could bear an average of six or seven children, but older siblings could be leaving home before the younger ones were born. Because the largest families, with 8 to 11 offspring, contained more children, we may conclude that more than half of America's early republican children grew up in large households.[14] Boys and girls slept three and four to a bed, sometimes in separate rooms and sometimes not, and many children were raised mostly by older siblings.

As internal commerce proliferated, in northeastern urban centers and the surrounding countryside the high birthrate of the colonial period was already slightly falling. The average of 7.4 children born to colonial mothers had fallen to an average of 6.4 for those who married in the late eighteenth century; women who married between 1800 and 1849 would bear an average of 4.9 children. Some northeastern parents were beginning to follow a new pattern of having several children early in the marriage according to the traditional two-year interval but then dropping off sharply when the mother reached the age of 30 or 35. Other couples were producing children in longer birth intervals, perhaps every three years instead of every two. These private decisions to limit family size began to be made as the northeastern economy was transformed by internal commerce and then industrialization. Nevertheless, as the nineteenth century progressed, the trend to limit births traveled south and west; by 1820 white birthrates in the upper South would reach the northeastern figure for 1800, a rate not reached in the new western states of Michigan and Wisconsin until as late as 1850. In 1800 the birthrate for enslaved black mothers was as high as that for whites; black birthrates would remain high throughout the antebellum period and not begin to follow the falling national trend until after emancipation, as late as the 1880s.[15]

Early republican mothers feared the dangers of childbirth; in the childbearing years, between the ages of 20 and 45, women's life expectancies continued to be lower than men's.[16] An experienced midwife like Martha Ballard, who practiced between 1785 and 1812, did not lose a single mother during the delivery of more than 800 babies; but five mothers did die during the lying-in period, a record of one maternal death for every 198 living births.[17] Mothers weakened by repeated births and burdened by a busy work schedule also succumbed more readily to chronic conditions and infectious diseases. In January of 1800, 27-year-old Louisa Adams Park, suffering from "Colds, want of appetite and weakness" in her drafty Massachusetts dwelling, was certain she would die during childbirth. "I have always, from the first, had a presentiment that I should never live to see May," she wrote her husband, "and it grows stronger every day."[18] After 1800, women of the Virginia gentry increasingly described pregnancy and birth as illness.[19] And in Philadelphia, as severely injured Molly Drinker Rhoads lost a breech birth and Sally Drinker Downing endured a "very sharp labour" to bring forth a "little pritty plump babe," their mother, Elizabeth Drinker, confided in her diary, "myself nor Daughters were never quick in this business; lingering, tedious, distressing times have always been our lots."[20]

To assuage fears and deal with these "distressing" births, well-to-do urban women increasingly turned to male physicians in post-Revolutionary decades. English male midwives and French physicians had assisted births with various styles of forceps in the eighteenth century. American doctors such as Dr. William Shippen Jr. of Philadelphia learned about such procedures when they trained in London with obstetrical experts. Dr. Shippen had established a training course for midwives as early as 1765, but between female midwives and the male medical community shared efforts gave way to considerable distrust and animosity.[21] Physicians had to combat prejudice against allowing men at the delivery and were annoyed by the female relatives, neighbors, and friends who gathered at the ritual of birth. Dr. Samuel Powel Griffitts of Philadelphia complained in 1795 that such groups of women crowd the house, obstruct the attendants, bother the patient with their noise, "and often, by their untimely and impertinent advice, do much mischief."[22] But midwife Martha Ballard found the 24-year-old professional Dr. Benjamin Page inexperienced and officious, objecting that he intervened in situations she would have waited out, administered laudanum (liquid opium) and practiced bloodletting instead of employing her comforting herbal remedies, and charged six dollars to her two dollars for a delivery. On one occasion she caustically commented that a Mrs. Kimball "was delivered of a dead daughter . . . the operation performed by Ben Page. The infants limbs were much dislocated as I am informed."[23]

Some children did not survive the birth process, perhaps due to trauma inflicted on them. Of the 814 births attended by Ballard, 14 children (1.8/100) were delivered stillborn and 20 (2.5/100) died as newborns.[24] Whether delivered by physicians in urban homes or almshouses, or by mid-wives in artisans' dwellings, on farms, or on plantations, other children entered the world bruised, injured, or considerably weakened. In 1781 45-year-old Elizabeth Drinker's seventh and last-born Charles was "alive and that was all . . . little more than skin and bone" at birth; his mother "did not expect he would survive many days." In 1795, when Dr. Shippen, who would warn attendants of a difficult birth by rattling the instruments in his pocket, assisted her oldest daughter Sally, Drinker recorded, "The little one seems hart whole, 'tho the blood is much settl'd in his legs, feet, etc., his feet almost as blue as indigo." "The dear little babe is bruised in many places in its lower parts—it eats and sucks well, but is hurt when the legs and feet are han-dled."[25] Louisa Adams Park did survive the birth of her son Warren in 1800 but continued to worry. "The little innocent that now lies sleeping in my lap, I wish was in better health," she reported to his father. "He is a slender child, and grows but little."[26]

Mothers watched carefully over newborns, considering the first two years of life the most dangerous. In 1811, Mary Palmer Tyler of Vermont, who called herself "the maternal physician," published one of the first indigenous manuals of child-rearing advice. Reporting that she felt "rapture" at the birth of each of her eight—by 1818 eleven—children, she admitted the "anxiety" she endured thereafter for their health. "Let your tenderness, then," she advised, "render you tremblingly alive to every appearance of danger." Born in Boston in 1775, Tyler had been raised with Lockean methods and later had read the enlightened medical literature. Yet, left alone when her husband, Royall Tyler, rode the circuit as justice of the Vermont Supreme Court, she also relied on her own observations and experience. Her manual contained both approaches. She recommended washing newborns in warm castile suds rinsed with cold water, and then dressing them in "clouts" or diapers and a "light and easy" gown. Following the advice of Dr. William Buchan's *Domestic Medicine*, Tyler suggested a "belly band" made of linen with a hole cut for the navel, drawn firmly but not too tight. Yet, supplementing enlightened advice with her own rural New England practices, she proposed covering the navel with a split raisin sprinkled with nutmeg and washed with sweet oil; if the navel discharged, she applied a cabbage leaf.[27]

Most American mothers breast-fed their own children. For mothers temporarily unable to nurse, New England relatives and neighbors followed the custom of exchange or courtesy wet-nursing. Martha Ballard arranged that two neighbors nurse the infant of Lucy Towne in 1793, when the new mother fell ill with fever a week after delivery.[28] In 1781 Elizabeth Drinker in Philadelphia "agree'd with Rachel Bickerton a shoemaker's wife next door to come in 4 or 5 times a Day" for four weeks to suckle her infant Charles while she recovered from a debilitating delivery. After employing three more wet nurses, Drinker felt it "a favour to be able to do that office oneself—as there is much trouble with nurses," and she was able to breast-feed Charles as long as two years.[29]

By the turn of the nineteenth century, some mothers attempted to prevent conception and lengthen birth intervals by nursing each child for a longer period. Quaker parents were among the first Americans to seek some control over fertility. In 1799 Elizabeth Drinker counseled her ill and despondent daughter Sally, in labor on her 39th birthday, "that this might possibly be the last trial of this sort, if she could suckle her baby for 2 years to come, as she had several times done heretofore."[30] Slaves nursed the children of South Carolinian Margaret Izard Manigault, who from her marriage in 1785 gave birth almost yearly until 1800 when she was 32; after that, she somehow managed to lengthen birth intervals to three or four years.[31] But Martha Laurens Ramsay, also of Charleston, followed enlightened advice and "suckled" all of her 11 children herself "without the aid of any wet nurse."[32]

In 1770, Landon Carter's daughter-in-law, who advocated new methods of child-rearing, had to fight to nurse her own child. Virginia gentry women of the next generation were more likely to breast-feed their infants themselves, perhaps in a futile effort to reduce their high average birthrate of 8.3 children.[33] "The maternal physician" Mary Palmer Tyler assumed in 1811 that mothers would breast-feed because of the positive pleasure of the experience.[34] Nevertheless, prolonged breast-feeding became less respectable as the nineteenth century progressed. In 1825, when Dr. William Potts Dewees published his immensely popular *Treatise on the Physical and Medical Treatment of Children,* he appealed not only to natural affections implanted in the female breast but also to guilt. Failure of a mother to nurse, the physician insisted, was "cruel and unnatural repudiation" of the child and was viewed by some as "absolutely criminal."[35]

Mary Palmer Tyler, whose father had participated in the Boston Tea Party, was keenly aware of her revolutionary heritage; her 1811 manual of child-rearing advice was dedicated to her own mother, who had fled the skirmish at Lexington with the author as a babe in arms. Implicitly recognizing republican responsibility, she urged mothers to encourage physical liberty and to stimulate mental alertness in their children. She had placed her newborns naked before the fire each day and had rubbed their bare limbs to "give a spring to the blood." Dressing her infants in soft and easy shirts and gowns, she had excited them to stretch, gently tossed them, and encouraged them to look about. She advised that older infants' "minds will appear to open much earlier" if they are carried outside daily to breathe fresh air. Urging mothers to talk to their children, she suggested that they stimulate babies by dangling in front of them bright and attractive objects.

The maternal physician recommended that the child be up and about by the fifth or sixth month, sitting upright and creeping when ready in order to develop an "elegant" form. Since "those pernicious inventions"—the walking-stools, go-carts, and leading strings used by earlier generations—were happily almost obsolete, a child could learn to walk naturally, according to his or her own inclination, with the carpet (beginning to appear in middle- and upper-class parlors) cushioning inevitable falls.[36] Colonial parents had encouraged their children to stand and not allowed them to creep (as animals did) through the use of such furniture as standing stools—stools or wooden boxes with holes for the child's waist—but by the early nineteenth century these items were disappearing.[37] Parents were advised to encourage autonomy in their children by allowing physical liberty and stimulating mental alertness.

If a child was healthy and not bothered too much by the red gum rash, thrush or sore mouth, "snuffles," or "wind," infancy could be relatively secure and comfortable. Even in poor homes and slave cabins, babies enjoyed maternal nursing, a spot by the fire, and the stimulation of a large family. Yet weaning and teething between the ages of 5 and 20 months was a dangerous and difficult time; mothers faced weaning with anxiety and considered teething a perilous new stage of development. Although Mary Palmer Tyler advised a mother to "steel" herself to giving up the "rapture" of nursing when the child reached the age of 9 to 12 months, children were actually weaned at any point up until the end of the second year. The health of the mother, the development of "bad" or "broken" breasts, as well as the desire to lengthen birth intervals, could determine timing for weaning: when Nancy Drinker Skyrin fell ill in 1802, she was forced to wean 16-month-old Mary sooner than she had wished. Urbanites and Southerners, reluctant to wean children during hot summer months, put off the process until early fall. When two-year-old Sally Rhoads was finally weaned in October of 1800, she did not like it. "Molly sent her daughter here forenoon," her grandmother recorded, "she looks the worse for her weaning."[38]

Some colonial New England women took a "weaning journey," perhaps to a relative's house, leaving the child at home;[39] in the early nineteenth century Mary Palmer Tyler still knew of children weaned abruptly through separation from their mothers. Nevertheless, she advised a gradual transition, as the mother slowly substituted meat broths and jellies, bread and cow's milk, for the breast. If the child seemed "dejected," it was all right for the mother to amuse him, carry him out, or keep him awake in order that he might sleep the night. If he was restless at night, she could give paregoric or a syrup of white poppies and even let him drink from the breast a little.[40]

Children undergoing weaning frequently experienced digestive problems as they encountered microorganisms in foods other than the mother's milk. Parents and doctors attributed such "flux" or "lax" to teething,[41] which they treated with further purging. The maternal physician had witnessed convulsions, fevers, and violent diarrhea during "the often painful and critical period of Dentition" and recommended that the bowels be "kept open" with doses of magnesia, syrup of elderberries, or rhubarb. She rubbed sore gums with honey and let her children play with an ivory or ebony corkscrew covered with a new cork. She was not afraid to lance swollen gums herself with a razor wrapped in a handkerchief ("always making it a point to feel the razor grate against the tooth") while the child slept on her lap.[42]

Dr. Dewees measured stages of childhood by the appearance of teeth and viewed weaning and teething as closely linked, the appearance of teeth an indication that the stomach was ready to digest solid food. He had observed diarrhea and convulsions, indeed "excessive" mortality, during teething and believed the process made the system irritable. He also recommended purges with such "gentle laxatives" as molasses or manna, but in extreme cases he prescribed a medicine as "brisk" as calomel, containing mercury. And he, too, instructed reluctant mothers to lance gums "with a bold hand and a sharp instrument" while the wiggling child was held firmly in a horizontal position on the lap.[43]

Problems of weaning and teething could be compounded for early republican children as parents began to replace previous indulgence with discipline. Following the Lockean methods used by her own parents, Mary Palmer Tyler began to teach obedience and regulation of desire with gentle but firm denials when the child was as young as eight or nine months. "After a few lessons of this kind," she asserted, "your word will no longer be disputed, while your children, thus early taught submission, will never require any severity whatever."[44] Calvinist parents still viewed early willfulness as a sign of human depravity that needed to be curbed. An anonymous article in *The Panoplist* in 1814 urged that wishes be crossed as soon as they were formed "by the time a child is two years old," if not "still earlier."[45] And most children lost their position of privilege in the household sometime in their second or third year with the arrival of a new sibling.

Letters and diaries are silent on issues of toilet training, which may have been casual in the early nineteenth century. Many rural houses did not have privies, and young children in loose shirts and gowns answered nature's call when and where they could. Substantial farmsteads and urban homes had backyard "necessaries," and families kept chamber pots to avoid a trip outdoors at night.[46] In his 1825 treatise Dr. Dewees suggested that children could learn to use the "chair" from older brothers and sisters. "[C]hildren will very early declare their wants as regards their evacuations, if they be frequently placed upon their chairs, whenever they seem to manifest a desire to relieve themselves," he counseled. A child placed on the chair at regular intervals—for example, morning, noon, and night—would soon acquire regular habits.[47]

Nevertheless, as direct external discipline declined in this increasingly democratic society, anxious parents could use this critical period of weaning, teething, and toilet training to introduce indirect controls. Although maternal nursing would create bonds of affection, and encouragement of physical liberty and stimulation of mental alertness would develop autonomy in children, during the period when children began to exhibit signs of willfulness, parents and physicians increasingly focused on the purge. Treating the digestive ailments that accompanied weaning and teething with purgative medicines, they gained considerable control over a child's elimination. During this same period, parents introduced behavioral lessons to subordinate children to adult authority. It would have been difficult for a stubborn two-year-old to resist an overwhelming parent by retaining his or her feces, when such resistance could so effectively be overcome with doses of rhubarb, molasses, castor oil, or even calomel.

During early childhood mothers treated both sexes alike; both boys and girls were relegated to feminine circles. In well-to-do homes, however, children of both sexes wore clothing different from that of adult females, distinguishing childhood—straight and loose haircuts with bangs, soft shoes, and casually belted muslin frocks[48] (see figure 5). Around the age of four or five, boys were encouraged to form a male identity; they gave up frocks and wore "Jacket and trowsers" for the first time. In 1799 Elizabeth Drinker recorded the "breeching" of four-year-old Henry Downing: "Sally has a Young Woman at work . . . making a little man of Henry—he is very pleas'd . . . one of the happiest days of his life."[49] Four-year-old Henry Manigault in South Carolina was similarly delighted with his new clothes. "Our son is hopping about me like a little bird," his mother wrote his father. "He has got his new clothes on & he asks if he does not look very pretty . . . He goes out with me to pay visits and behaves very prettily."[50]

Boys wore hussar or skeleton suits—long trousers and short jackets—modeled after soldiers' and sailors' uniforms, while girls continued to wear muslin frocks (see figure 6). In the 1790s girls as young as five were measured for stays, and the Drinker family owned an iron collar worn to correct the carriage of a "crooked" child.[51] After the turn of the century, however, the

Figure 5. *The Sargent Family.* Unknown American artist; Charlestown, Massachusetts, 1800. By the turn of the nineteenth century, children wore clothing which distinguished childhood: short haircuts with bangs, soft shoes, and casually belted muslin frocks. *National Gallery of Art, Washington, D.C.; gift of Edgar William and Bernice Chrysler Garbisch.*

enlightened preference for loose clothing prevailed, and such practices were abandoned. In 1825 Dr. Dewees could report that "stiff stays for female, and the tight waistbands of breeches for male children . . . have now yielded to the unconfined frock, in the one, and the modern invention of suspenders, in the other."[52]

Farm children owned relatively little clothing but followed similar gender differentiation. Daniel Drake in Mayslick, Kentucky, had a "suit of butternut linsey, a wool hat, a pair of mittens, and a pair of old stocking-legs drawn down like gaiters over my shoes to keep out the snow."[53] On farms where families produced their own cloth, men and boys wore long homespun frocks or shirts and trousers made of "towcloth"—coarse linen made from short flax fibers—or wool, or a combination of the two, "linsey-woolsey." Women and girls wore longer shirts under petticoats and dresses. Both sexes and all ages went barefoot until winter forced their feet into crude shoes, those of children sometimes so large that rags had to be stuffed in the toes. Slaves also

Figure 6. *The Children of Nathan Starr.* Ambrose Andrews; Middletown, Connecticut, 1835. The Starr children enjoy a game of shuttlecock in their well-ventilated central hall. Fifteen-year-old Emily and twelve-year-old Grace wear muslin frocks, while nine-year-old Henry and six-year-old Frederick have graduated to skeleton suits—long trousers and short jackets. The painting may have been commissioned to memorialize Edward, still dressed in feminine clothing, who died in 1835 at the age of three. *The Metropolitan Museum of Art, New York City; partial anonymous gift in memory of Nathan Comfort Starr (1896–1981) 1987.*

wore towcloth or later rough cotton: pants and a shirt for males, a gown or a dress for females. Former slave Frederick Douglass recalled, however, that on the Maryland plantation where he grew up, if children wore out the two shirts they received each year, they often ran about "almost naked."[54]

Gender identity was shaped and reinforced for children by tasks and toys. With the growth of internal commerce, itinerant portrait painters roamed the Northeast, as ordinary families sought to record for posterity their aspirations to middle-class gentility and status. In these portraits, even little boys still in frocks hold symbols of adult masculinity: Pearson Doty dangles his father's pocket watch; tiny twins Francis and John Fuller sport a riding whip; and Edward Gorham hammers tacks into a chair (see figure 7). Older boys wear skeleton suits or, by the 1830s, longer coats and trousers, and carry hammers or books. Girls of all ages, dressed in frocks, sit in small chairs holding books

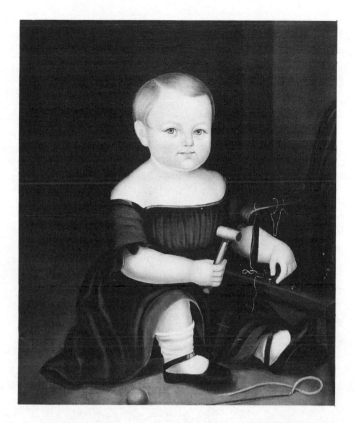

Figure 7. *Edward W. Gorham.* Joseph Whiting Stock; Springfield, Massachusetts, 1844. Edward W. Gorham, who died at the age of 20 months, was memorialized by this posthumous image. Although he is dressed in feminine clothing, his masculine identity is clearly indicated by his act of hammering tacks into a chair. *New York State Historical Association, Cooperstown.*

or dolls.[55] A study of portraits of children under seven painted by the 1830s reveals boys with balls or battledores; swords, bugles, toy soldiers, or drums; or wagons, hobby horses, or pony whips. Only 20 percent of the girls in the portraits hold toys at all, and when they do, they are always dolls or doll equipment—doll beds or tiny tea sets[56] (see figure 8).

Experts advised that both boys and girls run about in the open air, and rural children undoubtedly did so. Nevertheless, by 1825 Dr. Dewees included a long discussion of the controlled environment of indoor nursery space, directed to urban families of the new middle class of entrepreneurs, managers, professionals, and office workers who were supplanting the older "middling ranks" of artisans and farmers.[57] "The nursery should be the purest place in the house, as well as the one in which the children should most

Figure 8. *The Hobby Horse.* Unknown American artist, c. 1850. Once again, although a small boy is dressed in feminine clothing and both children have short haircuts, gender identity is clearly established. The older girl holds a bonnet, while the younger boy rides a hobby horse and carries a whip. *National Gallery of Art, Washington, D.C.; gift of Edgar William and Bernice Chrysler Garbisch.*

delight to be," he counseled, recommending the use of two rooms on an upper floor, "spacious, with a high ceiling, and perfectly dry." Doors and windows should be protected with "latticed half-doors" and "cross-bars," and ventilation a daily ritual to keep nursery air fresh and pure. Cooking, washing, or ironing should not be done in the nursery, to prevent not only accidents but also foul "vapours" caused by work.

In the controlled environment of the middle-class nursery, children would be allowed industrious play, amusement, and delight. Dr. Dewees recommended that games be provided: "a small backgammon table with men, but without dice," battledore or shuttlecock, a large cup and balls, a set of ninepins and ball, a rocking horse, slates and pencils, and assorted "dissected maps," Chinese puzzles, and tangrams. "A quantity of regularly shaped pieces of wood, of various sizes," would prove useful for children to arrange "with great ingenuity into houses, temples, and churches." As he sharpened the definition of maternal duty by providing rules for mothers to follow, the physician insisted that this isolated and protected environment be under the mother's constant surveillance. Dr. Dewees warned parents that "Children should never be left alone—their helpless condition requires constant care, especially when very young."[58]

In the 1820s middle-class children as young as seven kept diaries in which they revealed their internalization of gender identification and preparation for the adult roles encouraged by the parent of their sex. Seven-year-old Louisa Jane Trumbell of Worcester, Massachusetts, whose father was "Cashier of the Central Bank," spent her time drawing, making molasses candy, sewing for her doll, and making visits with her mother. Louisa's brothers Joseph and John dug in the dirt with shovels, but she and her sister Caroline played in the "wood-house," making tea and serving beans for cake.[59] Eight-year-old William Hoppin of Providence, Rhode Island, son of a merchant, tried very hard to adhere to the strictures impressed upon him by his father. Although he skated and went "slaying" in winter and played ball in spring, William felt guilty when he did so, remarking, "I think that boys in general do not fuly apprcciate the value of time, a thing which my Father has tried to impress seriously on my mind."[60]

These American children would grow taller than their European counterparts because of the increasing abundance—especially of vegetables—in their diets. Southern and western households still based their meals on pork, corn, and sometimes rice, turnips, or sweet potatoes, supplemented with eggs and "greens." Daniel Drake reported that in Kentucky in the late eighteenth century cornmeal mush or grits was the "standing dish for young children."[61] Northeastern farm families, on the other hand, were consuming wheat bread, beef, dairy products, and root vegetables—squash, onions, turnips, and cabbages—by the early nineteenth century. With the expansion of internal commerce, urban families could purchase these foodstuffs from the country more easily; more households had access to such imported items as spices, sugar, tea, and coffee.[62] Benjamin Rush believed that a "revolution" in diet had occurred by 1810, as meat, served only once rather than two or three times a day, was replaced by a "profusion of winter and summer vegetables."[63]

In 1825 Dr. Dewees recommended simple foods for young children— puddings and broths, breads, vegetables, and beef, mutton, or fowl—but he worried that fresh fruit would bring on disease. He also instructed mothers to supervise diet closely as an additional means of establishing indirect parental control. "It only requires a little firmness in the beginning, and that not of very long continuance," he advised, "to make children conform to the dictates of their parents, and to render them entirely obedient to their wills." Neither the child's "palate nor its caprice, is to be consulted—the parent must set before it for its meals, such articles of food as are judged best for it, and it is made to understand, that it must eat them or nothing." As the privatized nuclear family of the new middle class intensified its focus on slightly fewer numbers of children, and corporal punishment and use of communal shame declined, parents could resort to indirect means to maintain control through restriction of the child's diet, vigilant surveillance of controlled nursery space, and the use of purgative medicines.[64]

Although changes in diet and careful attention to methods of management may have improved the health of upper- and middle-class children, infant and child mortality remained high. Parents, who increasingly valued the individuality of each child, were forced to confront the reality of child death. From the 1790s through 1830 in Philadelphia, approximately 40 percent of all deaths were children under the age of 10. According to statistics kept by urban boards of health from 1815 through 1825, proportionate mortality of children under 10 was slightly higher in New York, at about 43 percent of all deaths, and in Baltimore, at about 44 percent. In Boston and Charleston, South Carolina, proportionate child death was slightly lower, at 38 and 36 percent respectively, although the difference in Charleston may have been caused by higher adult mortality. Only in smaller New England centers such as Salem, Massachusetts, and Portsmouth, New Hampshire, did the proportion of deaths under the age of 10 fall to as low as 30 percent of all fatalities.[65]

For children in all localities the first year of life was the most dangerous. Children under the age of one accounted for 15 to 25 percent of all deaths. Records kept by urban boards of health attributed these infant deaths to respiratory ailments, diarrhea, and less precise causes such as convulsions, "dropsy of the brain," "debility," or "decay."[66] In a study of records kept by six Philadelphia denominations from 1720 to 1830, Susan E. Klepp found that mortality under the age of one declined by more than 50 percent among the upper classes during the 110-year period. The greatest drop in mortality occurred during the first month of life and was perhaps due to improved management of newborns. Mothers restricting births in their late 30s may have reduced the high risk incurred by later pregnancies. Neonatal death rates fell among all classes, but remained high among the poor, who lived in increasingly crowded conditions as the nineteenth century progressed. While mortality fluctuated with epidemics in the colonial period, by the 1820s it followed economic conditions—lower in prosperous periods and increasing in hard times—as families living close to the margin of poverty struggled to provide for their children.[67]

While mortality rates fell for children in the first year of life, they remained high during weaning and teething. According to records kept by urban boards of health, 6 to 10 percent of all deaths were children between the ages of one and two. The largest number of deaths in the second year of life resulted from digestive ailments, as children undergoing weaning were exposed to microorganisms in foods other than the mother's milk.[68] Alarming to parents and physicians in Philadelphia, Baltimore, Richmond, and Cincinnati was the condition they labeled "cholera infantum" or "cholera morbus." Dr. William Currie of Philadelphia reported that cholera morbus began suddenly, as the child was stricken with severe diarrhea. The stomach would harden, a kind of "hooping" cough would appear, and death would follow in one or two days. Children who lingered eventually succumbed to dehydration from prolonged diarrhea. In 1792 Dr. Currie treated cholera morbus with "tonics, spirituous drinks, warm clothing, cleanliness, pure air, and moderate exercise, with occasional use of Laudanum [liquid opium], in very small but liquid doses."[69]

By the 1820s Philadelphia contained a free African-American community of approximately 12,000 persons, as slaves freed through gradual emancipation congregated in the city's southwest side and suburbs. Dr. Gouverneur Emerson observed that "numerous deaths" among infants and young children due to "bowel complaints" were "generally confined to the offspring of the poor, and especially among the blacks. Indeed, deaths by cholera infantum rarely happen in houses with large and well-aired apartments." As the nineteenth century progressed, the link between mortality in urban centers and poverty was evident in crude death rates calculated according to race. Dr. Emerson figured the mortality rate of white Philadelphians in 1820 as one death in about 50 individuals, but that of blacks as one in 19.[70]

Parents associated digestive problems with the presence of worms, and many early republican children and some adults did have worms. The symptoms ranged from diarrhea and vomiting to itchy nose, headache, and poor eyesight. Nancy Drinker Skyrin, who may have picked up worms while staying with a wet-nurse, was troubled by their presence throughout her life, as were her children. Dr. William Buchan's *Domestic Medicine* recommended treatment with Carolina pinkroot, but enterprising individuals who specialized in the treatment of worms might give a child a medicine as strong as calomel, containing mercury. After Eliza Skyrin was sent to the "worm doctor," her grandmother, Elizabeth Drinker, recorded that the four-year-old child "voided a worm 9-1/2 inches long. I cut it open with my sicers and found several young ones in it." The next day, however, Eliza continued to be ill from the medicine. "I expect there was mercury" in it, judged her grandmother, which "made her very sick."[71]

In all localities, children between the ages of two and five accounted for about 6 percent of all deaths. Children of these ages were particularly susceptible to childhood contagious diseases, many of which were fatal in the early nineteenth century. A major danger for children throughout the early republic was Cynanche Trachealis or "hives," either croup or the dreaded diphtheria, given its popular name by the "heaves" of a child struggling to breathe.

Doctors who dissected the bodies of children who died from hives found in some cases a "membrane lining the whole internal surface of the upper part of the Trachea." Cases in which the membrane was present were diphtheria, and there was little short of tracheotomy that could be done to save the child. Dr. William Currie treated hives with rather drastic measures, recommending bleeding, inducing vomit, purging, and blistering on the neck.[72] In 1784 little Charles Drinker, who "after diligent nursing had outgrown most of his weakness and promised fair to be a fine boy," died from hives 20 minutes after being treated by Dr. John Redman with a "gentle vomit" which "agatated him much." His mother recorded:

> [H]e expired aged 2 years 7 months and one day—about a week before, he was fat, fresh and hearty—he cut a tooth a day before he dyed—thus was I suddenly deprived of my dear little companion over whome I had almost constantly watch'd from the time of his birth.[73]

Mumps, measles, and whooping cough were epidemic. Although Sally Logan Fisher recorded in her diary that mumps was "an ugly disorder," it was rarely fatal.[74] Measles, however, could result in death; even Dr. Buchan, who advised against bleeding children, recommended initial bloodletting for this "inflammatory" disease.[75] Epidemics of whooping cough prevailed throughout the nation.[76] Urban mothers were advised to take their children to the country, but Mary Wistar recorded in 1817 that she had lost her "dear little Bartholomew" when "in bitterness of spirit" and "loaded with anxiety" she had fled Philadelphia with four sick children.[77] When scarlet fever—popularly called "canker rash"—swept through families, it could carry off several siblings in one or two days. In 1787, five children died when "canker rash" passed through Hallowell in northern Massachusetts. When Martha Ballard "laid out" William McMaster for burial, she commented: "Poor mother, how Distressing her Case, near the hour of Labour and three Children more very sick."[78]

Throughout the early republic children between the ages of 5 and 10 accounted for about 4 percent of all deaths. At these ages mortality was more likely to occur from contagious diseases attacking the population randomly. By the early nineteenth century, pulmonary consumption was the primary cause of death along the eastern seaboard. Most victims were young and middle-aged adults, but some children between the ages of 5 and 10 did succumb to the disease.[79] Epidemics of fever were receding in the Northeast but continued in the South and West. In 1793 a terrifying epidemic of yellow fever, spread by mosquitoes, killed more than 4,000 Philadelphian men, women, and children. By 1820, yellow fever had disappeared from New England but recurred in a more mild epidemic in Philadelphia; nevertheless, it still prevailed in Charleston, South Carolina.[80] Malaria or "bilious remitting fever" was epidemic in late summer and fall. By 1821 it was called "country fever" in Philadelphia, as citizens in the paved, central wards generally escaped the mosquito-transmitted disease. Malaria remained a serious problem, however, in the South and West; in 1815 Dr. Daniel Drake reported that it prevailed every autumn in Cincinnati.[81]

Smallpox, the scourge of the eighteenth century, was virtually eliminated among the upper and middle classes by the 1820s, although a small number of the poor continued to die from the disease.[82] In the 1790s, children were inoculated between the ages of eight months and five years, as dried material from the pustules of a patient with "truc" smallpox was inserted in an incision or puncture in the arm or leg. A few days after inoculation, the child would come down with some pox. Smallpox, however, was a serious disease; the effects of inoculation could last several months, and each year some inoculated children failed to survive. Prevention did not become safe until the process of vaccination with less serious cowpox was discovered in 1798, although the vaccine was not available in many American localities until as late as 1813.[83]

Other diseases that prevailed among the urban poor were typhoid fever, caused by contaminated water, and typhus, transmitted by fleas and lice. In 1818 "a bilious fever, of a typhoid and highly mortal character, almost exclusively confined to the blacks," swept Philadelphia's "narrow streets, courts, and alleys of the southwestern parts of the city and suburbs." Around the same time, typhus reached epidemic proportions in New York and Baltimore, as it had a few years earlier in Cincinnati.[84]

Suffering from these various ailments, American children were greatly affected by medical innovation, ironically, an adaptation of enlightened practice to a republican society. During the Philadelphia yellow fever epidemic of 1793, Dr. Benjamin Rush searched desperately for a remedy. Since 1789, he had been working with a "solidist" theory originally put forth by his former classmate at the University of Edinburgh, Dr. John Brown, who speculated that all disease was caused by "indirect debility"—excessive stimulation of the vascular or nervous system. As his patients suffered and died, Rush recalled a paper written in 1741 by Dr. John Mitchell of Virginia recommending treatment of yellow fever with quick and drastic purges. Remembering the strong purges with calomel, containing mercury, quickened with a dose of jalap given to soldiers in military hospitals during the Revolution, Rush determined to reduce "indirect debility" in his yellow fever patients with bloodletting and strong purges with "ten and ten"—10 grains of calomel and 10 of jalap. When his new treatment seemed effective, Rush was jubilant. "The effect of this powder not only answered but far exceeded my expectations," he wrote. "The disease was no longer incurable. Never before did I experience such sublime joy as I now felt in contemplating the success of my remedies . . . It was the triumph of a principle in medicine."[85]

More cautious Philadelphia doctors, following European "humoural" theory, were appalled by Rush's therapy, provoking a spirited newspaper controversy. Nevertheless, after the epidemic was over, Rush remained adamant in defense of his principle, for it fit neatly into his evolving philosophy of an appropriate republican medicine. Believing that the intellectual faculty and moral sense, as well as the vascular and nervous systems, were activated by external stimuli, Rush had argued that political systems could influence health. Since the Revolution, just as he had sought social arrangements and educational plans suited to a republican nation, he had pointed out that diseases varied in populations according to geography, diet, climate, and forms of government. Republics, he had claimed, were conducive to health, but only if citizens practiced industry, frugality, and sturdy virtue. Lingering loyalty to the trappings of royalty and a taste for aristocratic luxury, on the one hand, or a tendency to excessive liberty that became license, on the other, would have to be purged.[86]

Rush believed that the American Revolution had demonstrated the unity and simplicity of truth. Reason through the evolution of history had revealed one source of political authority—the sovereign people—and had discovered one source of disease—excessive stimuli—and one remedy—depleting measures. Drawing on his early education in evangelical Presbyterianism, Rush viewed political and medical truths in terms of God's millennial plan. Disease had entered human life with the Fall, and imperfect nature could not be trusted to heal it. Intervention by the physician was necessary in order to overcome nature and restore the human body to its original perfect state.[87] For Rush, the physician was an agent of God, and therapy resembled a conversion experience; the body was purified by the depleting measures of bleeding and purging and, cleansed of corruption, could gradually recover. By 1795, Rush was teaching his students at the University of Pennsylvania that "Medicine has caught the spirit of the times." Along with new principles in political and social life, a "revolution" had occurred "in the principles and practices of medicine."[88]

That same year Dr. Samuel Powel Griffitts, a friend and former student of Rush, decided that Dr. William Buchan's enlightened medical manual, consulted in America for more than 20 years, needed revising. "Doctor Buchan's *Domestic Medicine* has long since had a place in most families," Griffitts began, "yet it is evidently not sufficiently adapted to the climate and diseases of the United States of America."[89] His method was to reprint the original text and to add footnotes wherever his recommendations differed from those of the Scottish physician. Griffitts left Buchan's recommendations on physical management of the child essentially unchanged; he agreed that mortality might be reduced through "reasonable and natural" care. He differed from Buchan, however, in the treatment of disease, for he wove into the British text the innovations that constituted Benjamin Rush's "American Revolution" in medicine.

While Buchan's treatment of disease had been cautiously empirical, allowing nature to achieve the cure, Griffitts recommended active intervention by the physician. Disagreeing with Buchan's careful distinction between an "inflammatory" and a "debilitating" or "putrid" fever, he argued: "After all that has been said of this subject, it is not at all probable, that any fever can with propriety be called putrid. *They are always inflammatory at first.*" And because Griffitts viewed all disease as essentially fever, virtually all cases were to be treated with initial bleeding and purging. Intervention by the physician also meant very large doses of active medicines. Griffitts revised Buchan's cautious use of medicine, recommending calomel, the mercury purge, in almost all cases. He preferred red bark for malaria because it worked faster than the Peruvian bark (a crude form of quinine) recommended by Dr. Buchan. While the Scottish physician advised five or six drops of laudanum (liquid opium), adjusted to the age, constitution, and condition of a child, and considered 20 drops the maximum dose for an adult, Griffitts thought that "a person of skill" could administer 300 drops of laudanum in one dose. "Surely if a medicine is to produce any change in the body," he insisted, "it must be taken for some considerable time and in sufficient quantities."[90]

Professor of medicine at the University of Pennsylvania until his death in 1813, Benjamin Rush instructed as many as 3,000 students. In their dissertations for the degree of Doctor of Medicine, several of these students applied his vigorous therapies to the treatment of children's diseases. Diphtheria, diarrhea, and cholera infantum were all to be treated with depleting measures—blistering, bloodletting, and calomel, the mercury purge.[91] As these students returned to their homes to practice, the "American Revolution" in medicine was distributed widely throughout the mid-Atlantic, southern, and western states. Dr. David Ramsay, who learned Brown's theory in 1789 from his friend Benjamin Rush, also hoped that independence would bring a "revolution in medicine" when he introduced the "system of bleeding and using calomel" to Charleston, South Carolina.[92] Daniel Drake fulfilled a dream when he studied medicine with Rush in Philadelphia in 1805. On his return west he introduced his professor's therapies to Cincinnati, and in 1817 accepted a position at the new medical college of Transylvania University in Lexington, Kentucky.[93]

In letters and diaries, mothers and grandmothers of the early republic recorded their experiences with the active medical practice. In 1796 Martha Laurens Ramsay of Charleston did not resist bloodletting when her daughter, Eleanor, was "low" and "about to die" from fever. After Eleanor's fourth bleeding, "more copious than three preceding ones," the child did revive, allowing her mother, who did not hide the danger from her, to use the experience for religious instruction.[94] Elizabeth Drinker of Philadelphia knew of the controversy surrounding Rush and, fearful and critical of bleeding and purging, usually selected another doctor. Nevertheless, after some hesitation, she and her daughters usually followed physicians' instructions. When seven-month-old Eleanor Skyrin was bled for measles, her grandmother recorded, "[T]is a trying circumstance to a tender Mother to have a vein opened in an infant child. The opperator found it very difficult to find a vain, and did it partly by guess. Nancy was not present." Neither did Nancy Drinker Skyrin dare to attend the bleeding six years later of her youngest daughter Mary: "D[ea]r little Mary Skyrin is very ill. Nancy sent this morning for Dr. [Adam] Kuhn, he ordered two ounces of blood taken from her arm and a blister apply'd to her breast. Nancy sent for Sister who attended at these trying opperations—to blister and bleed a child of 7 months old is a great tryal to a mother."[95]

Henry Drinker Jr., however, was willing to undergo "heroic" treatment, and his family was treated by a Dr. Jardine. In 1797, when 22-month-old William was given purges every four hours with jalap and calomel, his grandmother reported that he "was extremely sick with it—swell'd much." "[P]oor dear child," she worried, "he will be brought down with a witness if he survives it." William survived his calomel purges, but his younger brother, Henry III, did not. At the age of three months, he was given calomel and "brought up great quantities of bile," according to his grandmother, "more than I ever saw a child void, upwards and downwards." "[T]he dear little babe is I hope much better," she recorded later, "it has been much work'd." Little Henry's digestive tract, however, never recovered from this and other assaults with the mercury drug, and before he reached the age of six months, the "baby was taken with a lax which soon carried it off." Another son, born in 1804 and named for the lost Henry III, survived heroic treatment, but, due to excessive purging, suffered at age three from a prolapsed anus; as his grandmother put it, his "body comes down," meaning that the intestine protruded several inches from the rectum.[96]

Heroic treatment even reached New England. In 1797 Dr. Benjamin Vaughan aggressively promoted solidistic therapies—vigorous use of bleeding and medicines such as laudanum, ipecacuanha, and calomel—in the portion of Massachusetts that became Maine. Martha Ballard, whose practice employed herbal remedies grown in her garden, may have protested when Dr. Daniel Cony's treatment of her grandchild in 1801 seemed excessive. "The babe is very sick indeed," she recorded. "Cony came. He proposed to put blister on the neck. He cast very hard reflections on me with out grounds as I think. May a mercifull God fogiv him. The Child faded away and gave up the ghost at 11 hour 55 minutes Evening with very little struggle." Having lost a grandchild and still smarting, later Ballard wrote in the margin of her diary, "the babe Expired . . . with a frown in his Brow."[97]

In Salisbury, Massachusetts, in 1801, when 11-month-old Warren Park's face and neck began to swell, perhaps from scrofula or the "King's Evil," a tuberculous disorder characterized by the degeneration of the lymph glands,

Louisa Adams Park confided in her diary, "I don't know what to do with it." Desperately seeking professional help as Warren's condition worsened and an epidemic of "canker rash" (scarlet fever) swept the neighborhood, Park watched Dr. Bradstreet of Newburyport treat the child with "an emetic," of which "it took an uncommon quantity to produce the effect," "antimonial wine, to make him throw off the phlegm when he coughed—a blister on his arm, and if no better, one on his throat from ear to ear." That night the young mother "sat up alone—I sometimes thought he would not live half an hour." Consulting with other physicians, Dr. Bradstreet prescribed for Warren "poultices to his feet—flannel wet with vinegar and rum on his bowels—a blister upon the whole of his breast—strong mercurial ointment on his throat. They gave calomel antimony when necessary—lemonade with salt of tartar ... Dr. Ordway saw him and pronounced him a dead child." Yet even after such assaults, his mother recorded, Warren "would have moments when he appeared to be at ease—would know me—kiss me—knew all that was said to him—would have his hands full of playthings to amuse himself—and his eyes had an unusual calmness and life in them." But finally, after a night of coughing "as long as his strength would allow it," six days after his first birthday, Warren Park "stretched himself out & ceased to breathe!"[98]

These assaults by physicians on desperately ill children would be repudiated in New England and New York even before Rush's death in 1813. Experiments in London demonstrated that when mercury "has been received into the constitution in too large a quantity, or under unfavourable circumstances, it has a tendency to create a specific and formidable disease," a finding with which Dr. David Hosack of New York's Columbia University agreed.[99] Pierre Louis in Paris used medical statistics to measure the effects of bleeding and purging, and by the 1820s this foreign research began to seep into American medical journals.[100] Nevertheless, Philadelphia's leading physicians and their colleagues in the South and West who had been students of Rush continued to defend the "American Revolution" in medicine.

In 1811, Dr. James Mease of Philadelphia argued that the energetic and entrepreneurial population of the early republic did not experience the "desolating low fevers, which so often prevail in the cities of Europe, among the laboring poor in confined courts and alleys," or "that long list of nervous disorders ... which abridge the lives of the higher class of society." Disease in democratic America had proved to be "inflammatory" in nature, and excessive stimuli necessitated the depleting measures of bleeding and purging:

Hence the lancet is oftener required than the stimulating draught; and hence, too the reason why the European physician, whose circle of observation may have been confined to disease of an opposite character, hears with astonishment of the depleting system of the United States and especially of Philadelphia.[101]

In 1820, in his "Prospectus" to the new *Philadelphia Journal of the Medical and Physical Sciences* (which became *The American Journal of the Medical Sciences* in 1828), Dr. Nathaniel Chapman elaborated on the argument. "Ever since the establishment of our *Independence,* it has become the habit of Europe, very wantonly to traduce our national character, our institutions and achievements," he complained. European physicians simply did not understand the unique American character and situation. "Neither perverted by prejudice, nor enfeebled by any undue reverence for authority," American doctors had been free to respond with "acuteness of penetration," "promptness of remedial resource," "vigor," and "efficiency." Dr. Chapman illustrated his position in the same issue with his article on "hives" (diphtheria), which he proposed to treat in children under the age of five with "directly depleting measures": repeated emetics with tartarized antimony, "copious" bloodletting, leeches and cups to the neck, and blisters to the throat. "Children, I have remarked," wrote the physician, "display an uncommon *tenacity of life* and strength of constitution. They often survive under circumstances which destroy adults," and "sustain better the operation of most active remedies, as vomiting, purging, sweating, blistering, and I add, without hesitation, *bleeding.*"[102]

Dr. William Potts Dewees, a student of Rush, summarized the American adaptation of enlightened medical advice in 1825 in his immensely popular *Treatise on the Physical and Medical Treatment of Children.* This indigenous American child-rearing manual would be consulted by families across the nation, incorporated into medical manuals by other physicians, and reprinted throughout the nineteenth century.[103] As we have seen, Dr. Dewees shared the faith of European enlightened physicians that infant and child mortality could be reduced through proper management. Rejoicing that a provident God had implanted in women emotions necessary for their difficult role, he sentimentalized the responsibilities of motherhood. Democratizing enlightened child-rearing for the commercial middle-class, he proposed new indirect controls. And, in his discussion of the "Diseases of Children," he defended the "American Revolution" in medicine, arguing that European advice was not suitable to the "climate, soil, manners, and habits" of the United States, where disease had proved to be "inflammatory" and had to "be met with promptitude, and with adequate force."

"Most of the diseases of this country, have a peculiarity of character, and intensity of force, and a rapidity of march, altogether unknown to European climates," Dr. Dewees insisted. Diseases of American children had proved to be "simple" and related to the digestive tract. "Hence, the necessity and success of evacuations in almost all of them." Dr. Dewees defended his practice against skeptical parents "who sometimes resort to the prescriptions of an old woman, rather than to the advice of a regular practitioner, from a persuasion, her remedies are the safer, because apparently, the more simple"; he advocated therapies of bleeding, blistering, vomiting, and purging with calomel for most childhood diseases. Local inflammations of ear or eye, even skin rashes, were to be treated with calomel purges. Diarrhea and cholera morbus were to be met with bleeding by leeches, blisters to the abdomen, and alternating purges with calomel and castor oil. Mumps, measles, whooping cough, and scarlet fever were to be confronted with emetics, calomel purges, and bleeding from a vein. "How often does the life of the child," the physician exclaimed, "depend upon the prompt application of the proper remedies!"[104]

4

The Spiritual World of the Child

From Virtue to Character

> *In America feelings vehement and absorbing . . . become still more*
> *deep, morbid and impassioned by the constant habits of self-govern-*
> *ment which the rigid forms of our society demand. They are repressed*
> *and burn inward till they burn the very soul . . .*
>
> Harriet Beecher Stowe, 1833

In post-Revolutionary decades the turbulent and chaotic democratic society that produced and responded to heroic medicine underwent parallel upheavals of religious enthusiasm that also impacted on the experience of children. New popular religious leaders, drawing on the rhetoric of liberty, challenged established clerical authority, urging ordinary people to choose salvation for themselves. Through the heightened emphasis on cataclysmic conversion, even individuals low on hierarchies of age and status could be empowered by the choice to acquire a "new heart."[1] As "new measures" of exhortation practiced by popular preachers influenced even respectable clerics, efforts to elicit conversion increasingly focused on children. Although colonial ministers, and even popular exhorters, expected communion or conversion in late adolescence or young adulthood,[2] the post-Revolutionary belief in the malleability of the child generated hope for the conversion of even the very young. Women had already assumed responsibility for religious education in the family, and much of the task of proselytization fell to mothers.

By the 1810s new "evangelical" methods and materials reached children of the urban poor and upper- and middle-class girls, penetrating or supplant-

ing enlightened or genteel educational experiments. Popular religious enthusiasm and efforts to channel it both contributed to the Sunday school movement of the Second Great Awakening, in which adults focused on "early
piety," hoping to elicit conversion experiences in children. One evangelical
"means" played on a child's real experience of illness and death to "awaken"
his or her spiritual awareness. Although during the colonial period the elderly
were revered for their "sharpened religious sensibility,"[3] as hierarchies dissolved, the dying child came to be seen as "the child redeemer," with special
access to spiritual insight.

In the 1820s, a national voluntary association, The American Sunday
School Union, employed new technologies of printing and distribution to
produce a children's literature for the national market. Reiterating fears for
stability and social cohesion in their expanding, democratizing society, Sunday School managers wove into their literature republican themes. Seeking a
national identity through allegiance to a common culture, they revised
imported British Sunday school materials "to accord with the idiom and sentiments" of an American population. In the context of developing capitalism,
however, they shifted the post-Revolutionary emphasis on virtue—subordination of private interest to the public good—to what the nineteenth century
would call character—industrious activity tempered by internalized restraint.
Hoping to appeal to children of the new middle class, they softened denominational distinctions and incorporated methods and materials of enlightened
child-rearing, imbuing them with a subtle evangelical message. Advocating
"animated affectionate appeals" by Sunday school teachers and by mothers,
not unlike Dr. William Potts Dewees in his *Treatise on the Physical and Medical Treatment of Children,* union managers elaborated definitions of the
maternal role and introduced new, indirect controls.

As children born in post-Revolutionary decades reached maturity, many
who had experienced intense proselytization reacted against it. Rejecting the
evangelical emphasis on individualized conversion, they stressed the formation
of character in a nurturing family environment. Democratizing older notions of
gentility with evangelical themes, a generation of authors defined respectability
for the new middle class. In the 1840s, as industrial capitalism transformed the
Northeast, this new middle-class domestic ideology achieved hegemony. As family life centered on the child, and infant and child mortality did not significantly
decline, the evangelical theme of the child redeemer took on heightened signifi-
cance. The cherished child dying young seemed capable of revealing spiritual
and cultural truth—a new romantic view of childhood that became "Victorian."

Nathan Hatch has argued that American culture was reshaped by "religious
populism" in the years following the Revolution, as new leaders, refusing to
defer to learned theologians and traditional orthodoxies, released the deep-
est spiritual impulses of ordinary people. Although they resisted enlightened
thought with their openness to signs, wonders, and the supernatural in

everyday life, these entrepreneurial Methodist, Baptist, or Disciples of Christ revivalists linked their goals with Thomas Jefferson's Democratic-Republicanism and were a liberating, modernizing force. Along with the entrepreneurial activity unleashed by the Revolution, they fueled democratic hope and the passion for equality; served to break up hierarchical bonds; and helped America become a liberal, competitive, and market-driven society. Although their appeal was primarily to adults, urging them to take religious matters into their own hands and rely on individual conscience, popular religious leaders also taught that access to spiritual truth, not unlike the moral sense, was less encumbered in the lowly, the uneducated, and the young.[4]

Late twentieth-century psychologists remind us that children, like adults, seek to understand "the nature of our predicament as human beings." Drawing on religious symbols and spiritual values in the world around them, they struggle to make sense of their experience. Many children feel moments of intense spiritual awareness.[5] When early American children memorized catechisms at age five or six, they probably did not understand the denominational doctrines they recited.[6] Yet they did imbibe religious language, image, and story, which fused with familial and natural surroundings and shaped their childhood dreams and fears. Religion blended with magic throughout the early republic. Families consulted almanacs and watched for signs and omens; parents gave instruction according to the collected wisdom of oral folk belief. Resisting or accepting the lessons taught by adults, children responded with empowerment or despair, frequently working out their own explanations as they grew.

In the 1790s Daniel Drake of Kentucky was instructed at the age of six in the Calvinist catechism at the knee of an itinerant Baptist preacher; the hymns of Dr. Isaac Watts were one of the family's few books, and Daniel memorized all of them. Yet his primary religious education was from his mother, who was "still more illiterate" than his father "but was pious, and could read the Bible, Rippon's hymns, and the Pilgrim's progress." She taught domestic and Christian duty mixed "with all our daily labours," and instructed her children in what sin was through her use of the word "wicked." "Her theory of morals was abundantly simple—*God has said it*! The Bible forbids this, and commands that, and God will punish you if you act contrary to his word!" It was "wicked" to be cruel, to neglect the cattle and sheep, to waste food, or to quarrel with or strike his sister Lizzy. "It was wicked to be lazy—to be disobedient—to work on the sabbath—to tell a falsehood, to curse and swear—to get drunk, or to fight." Some of these admonitions, however, were undermined by Daniel's father, illiterate and embarrassed about it, who told his son stories about his wild youth, played jokes on his wife, and did not participate in family worship.[7]

On the Kentucky fringe of settlement where Shawnee and Wyandot still lived, Daniel had fears based in reality as well as in religion blended with folk belief. "The children were told at night, 'lie still and go to sleep, or the Shawnees will catch you,' " and "nearly all" young Daniel's "troubled or vivid dreams included either Indians or snakes—the copper colored man & the copperheaded snake." Although the Virginians and Marylanders in Mayslick were mostly Methodists, and East Jersey folks like his parents tended to be Baptists, they all welcomed the illiterate but talented itinerant preachers who came their way. They also still believed in "omens, ghosts, and even the self motion of dead men's bones." For young Daniel, these ideas "were so established in my imagination, that I was always, when alone in the dark, in kind of expectation or fear that something would show itself from the world of mystery." Although nobody knew what the Zodiac was, his neighbors all believed in the influence of the moon on animal life and vegetation—the 12 signs of the Zodiac "presiding over the 12 different parts of the living body in the 12 months of the year." Things were done and not done accordingly, and "the almanac was a important book of reference. It would not be safe even to wean a baby without consulting the oracle."[8]

Most of Drake's neighbors expected the world to end with the coming of the nineteenth century. "I lived in expectation of it," he remembered. "So great was my dread on this point, that any uncommon appearance in the heavens always suggested that the time had arrived." In 1796, when Daniel was 11, a sudden lightning storm occurred in the afternoon while he was hoeing the corn: "Terror and awe of the most solemn kind were inspired in me." Drake's parents frequently "became solemn" and turned to the Bible during storms, inspiring in their children "a feeling of reverence converting terror into awe. We were in the midst of a great and sudden visitation of Divine power." This spiritual experience of nature was reinforced by a childhood spent in the forest, instilling a sense of wonder that later led Drake to the study of botany. "While yet unmutilated by the rude and powerful arm of the pioneer, the woods are a great school of beauty," he later concluded; the "influences of which I have spoken were molding forces of my own character."[9]

In 1800 and 1801, the great revival at Cane Ridge, Kentucky, in which as many as 12,000 to 25,000 people flocked to hear itinerant ministers, channeled and released these diverse spiritual yearnings. Peter Cartwright, the same age as Drake, grew up in Logan County, Kentucky, which was known as "Rogues' Harbor" because of the refugees from justice (and Carolina Regulators) who fled there. In 1794, when Peter was nine, an itinerant Methodist minister preached in his family's log cabin. "Jacob Lurton was a real son of thunder," Cartwright recalled. "He preached with tremendous power and the congregation were almost all melted to tears; some cried aloud for mercy, and my mother shouted aloud for joy." His mother joined a small Methodist congregation, but Peter remained "a wild, wicked boy" who "delighted in horse-racing, card-playing and dancing." Not until he attended the Cane Ridge revival in 1801 was 16-year-old Peter stricken with "an awful impression" "that death had come and I was unprepared to die." "I fell on my knees and began to ask God to have mercy on me," he wrote later. Withdrawing to a cave to weep and pray, "[a]ll of a sudden, such a fear of the devil fell upon me that it really appeared to me that he was surely personally there, to seize and drag me down to hell, soul and body, and such a horror fell on me that I sprang to my feet and ran to my mother at the house."

At an outdoor camp meeting three months later, Cartwright "heard a voice say, 'Thy sins are all forgiven thee.' " "Divine light flashed all round me, unspeakable joy sprung up in my soul. I rose to my feet, opened my eyes, and it really seemed as if I was in Heaven; the trees, the leaves on them, and everything seemed and I really thought were, praising God. My mother raised the shout, my Christian friends crowded around me and joined me in praising God." "I have never, for one moment," he wrote later, "doubted that the Lord did, then and there, forgive my sins and give me religion." After his conversion, Cartwright joined his mother's church and received a license from the Methodists to become an exhorter. By the age of 18 he was known as "the boy preacher" and regularly traveled the Methodist circuit.[10]

By the 1820s Cartwright had settled in the new state of Illinois, where he was known as a "rugged and fiery preacher," admired for his "wit, homespun sermons, and dedication to the Methodist cause."[11] In 1829 four-year-old J.B. and eight-year-old Oliver Orendorff attended a camp meeting he conducted in Blooming Grove in McLean County, Illinois, only seven years after the first white settlers had arrived in the area. Camp meetings were held for two to six weeks after the harvest in early fall; families looked forward to them with "interest and pride" and congregated from distances as far as 50 or 60 miles.[12] In the colonial period young children were often left at home when their parents traveled long distances to church,[13] but in the early nineteenth century impressionable children participated when whole families attended camp meetings.

As families gathered on the long log benches before the preacher's platform and the surrounding space called the altar, Cartwright exhorted them "to flee from the wrath to come." Those affected were called forward to take the "unction seat" while the audience sang and prayed, "several hundred voices singing as loud as they could sing." The Orendorff children sat spellbound as more came to the altar "crying, singing, praying, and shouting," while the audience "melted to tears." As the meeting continued into the early morning, J.B. Orendorff remembered, folks sang and prayed "until they all became exhausted. A few, while shouting, would fall to the earth as though they were struck dead; in some cases they remained in that condition for hours." The children watched one young couple, determined to go to heaven together, attempt to climb a small white oak sapling so slender they were forced to give up, although they continued shouting for two more hours until they could pray no more.[14]

Even in settled New England, imaginative children growing up in orthodox Congregationalism utilized magical thinking to combine the religion of their forefathers with a rich psychic life. Calvin Stowe, would work with the evangelical Rev. Lyman Beecher and marry his daughter Harriet, was born into a Natick, Massachusetts, family and raised by his widowed mother. When a young child in the 1790s, Stowe was fascinated by stories of Job, Daniel, and the Revelation, of witchcraft and demonic Indians, and of fiends and giants in John Bunyan's *Pilgrim's Progress*. He recalled, "As early as I can remember anything, I can remember observing a multitude of animated and active objects, which I could see with perfect distinctness . . . passing through the floors, and the ceilings, and the walls of the house . . . These appearances occasioned neither surprise or alarm except when they assumed some hideous and frightful form . . . for I became acquainted with them as soon as with any of the objects of sense." As a child Stowe saw visions of hell and devils, "well-dressed gentlemen" who in one dream terrified him as they attempted to carry off a "dissipated" local character. Another night he awoke to find "an ashy-blue human skeleton" in his bed, but he was calmed when going to another room by a vision of tiny fairies "in white robes, gamboling and dancing with incessant merriment."[15]

Lucy Larcom, born in Beverly, Massachusetts, a generation later, recalled: "The religion of our fathers overhung us children like the shadow of a mighty tree against the trunk of which we rested, while we looked up in wonder through the great boughs that half hid and half revealed the sky." Instructed in the Bible at age two or three, her earliest memories blended the religion she was taught with domestic life and the spiritual experience of nature. Larcom remembered a kind of ecstasy in "sitting on the floor in a square of sunshine made by an open window" while "dancing and wavering leaf shadows" talked to her "in unknown tongues." Carried outside to see the stars, she suddenly recognized, "*That* is the roof of the house I live in." Having memorized the passage, "Let not your heart be troubled; In my Father's house are many mansions," she thought of heaven as a rosy mist with vines and singing birds and "a great, dim Door standing ajar" to a home where she had lived "before I was a little girl, and came here to live."[16]

This capacity to blend on various levels of consciousness Christian doctrine with folk belief, the natural world, and the experience of everyday life was particularly marked in the spiritual life of African-American children. As Chesapeake slaves developed a more settled family and community life in the mid-eighteenth century, they also created a semiautonomous African-American culture, simultaneously adapting practices borrowed from whites and west African values and beliefs to the circumstances they found under slavery. Children grew up with a world view influenced by west African religions in which the sacred blended with the secular, individuals could have magical powers, and daily life was infused with the presence of the divine. By the 1780s this sacred African world merged with religious populism as slaves responded with joyful shouting, singing, and dancing to the promise of white Baptist and Methodist itinerant preachers that salvation was available to all who sought it. Magical folk beliefs and Christian doctrine both became sources of strength and release, as slaves created a shared spiritual space in which to survive an oppressive society.[17]

African-American cultural values and beliefs were transmitted to children through song and story. As slaves set the tempo of their work routines with music, through call and response they drew on both everyday experiences and Christian imagery to express deeply held feelings they could not otherwise reveal. Just as spirituals incorporated into the present elements of the divine, children experienced God immediately and intimately; a child could converse with the Lord, Christ, Satan, or other Biblical figures. "I first came to know of God when I was a little child," one slave reported. "He started talking to me when I was no more than nine years old." Yet adult slaves admonished children not only with Biblical images and Christian morality, but also with magical folk belief—omens, conjuring, and ghost stories. An old man could "work" a rabbit's foot on a child "till you take the creeps and git shaking all over." And disobedient children were warned by folktales like the story of the chick devoured by a hawk when he ignored his mother's call of "Crick, crick, kick, kick, kick!" "Dat was de . . . unruly chil' dat wouldn't min' his moder. De hawk get him. Like we get unruly chillun now."[18]

The appeal of religious populism would propel some young African-Americans toward freedom and increased acculturation. In the 1780s, as fresh, experiential Christianity spread from one plantation to another in the upper South, Methodist preachers not only welcomed blacks as full participants but also condemned slavery. "I had recently joined the Methodist Church," one slave reported, "and from the sermon I heard, I felt that God had made all men free and equal, and that I ought not to be a slave."[19] In 1777 Richard Allen, a 17-year-old Delaware slave whose parents and younger siblings had just been sold, was converted by itinerant Methodists. Convinced by circuit rider Freeborn Garretson that slaveholders would be found wanting on judgment day, his Methodist master urged Richard and his older brother to buy their freedom. Working as a sawyer and wagon driver, Richard rode the Methodist circuit, learning to exhort and joining the ranks of black preachers who would become community leaders. By 1786 Allen was preaching at St. George's Methodist Church in Philadelphia and holding outdoor meetings in suburbs where black families lived. By 1795, in a renovated blacksmith shop that became "Mother Bethel," the first congregation of the future independent African Methodist Episcopal Church, Allen and his congregation sought to reinforce the positive example of his experience by inaugurating a Sunday school for the instruction of black children.[20]

Adults who founded Sunday schools would attempt to shape and channel these spiritual experiences of children. During the colonial period, Anglican,

Congregational, and Lutheran ministers expected conversion or entry to communion to occur in the late teenage years or early 20s, and they did not attempt to elicit conversion experiences in children.[21] Post-Revolutionary popular religious leaders found their most receptive audience in teenagers and young adults. The first American Sunday schools for children were enlightened experiments based on philanthropic efforts in England in the 1780s to ameliorate the living conditions of the poor in new manufacturing centers.[22] When Benjamin Rush and other upper-class gentlemen founded Philadelphia's First Day Society in 1790, they intended to provide similar schools for children of the urban poor and implement enlightened methods to instill virtue in malleable children who would become republican citizens.[23]

As a delegate to Pennsylvania's ratifying convention in 1787, Rush focused millennial hope on improved forms of government—the new Federal Constitution. The following year he increased his effort "to prepare the principles, morals, and manners of our citizens for these forms of government." In a letter to clergymen of all denominations he proposed "a new species of federal government for the advancement of morals in the United States" through "a general convention of Christians, whose business shall be to unite in promoting the general objects of Christianity." One of his suggestions was the establishment of Sunday schools on the British model. "Who can witness," he wrote, "the practices of swimming, sliding, and skating which prevail so universally on Sundays in most cities of the United States, and not wish for similar institutions to rescue our poor children from destruction?"[24]

When Rush and the new Episcopal Bishop William White drafted the Constitution of the First Day Society in December of 1790, they clearly hoped to discipline children of Philadelphia's turbulent lower class. "Whereas the good education of youth is of the first importance to Society," they declared,

And whereas among the Youth of every large city, various instances occur, of the first day of the week, called Sunday,—a day which ought to be devoted to religious improvement, being employed to the worst of purposes, the deprivations of morals and manners: It is therefore, the opinion of the subscribers, that the establishment of First Day or Sunday Schools in this city and liberties would be of essential advantage to the rising generation . . .[25]

Yet Society members also sought to provide elementary education for the "numbers of children, the offspring of indigent parents" who did not have "proper opportunities of instruction, previously to their being apprenticed to trades." In a society meeting in October of 1791, the Catholic printer Mathew Carey moved that the group petition the legislature to establish free tax-supported schools throughout the state. "The proper education of youth is an object of the first importance," he argued, "particularly in free countries,

as the surest preservation of the virtue, liberty, and happiness of the people."
Success of the First Day schools would demonstrate "that schools established
at the public expense are, perhaps, the most effectual means of diffusing the
blessing of illumination among the mass of the people."[26]

Although its petition to the legislature was rejected in 1792,[27] the First
Day Society conducted three schools throughout the decade, attempting to
provide an example of how orderly habits, literacy, and skills could be taught
to children of the urban poor. In January of 1791, when Benjamin Rush and
the mayor of Philadelphia, the Quaker-turned-Episcopalian Samuel Powel,
were selected as a committee to draw up "Rules" for the schools, Rush was
able to implement his view that moral restraint and bonds of affection could
be instilled in future citizens through an education grounded in Christianity.
Children of all ages, both sexes, and all denominations were to be instructed
in reading and writing each Sunday morning and evening. During the break,
children were required to attend worship in their respective churches. The
Bible would be the only textbook. The rules stated: "As religious observation
of the Sabbath is an essential object of the Society, reading will be restricted
to the old and new Testament and to writing copies from the same."[28]

Yet children would be motivated to industrious activity through the states of
esteem and disgrace originally suggested by Locke. An annual public examination
would be held by the schools' distinguished Board of Visitors; orderly behavior
and scholarly progress would be rewarded with the Board's "esteem" and the present of a "premium," a little book. In the 1790s urban Philadelphia was enough of
a community that misbehavior could be punished with shame. The rules provided
that "If any Scholar be guilty of lying, swearing, pilfering [or] talking in an inde-
cent manner, . . . he or she shall be excluded from the school."[29]

As the decade progressed, members of the First Day Society considered
their experiment a success. The response from "indigent" families was enthu-
siastic; by 1795, 452 boys and 502 girls had been instructed. The three
schools continued to attract about 40 scholars each. In December of 1799, a
handbill distributed by the society declared: "the utility of this institution has
been much greater than could have been expected . . . the children of the
indigent poor . . . thus rescued from savage ignorance, acquire habits of order
and industry, and are thereby qualified to be good servants and good apprentices, and we hope they will become good masters and good citizens."[30]
Although attendance declined after 1805, the society continued to believe
that its schools prepared lower-class urban children for citizenship. "A recur-
rence to the early minutes," an 1810 report reflected, "has given in Evidence
that some of the Lads then steadily attended the School and received Premiums for good Behavior and Improvement in their studies . . . have since
become opulent and respectable Members of the community."[31]

In 1811 a competing method of Sunday school instruction appeared in
Philadelphia. During a three-month visit to the city, the Rev. Robert May of

the London Missionary Society conducted an evangelical Sunday school, reported by its admirers to be the first of its kind in America. May's "evangelical" educational methods had been worked out by a new generation of young men who had assumed the leadership of British Sunday schools when they founded the London Sunday School Union in 1803. Launching his experiment in the working-class suburb of the Northern Liberties, the Rev. May began with a Sunday evening meeting for prospective scholars and their parents. After a blessing, a hymn from the *Children's Hymn Book*, the reading of Scripture, and a prayer, he gave a short exhortation that must have been compelling. The minister recorded in his minutes of the school: "Such a sight was strange and wonderful to all. Children and parents who never bowed their knees before now were kneeling before their Maker . . . Many were in tears."[32]

On Sunday evenings in the following weeks, as May called roll each child was asked to recite a lesson memorized from Scripture or catechism. His system of rewards, worked out by the London Sunday School Union, taught children the values and procedures of a cash economy. A child who recited the lesson correctly earned a black ticket. A certain number of black tickets bought a red one; and a certain number of red tickets purchased a premium, usually a small hymnbook or catechism. In the minutes May kept of his school he compared his procedures to those of local schools conducted by the First Day Society. May's model offered only religious instruction, not secular elementary education. Assistant teachers volunteered their time, in contrast to the paid professionals of the First Day schools.

In addition, May deliberately attempted to evoke an emotional response from children. When scholar Hannah Lott was about to move with her family 200 miles away, he preached on the text, "There is a friend that sticketh closer than a Brother." About to leave the only locality she had ever known, Hannah was aware that the sermon was directed at her and was deeply moved. "She wept nearly all the time during the exhortation . . . and when a word of advice was given to her, she seemed to feel very much. She wept when she left the schoolroom." May chose this moment to offer Hannah a public reward; delighted with her tears, he gave her a hymnbook. The minister recorded: "This is the first and very pleasing instance . . . of the fullness of Sabbath instruction."[33]

May also sought to "awaken" children with sermons on the themes of death and judgment. After he spoke of "The General Judgment," he recorded: "The children in general were remarkably attentive." On another occasion, when he read aloud an address written by an English pastor entitled "Wicked Children Punished," he reported: "The children were very attentive while I was reading. Some of them were particularly attentive during prayer . . . The children were much more still and quiet than they had ever been before." Missionary May was much warmed and strengthened by the successful evening and felt that the young adults who assisted him should have been as well: "The committee went away this Evening (I trust) highly gratified and pleased with the Services of the Evening and the conduct of the Philadelphia children in general."[34]

By January of 1812, the children who attended May's school had learned to respond according to his expectations. By memorizing one entire chapter of Matthew, five girls and six boys earned enough tickets to purchase a hymn-book. When May would call out, "What is the one thing needful?" the children would respond, "A New Heart!" When May read aloud from James Janeway's *Token for Children,* a seventeenth-century classic recording the deaths of pious children, he found the children "never more attentive than they were this evening . . . I then lent three of Janeway's *Token for Children* to three of them and if I had brought a dozen with me I would have lent them all. The children who could not obtain the loan of one of them seemed to be much disappointed. May God bless them when they read it."[35]

May believed that most of the children he met had received little previous religious instruction, an opinion Benjamin Rush confirmed in an entry in his *Commonplace Book*: "Branch Green informed me that in a school lately opened in the Northern Liberties by the Revd. Mr. May, consisting of 120 children of different ages up to 10 years, not more than twenty knew who made them."[36] Yet at a time when the enlightened First Day Society was having difficulty attracting scholars, workingmen's children in the Northern Liberties flocked to May's exciting evangelical school. In the first month the school attracted 240 scholars, most of whom attended regularly during the three-month period. After May left the city, his committee of local assistants operated the school and the numbers of scholars continued to grow. By 1813 the roll listed 724 names; by 1814 there were 844; and by 1815 there were 1008.[37]

Although the Rev. May's evangelical methods had been worked out in England, they rode a crest of religious enthusiasm that permeated the urban working-class neighborhood of the Northern Liberties by 1815. The Rev. James Patterson, a 35-year-old Princeton graduate and an "original, bold, imaginative, and powerful" minister, "an evangelist of the school of White-field and Gilbert Tennent," had recently been called to the First Presbyterian Church. Employing the methods of popular exhorters—preaching in the fields and vividly describing the terrors of hell—Patterson generated an immensely successful urban revival. Membership in his church jumped from 52 to 1,100 converted souls, and "[h]e saw young converts going everywhere throughout the Northern Liberties to visit the poor, to hold prayer-meetings, and to organize Sunday Schools."[38] Although Patterson's revival caused a split among Presbyterian ministers in Philadelphia, by 1816 flourishing Sunday schools appeared in the churches of younger men who favored the "new measures."[39]

In 1817 this spontaneous burst of Sunday school activity was consolidated by the Male Adult School Association, a group of young men originally offering elementary education and moral direction to white working-class adults. As Sunday school teaching became the rage, they voted to change their name to the Auxiliary Evangelical Society and to concentrate solely on the religious education of children. Within a year, they had attracted 680 pupils and were conducting six schools. Encouraged by a visit from Mr. Divie Bethune, an importing merchant who had recently founded the New York Sunday School Union, in May of 1817 they invited delegates from Presbyterian, Baptist, Dutch Reformed, and Episcopal Sunday school societies to form the new interdenominational Philadelphia Sunday and Adult School Union.[40]

The growth of the new union was phenomenal; within a year 43 Sunday schools were conducted under its auspices, instructing 5,658 children and 312 adults. "An affectionate intercourse" was established with the London Sunday School Union; materials were imported, and teachers learned to follow the kind of educational methods introduced in 1811 by the Rev. Robert May.[11] Initially, children who attended the Sunday schools came from poor and working-class families, partly because urban revivals were held and the first schools were founded in the neighborhoods in which they lived, and partly because Sunday classes were still associated with charity education. By 1820, however, "scholars from all the grades and ranks of society" began to attend the schools. Union managers reported:

In November last [1819] 8 or 9 girls formed themselves into a class, came to the Spring Garden schools, and requested that they might be admitted into the school, furnish their own books, and 'receive religious instruction only.' What renders this circumstance more interesting, they are the children of wealthy parents.

Annual reports began to argue that evangelical Sunday schools were not charity education; their primary purpose was religious instruction that "might equalise advantages between rich and poor." "These schools are intended as much for the affluent as the indigent," managers insisted. "The great object is religious instruction . . . given without money and without price."[42]

The appearance and growth of evangelical Sunday schools can be traced in the minutes of the First Day Society. In 1815, the board reported that attendance at their school in the Northern Liberties had declined due to competition from Patterson's revival. Although they hired a new teacher who introduced a ticket system of rewards, enrollment remained low; the board complained, "the introduction of First Day or Sunday schools by two religious societies in that vicinity . . . was mostly preferred by the parents." By 1819 the upper-class Quaker, Episcopalian, conservative Presbyterian, or free-thinking members of the First Day Society, many of whom regarded evangelical fervor with some distaste, realized that their enlightened experiment was outdated. "In consequence of various Religious Societies of the city and districts having opened under their care First Day or Sunday Schools," the board admitted, "the schools under the care of this Society have in great measure been superseded." In 1820 the First Day Society abandoned all efforts to operate its own schools and donated $200 to the Philadelphia Sunday and Adult School Union.[43]

A similar introduction of intensive evangelical methods occurred in New England during the same years. Sarah Pierce was only 25 in 1792, when she inaugurated her Female Academy in Litchfield, Connecticut, a bustling county seat already boasting Judge Tapping Reeve's law school and beginning to become an intellectual center. Attracting teenage daughters of not only gentry families in New England and New York's Hudson Valley but also merchants and manufacturers, small-town professionals, farmers, and artisans, Sarah Pierce offered a curriculum based on eighteenth-century British authors. In the first decade of the nineteenth century students copied in their required journals extracts from the works of such British poets as Milton, Pope, Dryden, Cowper, and Thompson. Miss Pierce instilled taste and genteel values in her students by reading aloud selections from Joseph Addison's *The Spectator*; she wrote little plays for students to perform that combined Addison's admiration of domestic life and admonitions to female virtue with her own advocation of the prompt payment of debts, essential in New England's emerging cash economy. On Saturdays before the assembled group she pointed out faults she had "discovered" in each girl during the previous week. Disciplining her scholars through shame, she advocated sisterly affection, warned against pride as well as envy of those of higher rank, and suggested which style of bonnet would be more becoming.[44]

Students at Miss Pierce's school learned the genteel accomplishments, producing lovely drawings and watercolors of flowers and plants or neoclassical scenes, alphabetical samplers and elegant silk embroidery, and carefully drawn maps (see figures 9 and 10). Those who could afford to took music lessons from local teachers. Their lessons were suited to the new republic, stressing United States geography or classical examples of virtue from Rollins ancient history. In the arch Federalist society of Litchfield, where the Hamiltonian Secretary of the Treasury Oliver Wolcott retired in 1801, students at the female academy copied in their commonplace books extracts from Edmund Burke's *Reflections on the Revolution in France* and poems extolling "Adams and Liberty." They also read advice to women of quality by the English evangelical author Hannah More and were instructed in Miss Pierce's strict Congregationalism.

In 1809 when Catherine Van Schaak of Kinderhook, New York, attended the school, each Sunday evening she went to "conference" where Miss Pierce reminded the scholars of the "uncertainty of life," of the girls who "had attended her School that were now in the Silent grave. [C]ould they look

Figure 9. *Minerva Leading the Neophyte to the Temple of Learning.* Lucretia Champion; Litchfield, Connecticut, c. 1800. A student at Sarah Pierce's Female Academy in post-Revolutionary Litchfield, Lucretia Champion painted this watercolor depicting a neoclassical theme that celebrated female virtue and opportunity for education. *Collection of the Litchfield Historical Society, Litchfield, Connecticut.*

up\down and see us," wrote Catherine, "how would they intreat us to turn unto him in the day of our youth before the evil day draweth nigh." Sarah Pierce instilled female virtue by reading stories about women who were good and bad examples, admonishing her students that their "characters was like a piece of white Sattin if there was a single spot upon them they were spoilt forever." A visiting minister discussed the duties of mothers toward children, that they "impressed the first lessons in their tender Minds," imparting the "good advice" for want of which "the little Innocents" "would have to suffer eternal damnation."[45]

Nevertheless, religious instruction in Sarah Pierce's academy changed significantly when Lyman Beecher answered the call to Litchfield's Congrega-

Figure 10. *Pointing the Neophyte Toward the City of Knowledge.* Lucretia Champion; Litchfield, Connecticut, c. 1805. Lucretia Champion reworked her neoclassical watercolor in this elegant embroidery of silk and silver thread and watercolor on silk. She was able to display her proficiency in needlework through rows of satin and split stitches and expertly executed French knots. *Collection of the Litchfield Historical Society, Litchfield, Connecticut.*

tional church in 1810 and began to teach theology at the school in exchange for the tuition of his five, soon to be eight (and eventually 11), children. One of the first things Beecher did to establish himself in the new community was attempt to elicit a revival among Miss Pierce's students. His efforts were successful in the summer and autumn of 1815, when Abigail Bradley wrote to a cousin in Stockbridge, Massachusetts, "We trust that more than half the school have been made the subjects of unerring grace." Thirteen-year-old Caroline Boardman of Hartford recorded in her journal that the Rev. Beecher "wanted to tell them of the evil of their ways and how nigh their feet stood to the precipice of destruction and that if they would wish to escape the horrible pit and turn, Jesus Christ stood with open arms to receive them."[46]

When Caroline found it difficult to achieve conversion, Beecher selected her as an object of exhortation; "have you says he," she recorded, "given your heart to God, and do you love him? or are you still in the world? [M]y dear child now is the accepted time, now is the day of salvation . . . perhaps you will never have any more time given you, do improve this." Judge Tapping Reeve came to pray and read the story of Ruth to the students. Miss Pierce "made a division between the scholars those that had obtained a hope and those that had not," and Caroline's friends circled around her, urging her to become "one of Christ's flock." Nevertheless, Caroline did not submit to Beecher's exhortations in personal conferences and did not experience conversion. When the students were "sewing for Mr. Beecher to repay him in some measure for what he has done for us," she commented rather caustically, "surely we cannot have that for an excuse that we did not know our duty for we are told it every day by our ministers and other pious friends" (see figure 11).[47]

Lyman Beecher's intense proselytization at Sarah Pierce's school signified a theological shift. As we have seen, when Jonathan Edwards revitalized Calvinism in the eighteenth century, he insisted that true virtue was only that infused by God's grace. When conversions occurred among young people in his Northampton congregation in the 1730s, he attributed them to "the Surprising Work of God" rather than to his own terrifying descriptions of the fires of hell and warnings of the wrath to come. Although Edwards himself had not been reconciled to belief in hell as a child, as a young adult he had come to delight in thoughts of God's monarchical sovereignty, experiencing a loving acceptance of eternal punishment that became for him a test of conversion.[48] In the early nineteenth century, enlightened rationality and the concept of the moral sense influenced such ministers as William Ellery Channing at Boston's Federal Street Congregational Church, and Unitarianism seeped into Harvard University. Nevertheless, an evangelical Congregational minister like Lyman Beecher, converted and steeped in the works of Edwards and Samuel Hopkins at Timothy Dwight's Yale University, accepted and proclaimed the doctrines of "total depravity, regeneration by special grace . . . and eternal punishment."[49]

Beecher badgered his own children with reminders of sin and a vividly imagined hell. His son Charles later wrote to his brother Henry Ward: "Is eternal punishment a reality? Father thought so. He never doubted. Strike that idea out of his mind, and his whole career would be changed, his whole influence on us modified."[50] Nevertheless, Lyman Beecher conceded minor points in the theology of Edwards and Hopkins; although he believed in infused virtue, in the democratic context of the early republic, he thought that human beings could actively seek the necessary new heart. Like such "New School" ministers as Dr. Nathaniel W. Taylor of Yale, he allowed individuals enough free agency to *choose* to repent, a concept essential in a revival. He rejected the idea of infant damnation, thought children sinned

Figure 11. *Mourning Picture.* Elizabeth "Betsey" Catlin; Litchfield Connecticut, c. 1811–1815. As the nineteenth century progressed (and the Rev. Lyman Beecher came to teach theology), students at Sarah Pierce's Female Academy produced mourning pictures depicting cemetery scenes. In this large watercolor on silk Betsey Catlin memorialized her sister Achsah, who died on April 24, 1810 at the age of 17. *Collection of the Litchfield Historical Society, Litchfield, Connecticut.*

only when old enough to make moral decisions, and considered human depravity less a result of original sin than of "man's weak nature."[51]

The window opened for free agency by ministers such as Lyman Beecher allowed a new deliberate emphasis on "means" in evangelical educational methods employed in Sunday schools. In 1818, managers of the Philadelphia Sunday and Adult School Union—self-made, well-to-do merchants of the new middle class—drew up "Internal Regulations for the Sunday Schools." Their first goal was the spread of literacy. The union printed "alphabetical cards" and a spelling book, and the "Internal Regulations" suggested that children be divided into four classes according to their reading ability. Small classes of 10 were to be instructed in reading by volunteer teachers until students mastered the difficult Bible. Equally important was the formation of orderly habits; the "Internal Regulations" stressed industry, punctuality, and cleanliness. Union managers feared that democratic Americans lacked regularity of behavior; they warned teachers that creation of an orderly atmosphere would be the initial task of each Sunday school. "Order is delightful," they insisted, "and although it imposes restraint upon the scholars it will be found to be pleasing to them in practice."[52]

The primary purpose of the Sunday school, however, was to save souls. As adults began to focus on "early piety," they sought to elicit conversion experiences in children as young as seven or eight, even four or five years of age.[53] According to materials imported from the London Sunday School Union, each child was to be "awakened" emotionally in order to become receptive to religious instruction. *The Sunday School Teacher's Guide*, prepared in London and reprinted and distributed by the Philadelphia Union, suggested that children be "awakened" by evoking emotions of terror and pity. "By all that is awful and all that is pathetic in religion," it advised, "admonish and exhort the children . . . Endeavor to awe them by the terrors of the Lord and melt them by his mercies. Relate to them instances of early piety, and at other times cases of sudden and alarming dissolution."[54] According to the "Internal Regulations," Sunday School teaching required three methods. The "expounding" method was lecture, and the "catechetical" method was question and answer. Neither could be effective without "exhortation," through which the emotions of the child were "awakened" sufficiently that he or she would be receptive to religious instruction.[55]

By 1820 the Philadelphia Sunday and Adult School Union had discovered the value of the religious tract in manipulating the desired response. Union publications had increased greatly; in addition to publishing alphabetical cards and spellers, the voluntary association was printing 45,000 tracts a year. Managers had devised methods for tract distribution; not only were tracts the premiums purchased with reward tickets, but each month the child also received a tract to take home to his or her parents. Most of the tracts republished and distributed by the Philadelphia union, however, were British products and the managers were never fully satisfied with them. They objected that the tracts reflected British rather than American "civil government, manners, and customs," and they deemed it more "desirable that such works be written in our own country."[56]

One theme of the British tracts that made Sunday school managers uncomfortable was the advocation of contented poverty. Seeking to train children of the indigent to be "useful citizens" of "our common country," and hoping to attract upper- and middle-class children to evangelical Sunday schools, they searched for themes applicable across the barriers of social class.[57] Thus, they rejected Hannah More's *Shepherd of Salisbury Plain*, in which the child of impoverished parents rejoices because at least she has a

plate of potatoes for dinner. Perhaps more appropriate for an aspiring, democratic society, the tracts they did select sought to curb individual will through
voluntary submission to pain and death. Such tracts explained explicitly how
the experience of disease and death could be used as a "means" of awakening.

   Little Jane, the Young Cottager, by the British author Leigh Richmond,
illustrated how an adult could use reminders of death to awaken religious
concern in even the most healthy and carefree child. When the minister asks
little Jane, "What made you first think so seriously about the state of your
soul?" the child replies, "Your talking about the graves in the churchyard, and
telling us how many children were buried there." Jane explains the effect of
evangelical educational methods: "I remember you said one day, near twelve
months ago, 'Children! where do you think you will be an hundred years
hence? Children! where do you think you will go when you die? Children! if
you were to die tonight, are you sure you should go to Christ and be happy?'
Sir, I shall never forget your saying 'Children' three times together in that
solemn way . . . All the way as I went home, and all that night, those words
were in my thoughts."[58]

   In his masterpiece *The Dairyman's Daughter,* Richmond pointed out the
excellent awakening opportunity provided by a lingering fatal illness. "What
a field for usefulness and affectionate attention, on the part of ministers and
Christian friends," he wrote, "is opened by the frequent attacks and lingering
progress of consumptive illness." Elizabeth, the dairyman's daughter, exhibits
the bright eyes, flushed cheeks, and flashes of intelligence that indicate not
only the progress of consumption, but also her access to spiritual insight. Her
piety and submission to death touch all visitors to her bedside, awakening
them to their own need for religious concern. After the moving scene of Elizabeth's pious death, Richmond suggested that viewing her corpse could also
be used as a means of awakening. "It is not easy to describe the sensation
which the mind experiences on the first sight of a dead countenance," he
wrote. "Quickly a thought of glory breaks in upon the mind, and we imagine
the dear departed soul to be arrived at his long wished for rest . . . In another
moment the livid lips and the sunken eye of the day-cold corpse recall our
thoughts to earth and to ourselves again. And while we think of mortality,
sin, death, and the grave, we feel the prayer rise in our bosom."[59]

   The theme of pious death in Sunday school tracts was a means to awaken
religious anxiety, an essential part of the evangelical educational method. Yet
a brush with death was a real experience for early republican children of all
social classes. As we have seen, according to records published by various
urban boards of health in the 1820s, more than 40 percent of all deaths were
children up to the age of 10.[60] The evangelical conversion experience did parallel the active therapy of Benjamin Rush's "American Revolution" in medicine disseminated by Dr. William Potts Dewees in his *Treatise on the Physical
and Medical Treatment of Children* of 1825.[61] Several tracts compared the

minister to the physician; while one ministered to the health of the body, the other tried to "cure" the soul. Rush, whose notions of enlightened medical science and evangelical Protestantism were inextricably fused, had taught that the diseased body be treated with depletion by bleeding and cleansing by purging; after the patient had been reduced to great passivity, the purified body would slowly recover. In some tract stories ministers followed a similar pattern in "curing" the soul. During a lingering illness in which the patient's resistance was greatly weakened, the minister "prevailed" upon the individual, "badgering" him or her with intense questioning. When the patient was able to submit self-will entirely to the will of God, to accept pain and even welcome death, he or she experienced comfort and relief, in which the soul was "cleansed" of its disease or sins. Although the case could be a hopeless one and the body not recover, the cleansed soul could triumph and achieve salvation.

An example of this evangelical pattern in the Sunday school tracts was the *Memoir of Bowyer Smith*. Two ministers, who were "greatly interested and delighted with this conversation," "prevailed upon" the ill seven-year-old Bowyer with "intense catechetical questioning" for several days. At last the deeply anxious child was able to submit self-will to the will of God, purging the proud and wicked wishes of his sinful heart. Although the child's hopelessly diseased body would not recover, the ministers were convinced that their assault had purified his soul, insisting, "Surely, this may be considered as a genuine specimen of early piety."[62] In such tracts, the pious dying child usually accomplished the reformation or rebirth of his or her parents. The ministers who badgered Bowyer Smith considered the child a divine instrument; as the dairyman's daughter neared death, she seemed to have access to spiritual resources denied to the living. The child as redeemer had long been a Christian symbol; as one tract author wrote, "Have ye never read that out of the mouths of babes and sucklings thou has perfected praise?"[63]

Nineteenth-century children, like their twentieth-century counterparts, did face disease and death with the utmost intensity, as they struggled to make sense of what was happening to them.[64] Their moments of spiritual awareness, however, did not necessarily take the form of evangelical "early piety." A child who kept a diary might confront the sudden death of a beloved sibling by "talking it out," describing the illness and the individual in minute detail. The reading list of 10-year-old Louisa Jane Trumbell of Worcester, Massachusetts, born in 1822, contained novels of Sir Walter Scott, as well as religious tracts and evangelical children's literature. When her Grandmother died, Louisa Jane wrote pious formulas: "We of course feel very sad about Grandmother's death but we must think it is all best and look to *God* for consolation . . . We may feel assured that she is more happy as she was such a good woman." Six months later, however, when her "darling" four-year-old brother Johnny died quite suddenly from "dropsy on the chest" after a bout with "canker rash" (scarlet fever), Louisa Jane poured out her shock and grief in multiple-page entries minutely describing his illness and last moments, reconstructing almost desperately what Johnny liked, how he looked, and things he did and said. Only after the ritual of Johnny's funeral could she conclude, "now he is in heaven with God, and his holy angels . . . a place 'where there shall be no more pain or sorrow nor any separation.' "[65]

Their own illness and/or the death of a parent did cause some nineteenth-century children to become receptive to religious instruction. Twelve-year-old James Riker Jr. of New York City, also born in 1822, was embarrassed when encouraged by his father's clerk, a Methodist who shared his bedroom, to kneel in prayer and was ashamed to tell his family about the incident. When stricken with typhus fever on a visit to his grandfather's farm on Long Island the following summer, however, the delirious boy, "reduced to the verge of life," was soothed when his sister sang hymns she had learned at a Methodist meeting. James was still recovering on the farm in October when his mother in the city fell ill and died suddenly from cholera. The following year a protracted meeting was held and a "powerful revival of religion occurred" at the New York Seventh Presbyterian Church that the Rikers attended. As the "spirit of God descended upon the crowded audiences who nightly filled the sanctuary," young James felt ready ("with about 150 others") to make a "public profession" of faith, an act two of his sisters repeated the following summer.[66]

Other young people with similar experiences did not become "pious." When 15-year-old Mary Lorrain Peters, also born in 1822, attended Grove Hall school in New Haven, she recited a Bible verse each morning, checked out evangelical literature from her Bible class library, was taken on visits "to the Orphan Asylum across the way," and was required to attend Sabbath School and Presbyterian church services. "I think some of the girls in this school have become pious lately," she wrote, "and younger girls than I too." Mary was more interested in what she ate for breakfast and dinner, which she recorded dutifully, and what she wore to services—her brown silk dress. Intensely involved in her friendships, she found the visiting preachers occasionally "dull," and sometimes "could not remember anything about the sermon for I was so *sleepy*." When several "little girls and boys joined the church," she commented, "Oh! how red the latter [Frederick Smith] did turn when his name was called out, he blushed." Even when her friend Margaret Sherman professed religion, Mary wrote rather unconvincingly, "I wish I was good enough to join the church."

Mary was at home in New York in November of that year when her mother died very suddenly (perhaps from hemorrhaging) after childbirth. "I hastened with all my might into her room, and there she was, 'stricken on the bed of Death,' " she recorded. "I was the only one of her children that knew anything about Death that were there. Helen and the Baby were there what

could little children like them understand about such a thing?" Almost immediately the carefree world of Mary and her six siblings was shattered: her
father sold their home, boarded with some of the children at the Pearl Hotel,
and distributed others to different schools and families. When he remarried
within a year, Mary wrote, "I thought I should not like a stepMother at all,
but I don't know this one yet." She worried that her brother George was
"very much depressed in spirits." "Since our dear Mother's death he seems to
feel as if he had no friend in the wide world to whom he could confide his
affections." Even Mary, now at Mr. Picot's French school in Philadelphia,
admitted, "I have had one or two fits of homesickness, and missed my
lessons, once or twice, which is very uncommon with me." She still attended
Sabbath School and even an anniversary celebration of the renamed American
Sunday School Union. Nevertheless, although she now found the sermon
preached "expressly for children" "very interesting," Mary Peters continued
to resist conversion.[67]

By the 1830s, however, Sunday school materials had shifted emphasis as
managers employed new technology to distribute in a national market. In
1824 auxiliary societies of the Philadelphia Sunday and Adult School Union
conducted more than 700 Sunday schools in 17 states; more than 7,000
teachers instructed 48,000 students. In that year alone, the union republished
133,000 imported tracts, which it distributed not only in the mid-Atlantic
states, but north to New England, south to the Carolinas and Mississippi, and
west throughout Kentucky, Tennessee, Ohio, Indiana, and Missouri. Determined "to plant a Sabbath School wherever there is a population," and "to
circulate moral and religious publications in every part of the land," the
Philadelphia union reorganized into the American Sunday School Union, a
national voluntary association.[68] Seeking to design a message appropriate for
children throughout the United States, the new union established a Committee of Publications, which, "in order to accord with the idiom and sentiments
of our population," would not only localize but also censor and even revise
imported materials.[69]

   In its effort to design uniform materials for a national market, the Committee of Publications blended the evangelical message with assumptions and
methods of enlightened child-rearing, continuing the blurring of denominational boundaries and latitudinarian direction that would form a distinctly
American religious culture.[70] Reworking republican themes in the context of
developing capitalism in the 1820s and groping to define a national identity
through allegiance to a common culture, they steered the shift from post-
Revolutionary emphasis on virtue to what the nineteenth century called character. Although the committee had five members, between 1825 and 1827
most of the work fell to Joseph Dulles, a merchant who had picked up his literary skills and evangelical fervor at Yale when the Rev. Timothy Dwight was

the university's president. Dulles's pastor in Philadelphia would be Albert
Barnes of the First Presbyterian Church, who, like Lyman Beecher, united
revival techniques with Hopkinsian doctrines. In 1825 Dulles and the Committee of Publications voted to adopt a *Teacher's Manual* by W.F. Lloyd of
the London Sunday School Union. Lloyd incorporated enlightened assumptions as he stressed the malleability of the child. "Youth is the season of sus-
ceptibility," he wrote. "The heart is tender; the affections are lively and glow-
ing. The wax is warmed and softened by the heat of youthful feeling and
awaits the impression which we are desirous of fixing upon it . . ." The Sunday school teacher was instructed to emulate a "prudent and kind parent."
Rather than evoking emotions of pity and terror, exhortation of the child was
to consist of "striking, close, and animated" affectionate appeals.[71]

In their effort to design a literature appropriate for all American children,
the Committee of Publications rejected the blatant deathbed proselytizing of
the British tracts. Annotations initialed by Joseph H. Dulles in the committee's Commonplace Book judged a tract "too poor," "very poor," or "not
suitable for publication." The committee did approve *Memoir of Ann Eliza
Starr,* written by a New England clergyman and recommended by "friends in
New Haven." Ann Eliza, a Connecticut child, loses her father when she is
three and her mother five years later; by the age of 10 she has lived with three
different families in three locations. During her final lingering illness, this
"serious and thoughtful" child is comforted, made "genuinely happy," by the
promise that she will find stability with her mother in heaven. Although the
memoir was published with the committee's seal of approval, Joseph Dulles
recorded his opinion in the Commonplace Book: "I cannot say that I think
these narratives of death bed piety in children ought not to be much encouraged. This, for instance, has many interrogatories—that lawyers would call
baiting questions, the very object of which is to draw out something to be
repeated, and would not children be apt to say in regard to such, wait til I am
sick and going to die, and I will be pious too[?]"[72]

In 1825 the committee replaced the tracts with *Early Piety,* a British book
in which realistically portrayed children related deathbed scenes of pious children. Committee members preferred realism to fantasy in children's literature; John Fair commented in the Commonplace Book, "I do not like visions
when we can be furnished with realities." The committee revised *Early Piety*
to suit a republican society; "Master Billy and Miss Betsy" became William
and Betsy. It crossed out the lines saying that the children's teacher, Miss
Lovegood, "was very indulgent to them and never failed generously to
reward them when they did well," and substituted, "and being herself a very
pious and good woman she talked to them of Jesus Christ and his salvation
every morning and evening." But the primary message of *Early Piety* replaced
a child's real experience of disease and death with a sentimental formula. The
children staged a "little pious assembly"; overcome by their sad stories they

wept, sang hymns, and prayed. "Who could help crying," the author asked, "if they heard in what a pathetic manner the story was recited? All were dissolved in tears."[73]

Another British book selected by the Committee of Publications, *Winter Evenings' Conversations*, wove an evangelical message into the study of natural science. Employing the enlightened conversational method originally developed by the eighteenth-century author Anna Laetitia Aikin Barbauld, Father discusses with Henry and Eliza minerals, plants, and animals and the use of each to man. Man is an intelligent, admirable, and healthy creature; "we are," says Father, "fearfully and wonderfully made." Only at the end of the book, while discussing the soul as seat of the affections, does he mention the need to prepare for death. The committee's Commonplace Book recorded that this volume "has been read by Jos. H. Dulles and highly approved as a work particularly suited for youth of the higher classes; and well adapted to revive a knowledge of Natural History and natural philosophy in the minds of those who have formerly studied these objects."[74]

In 1826 Joseph Dulles's *Union Primer,* which the committee hoped would be accepted in all American schools, sought to form character in children throughout the expanding republic. As Benjamin Rush had advocated 40 years earlier, Dulles grounded instruction in literacy in Christianity. For example, children were taught to read the sentence, "Remember now thy Creator in the days of thy youth." After each child had spelled one word aloud, the teacher was to explain the meaning of the sentence and, with a little exhortation, "impress the lesson on the hearts of the children." By the 1820s, community in urban Philadelphia had deteriorated to the point that discipline could not be maintained through shame. Children throughout the expanding nation would internalize self-restraint through guilt. Stories in the primer contrasted tamed and untamed animals. Beneath a large engraving of a sheep, the child was told that the tamed sheep was an animal useful to man. By contrast, an engraving of a "fierce, cross, and shaggy" bear illustrated the destructive untamed animal. To help children tame their own animal natures, Dulles reminded them that God, the internalized surveillant parent, watched them all the time: "In every place by night and day, *He* watches all you do and say."[75]

Older children in the expanding democratic nation were taught the necessity of internalized restraint by *Election Day,* in which a group of Philadelphia boys show the local sights to a friend from New England. At the library the boys explain how Benjamin Franklin, the son of a candle-maker, rose through industrious activity to become a great citizen possessing riches, fame, and scientific knowledge. At the hospital an attendant comments that doctors treat the body, but "Jesus is the all powerful physician of souls; he can give the healing balm which will cleanse them from sin's corroding diseases." At the State House, because it is election day, the boys observe worthy and unworthy citizens. An honest and industrious man, the good father and good citizen instructs his sons and apprentices in duty to God and community, casts his independent vote for the man of his choice, and goes back to work. The bad father and undesirable citizen is swayed by the crowd, joining the drunken rioting around the polls and promising his vote to the candidate who furnishes the best liquor. The boys just happen to meet their Sunday school teacher, who, quoting Washington's "Farewell Address," points out that "religion and morality" are the "indispensable supports of the political community." And when they return home, an aged grandfather instructs the future citizens in the history of the republic, explaining that true liberty is not licentiousness, but voluntary submission to the laws of God (see figure 12).[76]

The Committee of Publications also commissioned Anna Reed to write a *Life of George Washington*. Reed's Washington displays qualities admired in earlier biographies of the first president written for children: industrious habits, productivity, and the ability to create order from the disorder of the Revolution. Yet, ignoring Washington's self-motivated effort to acquire stoic virtue, Reed attributed the formation of his exemplary character to the influence of his pious mother. Because she tamed the "manly superiority" of the young hero to "self-denying tenderness," she can say of his victory at Yorktown, "I am not surprised at what George has done, for he was always a very good boy." Washington's positive example is contrasted with the negative one of Benedict Arnold, a "follower of the path of pleasure" who, "overcome by the indulgence of ease," betrays his country. The Marquis de Lafayette, even though French, is able to curb "his naturally ardent temper" and practice a "prudent self-denial"; he is thus pained by the excesses of the French Revolution, during which "in the attempt to throw off the oppression of man, the restraints of morality were cast away, and human passions raged uncontrolled." "Young Americans!" Reed warns, "as you grow up to manhood, and enjoy the great blessing of freedom from all unjust and oppressive laws of man, beware of wishing to be free from the just and righteous laws of your Creator!"[77]

In the 1840s, the generation born after 1800 continued to rework inherited themes, consolidating this concerted effort to create a uniform national culture. Many of these new cultural leaders rejected the individualistic conversion experience, as well as the intensive proselytization they had experienced as children. Instead, they emphasized the nurturing role of women and the domestic environment in forming character. Born in 1800, Lyman Beecher's eldest child Catherine enjoyed a special relationship with her high-spirited father when he was a young, dynamic minister first on Long Island and then in Litchfield. Raised on a Connecticut farm, Lyman Beecher played pranks on his children, joined them in chopping wood and hoeing the garden, and participated with gusto in their rural tramps and games. He also taught them his robust Calvinism, which as a child Catherine interpreted to mean

Figure 12. *Great-Grandfather's Tale of the Reverend Zachariah Greene.* William Sidney Mount; Eastern Long Island, New York, 1852. In the nineteenth century Americans reworked their Revolutionary heritage as they intensified their effort to form character in malleable children. *The Metropolitan Museum of Art, New York City; purchase, Morris K. Jesup and Maria DeWitt Jesup Funds, gift of George I. Seney and bequest of Vera Ruth Miller, by exchange; and gift of Anita Pohndorff Yates, 1984.*

that God made me and all things . . . that he knew all I thought and did; that because Adam and Eve disobeyed him once only, he drove them out of Eden, and then so arranged it that all their descendants would be born with wicked hearts, and that, though this did not seem either just or good, it was so.

She knew that to be truly good she needed a new heart, and that if she died before conversion she would "go to a lake of fire and brimstone, and be burned alive in it forever."[78]

Catherine was also influenced by her genteel, well-read, and accomplished mother, Roxana Foote Beecher, and by the education she received from age 10 in eighteenth-century British authors, Addisonian admonitions to female virtue, and the genteel accomplishments at Sarah Pierce's Litchfield Female Academy. A lively and highly intelligent child, Catherine participated vigorously in school and community contests. When she reached her early 20s without experiencing conversion, Lyman Beecher pressed the issue until she fell ill. Yet Catherine could not feel guilty enough to submit. Her religious crisis intensified when her fiancé, Alexander Metcalf Fisher, died in a shipwreck, and her father intimated that the young man may have been damned. Catherine's loss became a theological confrontation with her father and her God. Unable to accept eternal punishment for those who died without conversion, she gradually concluded, after great travail, that salvation could be achieved through a blameless life, and she drifted away from evangelical Calvinism.[79]

Although, like many of her generation, Catherine Beecher rejected individualized conversion, she drew on evangelical themes as she shifted to social concerns and an emphasis on moral character. As she began to delineate a national role for women, she incorporated key concepts from eighteenth-century precedents. Beecher took seriously the genteel definitions of female virtue and domestic harmony, based on Joseph Addison's *The Spectator,* that Sarah Pierce pressed on students at her Litchfield school. "Let the leading females of this country become pious, refined, and active," she wrote to her friend and fellow teacher Mary Dutton in 1830, "and the salt is scattered through the land to purify and save." Immersing herself in the moral philosophy of the Scottish Enlightenment (which dominated American academic circles in the mid-nineteenth century), she came to see the family as a socializing force, and the cultivated conscience as an agency of moral authority appropriate for a democratic society.[80]

In 1841, Catherine Beecher wove these themes into her discussion of "The Peculiar Responsibilities of American Women," which introduced her *Treatise on Domestic Economy.* Her argument was not unlike that of Benjamin Rush as she urged women to support democratic institutions, which she considered identical to Christian principles. Nevertheless, to retain harmonious order in an increasingly democratic society, Beecher believed that hierarchical relationships involving "duties of subordination"—subject to magistrate, wife to husband, child to parent, pupil to teacher, and employee to employer—would have to be maintained. The difference between a democracy (in which wealth was open to all) and a traditional hierarchy (in which individuals were born into a particular status) was the insistence on responsible free agency she had learned from her father. In democratic America, inferiors could *choose* their superiors. Women could submit voluntarily ("with a sort of pride") to their husbands, making it "their boast to bend themselves to the yoke, not to shake it off."

Catherine Beecher acquiesced that American women would not participate in political and civil affairs. Yet, like Benjamin Rush, she allocated to
them the primary responsibility of molding the minds, morals, and manners
of their children. "In matters pertaining to the education of their children,"
she insisted, "and in all questions relating to morals and manners, they have a
superior influence." Their reward would be participation in the providential
plan, as "democratic equality" spread throughout the world:

> The woman who is rearing a family of children; the woman who labors in the
> schoolroom; the woman who, in her retired chamber, earns, with her needle the
> mite to contribute for the intellectual and moral elevation of her country; even the
> humble domestic . . . each and all may be cheered by the consciousness, that they
> are agents in accomplishing the greatest work that ever was committed to human
> responsibility.[81]

As Beecher instructed American women in principles of domestic economy (not unlike managers of the American Sunday School Union), she sought
to transcend the barriers of region and social class and create a national identity through allegiance to a common culture. Democratizing the genteel values with which she had been raised, she argued that refinement was compati-
ble with work. "Everything is moving and changing" in nineteenth-century
America, she wrote. "Persons in poverty are rising to opulence, and persons
of wealth, are sinking to poverty." People in new settlements live in log cabins, domestic servants are difficult to obtain, and individuals of all social
classes mingle with and emulate those of larger means. A "democratic lady"
in her neat oilcloth apron need not forego gentility even as she performs her
own domestic work. Mothers should teach daughters and teachers their
pupils that in a democracy "it is refined and lady-like to engage in domestic
pursuits."[82]

A second child of New England Calvinism who rejected individualized
conversion and emphasized formation of character in a genteel domestic
atmosphere was Horace Bushnell, who published his *Views of Christian Nurture* in 1847. Born on a Connecticut farm in 1802, Bushnell was influenced as
a child by his Methodist grandmother and went on to study Nathaniel W.
Taylor's "New Divinity" at Yale. Nevertheless, when he was called to the
North Church in Hartford in the 1830s, he avoided the theological debates
that consumed Lyman Beecher. Like others of his generation, he was drawn
to English romantic authors, especially the writings of Coleridge. This attrac-
tion to symbolic language and intuitive truth was strengthened in the 1840s,
when he was exposed to German romanticism on a trip to Europe.[83]

In *Christian Nurture*, Bushnell repudiated the "piety of conquest" of
"extreme individualism" (a "kind of public piety that is strenuous and fiery"),
and advocated a private piety learned through habit and early associations.

Espousing views not unlike those of the eighteenth-century Scottish Presbyterian John Witherspoon, Bushnell wrote that "the child is to grow up a Christian, not remembering the time when he went through a technical experience, but seeming rather to have loved what is good from his earliest years." Bushnell viewed human depravity as inclination to evil, but thought it wrong to consider a child a sinner incapable of good until God gives a new heart. Instead, the "plastic nature of childhood" could be formed through the faith and example of the parents, as children absorbed the nurturing atmosphere of a home that, "having a domestic spirit of grace dwelling in it," became a "church of childhood."[84]

Stressing "cultivation" of character in the child "by virtue of an organic power," Bushnell viewed moral behavior not as a matter of "separate and absolutely independent choice," but as a "state of being." "A pure, separate, individual man, living *wholly* within and from himself," he argued, "is a mere fiction." He defended infant baptism, which symbolized a spiritual link from parent to child, and also thought that wickedness in parents continued in their children. This support of infant baptism and retreat from the democratic implications of adult conversion, through which an individual could will to break with his or her past, bothered the managers of the Massachusetts Sunday School Union, who suspended the publication of his book. Bushnell's emphasis on a genteel domestic setting did restrict access to the new middle class in its implication that it was difficult to become what one's family was not. He also proposed that if the "spirit" of a "bad or irreligious family" was not in the best interest of the child, the child "most dismal thought! is to be delivered from their home." "If you will not be Christians yourselves," he admonished parents, allow your children to be sent "where another spirit reigns." "Understand how plastic their nature is." "If you yourselves will not fashion them for the skies, let others, more faithful than you, and more merciful, do it for you."[85]

By the 1850s cultural concern with forming character fused into a new romantic, organic concept of childhood, perhaps most clearly articulated in the novels of Harriet Beecher Stowe. Born in 1811, and only four when her mother, Roxana Foote Beecher, died, Harriet grew up a late-born child in the large and lively Beecher household. From the age of eight she attended Litchfield Female Academy after the arrival of Sarah Pierce's nephew, John Brace, who supplemented his aunt's "Johnsonian" curriculum with higher mathematics, the sciences, moral philosophy, logic, and Latin tutorials. With her siblings, she also devoured novels of Sir Walter Scott, as well as works of the English romantic poets. Harriet witnessed Catherine's wrenching religious crisis and rather easily achieved conversion at age 14. Yet her faith was shattered when she attended her sister's Hartford academy, and a minister challenged: "Harriet, do you feel that if the universe should be destroyed, you could be happy with God alone?"

Depressed rather than rebellious during the religious struggle of her teenage years, Harriet confessed to Catherine in 1827, "Sometimes I could not sleep and have groaned and cried till midnight, while in the daytime I tried to appear cheerful . . ." In 1833, after moving with the Beecher family to Cincinnati, she wrote to her friend Georgiana May:

> In America feelings vehement and absorbing . . . become still more deep, morbid, and impassioned by the constant habits of self-government which the rigid forms of our society demand. They are repressed, and burn inward till they burn the very soul, leaving only dust and ashes.

After her marriage to Calvin Stowe in 1835, Harriet bore five children—twins and three others, in rapid succession—while she struggled to pursue a writing career. In the 1840s, overwhelmed by her children's periodic illnesses and anguished by the suicide of her brother George, she did experience spiritual rebirth, coming to accept a simple faith in a loving Christ, and believing that only through the suffering of the lowly and oppressed would the kingdom of God arrive.[86]

During a cholera epidemic in Cincinnati in 1849, Harriet Beecher Stowe lost her sixth child suddenly, her beloved late-born 18-month-old Charlie. As concepts of child nurture and domestic ideology gained widespread middle-class acceptance in mid-nineteenth century America, families still experienced the tragic loss of child death. Pouring out both her grief over Charlie's death and her rage at the Fugitive Slave Act in the Compromise of 1850 in her novel *Uncle Tom's Cabin* (published in 1852) Stowe alerted the conscience of the nation to the immorality of slavery by applying middle-class domestic ideology to enslaved families. Influenced by Charlie's death, she also drew on the evangelical concept of the child redeemer. Little Eva, the genteel child of character, seems less to be formed by environmental influences than endowed with a special spiritual sensibility. As her premature death approaches, she becomes capable of intuition reinvigorating to adults. In the hands of Harriet Beecher Stowe, Little Eva reveals the profoundly democratic truth that Christ loves black Topsy as much as he loves her, an insight denied to both St. Clare, her Byronic father, and his cousin Miss Ophelia, who is steeped in rigid forms of New England Calvinism. With the meticulously drawn characters of such novels as *The Minister's Wooing* (1857), *Oldtown Folks* (1869), and *Poganuc People* (1878), Stowe would continue to explore nuances of her region's religious controversies in their social ramifications. Yet always central, freeing itself from hardened layers of Calvinism or redeeming a withered or despairing adult, would be the special spiritual insight of the child.[87]

5

Forming Character

Schooling

If we can but turn the wonderful energy of this people into a right channel, what a new heaven and earth must be realized among us.
William Ellery Channing to Horace Mann, 1837

We are shut up in schools and college recitation rooms for ten or fifteen years and come out at last with a belly full of words and do not know a thing . . .
Ralph Waldo Emerson, 1839

By the 1840s the task of forming character in children was increasingly allocated to American public schools. In post-Revolutionary decades such patriots as Thomas Jefferson, Noah Webster, and Benjamin Rush had sought to overcome diversity and create social bonds through uniform education. Although republican theorists believed the source of virtue was the widespread ownership of land, they also felt that education could inculcate republican principles, create affectionate ties among individuals, and instill the moral restraint essential for citizenship. Early plans in Virginia or Pennsylvania for the establishment of public schools, however, were rejected by state legislatures, largely because the United States was still a rural society, and a uniform system did not mesh with the existing social structure. Families headed by farmers or craftsmen relied more on their own than on hired labor; high fertility meant large numbers of children who were expected to work. Education occurred in family or workplace settings, and schooling could only be intermittent, fitted into those hours of the day or seasons of the year that the rhythms of an agricultural society allowed. Revolutionary rhetoric inspired interest in education, but actual practice followed the rural intermittent model. Enrollments did increase in locally controlled district or subscription schools. Academies throughout the nation proliferated, especially those like Sarah Pierce's Litchfield Academy, which focused on the education of girls.

Educational innovation in the early republic took place in urban centers where commercial relationships were replacing older familial arrangements with the wage. By the first decades of the nineteenth century older charity schools, such as those conducted by Philadelphia's First Day Society, were supplanted not only by evangelical Sunday schools but also by new methods of instruction for the poor. Under British Joseph Lancaster's monitorial plan, student monitors helped a single teacher instruct several hundred children. Marching according to commands and sitting in regimented rows, pupils in Lancasterian schools resembled workers in the new manufactories; motivated by competition and rewarded with tickets similar to those used in Sunday schools, they learned behavior appropriate for an emerging cash economy. Yet the Lancasterian model was popular throughout the nation. By 1817 these schools became the nucleus for tax-supported public education in Pennsylvania and New York, and also flourished in areas as remote and varied as Detroit; Cincinnati; New Orleans; and New Bern, North Carolina.[1]

By the 1820s and 1830s capitalism began to transform the northeastern economy and penetrate even rural households. Family members engaged in outwork, and older children took factory jobs. Rural women, burdened with productive and reproductive labor, began to adopt the domestic ideology of their urban sisters and limit family size. As rural crafts declined and even farmers hired labor, expectations of children's work began to change. Children in poor families continued to labor, but those in new middle-class or rural households tied to the market were free to engage in schooling that was no longer intermittent but full-time. In this economic context, by the late 1830s school reformers such as Horace Mann in Massachusetts, Henry Barnard in Connecticut, and Calvin Stowe in Ohio promoted consolidated systems of state-supported education, advocating 10-month terms, a uniform curriculum, and professional teachers trained in "normal" schools. Although they admired the Prussian system, which implemented Pestalozzi's interpretation of Rousseau, they still sought to prepare republican children for citizenship. In the new capitalistic context merit would be based not on land ownership but on character—industrious activity tempered by internalized restraint instilled through uniform state-supported and controlled nonsectarian but Protestant education.

By the 1850s school reform spread to the Midwest, a region undergoing similar economic and social change. In the South, however, where slavery held penetration of the household by capitalism at bay, school reform did not take root. While slaves were denied schooling, children of planters learned at home and in academies; those of yeoman families who retained rural culture and values continued the pattern of farm work interspersed with intermittent schooling.

In his study of western Massachusetts, Christopher Clark has discovered a "dynamism" in post-Revolutionary rural families, even while they continued to engage mostly in subsistence farming and participate in a culture based on barter and local exchange. As the birthrate remained high, fathers controlled the labor of large numbers of children and sought to improve their economic position in order to provide for these children when they became adults. These familial motivations, nevertheless, contributed to growth of the local economy. In this environment of high fertility and dwindling land resources, farmers worked their land more intensively and brought marginal areas under cultivation. Grown children for whom land could not be provided migrated north or west. Those who stayed acquired new skills and prepared for new careers, increasing household manufacturing and the demand for schooling.[2] In 1789 Massachusetts required towns of 50 or more families to provide "district" schools for at least six months of the year and towns of 200 or more families to provide a grammar school. The state did not provide financial aid, however, and both initiative for and control of a school remained with local parents. Yet enrollments rose in district schools in post-Revolutionary decades,[3] largely due to the dynamism of precapitalist rural culture.

Nahum Jones, a schoolteacher born in 1772 to a farming family in Gerry, near Worcester, Massachusetts, exemplified these trends. His father Jonathan Jones was a Revolutionary War soldier who had been active in incorporating the town in 1770; a middling farmer, Jones would be pressed to provide livelihoods for Nahum and his nine siblings. From the age of six Nahum attended "moving" or district schools in various homes and schoolhouses for two- to four-week terms. In winter a male or in summer a young female teacher (such as his favorite, 16-year-old Sally Rowe) taught him to read the Bible "tolerably well," to write, and to spell. By age 10, however, Nahum was working full-time on the farm, alternating "hard labor" with four- to six-week sessions of memorizing syllables in Dilworth's speller and learning to add "weights and measures." After honing his spelling and math skills, Nahum was ready to attend rural academies—New Ipswich Academy in New Hampshire and Williams Academy in Williamstown, Massachusetts—where he studied to become a teacher.[4]

By 1800 Nahum Jones had been "keeping school" for six years, alternating hard labor on the farm in Gerry with six- or seven-week sessions at different country schoolhouses. An Adams Federalist, he was keenly aware of political events, praising histories of New England or the Revolution by Thomas Hutchinson, Jeremy Belknap, or David Ramsay; considering patriotic literature by Joel Barlow, Timothy Dwight, and John Trumbell the "soul of taste"; and recommending republican texts such as Jedidiah Morse's geography and Noah Webster's speller. "Schools are established in every town, for some part of the year in every hamlet," he recorded in his diary. The town school committee supported Nahum's efforts by visiting his school regularly to hear pupils recite their lessons and short pieces from "the *male coquette,* a short comedy," and *The Columbian Orator.* "The performances met with the approbation of the visitants," the teacher proudly recorded. "The students for the time they have been to school have made very good proficiency."[5]

In 1801 Nahum was an active member of the town's Library Society. Nevertheless, by 1802, he was restless. Weary of hoeing corn and harvesting hay and perhaps aware that he would not inherit the Gerry homestead, he was eager to escape the farm. Exhibiting the kind of entrepreneurial activity that generated rural dynamism, he began shopping around for other localities where he could open a school. Finally settling in Provincetown at the tip of Cape Cod, he taught locally controlled private schools for five years, returning to Gerry only for regular visits. Nahum died in Provincetown in 1807 at the age of 35. Yet other young men of his and the following generation, as eager as he to escape hard labor on farms, would propel the skills they had honed in short terms of teaching into commercial careers, contributing to the regional economic activity that fueled the development of capitalism.[6]

In ungraded one-room district schools such as those taught by Nahum Jones, children as young as two or three mingled with older scholars; busy mothers, engaged in domestic production for large households, found school a convenient means of keeping toddlers out from underfoot. Henry Ward Beecher, born in 1813, was three, the seventh of her eight children, when his mother, Roxana Foote Beecher, died. Sent that year to Widow Kilbourne's school in Litchfield, Connecticut, he, like other children, brought along sewing and knitting to keep him occupied. His sister Harriet later described the "bashful, dazed-looking boy" who "pattered barefoot to and from the little unpainted school house, with a brown towel or a blue-checked apron to hem during the intervals between his spelling and reading lessons." Henry later wrote that the little boys "seemed to be sent to school merely to fill up the chinks between the bigger boys."

[We] were busy in keeping still . . . Our shoes always would be scraping the floor . . . All of our little legs together . . . would fill up the corner with such a noise that, every ten or fifteen minutes, the master would bring down his two-foot hickory ferule on the desk with a clap that sent shivers through our hearts . . . and then, with a look that swept us all into utter extremity of stillness, he would cry, "Silence in that corner!"

Having been raised on a Connecticut farm, Lyman Beecher expected his children to work; by age eight Henry combined his schooling with helping his father plant and hoe the garden, caring for the horse and cow, carrying wood, and drawing water from the well on winter mornings.[7]

Horace Greeley, born in 1811 into a "poor and hard-working" Londonderry, New Hampshire, farming family, was entertained by Scots-Irish stories and ballads and taught to read at age three by his mother while she spun flax. At four he boarded with his grandfather and was sent to district school with 60 other scholars, "many of them full-grown men and women." Already a good speller, he was selected for evening spelling bees even though his teammates had to rap him "sharply" to wake him up. By age five, however, Greeley was working the family's 40-acre farm, rising at dawn to ride the horse while his father plowed and rushing to school when the morning lesson was almost over. At age eight and nine he skipped the summer session entirely because his father, who had taken a larger farm on shares, depended on his labor. By age 11, Greeley hoped to apprentice with a printer, eager to leave hard labor on the farm. "I have asked myself," he later wrote, " 'How would you like to return to that cot on the hillside, and spend the rest of your days there?' My answer is that I would *not* like it" (see figure 13).[8]

For older children intermittent terms in district schools could be followed by attendance at a town grammar school or one of the many academies that appeared throughout the nation in post-Revolutionary decades. Some academies, attended by children from well-to-do or middling families, were essentially extensions of the schoolmaster's family. Busy wives and daughters engaged in extra labor to board scholars who came from longer distances for short periods of time. In 1817 11-year-old Samuel Parris of Kingston, Massachusetts, studied with 19 other children at the academy his minister father kept in their dwelling. Although he kept a journal in which to record his "faults that by looking on this I may remember them and do so no more," and studied math and Latin, Samuel preferred demonstrating his father's "electric machine." In this percolating rural culture curious "folks" came by "who wished to be Electerized." "Pa," Samuel recorded, "wished me to be charged. So I got on the bottles and he charged me. As he was turning the Wheel the phial slipped. I not thinking took hold of the phial to move it back [and] took a smart shock." Even after this experience the fascinated boy could not resist playing with the "machine" while his father was away, and "now," he lamented, "it does not work." A year later when his father took a church, 12-year-old Samuel recorded, "Pa says he thinks he shall set me teaching some scholars . . . But I hope he will not." "I hope we shall take no boarders," he had complained previously, "Ma is yet unwell."[9]

Some academies were coeducational. In 1799 Mr. Proctor Pierce conducted an academy in Greenfield, Massachusetts, attended by 14-year-old Sally Ripley, a few other girls, and "a large number of boys." Sally learned to

Figure 13. *School Boys Quarreling.* William Sidney Mount; Eastern Long Island, New York, 1830. In the 1830s William Sidney Mount recorded American rural life in humorous genre paintings. His realistic painting of lively school boys depicts the casual egalitarian atmosphere of the rural district school. *The Museums at Stony Brook, New York, Museums Collection.*

"cypher," and recited lessons in astronomy and American geography. She read Jeremy Belknap's *History of New Hampshire* and the "life of Mr. George Whitefield a Methodist minister." But the bulk of her reading was Anglo-American literature directed to girls which diffused Addisonian taste, filtered through the advice of Anna Laetitia Aikin Barbuald or the novels of the American Susanna Rowson. Sally learned genteel values suitable for a republic by acting in plays, copying her parts in her journal in order to memorize them. As Lemira in "The Insolvable Question," she learned from "Madame Sensible" that a lady is neither "too forward" nor "too prudish." As Emily in "The Spring for Flowers," she was told by "Mrs. Easy" that she need not marry, but it is possible to handle a husband's faults. As Nelly, a country girl in "The Mother of a Family," she was persuaded that education and gentility would suit her for motherhood. And as "Mrs. Allworthy" in "The

Female Gamesters," she repeated remonstrances from Joseph Addison's *The Spectator* against ladies of fashion, arguing that domesticity is preferable to public display. Thus, Sally and her classmates, both boys and girls, by memorizing parts and performing in plays, internalized the genteel values they would diffuse throughout what would become the new middle class.[10]

In 1810, when 10-year-old Catherine Beecher attended Sarah Pierce's Female Academy in Litchfield, Connecticut, students imbibed similar genteel values and accomplishments, in addition to instruction in grammar, geography, arithmetic, and ancient history. Four years later, however, Miss Pierce's nephew John Brace came to teach at the school and introduced a curriculum resembling that of academies for boys. Eight-year-old Harriet Beecher enrolled in 1819 for a course of study that included

> Morse's Geography, Webster's Elements of English Grammar, Miss Pierce's [Universal] History, Arithmetic through Interest, Blair's Lectures [literary criticism], Modern Europe, Ramsay's American Revolution, Natural Philosophy, Hedge's Logic and Alison on Taste.

Brace took the male students (including Henry, George, and Charles Beecher) on rock- and bug-hunting expeditions in the Connecticut hills and assigned essays for both sexes on topics as difficult as "The Difference between the Natural and Moral Sublime," "The Comparative Merits of Milton and Shakespeare," and "The Comparative Merits of the Athenian and Lacedaemonian Systems of Education." He divided the school into classes, each under a leader, and, Stowe wrote later, "at the close of every term came on a great examination, which was like a tournament or passage at arms in matters of the English language. To beat in this great contest of knowledge was what excited all our energies."[11]

Nevertheless, John Brace continued to instill Addisonian domestic genteel values in his female students. In 1827, when Laura Maria Wolcott attended the academy, she interspersed lessons in geography, philosophy, literary criticism, and the history of modern Europe with regular reading in the *The Spectator*. Laura recorded in her journal, "I do not know but Mr. Brace will think it foolish for me to write of what I remember from the Spectator." Brace, who made a point of checking each student's journal, penciled in after Laura's remark, "No—I approve of it much." The educational practices of Sarah Pierce and John Brace were immensely influential, for Catherine Beecher followed them closely when she inaugurated her Hartford Female Seminary in 1823. Later, in fact, John Brace complained that Catherine had "all her life . . . taken my best ideas, and by her imitations run away with the credit."[12]

Enterprising and mobile parents in the South and West also sought to provide educational opportunities for their children. As cotton became a staple crop and a planter class coalesced in the Southern backcountry, yeoman families migrated to upland regions or were pushed west. Some, perhaps owning a few slaves, moved into Tennessee and Kentucky. As a slave system took root in these regions, many, opposing or too poor to participate in slavery, moved on along the Ohio River to southern Indiana and Illinois. Others sought land in newly opened areas wrestled from Native Americans in Georgia, Alabama, or Mississippi. Sharing a rural culture not unlike that of their northern counterparts, Southern yeoman families engaged in barter and local exchange, participated in communal work "frolics," and depended on the labor of their numerous children. Arriving in areas still inhabited by Native Americans, they instigated or endured the violence that drove the Indians westward. But as soon as Indian resistance was broken and other white families poured in, they organized for their children locally controlled schools.[13]

When Daniel Drake's family arrived in Mayslick, Kentucky, in 1788 it was still Indian country; incidents of violence, "kept vividly alive by talking it over and over," terrified children and adults. In the early 1790s Major General Anthony Wayne pursued the Shawnees and their allies in Ohio, and not until their defeat at the Battle of Fallen Timbers in 1794 and the subsequent Treaty of Fort Greenville a year later did the Shawnees give up their claims to lands in Ohio and their hunting grounds in Kentucky. In 1794 "immense" emigration came through Mayslick on the Ohio River into Kentucky; "[g]reat quantities of merchandise . . . were hauled into the interior." Drake started school in 1790, when he was five, with a Scottish teacher named McQuitty in a log cabin schoolhouse with paper windows, a wooden chimney, and a puncheon floor. As migration into the area increased, children were taught by Jacob Beaden from Maryland's eastern shore, who himself had mastered only reading, writing, and cyphering up to the rule of three.

Beaden had students of all ages recite the same lesson aloud, gathering energy as they spoke, "until the high excitement would be spread throughout the whole school." Children also instructed each other: pouring over Dilworth's speller or the New Testament, "[t]wo boys or more would 'get' & say their spelling lessons together & so of their reading lessons." In later life Drake found he could concentrate in almost any situation and thought it an advantage that he had learned to study in the midst of noise. He also appreciated the natural mingling of boys and girls, who joined in running races and playing games such as "corner-ball," "hop, skip, and jump," or "Prison-base."

In the 1790s Southern children learned deference to adults, "to take off their hats and bow and courtesy to all whom they met, either coming or going." When someone came along the road, Drake wrote, "we all stepped aside, stopped in a row, took off our hats, and made bows as near as possible at the same time." His father, however, depended on the labor of his eldest son, and when the family moved to a larger farm, nine-year-old Daniel had to leave lessons to help clear land. When Daniel was 15, an injury to his father ended his intermittent schooling, and he worked the farm alone. Such would have been his fate had not his illiterate father been determined to have at least one educated child, sending him at age 16 to Fort Washington (Cincinnati) to study medicine.[14]

In the first decades of the new republic, federal policy toward Indians sought to convert them to yeomen and eventually citizens, through trading ties, intermarriage, and economic assistance. "Let me entreat you, therefore, on the lands now given you to begin to give every man a farm," Thomas Jefferson urged a delegation of Cherokees in 1808:

> [L]et him enclose it, cultivate it, build a warm house on it, and when he dies, let it belong to his wife and children after him . . . When once you have property, you will want laws and magistrates to protect your property and person . . . you will unite yourselves with us, join in our great councils and form one people with us, and we shall all be Americans; you will mix with us by marriage, your blood will run in our veins, and will spread with us over this great continent.

Jefferson, nevertheless, had promised Georgia in 1802 that if the state ceded its western claims (the territory that became Alabama and Mississippi) to the national domain, Indians within its borders would eventually be removed; his Louisiana Purchase of 1803 provided land across the Mississippi River for those who chose to pursue their traditional ways. Yet the policy to acculturate native people was successful among the Cherokees, who, after suffering defeat in 1794, were pushed back into an area covering western portions of the Carolinas, eastern Tennessee, and northern Georgia.[15]

Although chiefs in Lower and Upper Towns (the former in central and latter in northern Georgia) were deeply divided, some Cherokees did seek to teach their boys to be farmers and their girls to be farmers' wives. In 1801, Moravian missionaries Brothers Gaschwister Wohlfart and Gottlieb Byhan and Byhan's wife (later joined by Brother John Gambold and his wife) came from their settlement in Salem, North Carolina, to Spring Place in northwest Georgia. There they were protected by James Vann, a slave-owning half-blood planter and trader, one of the Upper Town chiefs who favored acculturation and a federal road through Georgia, while resisting removal and the relinquishment of additional land. Fifty white families had already settled on Cherokee lands in the area, and more demanded land across the Tennessee River; the missionaries reported: "Thus one piece of land is taken after the other is taken from them until they will finally be completely crowded off their land."

Upper Town chiefs such as Vann, The Ridge, and Chulio knew what they wanted from the missionaries. When by 1803 the Moravians, who came to preach, had not yet started a school, the chiefs insisted that they do so; "they had no ears for that but that we should go to their towns and hold schools," recorded Brothers Wohlfart and Byhan. The chiefs expected children trained in the schoolhouse built in 1804 to become interpreters, intermediaries between the old and new ways. When Tom brought his eight-year-old son, he told the missionaries "that he wished to name his son Agaruk, meaning whirlwind . . . We were told to teach his son English and not German" and asked to "be kind to his son." When The Flea brought his grandson to the school, he requested that the child board with the Moravians rather than with Vann, for "mostly Indian was spoken at Vann's and . . . he wanted him to learn English."[16]

Although the Moravian community in Salem held slaves, Africans as well as Indians could convert to the faith, and the little community at Spring Place attempted to achieve multiracial harmony. Pupils brought by the chiefs were full- and half-blood Indians; by 1806 white farmers also brought their children. "Mr. Rogers, who lives about 40 miles from here, brought his 12 year old daughter to us," the Moravians recorded. "He is anxious to have her learn to sew, knit, read and write." Slaves were not educated until they became converts, but the Moravian meeting was attended by "Mulatoes, Negroes, Indians, and half Indians." "Such a thing" as preaching to "the poor Negroes," the missionaries admitted, "is quite unusual in these parts."

Pupils, who boarded with the Moravians or Vann and usually numbered 8 or 10, learned to read the Bible, spell from Dilworth's speller, and sing hymns. They also learned to be farmers; following the example of the parent community at Salem, they were required to work in the cornfield and peach orchard. The missionaries recorded the Upper Town chiefs' pleasure with the children's progress. Chulio "admonished them to be obedient in all things as they would learn only good things from us. . . They should be very thankful for few Indians' children were as fortunate as they." Killjoly and The Ridge "told us that they wished that they might be young again and attend our school." Nevertheless, some of the Indian children ran off for short periods of time. Although on one occasion the Moravians "feared that they might have got lost in the woods," "[t]he next day the three [children] returned. They had gone to Rabit Trap to the larger pupil's home and stayed with his parents."[17]

During this period of transition, cultures clashed at Spring Place as Upper Town chiefs sought to defend their lands and define Cherokee identity through rebellion against Lower Town chiefs and the federal agent Colonel Return J. Meigs, who favored removal. The Moravians feared that Satan had complete control over Vann, as he cavorted with multiple wives, engaged in drunken bouts of violence, and informed them it was not their business if he drank, danced, and fornicated in his own house. When a ball game, council, or the annual Green Corn dance was held at Vann's plantation, the Byhans huddled in their dwelling, complaining on one occasion, "The night was terrible with Indians everywhere. Our kitchen and school house full of them.

They shouted and danced and were so noisy we could not sleep." Nevertheless, as division within the Cherokee Nation accelerated, when Vann was murdered in 1809, the Moravians admitted that he "had been an instrument in the hand of God for establishing our mission in this Nation. Never in his wildest orgies had he attempted to harm us." After his death they focused their energies on his first wife, the half-blood Peggy Scott, who moved into a new cabin and became their first Cherokee convert.

In 1810 The Ridge sent his children to the Moravians—Nancy and Sally to board with Peggy Scott Vann, and John to live at the school. They were soon joined by Gallegina or Buck Watie, son of The Ridge's brother Oowatie. Charles Hicks, later Second Principal Chief of the Cherokee Nation, sent his children to the Moravians and became their second convert in 1812. Hicks, Chulio and The Ridge served under Andrew Jackson in the Creek War in 1813, and The Ridge earned the rank of Major in the United States Army. In 1818, after Congregational missionaries from the American Board of Commissioners for Foreign Missions established their school in Chickamauga, Tennessee, John Ridge, Buck Watie, and then John Vann traveled to Cornwall, Connecticut, to enroll in the board's parent school, where they studied geography, history, rhetoric, surveying, natural science, and Latin. Buck Watie took the name of the President of the American Bible Society, Elias Boudinot, and he and Ridge married New England girls. On their return to the Nation, where they were wealthy planters and slave owners, John Ridge, Elias Boudinot, David and John Vann, and Elijah Hicks, all of whom began their education at the Moravian school, became highly acculturated leaders of Cherokee "renascence" and the tragic effort to save the eastern lands and the sovereignty of the Cherokee Nation from encroachment by Georgia law and white farmers in the 1820s and early 1830s.[18]

Jeremiah Austill's father, hired by the federal government "to teach the Indians civilization" in the Cherokee Lower Towns of central Georgia, was one of the white farmers who hoped to benefit from the acquisition of Indian lands. When "Jim Vann," "a celebrated chief or leading man . . . who had been opposed to the sale and removal of the Cherokees across the Mississippi," was murdered in 1809, the elder Austill "concluded the sale would then be made," and decided to move his family to Clarke County in southwestern Alabama, "which had been but recently bought of the Choctaws." Margaret Ervin, who later married Jeremiah Austill, was only three in 1811 when her father "determined to move" west from Washington County in Georgia. Traveling with two other families "and about one hundred slaves, men, women and children," the Ervins found the Cherokees "kind and friendly," "but as soon as we entered the Creek or Muscage [Muscogee] nation," Margaret recalled later, "we could see the terrible hatred to the whites." At night the party camped in a circle, with women, children, and slaves protected in the center. This group also arrived in Clarke County, where Margaret's father bought a farm with a small log cabin and began to plant sugarcane and corn.[19]

Engulfed by the Creek War in 1813, the Austill and Ervin families fled to a fort in the Choctaw Nation on the Tombigbee River, where they lived for six months while Red Stick Creek rebels "crossed the Alabama and burned houses, corn, destroyed cattle, killed people who were at home." "Time passed on with fear and trembling with the grown folks," Margaret recalled, "but we children enjoyed every moment. I was in every tent in the day." Nevertheless, when Fort Mims down the river fell in August and 500 whites were killed, "[e]very heart nearly became paralyzed with fear." Red Stick resistance was not broken until General Andrew Jackson and his army devastated the village at Tohopeka—Horseshoe Bend on the Tallapoosa River—where Cherokees led by Major Ridge cut off escape by destroying Creek canoes, and only 50 of 1,000 Creeks survived. In 1814, the treaty at Fort Jackson opened to white settlement territory from Tennessee to the Gulf of Mexico. Margaret Ervin Austill recalled, "people were pouring in by thousands. The country was filled with young men looking for land. School teachers getting up schools and the largest school in the territory was St. Stephens. There I was sent with many a poor little waif to learn grammar."[20]

Schools followed Native American defeat almost as quickly in the Northwest. Congressional Ordinances of 1785 and 1787 provided that one of 36 sections of land in each township be set aside to support schools, but this enlightened policy had little effect. School lands went unrented and school funds unused.[21] In the pattern followed throughout the nation, yeoman families made arrangements with teachers for intermittent schooling that could be combined with farm labor. In the 1790s, after the Battle of Fallen Timbers, the Kickapoo had withdrawn to the Illinois country. As whites filtered onto their lands, the Kickapoo joined the confederacy put together by the Shawnee leader Tecumseh and participated in the violence that wracked the Northwest from 1811 to 1815. Many of their people chose to withdraw across the Mississippi River when the war ended, but not until Illinois became a state in 1819 did the Kickapoo formally exchange their lands for tracts in Missouri. The first white families, migrating from the upper South through Kentucky, settled the Sugar Creek area of Sangamon County the same year. In 1820 they subscribed their support to a "subscription" school, which was taught by a succession of teachers in a log cabin.[22] Maria Dawson came with her family to settle Blooming Grove in McLean County, Illinois, in 1822, when Chief Machina's band of Kickapoo still lingered in the area. Later she recalled "their war paint, the red feathers in their headdress, glistening in the bright sun, their tomahawks and knives in their belts," when a party unexpectedly visited the family. By 1825, however, Maria attended a subscription school in a "new hewed log cabin" donated by her father. Nine years later the community, newly named Bloomington, already boasted a two-schoolroom academy.[23]

In the South as well as North, locally initiated and controlled schools were supplemented by private academies, many of which focused on the education of girls. Eliza Carolina Burgwin Clitherall (born in 1784 on a Wilmington, North Carolina, rice plantation) upon her mother's death was educated in England by Quaker relatives and at boarding schools. Although she married into a well-to-do Charleston family, when in 1814 her husband lost 72 slaves through a legal technicality, she was forced to help support her five children. Based on her English education, the school for girls she opened at Thornbury, her Wilmington plantation, was the first of several she conducted throughout her life in Smithfield, then in New Bern, North Carolina, and eventually in Tuscaloosa, Alabama.[24]

A more structured Female Academy was operated by the Moravians in their Salem, North Carolina, community after 1805. Moravian life was based on 10 "choirs," designated by age, sex, and marital status. Children, who were born with perfect souls, were allowed the freedom to develop on their own in the protected environment of the family, supplemented by the infants, little boys or little girls, or older boys or older girls choirs. Children attended day school as soon as they were weaned, learning to read through games and pictures. From age 6 to age 13, they studied writing, arithmetic, grammar, history, geography, nature studies, and vocal and instrumental music at their separate Little Boys or Little Girls School. At 14, older boys entered the Single Brothers House and older girls the Single Sisters House, where boys began farmwork or apprenticeship in skilled crafts and girls learned needlework and domestic production. As the Little Girls School took in boarders, this cherished yet structured childhood attracted students from throughout the South. One traveler reported in 1814: "The academy for young ladies is famous and many Girls are sent there from S. Carolina, Georgia, Virginia, and their own State," a practice that continued throughout the antebellum period.[25]

Innovation that led to systems of tax-supported education occurred in northeastern cities as commercial relationships eroded apprenticeship, and manufacturing concentrated in outwork shops and larger units. In post-Revolutionary decades, only Boston supported a system of public education. Responding to the Massachusetts law of 1789, Boston established an annually elected School Committee that supervised grammar schools for boys and girls ages 7 to 14 and a Latin school for boys over the age of 10. Only children who could already read were admitted to the grammar schools, and girls attended them fewer hours a day than boys, and for shorter terms. Children under seven learned to read in Private Dames' Schools, conducted in various homes by female teachers licensed by the city. Stanley K. Schultz has estimated that only about 12 percent of the city's children, mostly of the middle class, attended public schools. If well-to-do children attending academies are included, the figure rises to about 20 percent; additional children of the poor received some instruction in charity schools.[26]

Boston's public system, of which citizens were very proud, emphasized the arithmetic essential in a commercial city. Yet it differed only slightly from private schooling in Philadelphia and New York, where children of well-to-do and some middle-class families attended denominational academies or learned skills and genteel accomplishments from teachers who advertised short-term classes. Academy boys learned classical languages in preparation for college; girls could attend such innovative post-Revolutionary institutions as John Poor's Young Ladies Academy in Philadelphia.[27] Boys apprenticed to crafts were educated in workshops and on the streets. Before apprenticeship at age 12 or 14, they learned to read, write, and cypher at short-term schools, and some continued with evening classes. Stephen Allen of New York, whose father, a house carpenter, died in 1770 when Stephen was two, was taught to read by his mother. He attended intermittent terms under two schoolmasters, neither of whom he particularly liked, until his apprenticeship to a sail-maker at the age of 12.[28]

After 1800 efforts to develop systems of uniform schooling for large numbers of children occurred in experimental charity schools provided for the urban poor. Philadelphia's First Day Society, as we have seen, hoped to instill the orderly habits, literacy, and skills that would enable children of the poor to become "good servants and good apprentices" and eventually "good masters and good citizens."[29] By 1805, Quaker philanthropists also influenced by enlightened ideals, Thomas Scattergood in Philadelphia and Thomas Eddy in New York, championed a new educational model worked out in England by a fellow Quaker, Joseph Lancaster. In Lancaster's system, student monitors aiding a single teacher could simultaneously instruct several hundred children. Attracted by this method of teaching large numbers of poor children at minimum expense, Eddy founded New York's Free School Society, which opened the first American Lancasterian school in 1806. Scattergood followed with the Philadelphia Association of Friends for the Instruction of Poor Children, which introduced the method in the existing Quaker Adelphi School by 1808.[30]

Joseph Lancaster had developed his "improvements in education" for the benefit of "the industrious classes of the community" in 1798, when industrial manufacturing was celebrated in England. Lacking funds yet eager to teach literacy to children of the London slums who flocked to his school, he hit upon the idea of letting the most active older boys assist him as monitors. Arranging his ungraded school into small classes of equal ability, he placed one monitor in charge of about 10 boys, and found that monitors under one adult teacher could instruct several hundred pupils. Children began by learning letters of the alphabet and words of one to two syllables using dry sand. At the monitor's verbal command, they would copy the lesson in the sand; after their work was checked, they could smooth the sand with an iron bar and begin again. For more difficult lessons, students switched to slates. In order to save money on books, lessons were copied onto cards that were read aloud by the monitor and repeated by his circle of pupils. Passed from group to group, one lesson on a card could serve as many as 200 students.

The bedlam that could have resulted from the interaction of several hundred pupils in the same classroom was avoided by Lancaster through his insistence upon uniform, drill-like behavior. When the boys entered the large, spare classroom, they were told to "sling caps" by placing their caps on their shoulders. As monitors issued short commands of "In," "Out," "March," and "Show slates," the boys would march into their groups and prepare for their lessons. Lancaster argued that this constant marching, reciting, and responding to verbal commands prevented idleness, saved time, and taught the pupils to pay attention. Students were motivated by what Lancaster called "emulation"; they were encouraged to compete with each other and earned wages for their endeavor.

Seated in a circle next to someone who approximated his ability, each student wore a card with a number indicating his rank in the class. After each recitation, the boys exchanged numbers according to their performances; the "number one" card had a picture, which the winner took home as a prize. Lancaster also used a system of reward tickets not unlike that of the evangelical Sunday schools. Each ticket had an equivalent monetary value; when a boy earned a certain number of tickets, almost as though he had earned his wages, he could purchase a toy worth the amount he had accumulated. Lancaster did not believe in corporal punishment, but for repeated "misdemeanors"—infringements of cleanliness, order, or decency—he advocated confinement of physical liberty, including measures as awkward and humiliating as shackles on the legs, a wooden log around the neck, or tying the offender's left hand against his back.[31]

Admired for its economy, efficiency, and machinelike replicability, the Lancasterian system became the basis for the first public schools in Philadelphia and New York. Interest in tax-supported schools was stimulated by urban growth, economic change, and an attitude toward poverty increasingly emphasizing moral restraint. In 1815 both were commercial cities, although manufacturing was beginning to be concentrated in larger units. In small shops, capitalist innovation was under way.[32] After the War of 1812 renewed European competition in manufacturing and commerce brought economic depression to urban centers. Workers were laid off, and those with work took wage cuts; suffering among the lower classes became acute, and the number of families on poor relief soared. Prominent citizens, worried about the prevalence of vice and crime in poor neighborhoods, began to investigate the underlying causes of poverty. An 1817 report of the Pennsylvania Society for the Promotion of Public Economy distinguished the worthy poor, those temporarily out of work, from paupers, who, because of their undisciplined habits, were likely to remain on relief.[33] The society's Committee on Public

Schools, chaired by Quaker philanthropist Roberts Vaux, investigated how discipline might be instilled in the children of paupers at minimum public expense.

In 1817 about 4,000 Pennsylvania children from poor families were being maintained by county funds at existing pay and charity schools. Yet the Vaux committee considered the existing state law to be too expensive. The cost of educating each child was $10–$12 a year; under Joseph Lancaster's monitorial plan, the cost could be reduced to $4 per student per year. Although the economy of the Lancasterian system was its selling point, Chairman Roberts Vaux believed it should educate children of all social classes. Arguing in the bill presented to the legislature that the plan would inculcate not only habitual "attention, order, and obedience," but also "uniformity of principles and habits . . . essential to the formation of correct national feeling and character," he urged that Lancaster's methods be adopted as the foundation of a citywide public school system. "There is a disposition in the [American] people adverse to dependence," Vaux argued; "a parent will raise children in ignorance rather than place them in charity schools." "In place of Charity Schools," the legislature should establish "Public Schools for the education of all children, the offspring of the rich and the poor."[34]

However, when Pennsylvania legislators passed the law making the city of Philadelphia the first school district of the state, they provided tax-supported education only for "children of indigent parents." The Adelphi School, already applying the monitorial plan, became a public institution, and Lancasterian schools were established in Philadelphia suburbs where poor and working-class families lived. In 1818 Joseph Lancaster himself arrived from England to conduct a model school, and 2,845 "children of indigent parents" received tax-supported education, a number that almost doubled within three years.[35] Soon Harrisburg, Newcastle, Pittsburgh, and other Pennsylvania communities all had monitorial schools.

The Lancasterian method also flourished in New York, where by 1825, 11 free schools including the new monitorial high school had already instructed more than 20,000 children. Arguing that year that children of rich and poor would benefit from "common" schooling, and seeking to eliminate competition for state funds from denominational charity schools, members of the Free School Society proposed to the legislature that they be allowed to become the Public School Society and open their schools to all children.[36] In the 1820s New York teachers were called "operatives," and the machinelike replicability of the Lancasterian method was extolled as a means of expanding educational opportunity. Monitors as apprentice-teachers could become monitors-general and expand the system by starting their own schools. As Lancasterian schools gained in popularity, the method spread throughout the nation. Children learned their letters, drill-like behavior, and the practices of a cash economy in more than 150 Lancasterian schools in locations as distant as Cincinnati,

Detroit, and New Orleans. The monitorial system taught blacks in New York, children of the Cherokee Nation within the borders of Georgia and Tennessee, and children of the urban poor in Charleston, South Carolina.[37] Lancasterian methods instructed even children of southern planters at New Bern Academy in North Carolina.[38]

Although the Lancasterian system seemed an educational panacea in the 1820s, it was too mechanical to mesh with the emerging domestic ideology of the new middle class. In 1827 Joanna Bethune of the New York Sunday School Union introduced the English model of infant schools for children of 18 months to six years. Her Infant School Society opened a school for children of the poor that emphasized post-Lockean psychology and maternal affection. When the New York Public School Society took over the infant schools, which became the city's primary schools, society members agreed that small children needed a woman's affection, and eliminated monitorial procedures. By 1830, nine infant schools also flourished in Philadelphia, and the concept was introduced in Boston, Salem, and Worcester, Massachusetts; Providence, Rhode Island; Hartford and New Haven, Connecticut; and Charleston, South Carolina.[39]

Working-class families in Philadelphia also failed to find the rigid discipline of Lancasterian public schools attractive. Parents were reluctant to enroll their children, perhaps because of the stigma of poverty still attached to the schools. One English visitor attributed the unruliness he observed there to "the intractable spirit generated by republican institutions." "From what I saw of children in the United States," he concluded, "I do not believe that it would be practicable to get a set of monitors to work over hours as I have seen them work in England; they would not submit to the drudgery."[40] Riding the crest of evangelical enthusiasm, Sunday schools in Philadelphia's working-class suburbs surged ahead of Lancasterian schools in attendance, just as they had superseded schools conducted by the First Day Society. In 1824 Philadelphia Sunday schools taught 7,286 pupils, or 12 percent of the city's children, while Lancasterian schools instructed 5,369, or only about 9 percent.[41]

By the 1830s very different European educational methods seeking the organic development of each individual child, based on precepts of Heinrich Pestalozzi and the example of the Prussian schools that implemented them, were trickling into the United States. As a young man in Switzerland, Pestalozzi had been influenced by Rousseau's *Emile* when that educational treatise was published in 1762. At his farm, Neuhof near Bern, in the 1770s, he had attempted to apply the education Rousseau designed for a gentleman's child to 50 destitute orphans between the ages of 6 and 16. From that experience Pestalozzi wrote *Leonard and Gertrude* in 1781, followed by *How Gertrude Teaches Her Children* in 1811, in which he explained how self-generated activity based on cultivated sense impressions in an atmosphere of security and affection could allow the organic unfolding of a child's nature. Unlike Rousseau, Pestalozzi did not manipulate children; raised by his widowed mother and a beloved servant, he genuinely admired and trusted women. Like Rousseau's English disciples Richard Lovell Edgeworth and Thomas Day, he hoped for the reformation of society through the education of the individual child, an aspiration he applied to mass education and the most poor and destitute children.

From 1804 to 1825 Pestalozzi experimented with methods of education at Yverdon, creating a kind of teachers' institute for assistants and visitors who disseminated his ideas across the Continent, greatly influencing King Friedrich Wilhelm III's progressive state-supported system of education in Prussia. Americans visited both Yverdon and the Prussian schools. Pestalozzi's aide Joseph Neef applied the master's principles in a Philadelphia school for 100 boys as early as 1806; in the 1820s he established another school at Robert Owen's utopian community in New Harmony, Indiana. New York school reformer John Griscom visited Yverdon in 1818, informing Americans about the new educational methods in his ensuing report, *A Year in Europe*. In 1837 Calvin Stowe observed the Prussian school system in preparation for a report to the Ohio legislature, bringing home ideas that would influence the romantic concept of childhood which his wife, Harriet Beecher Stowe, would later popularize.[42]

Mechanical methods would be superseded, but the replicable uniform system of the Lancasterian schools would continue to be admired as capitalism transformed the northeastern economy. From 1820 to 1840 capitalist innovation affected even rural families, who, beginning to rely on distant markets, gradually replaced older patterns of barter and local exchange with cash transactions. Production of textiles left the household as women purchased factory cloth at country stores with income from the sale of surplus cheese or butter. Women and children engaged in new forms of outwork, earning cash or credit by processing items at home for merchant capitalists. As household production and consumption patterns shifted, mothers, perhaps influenced by evangelical religion, adopted domestic ideology and sought to curtail fertility. Fathers, participating in a cash economy, began to pay wages to hired workers, relying less on the labor of their children. As rural capitalism developed, property became more fluid, character became the source of credit, and children in slightly smaller families had more time to spend in school.[43]

These underlying structural changes provided the context for school reform in the 1830s, as middle-class reformers promoted state-supported and supervised systems of education, advocating standardized, uniform full-time schools taught by professional teachers. As middle-class children worked less and went to school more, character formation became increasingly associated with schooling. Born in 1796, Horace Mann lived through New England's

economic transformation; like other rural Massachusetts boys of his generation, he labored on the farm and intermittently attended district school. As
early as 1804 he and his sisters contributed to the family income by braiding
oat straw for a nearby hat manufactory. Mann escaped digging and plowing
on the farm through an opportunity to attend college at Brown University.
Later, he read law at Judge Tapping Reeve's school in Litchfield, Connecticut. By the 1820s he moved to Dedham, near Boston, where he conducted lit-
igation for mills and merchants, invested in factories, and campaigned for
temperance in his spare time. Elected to the Massachusetts legislature by
1828, Mann espoused a "positive republican" belief in active government,
which led him to advocate state support for such benevolent institutions as
the Massachusetts state mental hospital that he steered through the legislature
in 1830. A member of the new Whig party and president of the state senate in
1837, Mann seemed to Governor Edward Everett, who admired the Prussian
schools and had an educational fund to distribute, the ideal candidate to
appoint to the position of secretary of the new Massachusetts State Board of
Education.[44]

By 1837 Horace Mann was disillusioned with the vested interests con-
trolling Massachusetts politics yet was alarmed by the urban poverty and
crime accelerated by that year's economic panic. He agreed with the optimism of his friend, the Unitarian minister William Ellery Channing, who
wrote, "If we can but turn the wonderful energy of this people into a right
channel, what a new heaven and earth must be realized among us." In
the dynamic yet chaotic context of industrial transformation, belief in the
malleability of the child again provided hope for the maintenance of common
values and the reestablishment of social bonds. "Having found the present
generation composed of materials almost unmalleable," Mann wrote, "I
am about transferring my efforts to the next. Strength expended upon the latter may be effectual, which would make no impression upon the former."
Immersing himself in Scottish Common Sense philosophy and reports on
Prussian schools, Mann prepared to promote the nondenominational public
school, the purpose of which would be "to form character." Lecturing
throughout the state and lobbying the legislature, he advocated a state-
supervised system financed by taxation, a uniform curriculum, a continuous
10-month term, carefully designed school buildings, and normal schools to
train teachers.[45]

Battles fought by Horace Mann and other school reformers built widespread support by the 1840s for nonsectarian, yet Protestant, public schools
that would instill values of republicanism and capitalism. When Frederick A.
Packard of the American Sunday School Union promoted adoption of the
union's line of juvenile literature in 1838, Mann objected that evangelical
Sunday school books inspired fear. Like others of his generation, he rejected
the individualistic conversion experience and was attracted to the concept of

the cultivated conscience and the organic view of child nurture soon to be articulated by Horace Bushnell. Mann thought that "fundamental principles of Christianity may and should be inculcated" in common schools, but, as a Unitarian, he opposed instruction in the doctrines of any denomination.[46] As public schools that instilled Protestant and republican moral restraint (not unlike those originally advocated by Benjamin Rush) evolved and became permanent, denominational Sunday schools superseded the ecumenical American Sunday School Union. Reaching the same students who attended public schools, they abandoned teaching literacy and concentrated on denominational doctrines.[47]

As immigration increased and Irish neighborhoods burgeoned in Boston and Lowell, Philadelphia and New York, Catholic clergy objected to the Protestant thrust of public schools and responded by forming their own educational institutions. In 1840 New York Catholics petitioned the state legislature for school funds, protesting exclusive use of the St. James Bible, lack of Biblical explication, a negative image of Catholics, and slurs against the Irish in the city's common schools. After two years of rancorous division in both the Whig party and the Catholic church, local government took control from the zealous Public School Society; but New York schools retained their Protestant message. Acculturation of immigrants and consolidation of middle-class cultural hegemony would continue to be a function of American common schools.[48]

Neither would public schools recognize racial diversity. Since the colonial period, free schools for black children and adults had been established by benevolent whites in northeastern urban centers. With gradual emancipation in post-Revolutionary decades, free black leaders such as Richard Allen and Absalom Jones in Philadelphia organized their own schools and Sunday schools. Yet for black children, schooling remained intermittent and interspersed with work. When Philadelphia's Lancasterian public schools were established in 1818, black children were excluded.[49] Although public systems, including that of New York, absorbed some existing black schools, by the 1840s communities such as Lowell, Nantucket, New Bedford, Worcester, and Salem, Massachusetts, were unusual in admitting black pupils into predominantly white schools.

In Boston separate public schools for white and black children had evolved by 1830. Although middle-class blacks and white abolitionists pressed for integration, the Boston School Committee rejected their plea, fearing that white parents would withdraw their children from integrated schools. In 1849 black parents sued the Boston School Committee in *Roberts v. City of Boston*. A year later Charles Sumner argued before the state Supreme Court that racially segregated schools did not recognize equality before the law. Nevertheless, the school committee's decision was upheld. Not until 1855, after negative views of increased Irish immigration and the rise of the Know Nothing party shifted attitudes toward blacks, did the state legislature mandate integration throughout Massachusetts. Although Boston schools were finally integrated, no other Northern state followed the Massachusetts example.[50]

By the 1850s common schools dovetailed neatly with domestic ideology. As middle-class mothers assumed responsibility for character formation in early childhood, children under the age of six were excluded from graded public schools. Carl Kaestle and Maris Vinovskis have estimated that 40 percent of Massachusetts three-year-olds still attended school in 1840. Nevertheless, the percentage of children from birth to age 19 attending school declined by mid-century, as early childhood became more protected and very young children were kept at home. As public school systems consolidated, administrators sought to save money by hiring female teachers under the supervision of a male principal teacher. Teaching became more hierarchical and bureaucratized, but education in a normal school provided a professional opportunity for women, allowing single women to participate in the important national task of forming character. When school reformers and other social critics berated the increasing instability of family life, their comments often focused on the middle-class father who, "eager in the pursuit of business, toils early and late." By the 1850s the paternal role in forming character was increasingly assumed by the state, acting *in loco parentis* for the absent patriarchal father.[51]

As common schools focused on forming character, reworking republican goals for a new economic context, they prepared children for success in competitive careers and more disciplined routinized work. Pupils, engaged in memorization and drill with others their own age, focused on promotion from grade to grade. Studying for 10-month terms in large classes in quickly overcrowded new buildings, they probably did have a more impersonal experience than that of the community district school or rural academy. Ralph Waldo Emerson perceived the regimentation that graded state-supervised schools introduced into children's lives. Education "has frozen stiff in the universal congelation of society," he complained:

> We are shut up in schools and college recitation rooms for ten or fifteen years and come out at last with a bellyful of words and do not know a thing. We cannot use our hands, or our legs, or our eyes, or our arms. We do not know an edible root in the woods. We cannot tell our course by the stars, nor the hour of the day by the sun. It is well if we can swim and skate. We are afraid of a horse, of a cow, of a dog, of a cat, of a spider. Far better was the Roman rule to teach a boy nothing that he could not learn standing . . . The farm, the farm, is the right school . . . The farm is a piece of the world, the school-house is not.

Farmers in areas less affected by rural capitalism tended to agree, maintaining local control over their district schools and resisting consolidation in the mid-

nineteenth century. State legislators in Massachusetts who supported Horace
Mann and the Board of Education overwhelmingly represented commercial
areas where economic development was well under way. They also tended to
be Whigs favoring a positive role for the state, rather than Democrats, who
opted for local control.[52]

In states carved from the Northwest Territory, yeomen also opposed a
general tax for education and loss of local control. Where subsistence farming
and customs of barter and local exchange prevailed, families who depended
on their children's labor preferred voluntary intermittent schooling that
could mesh with agricultural work. Not until the 1850s, when railroads penetrated the Midwest, speculators bought up land, and tenant farming and hired
labor became widespread, did tax-supported public schools retaining strong
district control take root. As a cash economy and rural capitalism transformed the Midwest, northeastern patterns affected even families of Southern
background; second-generation women decreased fertility, and with hired
labor, middle-class children in smaller families had more time to spend in
school.[53]

Isaac Funk came with his parents and eight siblings from Kentucky
through Ohio to a log cabin in McLean County near Blooming Grove, Illinois, in 1823. After attending a local one-room subscription school, by the
1830s he was driving hogs and cattle purchased in Missouri to market in
Chicago. Famous locally as the "beef king" in the 1850s, he owned 25,000
acres of land farmed by tenants and hired labor, and livestock valued at one
million dollars. As a Whig county supervisor, he arranged the selling of
county swamplands that would bring the new state normal school to the
thriving agricultural area.[54] Six male and three female scholars enrolled to
study Horace Mann's *Lectures* and Henry Barnard's *Journal of Education* at
Illinois State Normal University when it opened in 1857; "our parents were
sad-faced, struggling pioneers of the prairies," one of them later recalled,
"but we were cheery, resolute, and happy in our life and work."[55]

Tax-supported public schools made some headway even in the South
before the Civil War. In Virginia and Georgia, legislative efforts to provide
common schooling for whites failed by close margins. In North Carolina,
where Whigs were prominent in the state legislature, Calvin Wiley, an active
state superintendent, administered a fledgling public school system by 1852.
Alabama, Louisiana, and Kentucky also appointed state superintendents in
the 1850s.[56] Perhaps the most successful effort occurred in Charleston, South
Carolina, where Irish and German immigrants composed 40 percent of the
white population by mid-century. When the state legislature named German-
born Christopher G. Memminger to the local school board, he spearheaded a
drive for public schools. Visiting Boston, Philadelphia, and New York and
consulting the Connecticut school reformer Henry Barnard, Memminger
brought to Charleston a male superintendent and two female principals from

Brooklyn. By 1857, three new buildings were completed housing two primary schools and a high school for girls. Extolled for elevating white labor and coalescing white supremacy in a slave society, the public school system flourished in Charleston until the Civil War when Yankee teachers left for the North and enrollments declined. Associated with painful racial issues, Charleston's common schools were not revived during Reconstruction years.[57]

Nevertheless, in the antebellum period slavery kept capitalistic transformation of the southern rural household at bay, preventing the development of the economic context in which parents and legislators advocated state-supported full-time common schools. Planters continued to educate their children at home or in academies, many of which provided military training by mid-century. Southern yeoman families continued older patterns of barter and local exchange, high fertility, and patriarchal control of children's labor. In Newton County in northern Georgia in the 1850s, James Monroe Adams, the eldest of 16 children, from the age of five planted and shucked corn, picked and hauled cotton, mended fences, and helped slaughter hogs on the family farm. Only during intermittent breaks from the labor directed by his father was he able to attend four- to six-week sessions of reading, writing, and cyphering at various locally initiated and controlled subscription schools.[58]

6

Re-forming Character

Work

> *Ask the magistrates of these courts, from whence come the children who are arraigned before them for pilfering, they will tell you that three fourths of them are from families, which have looked to these children* for a part of their means of support.
>
> Joseph Tuckerman, 1830

In the early American republic children were valued for their labor and expected to work. Production took place in hierarchical, patriarchal households where fathers and masters directed the labor of family members and helpers. Parents allotted tasks to children according to gender, which they learned to perform by watching and doing. Nevertheless, in the 1790s expanding commercial markets and revolutionary rhetoric were beginning to transform northeastern households. Rural parents, even in an economy of barter and local exchange, utilized their children's labor to supplement family income. In urban centers, as capitalism penetrated the trades, the nature of apprenticeship changed. As contractual arrangements in small shops eroded and some masters substituted apprentices for trained journeymen, children became a source of cheap, unskilled labor. Children who worked for wages in the new large manufacturing units were not apprentices to be educated by watching and doing but performers of limited, repetitive tasks. Yet the labor of children was an essential ingredient in various strategies employed by parents that began to produce a more dynamic economy.

By the 1820s and 1830s capitalism was transforming the Northeast. Merchants inserted themselves into patterns of exchange, providing new kinds of outwork for rural families. Textile factories on the Lowell model freed many girls from domestic cloth production, offering young women independence, cash, and a chance to escape the farm. Enterprising apprentices picked up innovations in technology faster than their masters did. Boys absorbed the entrepreneurial values penetrating popular culture and propelled themselves into the new middle class. Nevertheless, as class differences became more distinct, although some children profited from economic change, many parents struggled to survive or sought to benefit from children's labor. As crafts continued to deteriorate in expanding urban centers, families taking in outwork "sweated" their children in garret shops and cellars. Parents in the poorest urban families sent their children to fetch and scavenge in the streets.

Such "pilfering and vagrancy" alarmed well-to-do urban adults. In the 1820s, benevolent individuals who sought national founding of Sunday schools or supported public schools also hoped that character could be "reformed" in delinquent but still malleable children through regular habits and supervised work. Forming voluntary associations, they founded municipal Houses of Refuge through which the community intervened for "neglectful" parents. These innovative institutions were both prisons and schools, yet incarcerated children spent the bulk of each day in work; upon their release they were placed under indenture. By the 1830s overburdened parents used the Houses of Refuge to deal with children they could not handle. Yet the very presence of the reform school served to strengthen the opinion that delinquent or destitute children should be removed from their families and placed in institutions for their own and the community's good.

After the panic of 1837 and the depression that followed it, firms were increasingly highly capitalized, and opportunity lessened. As previous patterns of barter and local exchange were replaced by a cash economy, character—industrious activity tempered by internalized restraint—became a source of credit. By the late 1840s, immigration increased, and family shops and sweatshops proliferated. Destitute Irish fleeing the potato famine provided the cheap labor that allowed Boston to become an industrial city and transformed the workforce in Lowell. German immigrants, who outnumbered the Irish by 1850, utilized the labor of their children in deteriorating crafts. By midcentury, lessening opportunity and increased immigration contributed to concern about children on the streets. As concepts of child nurture, such as those articulated by Horace Bushnell, permeated American culture, urban charities began to advocate removing children from unsuitable families and placing them in new domestic settings. Massachusetts passed the nation's first adoption law in 1851. Legislators passed truancy laws requiring children to attend public school and founded new institutions—state reform or industrial schools—as the state assumed the paternal role in forming or reforming character.

In the early American republic, unless they were well-to-do, parents expected their children to contribute their labor to household survival. Seeking to secure a future for their children, they engaged in various strategies—making things at home, clearing marginal land, or migrating west. Pursuing such endeavors to stay even or get ahead, rural patriarchal fathers enlisted and directed the help of boys. In Mayslick, Kentucky, in the 1790s, Daniel Drake was about six when he began fetching the cow from the woods, grinding corn until his knuckles bled, and riding and guiding the horse while his father plowed. By the age of eight he was feeding as well as collecting the livestock, and dropping corn in plowed furrows for his father to cover with the hoe. When he was nine he left school to help his father clear land, grubbing up shrubs and bushes, cutting limbs off the trees his father felled, and tending brush fires and the charcoal pit late into the night.

At 10 Daniel began to participate in the rural economy of barter and local exchange, "toting" corn on his back to be ground by a neighbor's hand mill, or on horseback to a grist mill. He also helped his father and a neighbor build fences, setting stakes and marking the ground with a hoe, while the men followed laying rails. At 12 Daniel could lay rails himself, handle the plow alone, and join his neighbors in the wheat harvest. "When I was thirteen, fourteen, and fifteen years old," he later recalled, "I was able to do half a man's work with the sickle and I may add (boastingly) with the scythe also . . . In the harvest field my greatest ambition was to sweat so as to wet my shirt."[1]

"Harvest was a social labor, a frolic, a scene of excitement," Drake remembered, as boys joined men in rituals of male communal labor. At log rollings or corn huskings the "green glass quart whiskey bottle, stopped with a cob, was handed to everyone, man and boy, as they arrived, to take a drink." Two men or boys at the fall corn husking were chosen as captains, and teams sang, cheated, and fought as they competed to husk corn and build piles of cobs. Finally, "the victorious captain, mounted on the shoulders of some of the stoutest men, with the bottle in one hand and his hat in the other, was carried in triumph around the vanquished party, amidst the shouts of victory which rent the air." After dinner (prepared by women and girls) and a round of fighting, "by midnight, the sober were found assisting the drunken home. Such was one of my autumnal schools," Drake wrote to his children, "from the age of nine to fifteen years."[2]

Although mothers directed the work of girls, gender roles could blur in a rural late eighteenth-century household. As the eldest child in a poor family without hired help, Daniel helped his mother "as a matter of duty" until his sister Lizzy was old enough to supplant him. He did not milk—Lizzy "was taught that accomplishment as early as possible"—but he held the ears of the cows while his mother milked, he churned butter, and he helped make cheese. On washing days, he fetched water from the spring, kept up the fire, and helped his mother hang clothes on fences. Both Daniel and Lizzy did "scrubbing and scouring," using a "split broom" made from a hickory sapling and homemade "scrubs" for the Buckeye bowls and black walnut table. On days he did not work in the fields, Daniel could be found setting the table, turning the meat, or watching the cake while Lizzy dressed three younger children and his mother nursed the baby.

Daniel also helped his mother with cloth production; although he disliked shearing sheep, he rather enjoyed carding wool. It was his job to do the "doubling and twisting," walking backward and turning the rim of the big wheel while his mother spun. He "swingled" or prepared dried flax for his mother to spin on the small wheel, and spread the finished linen on the grass to bleach in the sun. He, Lizzy, and his mother then "colored" or dyed the finished cloth with materials they had gathered—inner bark of white walnut, hulls of black walnut, oak bark—or indigo they had purchased with goods. "My pride was in the labors of the field," Drake later recorded, "but taste and duty held me as occasion required, to the duties of the house."[3]

Like Lizzy Drake, girls as young as 10 were expected to be skilled in household tasks throughout the early republic. Instructed by their mothers or neighbors, New England girls learned to spin at age 8 or 10, and to weave a coverlet by age 14. Girls could produce prodigious amounts of textiles, carding wool, spinning yarn, and weaving cloth for weeks at a time. In 1791, 15-year-old Elizabeth Fuller of Princeton, Massachusetts, recorded in her diary that she spun for three weeks, producing 74 skeins of yarn (more than 40,000 yards). A year later, when she finished weaving 176 yards of cloth, she commented wearily, "Welcome Sweet Liberty, once more to me. How I have longed to meet again with thee."[4]

In her meticulous explication of Martha Ballard's diary, Laurel Thatcher Ulrich has demonstrated how in Hallowell, Maine, in the 1790s the labor of girls contributed to "the complex web of social and economic exchange that engaged women beyond the household." By the age of 15 Hannah and Dolly Ballard could spin on both the big wheel for wool and the smaller one for flax, producing thread their mother took to neighbors to weave. When the family obtained weaving equipment, Hannah and Dolly wove "check, diaper, huckaback, worsted, dimity, woolen 'shurting,' towels, blankets, 'rag coverlids,' and lawn handkerchiefs, as well as 'plain cloth.'" Ballard exchanged textiles produced by her daughters for items the family consumed—spices or brandy at the local store, or pumpkins, cabbages, pork, mutton, candles, or soap produced by neighbors. In times of necessity, daughters themselves were exchanged among households. The labor of girls in ordinary chores—laundry and soapmaking, scrubbing and scouring—also freed Ballard to conduct her thriving midwifery practice. When her daughters married and left home, Ballard had to cut back on both midwifery and textile production. Although Hannah and Dolly would use their skills as wives and mothers in their own households, their labor had benefited their mother, much as fathers benefited from the labor of their sons.[5]

Among New England households in the late eighteenth and early nineteenth centuries, as Christopher Clark has pointed out, these family strategies to stay even or get ahead contributed to the development of a dynamic regional economy; parents seeking to provide for their children utilized their children's labor to increase their economic activity.[6] Horace Greeley's father was one of many farmers in the 1810s who increased production by bringing marginal lands under cultivation. As young as the age of five, Horace picked stones from rocky New Hampshire fields, rode the horse "to plough," and killed "wire-worms and grubs" brought to light by his father's hoe. By six or seven he began to watch the charcoal pit and look forward to communal hop-picking, when men cut vines and laid out poles while teams of women and children competed in stripping hops to fill large bins. When his father's venture failed and creditors seized the farm, nine-year-old Horace and his eight-year-old brother went to Vermont with their father to work for wages, supporting the family by clearing additional new land for cultivation.[7] Other rural New England families increased their income by using children in the household manufacture of brooms, tools, and other wooden items. In 1810 in Amherst, Massachusetts, three young sons of Eli Dickinson helped their father make wooden faucets in a workshop on their farm.[8]

Initially, farmers in Lynn, Massachusetts, combined shoemaking with other rural endeavors. By the 1790s, however, distinctive to the community were "ten-footers"—little wooden buildings interspersed among dwellings—in which masters directed the labor not only of journeymen but also their own wives and children. While the master and journeymen cut leather and tacked and sewed "uppers" and soles, the shoemaker's wife and daughters did the binding, stitching the parts of the upper shoe together. Sons mingled with apprentices, helping with various tasks. By 1800, 200 workshops thrived in Lynn, producing shoes to exchange for provisions with local shopkeepers, who, in turn, exchanged them for goods with merchants, who distributed the shoes in an expanding market. As enterprising individuals inserted themselves into the process, coastal farming and fishing families were drawn into out-work. Merchants distributed cut out stock from workshops for binding by women and girls, and lasting and bottoming by men and boys, as families sought to benefit from the labor of their children.[9]

Changing economic relationships affected apprenticeship, the time-honored method of learning a craft. Sometimes as young as age 7 or 10, but usually about age 14, a boy would be placed by his parents or guardian under indenture. Serving until his early 20s, he would learn by doing, providing his master with labor in return for instruction in skills, some education in reading and writing, room and board mixed with paternal guidance, and perhaps a suit of clothes when he progressed to day laborer or journeyman. Only occasionally was an urban girl apprenticed to a seamstress or milliner; girls under indenture were more likely to be servants. European guilds regulating apprenticeship were not transferred to the American colonies; nevertheless, adherence to the practice was valued by both masters and journeymen in order to maintain quality of workmanship and monitor entry into the craft.

By the 1790s, capitalism—the response to an enlarged market, the use of cash, and the hiring of free wage labor—was beginning to penetrate the urban trades, and the old hierarchical personal relationships were changing. Disruption during the Revolution and hard times in the 1780s followed by commercial prosperity in the 1790s created a fluctuating urban economy that demanded flexibility. Long-term contracts became unprofitable; journeymen moved around, and artisans faced with high turnover shifted to paying wages and boarding workers outside the household. Under these conditions apprenticeship indentures omitted provisions for education or clothing, and occasionally included cash payments to parents; in good times masters took on additional apprentices in order to benefit from cheap juvenile labor.[10]

During the Revolution contractual arrangements had eroded and the authority of masters had been undermined. In 1779, when Stephen Allen of New York was 12, he and his older brother William were apprenticed to a sail-maker without a formal indenture; their widowed mother simply agreed verbally that each boy would stay until age 21. Stephen felt that he and the other apprentices were not "well clothed, well fed, nor well-lodged," for they ate in the cellar and slept in the garret of their master's house. As trade thrived in British-occupied New York, the master took on two more apprentices and moved them all into the sail-loft, where they ate breakfasts of cocoa and bread, and dinners of "bitter" and "burnt" warmed-up stew in the yard or on the street. Purchased from a "slop shop," the roundabout jackets and canvas trousers furnished by their master resembled sailors' clothing, and sometimes "English press gangs" chased the boys. Allen read his Testament and Dilworth's Speller, but his loose apprenticeship did not include education, and his formal schooling stopped at age 12. Although he excelled in cutting out sails, his master's Tory sympathies inflamed his resentment, and he rejoiced in 1783 when Tories fled with "the disgusting red-coats." A free laborer in hard times at age 15, Stephen found wage work at another sail-loft, even though journeymen there objected to the hiring of a boy who had not served a full apprenticeship.[11]

In post-Revolutionary decades apprentices continued to resent authority and assert their rights. When John Prentiss and apprentices in Thomas Adams's Boston printing shop were served moldy bread, they "talked *out loud loud* about it" to the mistress of the house, and later threw an offending loaf into a neighbor's yard. When 14-year-old Millard Fillmore objected to chopping wood and tending the charcoal pit and his master chastised him, the future president allegedly raised his axe and said, "If you approach me I will split you down." Some boys, empowered by religious populism, refused to submit to ungodly masters. Others sought liberty by moving around, escaping drudgery or harsh masters by running away.[12] Yet republican ideology also included apprentices in the community of citizen-craftsmen when they joined masters and journeymen in rituals that celebrated solidarity in the trades. Mechanics in leather aprons paraded in Philadelphia or New York, demonstrating their support for the new federal Constitution or celebrating the Fourth of July. Speeches affirmed the right of producers to personal independence, political equality, and a just competence. For, according to ideals of artisan republicanism, apprenticeship was only a temporary dependence on the path to independent master through instruction in skills and values in the small shop.[13]

Even while artisans appropriated republican ideology, deterioration in the crafts was under way. As New York surpassed Philadelphia as a commercial center, in both cities merchants with capital or entrepreneurial masters created larger units of production—expanded workshops or "manufactories" with as many as 10 or 20 semi-skilled workers. Wage-earning boys working in tanneries or girls making cigars were cheap, unskilled labor without the obligations due apprentices. In New York, tailors expanding from sailor "slops" to cheap, ready-to-wear clothing or shoemakers attempting to compete with the output from Lynn subcontracted a larger share of their finishing work to outworkers. Many small masters toiling in garret shops or cellars survived only by working their families, "sweating" their wives and children to finish garments and bind shoes. Children increasingly contributed to family income by working for very low wages in larger units of production or as outworkers in familial settings under the direction of a patriarchal father or master.[14]

These changing relationships of production affected apprentices in small shops when tailors, shoemakers, or printers, seeking to benefit from cheap or unpaid labor, substituted juvenile "helpers" for trained journeymen. Forced to "tramp," sometimes with families, in search of work, journeymen who hoped to become masters viewed "illegal" apprentices as symbols of their own declining prospects. As they drew together in a fledgling labor movement, they objected to declining standards of apprenticeship and the hiring of young, unskilled workers instead of their own skilled labor. In 1808, the New York cordwainers (shoemakers) general strike focused on the hiring of boys. In 1811 the city's journeymen printers circulated an appeal to masters, complaining that the employment of young "half-ways" led to declining quality and an "unnecessary multiplication" of workers in the trade.[15]

As free wage labor became more prevalent and apprenticeship declined, bound labor was degraded, reserved more exclusively for blacks emerging from slavery and orphaned or destitute children. In 1780, the Pennsylvania legislature was the first to emancipate slaves, yet it protected an owner's investment by allowing him or her to retain slaves born before the law went into effect and to keep in bondage until age 28 all children born to slave mothers thereafter. The result was a blurring of slave and indentured labor and a brisk market in black children not yet free who would serve for a large portion of their productive lives. The practice influenced indenture of free or manumitted blacks who also often served until age 28, rather than the usual term of age 18 for girls and 21 for boys. Although such indentures provided a source of cheap labor for white masters, they were also used by black parents emerging from slavery as they struggled to gain an economic foothold in Philadelphia or the surrounding countryside.[16]

In 1794, Quaker Elizabeth Drinker recorded that her family took from prison the black 11-year-old Scipio Drake at the request of his mother's mistress. When Scipio ran away, his father, who lived elsewhere, brought him back; "he advis'd and threatened him, wish'd us to keep him," Drinker recorded. Ten days later, however, she "signed over" the mischievous Scipio to a friend in the country, where he probably became an agricultural laborer. Not long after, the Drinkers bought for fifteen pounds each the indentures of three more black children, including seven-year-old Peter Wood from Virginia, whose father was probably free, as he arrived a few days later to take the boy to visit his mother. Although managing her new child servants kept her busy, Drinker knew their value; "these small foulk ought to be of service when they grow bigger," she wrote, even though "they are very troublesome when young to those who have their good at heart." Two years later, Peter's parents—proud of his ability to read the Bible—formally bound him to the Drinkers until age 21. He remained their domestic servant and then driver until a year after he became free, when he decided, to Elizabeth's trepidation, to go to sea.

In 1795, Nancy Drinker Skyrin took under indenture 12-year-old Patience Gibbs, a black child brought from Delaware to Philadelphia by her mother. Patience served the Skyrins until she became free at age 18; her father, Absalom Gibbs, described by Drinker as "a decent sensiable" man, came to take her home, "highly pleased with her education." Yet the decision to indenture children must have been a painful one, and some black parents were reluctant or divided. In 1796 Elizabeth went to check out "a little Negro girl" that her daughter, Sally Drinker Downing, wished "to bind," recording: "The child looks cleaver—the Mother is not willing to part with her, but the father and others insist on taking her from her mother. I gave no incouragement of S.D.'s taking her."[17]

Indenture also continued to be used, as it had been throughout the colonial period, to place orphaned or destitute children. Through the vendue system, rural towns in New England and New York as late as the 1820s literally auctioned off dependent children, often separating them from their families, to serve the household that made the lowest bid.[18] Urban areas, however, combined outdoor relief (food, fire wood, and sometimes cash) to destitute families with such institutional solutions as the almshouse. By 1815, private charities such as the Female Orphan Society in Philadelphia began to found asylums. Not unlike the humanitarian First Day Society of the 1790s, the Philadelphia group declared its intention:

> to rescue from ignorance, idleness and vice, destitute, unprotected and helpless children, and to provide for them that support and instruction which may eventually render them valuable members of the community.

In a rented house supervised by a hired governess, the society began taking in three-, four-, and five-year-old children, some of whom already lived in the almshouse. Within two years the group built a new asylum on Cherry Street that allowed them to admit as many as 90 boys under the age of six and girls under the age of eight. The children received religious instruction and learned reading, writing, and arithmetic through the Lancasterian system. Yet they also contributed to their own support, knitting stockings sold to benefit the institution. And as young as age 9 or 10, but usually at about age 12, boys and girls left the asylum when they were placed under indenture.[19]

Between 1822 and 1832, 132 children (75 girls and 57 boys) were "bound out" by the asylum for periods of 1 to 11 years. All but two of the girls were bound as domestic servants, with their trade listed as "housewifery"; one of the two exceptions was apprenticed to a milliner and the other perhaps to a seamstress. Thirty-one of the boys were bound to farmers to become agricultural laborers, and two to "gardners," but, with the exception of one sent to a merchant, most of the rest were apprenticed to trades ranging from cabinetmaker, shoemaker, or tailor, to specialized crafts such as Windsor chair–maker, silk dyer, coppersmith, jeweler, or ornamental gilder. Only one boy's trade was indicative of the transforming Philadelphia economy: machine-maker.

The board of the Female Orphan Society did attempt to keep track of children after they were bound out. When Eliza McCarty could not get along with the family she served, another place was found for her in the country. Rebecca Dominick was reported to be "severely treated," and received a new indenture. Charlotte Dobell was not bound to Wilfred Hall because he was a single man. When Robert Malony's indenture ended, he received tools and a loan from the board to begin his trade. Robert Williams, who was sent to sea as a cabin boy after bribing another boy with a hoop to set a trunk (and potentially the asylum) on fire, was followed for several years. On his return from sea, Robert was apprenticed to various trades, sent a donation by the society when he was sick in Mobile, Alabama, on his release from the navy, and eventually, "on application of the board," released from prison.[20]

As the crafts deteriorated and the cultural meaning of apprenticeship changed, some children worked for wages in new mechanized factories.

Samuel Slater, a former apprentice who smuggled plans for the spinning frame from England, established his mill to produce cotton yarn—in partnership with the merchant capitalists William Almy and Moses Brown—in Pawtucket, Rhode Island, in 1790. His first labor force consisted of children 7 to 12 years of age—Turpin, Charles, Eunice, and Ann Arnold; Jabez, John, and Sylvanus Jenks; Smith Wilkinson; and Otis Barrows. By 1801, 100 children from 4 to 10 years old worked at Slater's mill, cleaning raw cotton, tending spindles, removing and attaching bobbins, and knotting broken threads. These children, nevertheless, still labored as household members. Families with five or six children were encouraged to come to the mill, where they were provided with rental housing and paid according to age and gender—$1 a day for the father, 67¢ for the oldest boy, down to as little as 10 cents for the youngest girl. Account bills indicate that the combined wages of family members barely covered the provisions they purchased at the company store. Within 20 years, this "family system" (in which about half of the workers were children) spread throughout Rhode Island, eastern Connecticut, and southern Massachusetts.[21]

By 1810, textile mills employing children thrived not only in southern New England but also outside of New York City and in Philadelphia and Baltimore. Secretary of the Treasury Albert Gallatin counted 87 such mills in the United States, estimating that they employed about 4,000 workers, 3,500 of whom were women and children. Promoters of manufacturing lauded not only the cheapness of child labor but also the contribution made to the national wealth and their own support by children under the age of 10 (35 percent of the population in the census of 1810), who otherwise would be "idle." Nevertheless, their critics objected that factory labor lacked the training in skills, the provision for education, and the paternal guidance that ideally characterized apprenticeship. From sunrise to sunset six days a week children performed limited, repetitive tasks. The Connecticut legislature required in 1813 that children employed in manufacturing "be taught to read and write" and be "instructed in the first four rules of arithmetic," "that due attention be paid to the preservation of their morals; and that they be required by their masters or employers regularly to attend public worship."[22]

In the 1820s and 1830s, manufacturing surged forward and capitalism transformed the northeastern economy. Improved transportation allowed farm families to sell their produce and purchase commodities in distant markets. As merchants inserted themselves into patterns of exchange, cash payments began to replace local arrangements of credit and barter. Rural families set up stores, and boys sought positions as clerks or anticipated business careers in urban centers. Traders put out materials for household manufacturing, engaging women and children in new kinds of outwork. Since the 1790s, cotton mills operating on the Rhode Island system had distributed yarn for farming families to weave into cloth or knit into gloves and stockings. Other families split and braided palm leaf to sew and fashion into hats. In the 1820s, Massachusetts merchants began to distribute vegetable ivory, metal, and silk for women and children to form into cloth-covered buttons. Paid with goods at the local store or sometimes in cash, outwork, increasingly considered children's work, was a welcome supplement to family income. Making buttons in Buckland, Massachusetts, in 1841, the Graham children earned $70 the family needed to migrate west. In North Hadley, the four daughters of widow Judith Nutting fit the braiding of palm leaf into sewing and other household routines; one daughter earned 54¢ in one day for making six palm-leaf hats.[23]

Although outwork and about two-thirds of cloth production continued to be performed in households where children's work was directed by parents, in the 1820s the new cotton mills at Lowell, Massachusetts, offered New England daughters an opportunity to work outside the household, thus gaining personal independence and earning cash. The highly capitalized mills at the confluence of the Concord and Merrimack Rivers followed the system introduced by Francis Cabot Lowell in Waltham, Massachusetts, in 1813; use of the new power loom and improved machinery allowed all the steps of manufacturing cotton cloth to be accomplished in one location. Perhaps because the increased speed of production and heavier machinery would overtax children, the company sought the labor of young women, farm daughters away from home whom managers promised to protect in supervised boarding houses. In his analysis of the Lowell workforce, Thomas Dublin found that more than 80 percent of residents in Hamilton Company boarding houses in 1830 and 1840 were between 15 and 30 years of age; only about 3 percent of Hamilton workers were under age 15. Children at Lowell arrived with kin; 14.3 percent of workers from three New Hampshire towns in the 1830s were under age 15, most likely younger sisters accompanying older ones. Fourteen-year-old Caroline Ames arrived from Canterbury, New Hampshire, in April 1835 to work as a weaver with her 18-year-old sister Lucy Jane, who took a job in the dressing room. Yet Caroline, who earned about $1.25 a week and continued to live in the boarding house after Lucy Jane left, had made a decision to live and work separately from her family, unlike the children in Slater's mill who still labored as household members.[24]

Children who came with widowed mothers to live and work at Lowell learned to value the personal independence they gained from their ability to earn wages and their contacts with older coworkers. After Lucy Larcom's father died, her mother, "seeing no other opening for herself," sold their home in Beverly, Massachusetts, "and moved to Lowell, with the intention of taking a corporation-house for mill-girl boarders." At first, 11-year-old Lucy attended a Lancasterian school and worked at the boarding house, but in 1835 the needs of her large family demanded that she enter the mill to earn $1 a week as a bobbin girl. Her task, "just to change the bobbins on the spinning-frames every three quarters of an hour or so," left her time to play and talk with older girls. Nevertheless, she "never cared much for machinery," reporting later that the "buzzing and hissing and whizzing of pulleys and rollers and spindles and flyers around me often grew tiresome." Disappointed that she could not attend high school, Larcom gave serious thought to alternative careers. Encouraged by her sister and other workers to write for the "Operatives Magazine" and later the "Lowell Offering," she began to gain the personal direction that would lead to her writing career.[25]

At about the same time, Harriet Hanson Robinson also arrived at Lowell with a widowed mother who kept a boarding house; soon she, too, became a bobbin girl in the mill. In 1836 when operatives were planning to "turn out" to protest wage cuts, 11-year-old Harriet became an active participant. She later recorded:

> Then, when the girls in my room stood irresolute, uncertain what to do, I, who began to think they would not go out, after all their talk, became impatient, and started on ahead, saying with childish bravado, "I don't care what you do, I am going to turn out, whether any one else does or not," and I marched out, and was followed by the others.

Later in her life Harriet continued this pattern of activism as an advocate for women's rights and organizer of the General Federation of Women's Clubs.[26]

The Lowell mills provided an opportunity for New England girls to leave rural households and to participate as boys did in the dynamic movement from place to place that helped transform the regional economy. Many operatives alternated factory work with teaching summer terms in district schools. As commercial expansion increased the demand for a state system of education, Lowell managers came to believe that training in public schools produced attentive, industrious workers, and school became the avenue to mill employment. In 1835, the mill agent would not hire Lucy Larcom until he was assured that she had completed three months in the local Lancasterian school. In 1836, the Massachusetts legislature enacted the earliest compulsory school attendance law, mandating that children under 15 could be employed in manufacturing only if they had received three months of schooling during the previous year. Similar laws were passed in other New England states and Pennsylvania by the 1840s. Lowell agents continued to check for school certificates, but this was not the case in many factories. Critics charged that some parents evaded the laws by sending children to work in a different mill every nine months.[27]

As the Northeast shifted to a cash economy, apprenticeship was further undermined. Boys could learn the machinist trade by working for wages in a textile mill; by 1827 shops at the Lowell mills paid "apprentices" $25 the first year, $50 the second, and $75 the third. Other boys moved from one workshop to another, learning innovations in technology faster than their masters did.[28] Under fluctuating economic conditions, apprentices—paid in cash—could find themselves doing the work of journeymen. In May of 1822, 16-year-old David Clapp "went to Mr. John Cotton's in Boston to learn the printers trade." He did not board with his master but with "Mr. Bartholomew, blacksmith & engine builder in Water Street." Paid $2.50 per week to cover his board, David received an additional $10 a year for "the privilege of doing jobs." By July, Cotton fell into debt and his father took over the shop, retaining David, who struggled to print jobs alone, without supervision or further training. In December the boy lamented, "I still continue to work alone, with nobody but the mice, who scamper around the silent office as if they thought it had been deserted on purpose to oblige them." Six months later Cotton was in jail, and David, busily printing a Universalist hymnbook and the *Boston Medical Intelligencer,* had taught himself the trade.[29]

Fifteen-year-old Horace Greeley, who wanted to escape hard labor on the farm, arranged his own apprenticeship in 1826 with printers of "the Northern Spectator" in the country town of East Poultney, Vermont. According to verbal agreement, Horace would earn only his board for the first six months, but then be paid $40 a year plus clothing until he was 20. When the editor left and a mercantile firm took over the paper, the office was "laxly ruled," and "as to instruction, every one had perfect liberty to learn whatever he could." Greeley became one of the principal workers in the shop. "I had not been there a year," he later recorded, "before my hands were blistered and my back lamed by working off the very considerable edition of the paper on an old-fashioned, two-pull Ramage (wooden) press—a task beyond my boyish strength—and I can scarcely recall a day wherein we were not hurried by our work." Later in his life Greeley supported a 10-hour day for apprentices and wage-earning children.[30]

The growing labor movement of the 1830s, which focused on obtaining the 10-hour day, continued to protest the hiring of children. As masters and journeymen divided in their interests, apprentices could be caught between them. Masters employed young workers as strikebreakers, while journeymen opposed the use of cheap child labor. In some trades, workingmen sought to buttress traditional apprenticeship; when New York bakers went on strike in 1834, they demanded the enforcement of five-year indentures and limitation to one apprentice per shop. In the mid-1830s the labor movement was fluid and expansive, and workingmen supported strikes by women workers, some of which included children. In Lynn, Massachusetts, men aided female shoe binders; the General Trades Union of New York supported striking women and children who were silk spinners in Paterson, New Jersey. Nevertheless, the depression following the panic of 1837 destroyed labor activism. When labor organizing revived in the 1850s, workingmen advocated their own version of domestic ideology, seeking a family wage for men that would allow women to stay at home and children to attend public school.[31]

Structural change from 1820 to 1840 increased the demand for full-time public education and intensified class consciousness. Children of the entrepreneurial new middle class would labor less and have more time to spend in school. Yet many working parents kept their children out of public schools because they desperately needed their earnings to supplement family income. As crafts deteriorated, many urban children engaged in outwork—binding fancy shoes and making artificial flowers, fringe and tassels, parasols and umbrellas—for the growing market in luxury consumer items. According to Christine Stansell, mothers in New York City "assigned home work to their children just as they did domestic chores." Even young children could cut and glue boxes, dip matchsticks, or pull bastings and sew buttons. Children carried materials and goods to and from shops, cared for younger siblings while their mothers worked, and ran errands. As young as six or seven, they scavenged on city streets for chips of wood or coal, or food items—coffee, tea, sugar, or flour—spilled on the docks or from wagons. Older children searched for items to sell to junk dealers, who distributed them to artisans and manufacturers—loose cotton and rags to make paper or a cloth called "shoddy"; nails, cogs, and screws to sell to iron and brass founders; and old rope shredded and sold as oakum to caulk ships.[32]

The line between scavenging and pilfering could be thin, and increasing numbers of children, picked up for stealing or vagrancy on city streets, came before police courts. "Ask the magistrates of these courts, from whence come the children who are arraigned before them for pilfering," asked Joseph Tuckerman, a Unitarian who ministered to the poor in Boston in 1830:

> They will tell you that three fourths of them are from families, which have looked to these children *for a part of their means of support*. And if they have looked into these cases, they will tell you also, that some of these children have been kept from school that they might beg; and others, that by any service they might earn a dollar a week, to be appropriated for the payment of rent, or for the purchase of necessary food.

Children as young as seven, if judged to have the capacity to distinguish between good and evil, could be sent to prison. In the early 1820s the New York Society for the Reformation of Juvenile Delinquents discovered that about 75 boys between the ages of 12 and 16 were being sent to Bellevue prison each year, "most generally for petit larceny and vagrancy." In addition, "many females of tender age" (15 years and younger) came before the magistrates for prostitution. In 1827 the Boston Prison Discipline Society estimated that about one-seventh of prisoners in New England, many as young as age 12, were under the age of 21.[33]

In the mid-1820s, concerned citizens of New York, Boston, and Philadelphia formed voluntary associations to found Houses of Refuge or Reformation in which such children charged with crimes could serve their sentences apart from hardened criminals. Methods in the innovative institutions reflected contemporary views of prison reform, which had taken shape in the enlightened and humanitarian context of the late 1780s. Once again, seminal concepts were articulated by Benjamin Rush. As he had proposed educational plans and a theory of medical practice appropriate for a republican society, Rush had also criticized Philadelphia's sentencing of criminals to public labor, and advocated punishment similar to that of "the best governed families and schools." His plan to reform individuals who committed crimes was not unlike the pattern of his medical therapy, resembling the conversion experience. In a "house of repentence" separated from "kindred and society," the criminal placed in "solitary confinement" would be led to reflect on his behavior. As old habits were broken down through religious instruction and regimen—cleanliness, light diet, and supervised work—gradually the diseased moral sense could be cured and the individual prepared to return to society. In the 1790s, First Day Society members William White and Mathew Carey joined Rush in the Philadelphia Society for Alleviating the Miseries of Public Prisons, and attempts were made to implement reformed views in the Walnut Street jail.[34]

Nevertheless, as depression followed the War of 1812 and continued into the early 1820s, numbers of the poor soared and personal distribution of poor relief became more difficult in the growing city; fear of crime intensified and attitudes toward the adult poor hardened. Well-to-do citizens such as Roberts Vaux (who was preparing his report on indigence for the Pennsylvania Society for the Promotion of Public Economy) were more inclined to stress the moral failing of the poor and their responsibility for their condition.[35] As citizens concerned with minimizing costs despaired of reforming adults, they turned to the malleable child and focused on prevention. In 1817 Roberts Vaux proposed a system of tax-supported Lancasterian schools; the Male Adult School Association shifted to evangelical Sunday schools and a year later formed the Philadelphia Sunday and Adult School Union.

In 1826, after a visit to the newly opened New York House of Refuge, a Philadelphia Board of Managers composed of these same citizens—including school and prison reformer Roberts Vaux and five managers of the American Sunday School Union—proposed a similar model institution for their city. Echoing enlightened hopes of Benjamin Rush and members of the First Day Society, they sought to render the youthful offender into a "useful and honorable citizen." "If during any period of life or any stage of crime, these happy results are to be anticipated," the managers argued, "we surely ought to expect them during the season of youth; when the mind is yet comparatively tender, when its sensibilities are acute . . ." Although offenders would be committed by city magistrates, police, or courts, they would be considered "neglected and destitute children rather than degraded and hardened criminals," their offenses "in a great measure attributable to the bad example, the neglect, or the coercion of vicious parents, and not to any extraordinary depravity of disposition or turpitude of heart in the children themselves."[36]

Although managers considered the House of Refuge an extension of the public school and Sunday school, they adopted the program and building design of the penitentiary, the product of prison reform in the 1820s. The voluntary association would remove children from the influence of parents (who could visit only once a month) and seek reformation of character through opportunity for reflection and acquisition of orderly habits. Boys and girls would be housed in separate buildings in double rows of seven- by four-feet "cells." A clean and neat appearance, courteous manners, silence at meals, and marching from place to place in twos would be required. Children who excelled at the routine would be rewarded with privileges. Disorderly behavior would be punished by the deprivation of play, exercise, or meals; solitary confinement; corporeal punishment "if absolutely necessary"; and "Fetters and Hand Cuffs" in extreme cases. Before breakfast and after supper children would attend a Lancasterian school. Yet, eight hours each day would be spent in work to support the institution—girls engaged in mending, sewing, and other tasks of "housewifery," and boys in such endeavors as shoemaking or caning chairs. And, after a term of one to three years, children with reformed habits would be placed under indenture, girls as domestic servants and boys with sea captains or artisans, but, as apprenticeship declined, mostly farmers.[37]

Children committed to the Houses of Refuge in the 1820s were often American-born orphans or half-orphans who wandered from place to place until they were picked up on the streets. Boys could be runaway apprentices. Fifteen-year-old J.B., son of a widowed ship-rigger father who had remarried twice, ran away from his master to go to sea. After traveling through the mid-Atlantic states, he hung around the New York streets and was apprehended for stealing a pistol. Fourteen-year-old J.M., whose father had died and mother remarried, ran away from two different masters in Philadelphia and was imprisoned there for stealing shoes. In New York and hoping to go to sea, he picked a gentleman's pocket at the theater and was sent to Bridewell prison and then to the House of Refuge. Girls who became inmates scavenged on the streets or engaged in prostitution. Thirteen-year-old M.S., daughter of a widow who took in washing, was dismissed from service because she was "too small," and scavenged for chips for her mother until she was "taken up at the theater." A gang of 11- to 15-year-old girls, who had also been in and out of service, were apprehended spending the money they had gained by picking the pockets of the men they prostituted themselves with in doorways and cellars.

Although the well-to-do citizens who founded the Houses of Refuge sought to intervene for "neglectful" parents, by the 1830s parents increasingly used the municipal institutions to deal with offspring they could not handle. When 14-year-old M.A.P., who was "large for her age" with "the appearance of a woman," fell in with female boarders "who were not good characters," her widowed mother, a live-in domestic servant, "requested" that her daughter be sent to the almshouse and then to the House of Refuge. According to Christine Stansell, commitments to the New York House of Refuge initiated by parents or kin increased from 11.5 percent (nine of 78 children) in 1825 to 47 percent (78 of 166 children) by 1835.[38]

Yet placing one's own child in the new institutions could backfire. When Mary Ann Crouse was committed to the Philadelphia House of Refuge on her mother's request, the girl's father protested that she had been imprisoned without a trial and her constitutional rights violated. When *Ex Parte Crouse* reached the Pennsylvania Supreme Court in 1839, the justices, relying on the English concept of *parens patriae*—the right of the Crown to intervene in natural family relations to protect a child's welfare—disagreed. Arguing that the House of Refuge was not a prison but a school, and that public interest justified the removal of children from unsuitable homes, they stated:

> To this end, may not the natural parents, when unequal to the task of education, or unworthy of it, be superseded by the *parens patriae*, or common guardian of the community? It is to be remembered that the public has a paramount interest in the virtue and knowledge of its members, and that, of strict right, the business of education belongs to it. That parents are ordinarily entrusted with it, is because it can seldom be put into better hands; but where they are incompetent or corrupt, what is there to prevent the public from withdrawing their faculties, held, as they obviously are, at its sufferance? The right of parental control is natural, but not an unalienable one.

Convinced that Mary Ann "had been snatched from a course which must have ended in a confirmed depravity," the justices determined that she would stay in the House of Refuge and could then be placed under indenture. Viewing the reformatory as an extension of the public school, the court extended *parens patriae* to both institutions. For the important task of forming or reforming character, their own and the public interest could require that malleable children be removed from their families by the state.[39]

Financial panic in 1837 was followed by depression and unemployment that lasted through the 1840s; surviving firms were highly capitalized and opportunity lessened. Although popular culture extolled enterprising boys who propelled themselves into business or manufacturing careers, the fluid dynamism of post-Revolutionary decades began to harden. Mercantile agencies began to assess business risks, and the industrious activity and internalized restraints of character (supplemented by means) became a source of credit. Northeastern rural areas shifted to a cash economy, replacing older patterns of sociable local exchange. Independent households lost control of outwork, and endeavors such as New England button-making moved to village factories hiring labor. Farmers, who raised cash crops for commercial markets, depended on hired hands more than on family labor, releasing some rural children to attend public school. In urban centers apprenticeship persisted in only a few crafts—ship building or butcher shops. Trades employing new technology, such as steam-powered presses used in printing, no longer required the physical strength of journeymen, and relied more exclusively on child labor. Tailoring, shoemaking, and furniture-making continued to deteriorate through subcontracting, but by the 1850s outworkers struggling to survive by "sweating" their families were more likely to be immigrants: Irish and Germans whose numbers increased dramatically in the 1840s.[40]

Irish immigrants in the late eighteenth and early nineteenth centuries had been mostly Scots-Irish Ulstermen—Protestants with education, skills, and some capital. As the population soared in southern and western Ireland, and subdivision of land led to pauperization, by the 1830s more sons and daughters of Catholic farmers and cottiers sought "independence" in America, finding work as day laborers and domestic servants. Especially during the hard times after 1837, Protestant Irish joined native-born Americans in attacks on the Catholic newcomers. In 1840 when Catholic clergy protested the evangelical Protestant message taught in New York public schools, nativist issues infused local politics. By 1844, nativist American Republicans allied with Whigs swept elections in New York and Philadelphia; in the latter city, rioters in the working-class suburbs of Kensington and Southwark burned Catholic churches and destroyed blocks of homes. Yet not until after 1845 did the great potato famine begin to propel a million and a half Irish to the United States, nearly destitute rural smallholders, cottiers, and laborers, about half of whom arrived in family groups including children.[41]

Famine emigrants were mostly Catholic and one-fourth to one-third Gaelic-speaking; unaccustomed to an urban commercial and industrial society, they struggled to survive in American cities. Brought from Liverpool by new steam packet lines, 50,000 Irish (about 23 percent of the city's population) lived in Boston by 1855, where they clustered around the commercial center, the North End, and the Fort Hill area in converted old mansions and warehouses. As four-story tenements were hastily built and new structures clustered in former yards, families crowded into rooms, attics, and cellars where one hydrant and privy could serve as many as 100 people. In such conditions, smallpox revived, consumption increased, and cholera raged, and Boston's rates of infant and child mortality surged upward. By the 1850s children under the age of one accounted for about 24 percent of all deaths, compared to about 9 percent in the 1820s; deaths of children under the age of five rose to about 47 percent, from about 26 percent in the earlier period. Although the Irish were initially trapped in Boston with little means of employment, Oscar Handlin has argued that the availability of their cheap surplus labor stimulated economic expansion and allowed Boston to become an industrial city. Dennis Clark contends that Irish immigrants to Philadelphia (composing about 18 percent of the population in 1850) were able to find work in an industrial economic expansion already well under way; in a city of 130 square miles compared to Boston's four, they eventually found housing in less congested neighborhoods of red-brick row houses.[42]

About 85 percent of emigrating Irish who fled the famine were unskilled, and in America men found work mostly as laborers—driving carts or working in construction, and traveling outside the cities to build railroads and dig canals. Women and children contributed to family income as outworkers in "the needle trades"; when possible, as was the case in Philadelphia, they joined the labor force in textile mills. An Irish community had formed in Lowell, Massachusetts, in the 1820s, when construction workers and their families had built "paddy camps" of wood and sod shanties. By the 1830s an Irish middle class had emerged, St. Patrick's Church served 1,000 people, and about 300 Irish children attended Lowell's public schools. In 1835, priests who feared Protestant proselytization had reached a compromise with the local school committee that only Catholic instructors would be hired and approved books used. In the early 1840s, as the mills lost their technological edge and the New England labor movement collapsed, mill agents began to hire young Irish women educated in public schools—12 percent of the mill work force by 1845. The influx of famine immigrants from Boston and New York provided a steady flow of labor when the mills expanded at the end of the decade and agents ceased to recruit native-born women. As the Irish moved in, becoming about 50 percent of Lowell's population by 1860, the New England mill town became an immigrant industrial city.[43]

As the Lowell work force shifted, the proportion of children working in the mills increased; Hamilton Company jobs designated for children jumped from 3 percent in 1836 to 6 percent in 1860. For new positions created by innovations in technology, such as attending the mule spinner, mill agents hired boys. In 1850 boys under age 15 were 15.4 percent of Hamilton operatives, while girls of the same age were 2.7 percent. Nevertheless, the school certificate requirement for millwork continued to be enforced. In households of female mill workers in 1860, about 84 percent of children under age 10 attended school. Girls entered mill work around age 13, while boys went to work at 14 or 15, either in the mills or at other occupations. By the 1850s, however, priests at St. Patrick's abandoned their 1835 compromise with the local school committee and urged the formation of Irish Catholic identity and separate Catholic schools.[44]

In Boston, Philadelphia, and other American localities, as well as in Lowell, as priests sought to church famine immigrants in the context of the inflamed political nativism of the early 1850s, Irish-Americans created distinct ethnic communities and separate Catholic institutions. Much of this community-building was done by women as nuns provided social services and founded parochial schools for girls. Sisters of Notre Dame de Namur founded a girls' school in Boston's North End in 1849 and a female academy in Lowell three years later. By 1856, Sisters of the Holy Cross conducted an Industrial School for Girls in Philadelphia, where they taught housekeeping, sewing, and proper English. As parish schools for girls preceded those for boys, and more girls attended them while boys attended public schools, girls taught by nuns "the rosary, the pen, the broom, and the needle" internalized a deeply Catholic domesticity, which they, in turn, as mothers, transmitted to their children.

Nevertheless, Irish girls also learned American middle-class values through employment as domestic servants. In Kingston, New York, in 1855, of 254 wage-earning Irish women, 240 were servants; in New York's Sixth Ward at the same time, more than 50 percent of Irish female residents cooked and cleaned in middle-class homes. In localities where mill work was not available, Irish girls entered service at about age 13; in Buffalo, New York, in 1855, one-fourth of Irish girls aged 10 to 14 who had lived in the city one year or less worked as live-in domestics. Although Irish-American community leaders considered service in Protestant families a threat to Catholic religious life, these immigrant girls must have learned middle-class behavior and domestic ideology which, in turn, influenced those communities and eventually their own children.[45]

As immigration rose to unprecedented levels in the 1840s and 1850s, a million and a half Germans also entered the United States. Propelled in the 1830s by population growth and craft deterioration in home kingdoms, duchies, and provinces, and by potato blight and the failed political revolution of 1848, German craftsmen, small proprietors, and laborers arrived alone or with their families. Although they concentrated in northeastern cities from New York to Baltimore, many also followed transportation lines to the Midwest, forming a "German-belt" that would eventually extend from Ohio to Nebraska and from Missouri to Wisconsin. In 1855 about one German immigrant in 10 lived in New York City, composing 22 percent of the city's labor force; some worked in butcher shops or bakeries, but most were out-workers in tailoring, shoemaking, or furniture-making—rapidly deteriorating crafts.

German families struggled to survive by "sweating" their children; common knowledge in the 1850s was, "A tailor is worth nothing without a wife and very often a child." Horace Greeley's *New York Daily Tribune* reported of the new immigrants:

> We have been in some fifty cellars in different parts of the city, each inhabited by a Shoe-maker and his family. The floor is made of rough planks laid loosely down, and the ceiling is not quite so high as a tall man. The walls are dark and damp, and

a wide, desolate fireplace yawns in the center to the right of the entrance . . . In this apartment often live the man and his work bench, his wife, and five or six children of all ages; and perhaps a palsied grandfather and grandmother and often both . . . Here they work, here they cook, they eat, they sleep, they pray . . .

In Philadelphia one in five shoemakers who worked their families was German-born; cigar-making was also organized on the domestic system, and a work force of 4,000, many of them German women and girls, labored in small shops. In Cincinnati, which was 40 percent German in 1850, children in immigrant families worked binding shoes; one booster reported that "a woman with three boys in this business three dollars a week, and each of the boys, three more," and "an elderly man" with the aid of "three or four children" brought in "twenty dollars per week."[46]

Although native-born critics charged that German immigrants were prone to working their children, Germans complained to old country relatives, "The Americans want to see a lot of work done in a day, and anyone who thinks he can get by easy shouldn't come here." "It was always very hard to send the little one out in the streets to make a living," a German-born single mother said of her 12-year-old daughter, who entered domestic service in 1852, "but I couldn't help it; I must pay the rent some way." When a 14-year-old girl lost her place in service, her German father objected when she scavenged on New York streets; "I don't want you to be a rag-picker," he said, "You are not a child now—people will look at you—you will come to harm."[47]

His attitude reflected a strong patriarchal tradition; yet many German immigrants also espoused the liberal and democratic values of political movements fighting autocracy in Europe in 1848. Craftsmen and small property owners who organized German organizations such as the *Turnvereine* expressed ideals of progressive democracy radical in America, and societies of free-thinkers flourished. The infusion of German workers helped revitalize trade unionism in the 1850s, perhaps accounting for its patriarchal emphasis on "plebeian domesticity." Although Catholics as well as both conservative and evangelical Lutherans favored parochial education, many German immigrants were also staunch supporters of American secular public schools.[48]

German-Americans were advocates of bilingual education and pressed for instruction in the German language in public schools. Laws permitting the teaching of German in public schools were passed in Pennsylvania and Ohio even before 1840, and in some remote areas, such as rural Missouri, local school boards initiated German instruction in common schools without legal authorization. Nevertheless, some families designated at least one child to become proficient in English. When tenant farmer Wilhelm Stille left Lengerich in Westphalia in 1833, some of his siblings joined him. Following a chain migration pattern to Ohio, Stille settled on 80 acres in Monroe County, while his sister Wilhelmina and her husband Wilhelm

Krumme bought 80 more across the Ohio River near Wheeling (then Virginia). Although Stille wrote home, "I wouldn't tell any family to come here . . . when you first come to this country you don't know the language and face an uphill climb," he also thought that people who have "been here for a while," "get a feel for freedom." Ten years later he had lost through death his first-born child, his 19-year-old brother Rudolph, and his sister, Wilhelmina Stille Krumme, who left a three-year-old child, Johann.

During hard times in the early 1840s, Johann's father, Wilhelm Krumme, boarded his son with strangers and prevailed on his in-laws in Westphalia to send his wife's inheritance. When Johann was seven, his father could report: "[H]e now goes to the English school every day which costs 8 talers a year; he can already read pretty well, and I hope he'll take a shine to learning so he won't have to do any heavy work." Three years later he wrote of his 10-year-old son: "[H]e goes to school every day and he's a good pupil, that is in the English language since he can handle books fairly well but he doesn't know much German." Wilhelm Stille's sons would remain poor farmers, but Johann Krumme, assisted by money from his German relatives and his proficiency in English, assimilated into the American middle class. At 19 he clerked in a tobacco shop in Cincinnati; he eventually married a native-born girl and advanced at the tobacco company to foreman and then to agent-salesman.[49]

By the 1850s, the influx of Irish and German immigrants contributed to concern about children on the streets, who seemed to native-born Americans to symbolize the disturbing problems of their urban, industrializing society (see figure 14). In 1849, George W. Matsell, the first New York chief of police, called attention to the almost 3,000 "vagrant, idle and vicious children of both sexes, who infest our public thoroughfares, hotels, docks, etc":

> Children who are growing up in ignorance and profligacy, and ultimately to a life of misery, shame, and crime, and ultimately to a felon doom. The offspring of always careless, generally intemperate, and oftentimes immoral and dishonest parents, they never see the inside of a school-room . . . Left, in many instances, to roam day and night wherever their inclination leads them, a large proportion of these juvenile vagrants are in the daily practice of pilfering wherever opportunity offers, and begging where they cannot steal. In addition to which, the female portion of the youngest class, those who have seen some eight or twelve summers, are addicted to immoralities of the most loathsome description.

As apprenticeship all but disappeared and cheap adult labor became available, there probably were more children on urban streets. Priscilla Ferguson Clement has demonstrated that municipal outdoor relief (cash payments to destitute families) was either greatly reduced or eliminated altogether by 1850. To reduce costs, institutional solutions such as almshouses admitted males for short stays and curtailed aid to children. The number of private

Figure 14. *A Match Seller.* David Gilmour Blythe, c. 1859. By the 1850s working children on urban streets symbolized disturbing problems of American industrializing society. As middle-class domestic ideology and concepts of child nurture gained hegemony, private charities, courts, and state legislatures advocated intervention in families who deviated from prescribed ideals. *North Carolina Museum of Art, Raleigh. Purchased with funds from the State of North Carolina.*

charities increased by 1850, but Clement argues that they could not accommodate the burgeoning need and did not fill the gap created by reduced public support.[50]

As domestic ideology permeated the middle class, courts and state legislatures, as well as private charities, responded to the presence of children on the streets through intervention in families who deviated from prescribed ideals. In the expansive early republic, judges, through individual decisions, had forged a liberal and contractual family law that decreased patriarchy and extended the individual rights of wives and children. Viewing law as an instrument of social policy rather than as a set of eternal principles, judges began to use government in new ways and to view law as instrumental in the national task of forming character. Expanding the doctrine of *parens patriae* to challenge paternal custody rights, judges used the argument of "the child's best interests" to enlarge their own authority. As mothers assumed the central role in child-rearing, an increasing number of custody cases concerning daughters or children of "tender years" were won by mothers. By the 1850s, however, as views of child nurture such as those of Horace Bushnell became widespread, new standards of child welfare and parental fitness could reduce the rights of both parents. As judges enhanced their domestic authority, destitute or delinquent children who came before police courts began to be placed in more acceptable domestic settings or in new institutions founded by the state.[51]

The first state reform school for boys under age 16 was founded in Westborough, Massachusetts, in 1847. When the first compulsory school attendance law was passed by the Massachusetts legislature in 1852, habitual truants could be sentenced to the state reformatory. Westborough was built on the model of a House of Refuge, but by the 1850s critics charged that reformatories resembled prisons more than schools and did not mesh with dominant views of child nurture. School reformers—Horace Mann, Samuel Gridley Howe, and Henry Barnard—admired a new European model of the "family" reform school, in which children in cottages could form affectionate relationships with surrogate parents and other children. This domestic model was followed in the Massachusetts Industrial School for Girls, approved by the legislature in 1854. Its trustees insisted that the new institution would be "a *home*" for children:

> It is to educate, to teach them, industry, self-reliance, morality and religion, and prepare them to go forth qualified to become useful, and respectable members of society. All this is to be done, without stone walls, bars or bolts, but by the more sure and effective restraining power—*the cords of love.*

Ohio, Wisconsin, Illinois, and Indiana founded similar state reform schools in the 1850s modeled on the family setting.[52]

Reformers who worried about the instability of family life advocated not only the removal of "destitute and morally exposed" children from their parents but also the dissolution of natural ties and placement in an approved domestic situation through adoption, a solution legalized in Massachusetts in 1851. In the early 1850s, a private charity such as the Boston Unitarian Children's Mission still placed children under indenture. Thirteen-year-old William B., the native-born, "very active, intelligent" son of a "very poor" widow, and 13-year-old Patrick B., whose "very worthy" parents feared his association "with a large number of very bad boys," were placed, perhaps with subcontractors, "to learn the shoe business." But 10-year-old native-born Sarah R. ("found in the street begging for work, her parents were both intemperate, a very bright girl") and seven-year-old C., daughter of a prostitute, were taken from their families and put up for adoption. A mission newspaper advertisement announced the availability not only of boys age 7 to 14 to work for farmers and tradesmen but also "for adoption three nice healthy boys, one four and two seven years of age."[53]

At mid-century, the response to urban children by Charles Loring Brace both celebrated the enterprising popular culture of his New England boyhood and anticipated Darwinian theories of natural selection that would prevail in the post–Civil War era. Son of John Brace, the teacher who inspired Harriet Beecher Stowe at Sarah Pierce's Litchfield school, Charles grew up reading history and Sir Walter Scott's novels, fishing for trout, and climbing the Connecticut hills with his father. After the family moved to Hartford, he attended Horace Bushnell's North Congregational Church, where the minister's sermons on "Unconscious Influence," he later wrote, "affected my whole life." Although he studied at Yale to become a minister, a move to New York immersed Brace in the "*flood* of humanity" that swirled through urban streets. Preaching to paupers, prisoners, and prostitutes on Blackwell's Island, he concluded that New England religion affected "sadly so little any of our practical business relations," and gradually resolved to express Christian love in social ways, joining an urban mission in the notorious Five Points neighborhood. Like others before him, despairing of reaching hardened adults, Brace determined that "whatever was done there, must be done, in the source and origin of the evil—in prevention, not cure," and turned to the reformation of character in malleable children.[54]

When board members of the Children's Aid Society (founded in 1853) invited Brace to become their urban missionary, he immersed himself in New York's neighborhoods—the German "Rag-Picker's Den" at Pitt and Willett Streets, "Dutch Hill" or the Irish shantytown on 42nd Street, "the murderous blocks in Cherry and Water Streets," or "Corlear's Hook" near the waterfront. As he founded industrial schools for girls and the Newsboys Lodging-house, Brace came to admire the self-reliant and resourceful urban children, who, he thought, felt keenly "the profound forces of American life; the desire of equality, ambition to rise, the sense of self-respect and the passion for education." Convinced that each child "ought to labor with a motive," with "something of the boundless hope which stimulates so wonderfully the American youth," Brace was critical of the regimen of the House of Refuge or state reformatory.

The poor boy "has a child's imitation, a desire to please his superiors, and readiness to be influenced by his companions," he later wrote; in the asylum

he soon learns the external virtues which secure him a good bed and meal—decorum and apparent piety and discipline—while he practices the vices and unnameable habits which masses of boys of any class nearly always teach one another. His virtue seems to have an alms-house flavor . . . And, what is very natural, *the longer he is in the Asylum, the less likely he is to do well in outside life.*

Reiterating Horace Bushnell's emphasis on the unconscious influences of Christian nurture, Brace concluded that "the best of all Asylums for the outcast child, is the *farmer's home*." City children should be placed with "farmers, manufacturers, or families in the country," where farmers treated their "help" like members of the family and welcomed extra labor. Children sent to "the unlimited west" would not be placed under indenture, but rather would be free to leave or be dismissed by the families who received them.[55]

By 1857 the Children's Aid Society had placed about 600 city boys in western states, transporting them by train to farmers who selected them at railroad stations in Michigan, Iowa, or Illinois. In years to come, priests, who sought to church the famine Irish and develop ethnic communities, would charge the Protestant charity with kidnapping Catholic children, wrenching them from struggling families and weaning them from their faith. The New York Catholic Protectory, administered by the Christian brothers, would seek to protect children from the "foul injustice" of placement in western states, separated from "their early faith and filial attachment." Catholic charities, rather than removing children from "neglectful" or "immoral" parents, would provide temporary stable environments in order to buttress struggling families of their faith. Other critics of the Children's Aid Society would later charge that children sent west were exploited for their labor, that the charity failed to follow their fate, and that the plan benefited "neither farmers nor the children." Nevertheless, placing its faith in time-honored patterns of children's work and the entrepreneurial energy of children themselves, before the fabric of the nation was rent by Civil War, the Children's Aid Society sent to rural western homes as many as 5,074 urban children.[56]

7

Black and White Children in the South

With ten [white] chillun springin' up quick lak dat and all de cullud chillun comin' along fast as pig litters, I don't do nothin all my days but nuss, nuss, nuss.

                                        Ellen Betts, Louisiana

They was money tied up in little nigger young-uns.

                                        Cato Carter, Alabama

$\mathbf{S}$outhern Americans in post-Revolutionary decades recalled their experience in the war for independence and continued to rework their revolutionary heritage, yet they did not wholeheartedly espouse capitalistic values as many Northerners did. The majority of the white population continued to live in yeoman households, engaging in local barter and exchange and benefiting from the labor of their large numbers of children. Nevertheless, as the cultivation of cotton expanded rapidly, the plantation system based on slave labor spread to the Southwest. In the 1790s, as speculators bought backcountry land and slaveholding planters gained dominance in South Carolina and Georgia, squatters, roving hunters, and more substantial yeoman families were pushed west or north. In the cotton boom following the War of 1812, as Cherokee, Creek, and Choctaw lands were surrendered to the encroaching tide, farmers and planters poured westward, filling Alabama and Mississippi, mingling with the Creole inhabitants of Louisiana, and seeping into Spanish and then Mexican Texas.[1]

Expansion of the plantation economy increased the demand for slaves. In addition to the 250,000 Africans brought to the mainland in the colonial period, almost 100,000 more landed in Charleston, Savannah, New Orleans, or Natchez between 1783 and 1807, allowed by the provision in the federal Constitution stating that the trade could not be prohibited for 20 years. When Congress did end the African trade on January 1, 1808, trade on the domestic market increased, transferring the surplus of slaves on Chesapeake plantations west and south. This demand for slaves increased the value of African-American children, viewed as a commodity and recognized by both whites and blacks as a source of a master's wealth. Westward migration of a labor force and the domestic trade increasingly focused on children, whose capacity for labor and monetary value would augment as they grew. Slave mothers were encouraged or forced to reproduce, while the threat of sale made familial relationships increasingly perilous. Although capitalistic values encouraged the slave trade, these values did not penetrate Southern households; unlike their Northern counterparts, white rural couples had little incentive to limit births. White mothers bore large numbers of children, who were valued on farms for their labor and cherished on plantations as heirs. Ironically, enslaved children, who were denied aspiration in American life, became an investment and source of income that southern planters relied on to educate and provide an inheritance for the children of their own burgeoning families.[2]

As the Atlantic slave trade to the mainland colonies increased in the 1680s and exploded from 1700 to 1740, by the mid-eighteenth century relatively stable slave societies took root in both the Chesapeake area and Low Country Carolina. As Africans accommodated to slavery and the ratio of males to females became more balanced, the enslaved population began to increase naturally, allowing on large plantations some stability in familial relationships and community life.[3] Nevertheless, trade in slaves was an integral part of the colonial economy, engaged in by well-to-do and often distinguished planters and merchants. Although the Atlantic trade was tapering off by the 1770s, a local domestic trade—especially of the native-born—continued, as slaves were sold to settle an estate, pay debts, or raise needed cash. Enslaved families could be sundered by inheritance patterns or sale, but individuals rarely were moved more than 20 miles from their birthplaces. Husbands could visit wives and adolescent children their parents by following the "Negro road," an almost hidden network of paths around fields and through woods.[4]

Steven Deyle has pointed out that in the colonial period neither the Atlantic nor the domestic trade focused particularly on children. Planters who sought to build a labor force quickly preferred healthy males between the ages of 15 and 25. Females were purchased largely for field work, and an ideal slave cargo, according to one Charleston merchant, contained "Boys &

Girls of about 15 or 16 years of Age of which 2/3 Boys & 1/3 Girls." Slaves on the domestic market tended to be between the ages of 14 and 20, and small children were generally considered a liability. Especially in the urban market, North and South, a female domestic servant could be sold because she "breeds too fast," for owners did not want the inconvenience of "a breeding Wench in the Family." Although planters were more likely to take the long view, even they considered small children a nuisance and sold them because of their undesirability. In 1769 the *Virginia Gazette* advertised a parcel of 30 "Boys and Girls from 14 or 15 down to the ages of two or three years" simply to be disposed of through sale.[5]

By the time of the American Revolution, however, Chesapeake planters were beginning to recognize the value of their surplus slaves. As Tidewater tobacco lands deteriorated and planters shifted to wheat, slaves no longer needed were moved to piedmont regions by planters or their sons migrating west. When the African trade was disrupted by the Revolutionary war, Virginians argued that it not be continued, prohibiting the importation of Africans to their state in 1778, and leading the fight against the international slave trade at the Constitutional convention in Philadelphia nine years later. In the diatribe eliminated from his original draft of the Declaration of Independence, Thomas Jefferson linked the trade to evils perpetrated by George III; he and other Virginia planters deplored the effect of slavery on white owners and their children. Yet Deyle argues that Chesapeake planters also spoke from their own economic interest; by the 1780s it was clear that one solution to the decline of their region in agricultural productivity would be sale of their surplus labor through the domestic trade.[6]

From 1790 to 1810 residents of Virginia and Maryland pushed into Kentucky and Tennessee; although many migrants were poor whites or yeomen owning one or a few slaves, planters or their children also relocated in the West, sometimes bringing with them as many as 100 slaves. As some 75,000 Chesapeake slaves were transferred west in this 20-year period, children were increasingly affected by both migration and the domestic trade. Not only were older slaves needed at home, but a force composed of 10- to 14-year-olds could engage in productive labor for another 20 years. As the value of these young slaves increased, attitudes toward child-bearing female slaves also shifted. Chesapeake sale announcements began to promote "likely young breeding NEGRO WOMEN." By 1820 even Jefferson reached the conclusion that "a woman who brings a child every two years" is "more profitable than the best man of the farm."[7]

While Chesapeake slaves were transferred west, demand for slaves in the lower South was met largely through the importation of Africans. Booming land speculation in South Carolina and Georgia in the 1790s opened large tracts to backcountry planters. Cotton production spread rapidly, fueled by the development of the cotton gin in 1793 and the boom in English textile manufacturing of the 1780s and 1790s: in 1791 the United States exported only 889 bales of cotton; by 1795 the figure had jumped to almost 28,000 bales, and by 1801, nearly 92,000. The resulting demand for labor was met by the revival of the Atlantic slave trade; in the 1790s about 30,000 Africans were brought directly to the United States, followed by 63,000 more by 1807. Dominated by Low Country planters who feared insurrection, the South Carolina legislature prohibited the trade in 1787; yet slaves continued to pour into the region by way of Savannah until Georgia followed suit 10 years later. In 1803, backcountry pressure reopened the port of Charleston to the trade. Spanish and then British ships brought African slaves to Louisiana from 1790 to 1795 and 1800 to 1803, until the trade was closed by the Louisiana Ordinance in 1804.[8]

When Congress, responding to the provision in the federal Constitution, abolished the African slave trade on January 1, 1808, the demand of the cotton frontier for labor accelerated the domestic trade. In the 1810s, as millions of acres of Cherokee, Creek, and Choctaw lands were conquered or obtained through treaty, white farmers and planters poured through Georgia into Alabama, Mississippi, and Louisiana. Allan Kulikoff has estimated that about 137,000 slaves were sent from the Chesapeake states and North Carolina, 60 percent of whom would meet the labor needs of this frontier South. Far fewer Virginia and Maryland planters migrated these longer distances; most sold their surplus slaves to professional traders, who increasingly dominated the domestic trade. Traders also transported Kentucky slaves down the Ohio and Mississippi Rivers for sale in Natchez or New Orleans. As the New England textile industry created additional demand in the 1820s and 1830s, between 350,000 and 450,000 slaves were transferred from the upper to the lower South, to be used largely in cotton cultivation. Following the flush times of the early 1830s, more than a third of the population in cotton frontier counties was enslaved by 1840.[9]

As eastern lands deteriorated in post-Revolutionary decades, Chesapeake planters struggled to retain the privileged status of their families. Seeking to fulfill their obligations to their children, they hoped to provide each child with "independence," or an estate that could sustain a family in accustomed comfort. Birthrates among Virginia gentry families began to fall slightly after 1800, but mothers still "suffered" births of seven or eight children. Faced with high rates of infant and child mortality, parents doted on those who survived. Family life became more privatized and sentimental, and the stoic virtue of a George Washington yielded to affectionate indulgence. Nevertheless, children of Chesapeake planters still grew up surrounded by supportive kin, and were socialized by loving grandparents, aunts, uncles, and cousins. Waited upon by slaves, they enjoyed free run of rural plantations.[10]

As Thomas Jefferson commented in *Notes on Virginia*, Chesapeake children observed the "storms" and "boisterous passions" of parents struggling to control a dependent labor force, and could imitate "those same airs in the circle of smaller slaves." They also found it difficult to develop industrious habits, for, as Jefferson observed, "in a warm climate no man will labour for himself who can make another labour for him." Parents expected to provide a livelihood for their children, and did not encourage youthful self-reliance and enterprising activity. Yet they also expressed alarm and disappointment at the indolence and idleness they observed in their children.[11]

Jan Lewis has argued that these children were ill prepared to confront the economic decline of their region, which accelerated by the 1820s. While some parents warned children to circumscribe expectations, Jefferson's cherished granddaughter, Ellen Wayles Coolidge, perceived that her own "present uneasiness" grew from an indulged childhood. "Nature gave me a timid and affectionate temper, great flexibility and docility, quick feelings, & a lively imagination," she wrote. "As severity was evidently unnecessary in the education of one so ready to yield & to obey," her fond relatives "neglected to enforce even the wholesome discipline which was wanting to give strength to my character ... The voice of affectionate commendation was sounding always in my ears—I was constantly hearing my own good qualities." As a result she had become "a sluggard, fond of ease, averse to any employment which does not happen to fall in with the humor of the moment." Upon reading a children's book published in Boston, Coolidge determined to instill in her own children "the *habit* of energy." Other Virginians also embraced industrious habits or evangelical concepts of character in the 1820s, but most planters associated the entrepreneurial energy of the North with commercial values they had come to disdain. Caught in a dilemma and determined to maintain their genteel lifestyle, many found it easier to raise needed capital by recognizing the value of their surplus slaves.[12]

These native-born Chesapeake slaves were the most highly acculturated African-Americans; as the institution of slavery weakened and became more flexible in the upper South, many slaves imbibed white culture and values and still more converted to Christianity. Some masters had responded to the 1782 act of the Virginia Assembly, which legalized manumission, by voluntarily freeing anywhere from a few individuals to their entire labor force. This created a small contingent of free blacks who lived between plantations, drifted to Richmond or Baltimore, or traveled north to Philadelphia. By 1806, however, manumission had become more difficult and slaves freed thereafter were required to leave the commonwealth within a year. Yet masters continued to hire out their skilled surplus labor, collecting the wages of artisans, boatmen, or servants, and sometimes allowing slaves to hire out themselves. Baptist and Methodist preachers exhorting among the enslaved converted many individuals to Christianity. Although only a small percentage of black adults actually joined Baptist or Methodist Churches, a far greater number participated in and were affected by evangelical revivals.[13]

Most enslaved children in the Chesapeake area grew up in relatively stable communities in which a distinct African-American culture simultaneously borrowed from whites, drew on west African beliefs and values, and adapted to conditions of slavery. On Tidewater plantations, in areas where slaves accounted for 25 to 50 percent of the entire population, native-born generations, perhaps descended from one or two aged females, lived enmeshed in complex family ties. In a study of four Chesapeake plantations, Allan Kulikoff found that about half of the young children lived with both parents. Those whose fathers and older siblings lived on nearby plantations or farms remained with their mothers and other relatives. Children grew up surrounded by grandparents, brothers and sisters, uncles and aunts, and maternal and paternal cousins. Kinship ties were reinforced by shared daily life. Families and relatives lived in "quarters" of double rows of one- or two-room log or clapboard cabins, where children slept with siblings in lofts, on pallets or in trundle beds. Sharing a common yard, slaves cooked and ate communally, one cook providing hoecake (cornmeal slapped on a hoe and cooked in ashes) or cush (corn bread crumbled in pot liquor and steamed) to children fed from a single skillet. On some plantations the young children ate together, like livestock, from a wooden trough.[14]

As the nineteenth century progressed, enslaved Chesapeake children could be put to work as early as age five or six or be allowed to play until age 7 to 10. Working with kinship groups, children began with simple tasks in which they were instructed by parents or other relatives. Both boys and girls began field work by "running" crows, helping stack wheat, or picking worms off tobacco plants. If the master or overseer was present, a child could be forced to bite or eat missed worms. As they grew older, children picked tobacco and cradled wheat. Boys minded cows or chickens, cared for horses, toted drinking water to the fields, used mud or sticks to mend fences, or guided oxen when fields were plowed. Five-year-old girls began dusting, cleaning silver, or setting the table at the big house. At 8 or 10 they cared for their master's offspring—rocking babies, telling stories, and putting children to bed at night.[15]

Enslaved and white Chesapeake children grew up playing together. Infants could nurse at the same breast, and children could eat together and sleep in the same beds. White and black boys and girls played in the woods, turning such tasks as gathering bark to put under the hot iron into games. Boys wrestled and got into mischief together, while girls made doll clothes and played house. Some white children played school by teaching slave children their letters, occasionally whipping them when they forgot their lessons. Enslaved children could first learn their status from this kind of play, at age four or five when girls playing house relegated them to the quarters, at seven or eight when mistresses whipped them for learning to read, or by age 10 when play ceased and they became children's nurses or were sent to the fields. And whites playing with black children could be deliberately cruel, enticing dogs to bite their toes, or purposely frightening them with actions and tales.

Enslaved Chesapeake children playing by themselves in the quarters or woods sometimes imitated or improvised upon white behavior: they rode sticks pretending they were horses, used scraps of material to make clothes for stick dolls, or played a game they called "Hide the Switch." Frederick Douglass understood that slave propensity to use the whip was learned by black children observing white behavior. "Everybody, in the South," he commented, "wants the privilege of whipping somebody else." But enslaved children also roamed the woods together, digging for worms and hunting possum; in the yard they played ring games of their own devising, based on songs they improvised much as their parents and kinfolk did. Older children were particularly fond of dancing—singing and dancing all Saturday night to fiddles in the yard, or anticipating and preparing for weeks for a frolic at an old cabin in the woods (see figure 15).[16]

Interaction with white culture as children could create psychological conflict for Chesapeake slaves. When six-year-old Frederick Douglass left his grandmother's Tuckahoe cabin in 1824 and found himself on Colonel Edward Lloyd's plantation on Maryland's eastern shore, he entered a self-sufficient community embracing 13 farms and more than 500 slaves. Yet he gravitated toward what he later described as "the grandest building my eyes had then ever beheld . . . the 'Great House' occupied by Col. Lloyd and his family." Paternalistic Chesapeake planters reinforced the dependence of their slaves by parceling out rations, and Fred was hungry much of the time. Associating the great house with an abundance of food, he finagled bread and butter by singing beneath the window of the daughter of his master (the manager of Lloyd's farms), who may have been his father. He also made friends with Lloyd's son, Daniel, five years his senior, whose Massachusetts tutor struggled to cure the white boy of speaking like a slave. In the company of the New England tutor, forming words along with Daniel, Fred learned the power of literacy and cultured English speech. Imbued with the ambition of learning to read, he also began to wonder why God, as he was told, "made *white* people to be masters and mistresses, and *black* people to be slaves."[17]

When 10-year-old Fred was sent to Baltimore as a gift and caretaker for a two-year-old relative of his master, he enticed reading lessons from his kind mistress until stopped by her incensed husband. Nevertheless, in the more flexible environment of urban slavery, "when sent of errands, or when play time was allowed me," he continued his spelling lessons by bribing white boys with the bread he had learned to cherish. By age 11 he could read well enough to match letters on boards in the shipyard with those in his young master's Webster's speller, in stolen moments teaching himself to write. About a year later he bought a copy of *The Columbian Orator* with 50 cents he had earned, steeping himself in selections celebrating virtue—speeches by

Figure 15. *Unidentified Boys.* n.d. Enslaved Chesapeake children could be put to work as early as age five or six or be allowed to play until age seven to ten. Boys such as these cared for each other and played around the quarters or in the woods. *Valentine Museum, Richmond, Virginia.*

Cicero or Cato, English Whigs or George Washington—and dialogues on slavery. Although he later renounced religion, about this time he was converted by Methodists. Once he achieved self-education in the heady atmosphere of Baltimore, Douglass became a teacher of other slaves; even as his master attempted to force him back into plantation slavery, he was determined to achieve the self-emancipation that launched his anti-slavery career. Yet all his life, although he became the most distinguished African-American of his generation, Frederick Douglass negotiated limits imposed by race. Like others who became assimilated in the flexible periphery of Chesapeake slavery, even while he emulated the genteel values of the great house, he also regarded it with mixed anxiety and deep resentment.[18]

For other acculturated Chesapeake slaves less fortunate than Frederick Douglass, contacts with genteel white culture became even more poignant when masters offered them for sale on the domestic slave trade. George Carter grew up on a large Virginia plantation in a two-parent household; as a child he picked worms from tobacco leaves until he was selected by his master (of the distinguished Carter family) to be trained as a houseboy. Yet, at age 16 George was sold with other slaves to professional traders or "speculators," who took him to Savannah in chains. " 'Cose us ain't want tuh go," he later remarked, "but us hab tuh."[19] Ignoring fathers off the plantation and networks of kin, masters and traders defined a slave family as a mother and her children. Infants and toddlers, too young to work on their own, were often sold with their mothers; when Josephine Smith was "put on the block at Richmond" as a "just toddling child," she and her mother together "brought a thousand dollars." Her father, she recalled, "belonged to somebody else, and we was just sold away from him just like the cow is sold away from the bull."[20]

As the domestic slave trade increased, special attention was paid to females in their child-bearing years, which usually began in their mid- to late teens. Thomas Hall recalled: "A woman who could produce fast was in great demand and would bring a good price on the auction block in Richmond . . ." By the 1850s in Richmond or Lynchburg, a young child-bearing woman brought $800 to $1,000.[21] Yet masters treated "a good breedin' woman" with care; understanding her potential to increase familial wealth, they often kept her on the plantation or presented her to one of their own children as a gift or legacy. Although enslaved women (who could not legally marry) were encouraged to form long-lasting unions, West Turner reported that his master in Nansemond County designated a particular man for breeding and hired him out to other plantations for that specific purpose. Enslaved Chesapeake women bore prodigious numbers of children; many enslaved women produced 9 to 15.[22]

As the interstate slave trade developed, mothers and even young children could be separated. As early as 1789, upon the death of his master, four-year-old Charles Ball of Calvert County, Maryland, watched as his mother and siblings were sold separately to a Georgia trader. Sixty years later he vividly remembered how she walked beside the horse of his new master, beseeching him to buy her and the rest of her children.[23] In the 1840s, also on his master's death, two-month-old Charles Grandy was sold in Norfolk with his mother and sent to Mississippi, but his six siblings were sold elsewhere or left behind. Virginia Hayes Shepherd remembered a mother who, sold to Richmond traders, "just had fits right there" when she was "wrenched from her baby."[24] And Mandy Long Roberson was still a toddler when her mother and infant brother were sold to traders who took them to New Orleans. "I was little den," she recalled, "but I recollects how de traders useter come an' buy

Figure 16. *After the Sale: Slaves Going South from Richmond.* Eyre Crowe, 1853.
After the Atlantic slave trade was prohibited by Congress in 1808, the domestic slave
trade accelerated. As enslaved children increasingly became recognized as a valuable
commodity, families could be separated and children sold away from their parents
and siblings. *Chicago Historical Society.*

our folks an' take 'em away an' leave us chilluns a-crying' an' a-weepin', but it
neveh done no good, they took 'em on anyhow" (see figure 16).[25]

As Chesapeake slave children grew up with the threat of sale, they experienced or witnessed professional trading activity. Eight-year-old Amos Abner
Cotton "fell into the hands of Adam Dupree, a speculator," on the death of
his master. Even though his artisan father had made enough money by hiring
himself out to buy back his son, the trader refused, admonishing the
anguished father, "he must think himself white." Sold to Kentucky, Amos was
put to work cradling and binding wheat.[26] Surplus slaves on the plantation on
which Baily Cunningham grew up were either hired out to tobacco factories
or sold to traders. Israel Massie recalled, "Some nights house servants would
come down to de quarters wid long faces an' tell de fiel' hands Marsa an'
Missus been talkin' 'bout money. Dey know dat mean dey gonna sell some
slaves to de nex' nigger-trader dat come 'roun' . . . Marsa he ain't ask you
nothin' 'bout wantin' to be sol'; he gwine sell you, an' you got to go whar dey

take you." When Nancy Williams remembered the mother she watched separated from her husband and baby and sold to traders, she recalled her own fears as a child: "Ise so fraid dey gonna tek me!"[27]

Enslaved children were deeply impressed as they watched the gangs of slaves taken south. Bailey Cunningham remembered: "They were chained together, a chain fastened to the arm of each one and they went afoot to North Carolina, South Carolina, or Georgia, driven by their new master." Robert Williams recalled when he was "a little boy wukin' 'round de house," "I done seen groups of slaves, women, men and children walking down the road, some of the women wid babies in dey arms and some on ox-carts wid babies all on dey way to de cotton country . . . De white folks would come up from de cotton country and buy slaves and carry dem back in droves."[28] As a boy, W.L. Bost worked at his master's hotel in upcountry North Carolina where traders stayed on their way south. "I remember when I was a little boy, about ten years," he recalled, "the speculators come through Newton with droves of slaves. They always stay at our place. The poor critters nearly froze to death. They always come along on the last of December, so that the niggers would be ready for sale on the first day of January. Many the time I see four or five of them chained together. They never had enough clothes on to keep a cat warm . . . They never wore any shoes. Just run along on the ground, all spewed up with ice. The speculators always rode on horses and drove the poor niggers . . . [T]hem slaves look just like droves of turkeys running along in front of them horses."[29]

Ironically, as Chesapeake planters strove to maintain their genteel lifestyle and provide independence for their own large families, painful separations of enslaved families could directly benefit privileged white children. Fannie Berry recalled the division of slaves by lottery on her master's death. When the youngest child, "George Blood a lad of six or seven," drew her mother's husband, the man was sold to a trader to provide funds for a trust. Allen Wilson as a child was given to his master's son as a reward for graduating from the country school. The youth hired Allen out to a tobacco factory and benefited from collecting his salary. Fifteen-year-old Elizabeth Sparks was given to her master's daughter as a wedding present. Almost immediately she was "married" to a man on another plantation, but she still stayed with her mistress and slept in her room "on a carpet, an ol' rug, befo' the fiahplace." When Louise Jones as a child was given to a daughter on her master's death, she was set to work tending the prolific number of both white and black babies. "I uster set on a pallet an' 'tend to de babies," she recalled. As Louise matured, her mistress hired her out as a nurse to another family, gaining needed cash by collecting her wages.[30]

On rice and sea island cotton plantations in Low Country Carolina and Georgia, slaves also established complex families and stable communities, but

African-American culture contained more African elements than in the Chesapeake. By 1740 two-thirds of the settlers of South Carolina were African, and in some coastal parishes nearly 90 percent of the inhabitants were enslaved. As Africans imported through Savannah and Charleston from 1783 to 1807 blended with this population, African cultural patterns were constantly renewed. Merchants and planters who engaged in the Atlantic trade clearly distinguished west African ethnic groups. Although they preferred slaves from the Gambia and Senegal regions, as well as others from the Windward Coast familiar with rice cultivation, as many as 70 percent of slaves brought to South Carolina in the formative 1730s came from the Congo-Angola region. In the early nineteenth century Africans continued to be imported from Senegambia, the Windward Coast, and the Congo-Angola area. Perhaps Gola or Angola accounts for the nineteenth-century term "Gullah," designating the Low Country people and their unique language. Applying his concept of "creolization" to both language and culture, Charles Joyner argues that Africans initially used a pidgin language in order to communicate with English speakers and with each other. However, passed on to succeeding generations as a native tongue, Gullah became a creole language, in which, although the lexicon or vocabulary was English, the grammar or underlying meaning remained deeply African.[31]

Gullah language, as well as culture and world view, influenced white children who grew up in planter families greatly outnumbered by their slaves. Folks said of Benjamin Allston Sr., who grew up in lower All Saints Parish between the Waccamaw River and the sea, that "his language was like a negro's, not only in pronunciation, but even in tone." But planters and their slaves also shared the deeply rural rhythms of plantation life, in which cycles of birth, growth, sickness, and death encompassed alike livestock, slaves, and white families. With little incentive to limit births, white as well as black mothers bore large numbers of children. White plantation women of the lower South born between 1765 and 1815 were more likely than their northern counterparts to marry as young as their late teens, to bear as many as 10 or 12 children, and to die in their child-bearing years.[32]

Privileged Southern white women who wrote letters and kept diaries recorded that they faced their succession of 8, 10, or 12 pregnancies with dread.[33] Physicians educated at the University of Pennsylvania diffused Benjamin Rush's "American Revolution" in medicine throughout the South; after 1825 families consulted Dr. William Potts Dewees's *Treatise on the Physical and Medical Treatment of Children,* and doctors followed its active therapy long after heroic measures were repudiated in the North. Pregnant women took large doses of dangerous medicines, were treated with bleeding and calomel purges, and eased their pain with opium. After repeated pregnancies, miscarriages, ill health, and loss of children through high mortality, some women found themselves dependent on opium, morphine, or even snuff.[34]

Mary Thompson McDowell, a white woman born in 1823, married Thomas Chaplin of Tombee plantation on St. Helena Island when she was 17. After bearing seven children, three of whom died in childhood, she suffered from prolapsus of the womb, filled her mouth with snuff to forget her pain, and died at age 29, two years after the birth of her last child. Yet her husband believed, as other planters did, that his wife suffered in childbirth "for him," and even when she was clearly ill, the couple welcomed additional children. If Mary Chaplin had lived, she might have borne more, for neighboring wives had nine children in 16 years, "suffered" 12 births or even 14. The English actress, Fanny Kemble, visiting her husband's Georgia Sea Island plantations in 1839, found enslaved women who also suffered from "falling of the womb and weakness of the spine," having returned to field labor only three weeks after childbirth. Yet these women, mothers at 16 and grandmothers at 30, also bore 9 to 16 children, one-half to two-thirds of whom did not survive. And they, too, knew that their "suffering" benefited their master, calling out to Kemble, " 'Look, missus! little niggers for you and massa; plenty little niggers for you and little missus!' "[35]

Low Country plantations could be isolated and lonely places for white families; children suffered not only from childhood diseases—measles, mumps, whooping cough, scarlet fever, croup, and colds—but also from the fevers that prevailed in late summer and early fall—malaria and sometimes yellow fever. Families who could afford it fled to Charleston, Savannah, or smaller towns, or encampments of rustic log and clapboard houses in the pine barrens. Around 1805 Eliza Burgwin Clitherall reported an epidemic of "bilious" fever on Edisto Island, which took her sister-in-law and four of her nieces and nephews from 4 to 14 years of age. After her family moved to Thornbury, a rice plantation on the Cape Fear River, where "the Yellow flies & Moschetoes were very annoying," Clitherall herself lost four-year-old James to an epidemic of yellow fever in 1812, and seven-year-old Emily to "fall" fever two years later. In the 1840s, after the death of four-year-old Maria, Thomas Chaplin sought funds to move his growing family to St. Helena village for the summer; in 1851, when they stayed on the plantation, his youngest child, two-year-old Mary Frances, died. Parents and physicians treated childhood ailments with the ubiquitous calomel and castor oil, blisters and bleeding, although by the 1830s quinine was available for young victims of fever.[36]

Black as well as white children died from fever. In July 1846 Thomas Chaplin complained of a "good deal of sickness both with white and black" in addition to an epidemic of distemper that took six of his horses. Shortly after, "a little Negro," "Sylvia's child, Sarah," died. Enslaved as well as white children experienced the epidemics of childhood diseases that swept through plantations; living in drafty and sometimes damp cabins, they were prone to respiratory ailments—croup or pneumonia. Roaming the quarters and yard, where garbage accumulated, and eating contaminated food and water, they expired quickly from diarrhea or dysentery, and generally had worms. Treatment for their various ailments included heroic therapy as well as folk remedies: Sam Polite was given calomel and a powder for worms by the doctor, but "Juse-e-moke" (Jerusalem artichoke) by his mother, and Savilla Burrell recalled a bleeding by one of the many South Carolina planters who was also a physician.[37]

Planters, who knew the value of enslaved children, considered their high mortality a personal affront. Struggling to provide for and educate their own large numbers of children, they counted on the fecundity of their slaves to turn a profit. A self-made planter who made an advantageous match, James Henry Hammond of Silver Bluff on the Savannah River worried about placing his eight children (five of whom would live to adulthood) "above the fear of poverty." As he struggled to build his plantation in the 1830s, 72 percent of the enslaved children died before the age of five. By 1841, having lost 10 percent of his labor force within a year, Hammond exploded in his diary:

> For ten years I have been working hard, overwhelmed with anxiety and care, and all I have made has been regularly swept off by death. Other people consider the shower of increase one of the greatest sources of profit to them . . . But a cruel fate overwhelms me by making this a source of ruin and takes all my earnings to repair the havoc of life . . . Negroes, cattle, mules, hogs, every thing that has life around me seems to labor under some fated malediction.

Although he originally treated his slaves with heroic practices, Hammond began to experiment with herbal remedies, steam baths, and rest, and introduced sanitary measures such as garbage removal, annual whitewashing of housing, lime on compost, and supervision of the water supply. He also increased milk in children's diets, and cared for children in a special building. Gradually child mortality on Silver Bluff declined to 56 percent under the age of five in the 1840s and 26 percent in the same age group in the 1850s. Visiting physicians confirmed Hammond's suspicion that his slave community may have suffered from some "hereditary venereal" disease, which may have contributed to the very high rate of infant and child mortality on his plantation.[38]

Although Hammond's scientific management and vast wealth helped him weather the falling price of cotton after the Panic of 1837, other planters struggled in the 1840s to make ends meet. As public education failed to take root in the South, they faced considerable expense in sending their numerous children to board at various schools. Ernest Chaplin on St. Helena Island was not sent to school until age 11, and even then his schooling was intermittent; at age 12 he still could not write. As his three younger siblings also went off to school, their father was hard-pressed for cash and complained bitterly when he lost a valuable slave child. Desperate even during the more prosperous 1850s to support his four children boarding out, Thomas Chaplin fumed, "This is the fourth Negro child I have lost since last fall. There is something wrong, & I will find it out yet, the one that is to blame had better be in hell."[39]

By the 1820s and boom years of the early 1830s, South Carolina planters looked to fertile western lands to improve their fortunes, and the state began to export slaves. Familial and kin relationships among the Low Country Gullah could be increasingly disrupted through migration and sale. Slaves looked to the birth of children—both black and white—to protect them from painful separation. A mother who bore large numbers of surviving children increased her value and status on the plantation, and perhaps that of her husband. And the birth of white children provided heirs, who, should they stay on the plantation, could ensure family and community life among the enslaved some measure of security and continuity. Slaves on Butler Island had labored for years under a negligent overseer, and Fanny Kemble reported that they welcomed not only her and her husband, but also their three-year-old daughter, giving "fervent thanks to God" that they "had made young missus for them." One elderly woman exclaimed, "Oh, missis, I glad now; and when I am dead, I glad in my grave that you come to us and bring us little missis."[40]

The Gullah lived on some of the South's most wealthy plantations, where blacks could outnumber whites by a ratio of nine to one, and a single labor force could number 100 to 1,000 slaves. Slave quarters, called "the street," were settlements of single- or double-pen log or clapboard cabins with broad front porches, resembling an English or African village. On Butler Island Fanny Kemble described 12- by 15-feet one-room cabins, separated within by wooden partitions to create sleeping quarters. Slaves could raise vegetables in each cabin's small garden, and keep poultry—chickens and ducks—which wandered in and out through open doors. "Firewood and shavings lay littered about the floors," Kemble wrote disparagingly, "while half-naked children were cowering around two or three smouldering cinders." Yet, former slaves, who grew up on the street, remembered their cabins with affection. Zack Herndon recalled the rope beds, tables, and benches his father made to furnish their "one-room log house." George Briggs remembered the large fireplace made "to take care of the chilluns in the cold weather. It warm the whole house," he said, "'cause it was so big and there was plenty wood." And Isaiah Jefferies recalled banking "taters, rutabagas, beets, carrots, and pumpkins" in his family's garden, and the fire kept going "all day and all night," by which children sat "in the winter and popped corn, parched pinders [peanuts], and roasted corn ears."[41]

Although some planters were notorious for their brutality and for underfeeding their slaves, most Gullah enjoyed an adequate diet in which rice, grits, hominy, and corn bread were supplemented by molasses, dairy products, and meat, as well as garden fruits and vegetables, and seafood and game acquired from surrounding waters and woods. On large plantations one cook prepared the midday meal for adults, and a separate children's cook provided about half the same rations for the children. Usually there was no breakfast, and cold food was carried back to the cabins for supper. On Cedar Shades, where Robert Toatley grew up, the cook would blow a cowhorn and 50 or 60 children would "run out the plum bushes, from under the sheds and houses, and from everywhere" to eat with their hands or scoop up with clamshells scraps doused with buttermilk and "potlicker" from long wooden troughs. "Each one take his place and souse his hands in the mixture," he said, "and eat just like you see pigs shoving around slop troughs." Savilla Burrell recalled that "flies would be all over the food and some was swimming in the gravy and milk pots," but "Marster laughed about that and say it made us fat."[42]

On large self-sufficient plantations slave women working full-time as weavers and seamstresses, supervised by their mistresses, made clothing for all the slaves. Early in the new year children were allocated yardage of red flannel or homespun according to their size. The benevolence of a master or mistress could be demonstrated by rituals in which both white and enslaved children participated. Robert F. W. Allston's daughter recalled that little girls "dropped a courtesy" to the white children and their mistress, "Maum Mary," when they "stood before her to be measured" for their homespun clothes. Ben Horry of Brookgreen on the Waccamaw Neck remembered when his master and mistress bought enough "of this cloth they call blue drilling to make a suit for every boy big enough to wear a suit of clothes and a pair of shoes for every one. I thought *that* the happiest setup I had in boyhood. Blue drilling pants and coat and shoe."[43]

White children grew up enmeshed in Gullah culture, but uneasy Low Country parents attempted to draw a firm line between their own offspring and the slaves who surrounded them. When Mary Chaplin had difficulty nursing Eugene, her fifth child, her husband commented in his diary: "Child sucked well this morning. Hope to God it will not have to suck a bottle & what is *ten times worse, a Negro*." When Ernest and Daniel Chaplin played with slave children, their mother accosted their father, "Good man, the little Negroes are ruining the children, I couldn't tell you half the badness they learn them. That little demon Jack must be sent out of the house, he *shan't* stay another day." Eight-year-old Rebecca Jane Grant was whipped by her mistress with a "raw cowhide strap" when she forgot to address a white child as "Master." "Marster Henry was just a little boy about three or four years old," she later exclaimed. "Come about halfway up to me. Wanted me to say, 'Marster' to him—a baby!" But Fanny Kemble feared such "little gestures of command" on the part of her own three-year-old. "I do not think that a residence on a slave plantation is likely to be peculiarly advantageous to a child like my oldest," she wrote. "[T]hink of learning to rule despotically your fellow creatures before the first lesson of self-government has been well spelled over! It makes me tremble . . ."[44]

On sea island cotton and rice plantations slaves worked according to the task system, through which the owner or overseer assigned each slave a task in the morning. When the tasks were finished, the slave could do whatever he or she wished for the rest of the day. Children played or cared for babies and younger children until they were 12 or 13, when they started field work as three-quarter-task hands, which could mean helping to plant or harvest rice or hoeing 12 rows or picking 30 pounds of cotton. Peter Clifton said that Low Country planters were "careful of the rule that say: You mustn't work a child, under twelve years old, in the field." Some children were designated to be house servants for wealthy white families. As a houseboy, Alexander Scaife "helped carry out things, take up ashes, fetch wood, and build fires early every day." He learned to "set the freshly polished shoes at the door of the bedroom. Get a nickel for that and dance for joy over it." Zack Herndon was taught to "mind the flies from the table," "tote dishes to and fro from the kitchen," and "help wash the dishes." Rebecca Jane Grant washed and ironed the long white embroidered dresses that white babies wore. Adeline Johnson dressed her young white mistresses and combed their hair, put flowers on the breakfast table, placed the Bible near her master's chair, and waited on table. "That was a happy time," she remembered, "with happy days."[45]

Yet field hands and house servants alike grew up on the street enmeshed in a rich creolized culture that retained deeply felt elements of a west African world view. Around the fire in the cabin, kept going with plenty of wood, African-born slaves related to children animal trickster tales they shaped to the experience of slavery. Buh Rabbit or Buh Cootah (Cooter, a small turtle) might outwit the large and powerful Buh Bear, but in confrontation with a small adversary like Buh Pa'tridge, the trickster himself could be tricked. Such tales were deeply instructional, teaching children not only cunning and deceptive behavior toward the master, but also to shrewdly assess actions of other slaves. They also underscored communal obligations. In the "Tar Baby" tale, during a drought Buh Rabbit fails to share water from a secret well, and his confrontation with the tar baby is arranged by the other animals to punish him not only for his vanity and boastfulness, but also for his selfishness.[46]

In another cycle of tales Buh Rabbit is replaced by the slave John, who matches wits with Ole Maussa. John, engaged in conflict and an uneasy partnership with his master, faces the danger of becoming too much like him. In one tale, John lures an old woman to replace him in a sack and be drowned; he, too, has become selfish and cruel and has violated another human being. Tales about John could end with his delivery and thanks to the Lord; in one instance, when he frees himself from a rock tied around his neck and escapes being drowned in the mill pond, he says, "Maussa, I trust the Lord. Lord take care o' John." The storyteller concludes, "And John's faith turned them all to Christian. They all got to believin' Christian like John."[47]

As early as the 1740s, ministers of the Great Awakening converted by George Whitefield had preached among Low Country slaves; by the 1770s two black Baptist churches with slave preachers were founded in Savannah and at Silver Bluff, up and across the river. By 1817 blacks in Charleston established ties with Philadelphia's African Methodist Episcopal Church, and Methodists exhorted on plantations in the 1820s and 1830s. Yet Margaret Creel argues that the Gullah did not fully embrace Christianity until the 1840s when planters, responding to abolitionist criticism in the North, allowed and sometimes encouraged Baptist "black societies." Directed by black elders and based on precedents of African secret societies, these informal organizations both regulated conduct and allowed the Gullah to practice their own version of Christianity.[48]

Planters influenced by evangelical concepts of character sought to instill internalized restraint in the enslaved. Tracts distributed in the South by the Philadelphia Sunday and Adult School Union extolled slaves who learned through conversion their Christian duty to submit to authority. Enslaved children in Beaufort attended "Sabbath school" on a white master's porch, where, according to Rebecca Jane Grant, they learned the "Sabbath catechism" and were "taught they must be faithful to the missus and marster's work like you would to your heavenly Father's work." Yet in "black societies" on plantations the Gullah were able to create their own religious vision, fusing Christianity with a multiplicity of African beliefs, rites, and practices.[49]

Religious practices on plantations could parallel west African initiation rites and ceremonies. Some children became "seekers," wearing a "little white cloth or string" around their heads and shunning all "social or worldly pleasures" in solitary pursuit of visions and dreams. According to one account from Hilton Head Island, "[i]n the winter most of the children were 'seeking and praying.' The older people said, 'They do hang their heads and pray'; and they were not allowed to do much of anything else for fear they would be turned back . . ." Reintegration into society would occur in the form of Christian conversion, yet Creel argues that seeking was closely linked to initiation into west African male and female cultural societies, in which boys and girls would enter the bush to converse with ancestors or spirits, experiencing a symbolic death as an individual before rebirth into the community. The Baptist practice of emersion, through which 100 Gullah of all ages could be baptized simultaneously in a river or stream, resonated with west African concepts of "water burial," through which a renewed individual emerged as a full member of the community. Those baptized were eligible to participate in the "shout," in which slaves shuffled along in a circle, first singing a spiritual slowly and then the refrain faster and faster, until the excitement climaxed with "furious" stamping and clapping. Children learned and reveled in the ring shout at an early age but could not participate at the Praise House until they were baptized and became full members. The ring shout involved an altered state of consciousness not unlike a possession trance, which was also characteristic of west African initiation practices.[50]

Coexisting with this distinctive Christianity was belief in haunts (spirits of the dead who returned to trouble the living) and hags or witches, who flew through the air and "rode" or victimized the young and the very old. Slaves disputed which were the most frightening, but children took haunts in stride. "Dat was a common thing," Amos Long commented, "to hear somebody walkin' up de front steps, in de hall [of the Big House], and dey wouldn't be nobody dere." Lettice J'yner insisted, "Ha'nts? Cou'se dey's ha'nts! I's seed plenty of 'em, but I ain't never been scared o'none. Day ain't no harm in a ha'nt; dey's jus' dead folks come back to deir old range." Witches, more malign spirits of the dead or malevolent individuals able to leave their bodies, were more ominous. Liza Williams attributed their origin to the fallen angel Lucifer, and explained, "Dey is dead spirits what cum an' ride yuh when yuh is asleep. Dey take different shapes, sometime dey is men sometime women an' sometime animals. When yuh wake up dey is chokin' an' smotherin' yuh. When dey sees yuh is awake, dey jump off an' go way."[51]

Contrary to the doctrines of Christianity, even an alternative religious system, were African beliefs in sorcery and conjuring, called voodoo or hoodoo in the New World. Conjurers could offer protection, perform cures, or engage in malevolent activity. Their ability was said to result from peculiar circumstances of birth; a child born with a caul over the face was believed to have second sight, which allowed him or her to see spirits. Some midwives used a counter-charm to remove the gift in order that children would not "grow up scared," "seeing things" all the time. But children with the caul were also designated for instruction in conjuring lore. Benjamin Johnson "could do and see things too," even when he "was very small." "God Almighty fixed me so I could," he said. "I didn't study no books to learn, that is a gift just handed down from my forefathers. You know, even before we was brought here from Africa by the white folks, and heathens as they say we was, there was that gift shown in many ways." Lettice J'yner reported, "My mammy always told me I'd see things 'cause I was bo'n wid a veil over my face." Because Liza Williams was "born wid a caul" she could see spirits "all duh time. Lots ob time I is walkin' long duh road," she said, "an' dere is a spirit right nex' tuh me, talkin, jes like a person."[52]

Somewhat removed from this plantation culture were the more highly acculturated mulatto children, fathered by their masters, a master's son, or perhaps an overseer. Many white men denied paternity of children born to enslaved mothers, but their obvious presence caused a painful dilemma for white, as well as black, families. Savilla Burrell reported, "Old Marster was the daddy of some mulatto chillun. The relations with the mothers of those chillun is what give so much grief to Missus. The neighbors would talk about it, and he would sell all them chillun away from they mothers to a trader." Other masters gave mulatto children who remained on their plantations preferential treatment. Sylvia Cannon remembered, "They learn the yellow chillun [to read], but if they catch we black chillun with a book, they nearly 'bout kill us. They was sure better to them yellow chillun than the black chillun that be on the plantation."[53]

Planters who sought to provide for their mulatto offspring often bequeathed the responsibility to their white children. In 1839 James Henry Hammond purchased 18-year-old Sally, who had an infant daughter Louisa, to be his mistress. At the age of 12, Louisa became Hammond's concubine, a situation that so distressed his wife, Catherine, that she temporarily left him. Hammond believed Louisa's children should remain in the care of their white half-siblings, as slaves. In 1856 he advised his son Harry, "Slavery *in the family* will be their happiest earthly condition."[54] In 1800, manumission in South Carolina required scrutiny of a slave's character by five witnesses; manumission became almost impossible after 1820, when a special law was required in each case. Nevertheless, an occasional master who took a slave concubine manumitted his illicit family, allowing them to join the 2 or 3 percent of the state's black population that was free, and mingle with Charleston's elite mulatto community.[55]

Two years before his death in 1815, Arnoldus Vanderhorst II of Kiawah Island manumitted Hagar Richardson and her three children, two of whom, eight-year-old Eliza and six-year-old Peter, he had fathered. On Hagar's death in 1816, income from lots and buildings in Charleston willed for her support was employed by his white children to board and educate Eliza and Peter, who shared the surname Vanderhorst. Eliza was purchased calico frocks, "a neck Handkerchief," "a merino shawl," shoes and stockings, bonnets, "a Leghorn hat," gloves, a small umbrella, ribbons, and "Jewels." Peter wore waistcoats, pantaloons, a "Bombarette coate," shoes, suspenders, and vests, and also carried an umbrella. Both had their washing done, their teeth drawn, and their hair cut. Their illnesses were treated by professional physicians, and from various teachers they learned to read, write, cypher, and speak French. Funds were allocated for their pocket money as well as for the tax on "free colored persons," which amounted to about $1.50 a year in the 1820s. In 1826, 21-year-old Eliza married G.A. Miller, "a free man of color," and 19-year-old Peter, like many other free blacks in Charleston, became a "mechanic." Two years later they received the balance on their estate, releasing their white half-siblings from their "obligation" to their father's will.[56]

After Cherokee, Creek, and Choctaw lands were surrendered through conquest or treaty following the War of 1812, whites from the Chesapeake states, the Carolinas and Georgia, Kentucky and Tennessee, rushed south and west into Alabama, Mississippi, and Louisiana in search of profit from the cotton boom. Joining the white Creole inhabitants of the Louisiana bayous, they built double log houses and rapidly began to assemble or augment a labor force. In 1810, half the population along the Mississippi River around Natchez already was enslaved, as those brought by slaveholders mingled with others recently imported from Africa. Migrating planters preferred a labor force that peaked in numbers from age 10 to 14. As these grew and were joined by the age group that accounted for nearly half of the domestic slave trade, age 14 to 26, they began to form families; by 1820 there were already 1.5 children under the age of 14 for each slave woman in Mississippi.[57]

Although population growth slowed somewhat during the depression of the 1820s, Alabama, Mississippi, and Louisiana were still consumed by cotton fever, while sugar production increased in the Lower Mississippi Valley. High prices of both commodities in the 1830s brought dynamic economic expansion, as the domestic slave trade accelerated and planters engaged in capitalistic, market-oriented behavior. Dr. James Foster married Sinah Ann Caroline Guillard of Adams County, Mississippi, in 1834 at the peak of the cotton boom. Immediately, he began to augment the labor force she inherited, purchasing 32 slaves for $20,000 in the next 13 years, almost half of whom were between 10 and 20 years of age. Three couples were already married, two women had two children each under the age of six, and nearly half the females were between age 14 and age 26—prime child-bearing years.[58]

Ann Patton Malone has argued that entrepreneurial activity by planters in the 1830s brought "a state of flux," "serious instability and disorganization," to the lives of slaves. One-third of slaves brought to some Louisiana cotton parishes were "solitaires," young people separated from family members or kin. While women and girls were purchased to pick cotton, as many as two-thirds of the solitaires engaged in heavy labor on a sugar plantation were male. On either type of new plantation a rapidly assembled labor force was surprisingly young; almost half of the individuals could be under age 17. As existing couples and families struggled to incorporate new purchases, discipline problems were rife, and much grief and homesickness prevailed. Not until the 1840s, when depression followed the Panic of 1837, did speculative activity taper off, allowing families to form, kinship networks to mature, and communities to develop. When prosperity returned in the 1850s, the price of slaves increased and speculative activity resumed; yet slave communities had reached the maturity and stability characteristic of seaboard areas, where multiple generations mingled and about half the young children lived in two-parent families.[59]

Joan Cashin points out that this dynamic migration to the Southwest in the flush 1830s also caused considerable disruption to planter families. As young men from Chesapeake states and the Carolinas escaped seaboard economic decline to seek independence in the West, they embraced individualistic, competitive, risk-taking behavior. Women were separated from the kin networks that had provided them a supportive social life, while children were removed from the grandparents, uncles, aunts, and cousins who had contributed significantly to their socialization. The nuclear family became the norm in the Southwest; on large landholdings and separated from kin, its members became isolated and dependent on each other. Without the moderating influence of older relatives, men were freer to behave aggressively, and children grew up lacking social graces, deference to authority, and emotional stability. Planters who sought profit in the competitive market could be tempted to drive their slaves more harshly, abandoning the paternalistic rituals and obligations established in the East.[60]

White women in the Lower Mississippi Valley, surrounded by slaves and enmeshed in rural rhythms of plantation life, did record feelings of loneliness and isolation. In 1843, while her husband took the steamboat to Natchez or New Orleans, Charlotte Beatty stayed with six-year-old Taylor and four-year-old Sara on their cotton plantation near Thibodaux, Louisiana, reading, sewing, and walking in the evening. She took her child-rearing seriously, confiding to her diary, "I am greatly blest in my children, Our Father in Heaven, help me to be faithful to this charge." Yet, "at home and lonely," she also felt "anxious and restless" and "melancholy." Perhaps dreading additional births, on the anniversary of the death of her first-born daughter, she lamented, "Oh the memory of this night 4 years ago," and copied the verse:

> Tho earthly ties are round me bound
> And earthly feelings fondly nursed
> Yet still the spell is not unwound
> That linked me to my first—my *First*!

In 1846 Eliza L. Magruder, an unmarried young woman visiting her uncle on Locust Plantation, near Natchez, kept herself busy—reading, knitting, sewing, vaccinating slave children, and visiting the quarters. Yet, she, too, while recording births and deaths of slave children and deaths of white mothers with four and five offspring, confessed her sense of uneasy isolation: "every Soul in the house black and no one in bed but me."[61]

Children in these privileged families grew up with the run of the plantation; both boys and girls reveled in country life and chafed at their parents' efforts to educate them. On his father's plantation near New Orleans in 1845, 12-year-old Nicholas (Azby) Destrehan, descendant of a distinguished French family, hung around the Sugar House, where he was fascinated by the machinery. He also cultivated his garden and amused himself with his horse, dog and gun, ducks and geese, fishing tackle and little boat. When his father attempted to instruct him "in reading and in figuring," he admitted five years later, "I felt miserable at being called from my little amusements, I would sometimes get right mad and often damned my father . . . but this fit of madness only lasted during the time I was occupied at study; for as soon as I left the room I was as happy as ever." On Good Hope plantation near Natchez in 1850, 12-year-old Mary Susan Ker sewed and made preserves, cake, and candy, but also rode horseback, enjoyed "lazy days," and fished for perch from a skiff with her little brother Willie. Intermittently, she did recite her lessons with her tutor, but commented, "I did not know my Latin lesson today very well and I had a very bad time in school altogether. I was very angry because I had to write a journal. I did not write my arithmetic either . . ."[62]

Parents employed tutors, often from the North, who lived on plantations and sometimes put together a school with neighboring children. A French governess from Pennsylvania, on a plantation near Belfield, Mississippi, in the 1830s, taught Northern domestic ideology to her female pupils but struggled with the mosquitoes, and her own boredom, exhaustion, and melancholy. "[E]verybody has an easy time here," she complained, "children, negroes, cats, dogs, all do just as they please." Astonished at the rapid and extravagant growth of Natchez, where "every man is building a villa, or a castle, or a palace," she lamented her own low salary and "cheerless" state. Parents without the services of a tutor boarded their children in Natchez at "great expense," fearing they would grow up without "improvement." In 1840 Judge Edward Turner exhorted his daughter Fanny: "You have been long absent from your studies, my dear child, & you must try to make up lost time; for you are growing very fast, & will soon be a woman. But if you get your growth before you get your education, you will be unhappy, & your friends will be mortified. The *mind* is what distinguishes *us* from the *brute* creation, and if that is not cultivated, improved, & adorned, we shall be like the savages."[63]

Enslaved children on southwestern plantations knew adults from "Ole Virginny" or Africa, or had themselves migrated with a labor force. They were keenly aware of the domestic slave trade and feared the "speculators," who stopped by plantations to swap, buy, or sell. Mary Reynolds recalled that her master in Louisiana "bought the bes' of niggers near every time the spec'lators come that way. He'd make a swap of the old ones and give money for young ones what could work." Having migrated from Georgia with his master at age "nine or ten," Jack Maddox observed, "Seems like there was a lot of speculators got to coming through Texas. I seen speculators coming by with womens and chilluns, as well as men." Calvin Moye, who also migrated to Texas at age "eight or ten," recalled his own fear: "Dey was lots of dem speculators coming by de road in front of de plantation, and ever' time I see dem coming, cold chills run over me till I see dem go on by our lane." Katie Rose of Arkansas remembered, "De traders all had big bunches of slaves and dey have 'em all strung out in a line going down de road." "I seen chillun sold off and de mammy not sold, and sometimes de mammy sold and a little baby kep on de place and give to another woman to raise. Dem white folk didn't care nothing 'bout how de slaves grieved when dey tore up a family."[64]

Hoping to increase their labor force, southwestern planters expected enslaved girls in their mid-teens to begin bearing children. When Rose Williams of Bell County, Texas, was sold on the auction block, her new master told her she would live with Rufus. "I's 'bout sixteen year old and has no larnin', and I's jus' a igno'mus chile," she protested. "I's thought dat him mean for me to tend de cabin for Rufus and some other niggers." When Rufus crawled into her bunk, she chased him with a poker and ran to her mistress, but "de missey say dat am de massa's wishes. She say, 'You am de portly gal and Rufus am de portly man. De massa want you-uns for to bring forth portly chillun.'" When Williams still went to bed with a poker, her master threatened a "whippin' at de stake." "What am I to do?" she said, "I 'cides to do as de massa wish and so I yields." Rachel Cruze remembered that the planter across the river would tell a "well-built, tall, husky man," "'You can come over and see my gals anytime you want. You're of good stock.'" Mollie Dawson of Texas said, "[E]very slave darkie woman had ter do dat whether she wanted to or not." "[I]f de woman wouldn't have de man dat picks her, dey would take her ter a big stout high husky nigger somewhere and leave her a few days, jest lak dey do stock now'days, and she bettah begin raisin' chilluns, too." For as Cato Carter of Alabama put it, and all the slaves knew, "They was money tied up in little nigger young-uns."[65]

Unlike the Low Country task system, on southwestern cotton plantations work was done by slaves divided into gangs; by the 1840s and 1850s, when families formed and communities developed, kinship groups worked the fields together and went home to rows of log or pine cabins in the quarters. Children as young as five went to the fields with their parents during the busy cotton harvest. Calvin Moye remembered, "When de cotton pickin' time come on, everybody dat was big enough to pick cotton was put in de field . . . De littlest chilluns would pick wid deir mamas or papas." Thomas Cole recalled, "De little chilluns would pick and put de cotton in a basket wid some older person, so de older person could move de basket 'long." Five- to ten-year-olds were put to work with the hoe, sometimes threatened by other slaves to keep up the work pace. Mary Reynolds remembered, "I helt a hoe handle mighty onsteady when they put a old woman to larn me and some other chillun to scrape the fields . . . She says, 'for the love of Gawd, you better larn it right, or Solomon (the slave who directed work as a driver) will beat the breath out you body.'" Aunt Sally Brown recalled, "They made me hoe when I wuz a child and I'd keep rat up with the others, 'cause they'd tell me if I got behind that a run-a-way nigger would git me and split open my head and git the milk out'n it. Of course I didn't know then that wuzn't true—I believed evything they tol' me and that made me work the harder."[66]

Enslaved children on cotton plantations toted wood and water, swept yards, picked up brush, fed livestock, and brought "taters" from the fields. Girls as young as seven or eight tended both white and black babies. Ellen Betts of Louisiana exclaimed, "With ten [white] chillun springin' up quick lak dat and all de cullud chillun comin' along fast as pig litters, I don't do nothin' all my days but nuss, nuss, nuss." Some boys were trained in crafts; Calvin

Moye was sent by his master to an elderly slave to learn woodworking and blacksmithing. "So de next morning," he recalled, "I was down to de shop befo' Uncle Zeke was, 'cause I sho' was glad to gits out of dat field work, and I knows I would like dat blacksmith work."[67]

Boys in the quarters "th'owed horseshoes, jumped poles, walked on stilts, an' played marbles." In the woods they made "bows and arrows" and dared each other to jump from one tree limb to another. Girls made rag and "shuck" dolls and played "church" by "singin' and prayin' and dyin'." Lessons learned from play with white children could be cruel. Katie Sutton was told that the stork brought white babies, but slave children hatched from buzzards' eggs. Thomas Cole went on fishing trips with his young white masters, but he had to obey their imperious commands. On one occasion, when he was "jest a little kid," they told him to jump off the barn and were terrified when he was badly hurt. Mollie Dawson remembered that her master's children "sho' was pretty little gals and dey was smart, too. Dey played wid de little slave chilluns all de time, and course day was de boss, same as deir mother and father." Slave children played in the quarters games they learned from white children—"base" and "puss wants a corner." But they also played games of their own devising—"shoo shoo," "a game about a old hen fluttering 'round to keep the little chickens from the hawks," and "warm jacket," which "was worked by each one gitting a brush from a tree or bush, and flailing de other'un till it got too hot fer him."[68]

Enslaved children could feel the whip administered by the overseer or driver if they failed to keep up with the gang in the cotton fields. They were also profoundly aware of punishments they either heard about or witnessed. Thomas Cole carefully described the procedure of a nearby master who "was beatin' on some of his slaves all de time." After stripping a slave naked, the master would tie his hands and feet, run a pole between his bent elbows and knees, and whip him with a "cat-o'-nine tails" (rawhide leather braided on an eight- or 10-inch wooden handle and knotted near the end to make a tassel called the "cracker") until the blood ran. After the whipping it was common practice to put salt in the wounds, perhaps for cleansing, but also to cause excrutiating pain. Curious children ran to the spot when they heard a whipping, and they were sometimes sent to the kitchen to fetch the salt. William Colbert knew when his older brother was whipped for staying out too late "seein' a gal on de next plantation," and recalled, "all de while, I sat on my mammy's and pappy's steps a-cryin'." When William Moore saw his mother whipped, he "run around crazy like" and threw a rock at his master. Yet, throughout the South enslaved children themselves were more likely to be punished by the master's wife, and recalled many an exasperated or cruel mistress who shook them, whipped them with a wooden paddle or leather strap, held their heads between her knees and "whacked" their bare backs, tied their wrists and lashed them with a rope, or rubbed snuff in their eyes.[69]

Throughout the antebellum South a majority of the white population continued to live in yeomen households, on smaller farms of less than 200 acres on the less desireable land between plantations—Low Country swamps, sand hills, or pine barrens—or in Upcountry regions of the cotton belt. On these holdings, whether or not they owned slaves, fathers worked the fields themselves, directing the labor of their large numbers of children. Producing most of the food their families consumed, they traded with neighbors for other foodstuffs, and raised a small staple crop to obtain credit at the local store. These households would not be transformed by rural capitalism before the Civil War, as were their counterparts in the North. Small masters within the slave society, Southern yeomen shared with planters the position of household patriarch. They worked to provide their children with inheritance, but the independence they cherished and protected ultimately depended on those children's labor.[70]

In yeomen households that included a few slaves, black laborers and white children worked the fields together. James Monroe Adams, the eldest of 16 children, grew up in a four-room, two-story log house in Newton County, in northern Georgia. Aaron, a slave given by his grandfather to his father, and Hester, inherited by his mother, lived in a nearby log cabin with their children. Adams recalled, "I never loved to work when I was a boy, yet I picked fifty pounds [of cotton] before I could tote it at all, in half of a day." Interspersed with lessons in various subscription schools, he planted corn; pulled, tied, and stacked "fodder"; mended fences; and slaughtered hogs. Adams's father, who was his own overseer, directed gangs composed of a few male and female slaves working with his own 10 sons; because they never knew when the patriarch might come by, they all just kept on working.

The elder Adams "always had good order and attention in the home as well as in the fields," his son remembered, and "did not equalize himself with Negroes nor children." Setting an example "for the other nine Boys to imitate," when James broke his hoe handle his father arranged "a settlement just as if I had been a slave," to which his son "submitted with as much grace as was possible under such circumstances." But Aaron, as the slave leader, also directed labor in the fields, deciding when it was time to drink from the gourd (which the white boys drank from first), and occasionally disciplining his master's children. One time when they were slaughtering and James got in his way, Aaron said, "[G]it out of my way or I'll hang you higher than your daddy ever hung any meat, for your mammy to cut down."[71]

Elmina Foster Wilson grew up in her grandfather's two-story log house with full-length porch in Guilford, North Carolina. As a child she picked cotton, ran errands, helped carry pans to the separate kitchen to bake bread, corn pone, puddings and pies, and washed pewter plates and iron kettles and skillets after dinner. Engaging in domestic production, she helped her grandmother spin flax and was "required to knit a certain number of rounds" on stockings "each night before going to bed." She also dyed yarn and prepared the loom for weaving, filling the quills for the weaver's shuttle, which she found "a monotonous job and very tiresome," and selecting threads for the warp, which the weaver would "put through the gears or sleigh." Although neighbors were slaveholders, African-Americans worked on the farm of her Quaker grandparents as "hired help." Elmina and her siblings worked along with them, and "in the loom house or by the spring washing" "eagerly listened" to stories they told of headless men and witches "riding through the air."[72]

Throughout the antebellum period as many as 30 to 50 percent of Southern whites were landless, composing a shifting, mobile population engaged in tenant farming or seeking work as hired labor. Not only did the institution of slavery limit access to wage jobs and keep wages low, but also the barter economy did not favor those who lacked credit or whose credit at country stores failed to cover the supplies they needed to survive. Children in these often fragmented families worked in the fields along with their parents for landlords or as hired labor. According to one son of tenant farmers in Tippah County, Mississippi, "My father did general farm work and my mother general housework. They and us children went to work at daybreak and worked till late night." Children of the landless also worked for low wages, boys in mines or shoe factories, and girls as domestics or in cotton mills. Racial barriers remained, yet distinctions blurred as landless whites and their children socialized and engaged in underground trade with free and enslaved blacks, often exchanging foodstuffs that planters complained had been pilfered from plantations.[73]

By the 1850s, as the number of landless whites was augmented by Irish and German immigration, planters intensified efforts to buttress their slaveholding society by elevating the character of this white population. Enlightened and patriotic citizens of Charleston, South Carolina, had founded the nation's first public orphan asylum in 1790. The four-story brick building of the Charleston Orphan House proudly symbolized the commitment of Protestants, Catholics, and Jews to the abandoned and homeless but malleable white children. Orphan house comissioners sought to create a family atmosphere in the asylum and to offer the children full participation in Southern society. Boys were apprenticed to merchants or tradesmen, and those showing special talent were supported at the University of South Carolina, where they mingled with the sons of wealthy planters. Girls, viewed as future wives and mothers, were trained in domestic skills and the care of younger children. In 1855, as planters sought support for slavery and to sharpen distinctions between blacks and landless whites, the asylum building was renovated and enlarged, and the commitment to "inculcate moral and religious principles" among "the fatherless running to ruin in our streets" was renewed.[74]

Evangelical Southerners had joined Northerners in voluntary associations of the 1820s that sought to form character. As the American Tract Society flooded the region with materials, and the American Sunday School Union extended its efforts to create a national culture, benevolent individuals in Southern cities and towns founded Sunday schools. After Protestant denominations split over the issue of slavery in the late 1830s and 1840s, membership in the nondenominational American Sunday School Union remained one of the few avenues through which Southerners could participate in national cultural activity.[75] Northern organic concepts of child nurture had also taken root in the South. Caroline Howard Gilman, born in Massachusetts and married to Charleston's Unitarian minister, had published *The Rose Bud* in the 1830s, a "juvenile newspaper" based on the model of Lydia Maria Child's *Juvenile Miscellany,* a successful Northern periodical for children. *The Rose Bud,* which grew to seven volumes, along with Gilman's novels and tales, attempted to transplant Northern domestic ideology in the Southern setting.[76]

Although public schools did not become widespread, concepts of educational reformers had also been advocated in the South. Influenced by the ideas of Pestalozzi, manual labor schools had been founded in Virginia, North Carolina, and Georgia in the 1830s, and in Arkansas in the 1840s. In the 1850s German-born Christopher G. Memminger, raised in the Charleston Orphan House and selected by its commissioners to receive an advanced education, advocated tax-supported public schools for children of Charleston's white working class. As Irish and German immigrants came to compose 40 percent of the city's population, citizens argued that "elevation of white labour" was essential in a slave society to preserve the distinction between whites and blacks. Yet Memminger's vision was inspired by a visit to Charleston of Connecticut school reformer Henry Barnard; on a trip north to observe state systems of common schools Memminger recruited a superintendent and two female principals from Brooklyn to help institute 11 new public schools and the Female High and Normal School founded in Charleston by 1859.[77]

Nevertheless, by the 1850s, as the plantation economy boomed from the Low Country to Texas, Southerners could not reconcile national concepts of character—the industrious activity and disciplined self-restraint appropriate to an economy of developing capitalism—with their regional commitment to slavery. Rejecting Northern commercial values, Southern cultural leaders reiterated their version of republican ideology, in which the independence of planter or yeoman was preserved by those who labored as dependents in his household. They also refashioned behavioral ideals of the eighteenth century, exhorting children to display genteel values and benevolent sympathy toward inferiors. A *Southern Reader* produced in Charleston taught children to dominate and command through stories of George and Clara, who, on a visit to a plantation, reward enslaved children with candy for learning to curtsy and bow, teaching them to "obey" "like so many soldiers." The white children are shamed for cruelty in their play. When George swings little Toney on a grapevine in an attempt to frighten him, Clara reminds him that Toney "has as much feeling as you" and protects the slave child. Such stories were alternated with *"home history,"* regional "anecdotes of patriotism and bravery" during the American Revolution. Tales of George Washington, General Francis Marion and his men holding out in the swamps, and Mrs. Motte of the Congree River, who burned her home to defend it from the British, instructed both boys and girls in republican self-sacrifice, protection of the household, and defense of home territory. "Such patriots," proclaimed the Southern schoolbook, "can never be conquered."[78]

Epilogue

Throughout the early nineteenth century, Americans across the nation reworked their revolutionary heritage. In the deeply divisive and painful but heady years of the Revolution, the aspirations of ordinary people had been unleashed as they rejected external authority and demanded their right to rely on their own judgment. Young people married without the consent of patriarchal fathers, producing large numbers of children until half the population was under age 16. Migrating west with their families, helping clear land, entering loosening arrangements of apprenticeship, engaging in outwork, making textiles, or laboring on farms and plantations, these children contributed to strategies of parents and masters that produced dynamism in American life. Responding to religious exhorters, engaging in entrepreneurial popular culture, or simply moving around, they could not escape imbibing a sense of independence—one's right to make choices for oneself.

Yet cultural leaders who came of age during the Revolution feared the loss of common social bonds. Seeking to implement republican ideals and to channel the raw energy around them, they proposed allegiance to a common culture. If the malleable child described by enlightened thought could be shaped not only for autonomy but also for virtuous self-restraint, perhaps the children evident everywhere could actually become responsible citizens and citizens' wives. While individuals pursued divergent paths with industrious activity, affectionate loyalty to common ideals would confer worth and convey meaning, engaging voluntary adherence to some measure of social order. Church and state would be separated, but most still viewed religion as the source of public harmony. In the 1780s and 1790s, as patriots sought to stabilize the new republic, they adapted European thought to American experience, blending concepts of enlightened child-rearing with Protestant belief.

Americans who produced their own child-rearing materials in the 1820s drew upon these post-Revolutionary themes. As capitalism transformed the Northeast, farmers and planters poured west, and traders transported the enslaved across the South, for many the need to impose order and coherence on a chaotic environment and pluralistic population became even more pressing. A new generation of cultural leaders, struggling to define a national identity, continued to focus on the malleability of the child, reworking concepts of republican virtue into a new concern with character. In the context of developing capitalism, physicians, Sunday school managers, educational reformers, and philanthropists sought to channel the dynamism around them by tempering industrious activity with internalized restraint instilled through new institutions and new indirect controls.

These efforts by adults to shape and to control produced ironic consequences as they reached the lives of real children. Methods of physical management may have improved for upper- and middle-class children, but rates of infant and child mortality remained high. An "American Revolution" in medicine treated children with dangerous and frequently fatal depleting measures. Capitalism created a new middle class, but increased consumer demand exploited the labor of rural and poor urban children, who were drawn into outwork or large manufacturing units. Concepts of child nurture permeated the middle class, prompting the removal of poor urban children from their living natural parents. Slavery spread to the Southwest, a professional slave trade developed, and the increased value of enslaved children provided income to educate and provide an inheritance for their privileged white counterparts.

In the complex American society of the mid-nineteenth century, children growing up in middle-class homes, on urban streets, on yeoman or capitalized farms, in big houses, or in slave quarters on plantations experienced very different childhoods. Only remotely were many of them touched by efforts to create allegiance to a common culture. Yet children, even slaves who were denied it, still imbibed the heady aspiration that permeated American life. Working with children of immigrant parents in notorious New York neighborhoods in the 1850s, Charles Loring Brace observed:

> In the United States a boundless hope pervades all classes; it reaches down to the outcast and vagrant. There is not fixity, as is so often the fact in Europe, from the sense of despair. Every individual, at least till he is old, hopes and expects to rise out of his condition.

Even the daughter of a rag-picker could keenly feel "the profound forces of American life; the desire of equality, ambition to rise, the sense of self-respect and the passion for education."[1]

Perhaps no individual better summarizes the themes of childhood in American culture from 1775 to 1850 than Harriet Beecher Stowe. From her father Lyman Beecher, who was born in 1775, she inherited her concern with creation of a national culture. Although imbued with evangelical fervor, she rejected the intense conversion experience expected by her father and shifted to a social concern with character. Yet her concept of character was softened by the genteel behavioral ideals she learned first from her mother, Roxana Foote Beecher, and then as a student at Sarah Pierce's Litchfield Female Academy. The sixth of her father's 11 children, Harriet also enjoyed the physical liberty of rural children, romping in the Connecticut hills, picking berries, and helping her brothers chop wood. Her mental alertness was honed by the innovative teaching of John Brace, father of Charles Loring and teacher at Sarah Pierce's school.[2]

Later in her life Stowe would re-create her New England childhood through meticulously drawn sketches of religious belief in its social ramifications; yet she transcended her regional roots when she followed her father to Cincinnati in 1832. There she married school reformer Calvin Stowe—bearing twin daughters within a year and a son the next—and embarked on the struggle to rear her children while pursuing a literary career. Stowe raised her seven children with enlightened methods and suffered the consequences of heroic medical therapy. Her physical health was endangered not only by closely spaced pregnancies but also by probable mercury poisoning from the little blue pills of calomel prescribed by her friend and physician Dr. Daniel Drake. In the early 1840s, burdened by the illnesses of her children and devastated by the suicide of her brother George, Stowe experienced spiritual rebirth. Rejecting her father's Calvinism in favor of a Christianity founded on her own experience as a woman and mother, she came to believe in a simple imitation of Christ and that through the endurance of the lowly in the daily struggle to live, the kingdom of God could be achieved.[3]

In Cincinnati, the junction of the American South and West, Stowe developed her literary skills. Beginning to write on the model of Joseph Addison's *The Spectator,* she democratized the Anglo-American literary tradition with the inclusion of the voices she heard around her. Witnessing the flight of slaves across the Ohio River to freedom, she grasped the cruelty of the domestic slave trade to human beings with feelings not unlike her own. Stowe's identification with enslaved mothers whose children were sold away from them was felt most fully after the death of her beloved 18-month-old sixth child, Charley, from cholera in 1849. She wrote in 1852: "There were circumstances about his death of such peculiar bitterness, of what might seem almost cruel suffering, that I felt that I could never be consoled for it, unless it should appear that this crushing of my own heart might enable me to work out some great good to others." "It was at *his* dying bed, and at *his* grave that I learnt what a poor slave mother may feel when her child is torn away from her."[4]

This accumulated emotion and experience enabled Harriet Beecher Stowe to portray slave relationships in terms that Northern middle-class Americans deeply understood. Articulation of concepts of child nurture and wide acceptance of domestic ideology occurred during a period in which almost every family still experienced the tragic loss of child death. When the Compromise of 1850 achieved only an uneasy truce among deeply disturbing sectional divisions in the American republic, Stowe moved the energy of this cultural focus on the child into the political arena. Pouring out her grief over the death of her child and rage against the Fugitive Slave Act in serialized segments of *Uncle Tom's Cabin, or Life Among the Lowly,* she held the domestic slave trade up to public scrutiny. Drawing on the Scottish Enlightenment notion of the moral sense, she viewed slaves as particularly capable of domestic attachment and deeply affected by loss. Expressing themes of pity and terror from her Calvinist evangelical childhood, she warned of divine vengeance for collective sin.

Yet in *Uncle Tom's Cabin,* Harriet Beecher Stowe also delineated a genuinely democratic concept of the child. Four-year-old Harry, child of the mulatto, Eliza, is remarkably beautiful; his father, George, a man of entrepreneurial energy, chafes at limits imposed on him by race. When the enslaved mother flees across the icebound river to save her precious child from the professional trader, her action symbolizes a universal human aspiration to liberty. Eight-year-old enslaved Topsy is the neglected child whose character can be reformed through adoption. Uncle Tom expresses Stowe's own spiritual discovery, as he endures the bitter struggle of daily life to prevail in death through a simple faith in Christ. And little Eva, the beloved child who dies too soon, is the child redeemer, recognizing in premature death the profound truth of racial equality—that Christ loves Topsy as much as he loves her—to become the conscience of an erring nation.[5]

Chronology

1688	Glorious Revolution occurs in England.
1693	John Locke's *Some Thoughts Concerning Education* is published.
1711–12	Joseph Addison publishes *The Spectator* papers.
1725	Francis Hutcheson's *Inquiry Into the Original of Our Ideas of Beauty and Virtue* is published.
1740	Samuel Richardson publishes *Pamela, or Virtue Rewarded.*
1744	John Newbery publishes *A Little Pretty Pocket-book.*
1747	Dr. William Cadogan's *Essay upon Nursing and Management of Children* is published. Samuel Richardson publishes *Clarissa, or the History of a Young Lady.*
1762	Jean-Jacques Rousseau's *Emile* is published.
1769	Dr. William Buchan's *Domestic Medicine* is published.
1770s	Enlightened child-rearing is apparent in colonial regional cultures. Family change is influenced by pressure on eastern lands, commercialization of colonial economies, unprecedented movement of people, and pietistic religion. Colonial break with England is argued in terms of the family analogy.
1775–83	American Revolutionary War.
1787	Constitutional convention at Philadelphia.
1780s, 1790s	Americans adapt enlightened child-rearing to their new republican society.
1783	Noah Webster's *A Grammatical Institute of the English Language* is published.
1784	Benjamin Rush's *Thoughts upon the Mode of Education Proper in a Republic* is published.

1790	Philanthropic gentlemen found First Day Schools in Philadelphia. Boston founds system of public schools. Enos Hitchcock's *Memoirs of the Bloomsgrove Family* is published.
1792	Sarah Pierce establishes Litchfield Female Academy.
1795	Dr. Samuel Powel Griffitts incorporates "American Revolution" in medicine into Buchan's *Domestic Medicine.*
1790s	Conditions of apprenticeship decline. Rural dynamism develops in New England. Samuel Slater employs children in cotton mill. Cotton cultivation expands rapidly in the South.
1801	Moravians send missionaries to Cherokees in Spring Place, Georgia.
1808	Congress ends African slave trade, and domestic trade accelerates.
1811	Mary Palmer Tyler's *The Maternal Physician* is published. The Rev. Robert May introduces evangelical Sunday school to Philadelphia. The Rev. Lyman Beecher teaches theology at Litchfield Female Academy.
1812–15	War of 1812.
1815	Asylum is founded by Philadelphia Female Orphan Society.
1815–19	Economic depression occurs in northeastern urban centers, yet country experiences economic boom. Indian lands are ceded to the federal government. Families pour into the Northwest and Southwest.
1817	Philadelphia Sunday and Adult School Union is founded. Lancasterian public schools are established in Philadelphia.
1819	Financial panic is followed by depression.
1822	Cotton mills are established in Lowell, Massachusetts.
1824	American Sunday School Union is organized.
1825	Dr. William Potts Dewees's *Treatise on the Physical and Medical Treatment of Children* is published. Public School Society is reorganized in New York. New York House of Refuge is founded.
1826	Philadelphia House of Refuge is founded.
1830s	Cotton boom stimulates migration to the Southwest.
1837	Financial panic is followed by depression, north and south. Horace Mann is appointed Secretary of Massachusetts State Board of Education.
1840	New York Catholic priests protest Protestant thrust of public schools.

1841   Catherine Beecher's *Treatise on Domestic Economy* is published.

1840s Irish fleeing potato famine emigrate to United States. Immigration of Germans increases.

1847   Horace Bushnell's *Views of Christian Nurture* is published. State reform school for boys is established in Westborourgh, Massachusetts.

1849   In *Roberts v. City of Boston* black parents protest segregation in public schools.

1851   Massachusetts passes the first state adoption law.

1852   Harriet Beecher Stowe's *Uncle Tom's Cabin, or Life Among the Lowly* is published.

1853   Charles Loring Brace becomes urban missionary of the Children's Aid Society.

1854   Family style Massachusetts Industrial School for Girls is founded.

Notes and References

Introduction

1. Richard L. Bushman, *The Refinement of America: Persons, Houses, Cities* (New York, 1992).
2. J.G.A. Pocock, *The Machiavellian Moment: Florentine Political Thought and the Atlantic Republican Tradition* (Princeton, N.J., 1975); Gordon S. Wood, *The Radicalism of the American Revolution* (New York, 1992).
3. Nathan O. Hatch, *The Democratization of American Christianity* (New Haven, Conn., 1989).
4. Patricia U. Bonomi, *Under the Cope of Heaven: Religion, Society, and Politics in Colonial America* (New York, 1986); "Religious Dissent and the Case for American Exceptionalism" in Ronald Hoffman and Peter J. Albert, eds., *Religion in a Revolutionary Age* (Charlottesville, Va., 1994), 31–51.

Chapter 1

1. Lawrence Stone, *The Family, Sex, and Marriage in England, 1550–1800* (New York, 1977), 221–269.
2. Richard L. Bushman, *The Refinement of America: Persons, Houses, Cities* (New York, 1992).
3. The Anglo-American revolt against patriarchy has been discussed by Jay Fliegelman in *Prodigals & Pilgrims: The American revolution against patriarchal authority, 1750–1800* (Cambridge, 1982).
4. Maurice Cranston, *John Locke, A Biography* (New York, 1985), 205–213.
5. John Locke, *Two Treatises of Government* (London, 1690; New York, 1963), 345–348, 362–365.
6. Cranston, *John Locke*, 232, 239.

7. John Locke, *Some Thoughts Concerning Education* (London, 1693; Woodbury, N.Y., 1964), 10, 18, 24.
8. Ibid., 25, 29.
9. Ibid., 35.
10. Ibid., 133.
11. Cranston, *John Locke,* 371.
12. Peter Smithers, *The Life of Joseph Addison* (Oxford, 1954), 98.
13. Ibid., 91–92, 160–163, 179, 262.
14. *The Spectator,* No. X, March 12, 1711.
15. Smithers, *Life,* 216.
16. *The Spectator,* No. 89, June 12, 1711.
17. *The Spectator,* No. 33, April 7, 1711.
18. *The Spectator,* No. 15, March 17, 1711.
19. *The Spectator,* No. 57, May 5, 1711; No. 81, June 2, 1711.
20. *The Spectator,* No. 66, May 16, 1711; No. 71, May 22, 1711.
21. Smithers, *Life,* 219, 244, 231.
22. *Selections from the Spectator, Tatler, Guardian and Freeholder; with a Preliminary Essay by Mrs. Barbauld* 2 vols. (London, 1849), vi, vii.
23. Francis Hutcheson, *An Inquiry Into the Original of Our Ideas of Beauty and Virtue* (London, 1726; first edition, 1725), xiv–xviii, 75, 80, 82.
24. Ibid., 19, 34–36, 47, 65, 104.
25. Ibid., 113–116, 125, 133, 140, 155–156, 177, 183–195, 205, 271.
26. Ibid., 215–230, 269.
27. William Cadogan, *An Essay upon Nursing and the Management of Children From their Birth to Three Years of Age, by a Physician, in a Letter to one of the Governors of the Foundling Hospital* (London, 1748, first edition, 1747), 2.
28. Ibid., 9, 12.
29. Ibid., 34.
30. William Buchan, *Domestic Medicine or the Family Physician: Being an Attempt to Render the Medical Art More Generally Useful . . . Chiefly Calculated to Recommend a Proper Attention to Regimen and Simple Medicines* (Edinburgh, 1769). Page numbers have been obtained from the following Philadelphia reprint: William Buchan, *Domestic Medicine, or a Treatise on the Prevention and Cure of Diseases by Regimen and Simple Medicines with an Appendix containing a Dispensatory for the Use of Private Practitioners* (Philadelphia, 1784), preface.
31. Ibid., 45.
32. Ibid., viii, 112, 179, 423.
33. Bernard Fabian, "English Books and Their Eighteenth-Century German Readers," in Paul J. Karshin, ed., *The Widening Circle: Essays on the Circulation of Literature in Eighteenth-Century Europe* (Philadelphia, 1976), 166–170. In the same volume see also Robert Darnton, "Trade

in the Taboo: The Life of a Clandestine Book Dealer in Pre-revolution-
ary France," 13–83; and Roy McKean Wiles, "The Relish for Reading
in Provincial England Two Centuries Ago," 87–115. James D. Hart,
The Popular Book: A History of America's Literary Taste (New York,
1950), 19, 25, 28, 47–48, 50–51. Frank Luther Mott, *Golden Multi-
tudes: The Story of Best Sellers in the United States* (New York, 1947),
34. According to Mott, changing habits and tastes occurred in urban
centers in America throughout the eighteenth century.

34. From 1740 to 1802 the Newbery firm at the sign of the Bible and the
    Sun, St. Paul's Churchyard, London, produced at least fifty titles of lit-
    tle books for children. Charles Welsh, *A Bookseller of the Last Century:
    Being Some Account of the Life of John Newbery and of the Books He
    Published* . . . (London, 1885), 337–347.

35. M.F. Thwaite, *A Little Pretty Locket-Book* (London, 1969; first edition,
    1744), 9.

36. *The History of the King Pippin* (Philadelphia, 1786), 8.

37. *Nurse Truelove's New Year's Gift* (Worcester, Mass., 1786).

38. Samuel Richardson, *Clarissa, or The History of a Young Lady* (London,
    1985; first edition, 1747–48), frontispiece, 15–17.

39. Ibid.

40. Dr. William Buchan, whose *Domestic Medicine* was written in 1769, indi-
    cated that he had read Rousseau. Thus, it is more likely that Rousseau
    influenced the Scottish physician rather than the other way around.

41. Jean-Jacques Rousseau, *Emile, or On Education* (New York, 1979; first
    edition, 1762), 37, 45–46, 48–49, 59–60, 66.

42. Ibid., 79–80, 84, 100–101.

43. Ibid., 136–163, 165–166, 168, 173–175, 184–185, 195–202.

44. Ibid., 211–214, 220–229, 234, 244, 248–249, 253.

45. Ibid., 260, 273–294, 308, 316–329, 340–344.

46. Ibid., 360–387, 395, 477–479.

47. Ibid., 399–402, 412–420, 442–450, 473.

48. David Lundberg and Henry May, "The Enlightened Reader in Amer-
    ica," *American Quarterly* 28 (1976): 273.

49. Fliegelman, *Prodigals and Pilgrims,* 4–5.

50. Smithers, *Life of Joseph Addison,* 454.

51. Rodris Roth, "Tea-Drinking in Eighteenth-Century America: Its Eti-
    quette and Equipage," in Robert Blair St. George, ed., *Material Life in
    America, 1600–1860* (Boston, 1988), 441–442.

52. Garry Wills, *Inventing America: Jefferson's Declaration of Independence*
    (New York, 1978).

53. Fliegelman, *Prodigals and Pilgrims,* 87; Charles Evans, *American Bibli-
    ography: A Chronological Dictionary of* . . . *Publications Printed in the
    United States* 14 vols. (New York, 1941–1959).

54. These themes have been discussed by Bushman, *Refinement of America;* and T.H. Breen, "Narrative of Commercial Life: Consumption, Ideology, and Community on the Eve of the American Revolution," *The William and Mary Quarterly* 3rd. series, vol. L, no. 3 (July, 1993): 471–501.

Chapter 2

1. David Hackett Fischer, *Albion's Seed: Four British Folkways in America* (New York, 1989); Gordon S. Wood, *The Radicalism of the American Revolution* (New York, 1992); J.C.D. Clark, *The Language of Liberty, 1660–1832: Political discourse and social dynamics in the Anglo-American world* (Cambridge, 1994).

2. Patricia U. Bonomi, *Under the Cope of Heaven: Religion, Society, and Politics in Colonial America* (New York, 1986); Clark, *Language of Liberty.*

3. Fischer, *Albion's Seed,* 6–7.

4. Fischer, *Albion's Seed,* 97–102. See also John Demos, *A Little Commonwealth: Family Life in Plymouth Colony* (New York, 1970); and Edmund S. Morgan, *The Puritan Family: Religion and Domestic Relations in Seventeenth-Century New England* (New York, 1944).

5. Philip J. Greven, Jr., *Four Generations: Population, Land, and Family in Colonial Andover, Massachusetts* (Ithaca, N.Y., 1970), 72–99.

6. Greven, *Four Generations,* 222–258.

7. Robert A. Gross, *The Minutemen and Their World* (New York, 1976), 100.

8. Greven, *Four Generations,* 209.

9. Norman Fiering, *Jonathan Edwards's Moral Thought and Its British Context* (Chapel Hill, N.C., 1981), 15–19, 24, 65–68, 106, 118, 127, 132, 309, 319–321.

10. Samuel Hopkins, *The Life and Character of the Late Reverend, Learned, and Pious Mr. Jonathan Edwards, President of the College of New Jersey, Together with Extracts from his Private Writings and Diary. And Also Seventeen Select Sermons on Various Important Subjects* (Northampton, Mass., 1804), 57, in Philip J. Greven, Jr., ed., *Child-rearing Concepts, 1628–1861* (Itasca, Ill., 1973), 72.

11. Sereno E. Dwight, ed., *The Works of President Edwards: With a Memoir of his Life* (New York, 1829), Vol. 1, 126–30, in Greven, *Child-rearing Concepts,* 76–78.

12. Fischer, *Albion's Seed,* 207–216; Bushman, *Refinement of America,* 30–36; Cornelia Meigs, Anne Thaxter Eaton, Elizabeth Nesbitt, Ruth Hill Viguers, *A Critical History of Children's Literature* (London, 1969), 29–31.

13. Allan Kulikoff, *Tobacco and Slaves: The Development of Southern Cultures in the Chesapeake, 1680–1800* (Chapel Hill, N.C., 1986).

14. Daniel Blake Smith, *Inside the Great House: Planter Family Life in Eighteenth-Century Chesapeake Society* (Ithaca, N.Y., 1980), 21–22.
15. Karin Calvert, *Children in the House: The Material Culture of Early Childhood, 1600–1900* (Boston, 1992), 79–80.
16. Smith, *Inside the Great House*, 40–44, 120, 295.
17. Fischer, *Albion's Seed*, 311–320; an example of adaptation of Chesterfield's *Letters,* first published in London in 1774, is Philip Dormer Stanhope Chesterfield, *Principles of Politeness and of Knowing the World with Additions by the Rev. Dr. John Trusler for the Improvement of Youth* (Philadelphia, 1781).
18. *George Washington's Rules of Civility & Decent Behaviour in Company and Conversation* (Chester, Conn., 1988).
19. Peter Smithers, *The Life of Joseph Addison* (Oxford, 1954), 26–27, 256–268.
20. Fischer, *Albion's Seed*, 315–317.
21. Kulikoff, *Tobacco and Slaves*, 358–371.
22. Garry Wills, *Inventing America: Jefferson's Declaration of Independence* (New York, 1978), 177–180.
23. Thomas Jefferson, *Notes on Virginia* in Adrienne Koch and William Peden, eds., *The Life and Selected Writings of Thomas Jefferson* (New York, 1944), 210–211, 261, 278.
24. These issues have been sensitively discussed by Jan Lewis in *The Pursuit of Happiness: Family and Values in Jefferson's Virginia* (Cambridge, 1983), 130.
25. Fischer, *Albion's Seed*, 507–513; Barry Levy, *Quakers and the American Family: British Settlement in the Delaware Valley* (New York, 1988), 58–61, 66–72; J. William Frost, *The Quaker Family in Colonial America* (New York, 1973), 66, 77.
26. Levy, *Quakers and the American Family,* 132–137, 243–248, 251–255. See also Sydney James, *A People Among Peoples* (Cambridge, Mass., 1963); Jack D. Marietta, *The Reformation of American Quakerism, 1748–1783* (Philadelphia, 1984); and Jean R. Soderlund, *Quakers & Slavery: A Divided Spirit* (Princeton, N.J., 1985).
27. Fischer, *Albion's Seed*, 605–609; Carl Bridenbaugh, *Myths & Realities: Societies of the Colonial South* (New York, 1974), 122–124; Benjamin Davies, *Some Account of the City of Philadelphia . . .* (Philadelphia, 1794); J. Thomas Scharf and Thompson Westcott, *History of Philadelphia, 1609–1884* (Philadelphia, 1884); Stephanie Grauman Wolf, *Urban Village: Population, Community and Family Structure in Germantown, Pennsylvania, 1683–1800* (Princeton, N.J., 1976).
28. Gary B. Nash, "Up from the Bottom in Franklin's Philadelphia," *Past and Present* 77 (November, 1977): 57–83; *The Urban Crucible: The Northern Seaports and the Origins of the American Revolution* (Cam-

bridge, Mass., 1979), 155–166; Billy G. Smith, "The Material Lives of Laboring Philadelphians, 1750 to 1800," *The William and Mary Quarterly* 3rd ser., vol. 38, no. 2 (1981), 177; and "Inequality in Late Colonial Philadelphia: A Note of Its Nature and Growth," *The William and Mary Quarterly* 3rd ser., vol. 41, no. 4 (October, 1984): 629–645.

29. Larzer Ziff, ed., *Benjamin Franklin's Autobiography* (New York, 1959), 12, 14, 78–87.

30. Garry Wills, *Inventing America: Jefferson's Declaration of Independence* (New York, 1978), 176.

31. John Witherspoon, *A Series of Letters on Education* (New York, 1797), 13–23, 25–36, 39–42, 47, 63, 52.

32. Thomas Paine, *Common Sense* (Philadelphia, 1776; reprint, New York, 1973), 30–31, 48–49.

33. Alice Morse Earle, ed., *Diary of Anna Green Winslow: A Boston School Girl of 1771* (Williamstown, Mass., 1894, reprinted, 1974), xi–xiii, xix, 13, 71.

34. Abigail Adams to John Adams, June 18, September 25, October 1, 1775, in L.H. Butterfield, ed., *Book of Abigail and John: Selected Letters of the Adams Family, 1762–1784* (Cambridge, Mass., 1975), 90, 107–108.

35. Elizabeth Drinker, "Diary," AMs, September 9 and 13, October 17, and December 31, 1777, Historical Society of Pennsylvania, Philadelphia.

36. Henry Laurens to Martha Laurens, February 29 and August 17, 1776, in David Ramsay, *Memoirs of the Life of Martha Laurens Ramsay* (Philadelphia, 1811), 66–67, 71.

37. John C. Thomas, "Memoirs of Stephen Allen," Ts, November, 1825, 6–13, 18, 23, New York Historical Society, New York.

38. For discussion of these themes, see Gordon Wood, *The Creation of the American Republic, 1776–1787* (New York, 1969); *Radicalism of the American Revolution;* J.G.A. Pocock, *The Machiavellian Moment: Florentine Political Thought and the Atlantic Republican Tradition* (Princeton, N.J., 1975); Clark, *Language of Liberty.*

39. Bonomi, *Under the Cope of Heaven;* "Religious Dissent and the Case for American Exceptionalism" in Ronald Hoffman and Peter J. Albert, eds., *Religion in a Revolutionary Age* (Charlottesville, Va., 1994), 31–51.

40. *The History of Little King Pippin with an Account of the Melancholy Death of four Naughty Boys who were devoured by Wild Beasts and the Wonderful Delivery of Master Harry Harmless by a Little White Horse* (Philadelphia, 1786).

41. Lucy Aikin, *The Works of Anna Laetitia Barbauld: With a Memoir* 2 vols. (London, 1825); Betsy Rodgers, *Georgian Chronicle: Mrs. Barbauld and Her Family* (London, 1958), 16–56.

42. *Lessons for Children from Two to Four Years Old,* (Philadelphia, 1788); *Lessons for Children of Four Years Old* (Philadelphia, 1788).

43. *Lessons for Children from Four to Five Years Old* (Philadelphia, 1788), 3–4.

44. *The New England Primer, Much Improved; Containing a Variety of Easy Lessons for Attaining the True Reading of English* (Philadelphia, 1792).

45. John Ely, *The Child's Instructor: Consisting of Easy Lessons for Children on Subjects which Are Familiar to them, in Language Adapted to their Capacities* (Philadelphia, 1793), 11, 17.

46. George Warren Gignilliat, Jr., *The Author of Sandford and Merton: A Life of Thomas Day, Esq.* (New York, 1932); Thomas Day, *The History of Sandford and Merton: A Work Intended for the Use of Children* 3 vols. (Philadelphia, 1788).

47. *The Life of Gen. Washington, Commander in Chief of the American Army during the Late War, and Present President of the United States* (Philadelphia, 1794), 9.

48. *The Life of Judas Iscariot: Who Betrayed His Lord and Master* (Philadelphia, 1794).

49. Enos Hitchcock, *Memoirs of the Bloomsgrove Family. In a Series of Letters to a respectable Citizen of Philadelphia. Containing Sentiments on a Mode of Domestic Education, Suited to the present State of Society, Government, and Manners in the United States of America: and on the Dignity and Importance of the Female Character Interspersed with a Variety of Interesting Anecdotes* vol. 1 (Boston, 1790), 15–17, 53.

50. Ibid., 79–89, 93–95, 103, 105–115, 117–119.

51. Ibid., 121–123, 126–132, 141–146, 150–151.

52. Ibid., 161–169, 197–200, 207–211, 227–230.

53. Ibid., 239, 245–246, 251–256.

54. Hitchcock, *Memoirs* vol. 2, 29–31, 35, 48, 86–87, 89.

55. Ibid., 195–198, 223–226, 203, 293.

56. Charles Coleman Sellers, *The Artist of the Revolution, The Early Life of Charles Willson Peale* (Hebron, Conn., 1939), 4, 193, 207–210, 219; Brooke Hindle, "Charles Willson Peale's Science and Technology," and Lillian B. Miller, "Charles Willson Peale: A Life of Harmony and Purpose," in *Charles Willson Peale and His World* (New York, 1982), 108, 175, 182, 187, 230; and "Memoirs of Charles Willson Peale from his Original MS. with Notes by Horace Wells Sellers," Ts, American Philosophical Society Library, Philadelphia, 1, 42–45, 59, 79–89, 125.

57. Sellers, *Artist of the Revolution,* 6–7, 39; Peale, "Memoirs," 12, 140, 221.

58. *Charles Willson Peale and His World,* 198–199, 66, 88.

59. Noah Webster, "Memoirs," in Richard H. Rollins, *The Autobiographies of Noah Webster* (Columbia, S.C., 1989), 133, 136.

60. Noah Webster, *A Grammatical Institute of the English Language, comprising An easy, concise, and systematic Method of Education, Designed*

for the Use of English Schools in America Part I (Hartford, Conn., 1783), 15, 101, 104.

61. George W. Corner, *Autobiography of Benjamin Rush, His "Travels through Life" together with his Commonplace Book.* 46.

62. Benjamin Rush to Richard Price, May 25, 1786, in David Freeman Hawke, *Benjamin Rush, Revolutionary Gadfly* (New York, 1971), 341.

63. Benjamin Rush, *A Plan for the Establishment of Public Schools and the Diffusion of Knowledge in Pennsylvania; to Which Are Added, Thoughts upon the Mode of Education, Proper in a Republic* (Philadelphia, 1786), reprinted in Frederick Rudolph, ed., *Essays on Education in the Early Republic* (Cambridge, Mass., 1965), 10.

64. Ibid., 10–11, 14.

65. Ibid., 16–18, 22.

66. Benjamin Rush, *Thoughts upon Female Education, Accommodated to the Present State of Society, Manners, and Government in the United States of America* in Rudolph, *Essays,* 27–30, 32.

67. Ibid., 35–36, 37–38.

Chapter 3

1. Linda K. Kerber, *Women of the Republic: Intellect & Ideology in Revolutionary America* (Chapel Hill, N.C., 1980), 11.

2. In "The Republican Wife: Virtue and Seduction in the Early Republic," *The William and Mary Quarterly,* 3rd ser., 44, 4 (October, 1987): 689–721, Jan Lewis has argued that republicanism offered women the role of wives, while democratic liberalism extolled the political dimensions of motherhood. See also Ruth Bloch's statement that little attention was paid to republican dimensions of motherhood in the time period 1785 to 1815 in "American Feminine Ideals in Transition: The Rise of the Moral Mother, 1785–1815," *Feminist Studies* 4 (1978), n. 67, 125–126. Recently even Linda Kerber seems to agree: "Republican motherhood was a conceptualization which grafted the language of liberal individualism onto the inherited discourse of civic humanism" and did not in and of itself "effectively describe an active role for women in the republic," "The Republican Ideology of the Revolutionary Generation," *American Quarterly* 37 (1985), 486, 484. Both sources are cited by Lewis, "Republican Wife," n. 2, 690.

3. Patricia U. Bonomi, *Under the Cope of Heaven: Religion, Society, and Politics in Colonial America* (New York, 1986), 111–115.

4. Abigail Adams to John Quincy Adams, August 19, 1774; June [10?], 1778; Abigail Adams to John Thaxter, Feb. 15, 1778; in L.H. Butterfield et. al., eds., *The Adams Family Correspondence* 4 vols. (Cambridge, Mass., 1963–73), vol. 1, 142–143; vol. 3, 37; and vol. 2, 390; in Edith B. Gelles, "Mother and Citizen: Abigail Adams and John

Quincy Adams," unpublished paper delivered to the Bay Area Seminar on Early American History and Culture, October, 1991; *Portia: The World of Abigail Adams* (Bloomington, Ind., 1992).

5. David Ramsay, M.D., *Memoirs of the Life of Martha Laurens Ramsay* (Philadelphia, 1811); 27–29, Martha Laurens Ramsay to David Ramsay, Jr., May 7, 1810, 281.

6. Margaret Izard Manigault to Gabriel Manigault, AMs, November 28, December 1, December 4, 1792; Gabriel Manigault to Margaret Izard Manigault, December 7, 1792; Manigault Family Papers, AMs, South Caroliniana Library, Columbia, South Carolina, Box 2, Folder 16.

7. Elizabeth Drinker, "Diary," AMs, August 7, September 5, and December 5, 1795; February 29, April 22, June 20, and August 24, 1796; September 12, 1797; April 27, October 3, December 7–12, 21, 28, and 30, 1799; January 20 and 25, March 5, and December 3, 1800; January 31 and August 26, 1801; May 11 and 13, 1802; February 6 and May 30, 1803; January 5, March 25, and August 9, 1804; June 22 and July 9, 1805; Historical Society of Pennsylvania, Philadelphia.

8. Sally Logan Fisher, "Diary," AMs, June 11, 14, 15, 18, 20, and 22, August 8, 1779; January 12, 1783; Historical Society of Pennsylvania, Philadelphia; Ethel Armes, ed., *Nancy Shippen: Her Journal Book* (Philadelphia, 1935), entry for May 24, 1783, 147–48.

9. Drinker, "Diary," September 4, 1777 through April 25, 1778, June 16 and September 14, 1779; Fisher, "Diary," September 3, 1777, May 18, 1779, October 19, 1780.

10. Fisher, "Diary," October 2 and 3, 1778; November 19, 1780; June 1, 1785.

11. Laurel Thatcher Ulrich, *A Midwife's Tale: The Life of Martha Ballard, Based on Her Diary, 1785–1812* (New York, 1990), 17, 32.

12. Daniel Drake to his children, December 31, 1847, in Edward D. Mansfield, *Memoirs of the Life and Services of Daniel Drake, M.D.* (Cincinnati, Ohio, 1860), 17.

13. Jack Larkin, *The Reshaping of Everyday Life, 1790–1840* (New York, 1988), 110–115; Cary Carson, Norman F. Barka, William M. Kelso, Garry Wheeler Stone, and Dell Upton, "Impermanent Architecture in the Southern American Colonies," in Robert Blair St. George, ed., *Material Life in America, 1600–1860* (Boston, 1988): 113–158.

14. Larkin, *Reshaping of Everyday Life,* 11; Robert V. Wells, *Revolutions in Americans' Lives: A Demographic Perspective on the History of Americans, Their Families, and Their Society* (Westport, Conn., 1982), 50–52, 80.

15. Wells, *Revolutions in Americans' Lives,* 50, 92–93; Nancy Osterud and John Fulton, "Family Limitation and Age at Marriage: Fertility Decline in Sturbridge, Massachusetts, 1730–1850," *Population Studies* 30

(1976): 481–494; Robert V. Wells, "Family Size and Fertility Control in Eighteenth-Century America: A Study of Quaker Families," *Population Studies* 25 (1971): 73–82; reconstituting 744 families from church records of six Philadelphia denominations, Susan E. Klepp found that women who began to limit births were married to professional men—lawyers and white-collar workers, *Philadelphia in Transition: A Demographic History of the City and Its Occupational Groups, 1720–1830* (Philadelphia, 1989), 159–160, 188–189.

16. Larkin, *Reshaping of Everyday Life*, 78. Among the Philadelphia women she studied, Susan E. Klepp found decreasing percentages of upper-class women dying in childbirth, except among later births for older women, while maternal death increased among lower-class women (perhaps partly due to early underrecording). In the post-Revolutionary period, maternal death rates were 97.1 per 10,000 live births among upper-class women, compared to 193.4 per 10,000 live births for lower-class women. A comparative contemporary figure would be 2.2 maternal deaths per 10,000 live births in 1970, *Philadelphia in Transition*, 184–186.

17. In 1930 there was still one maternal death for every 150 births in the United States, but today the rate is one death per 10,000 births. Estimates from parish registers from seventeenth- and eighteenth-century English villages show from ten to twenty-nine maternal deaths per thousand births. Ulrich, *A Midwife's Tale*, 170–173.

18. Louisa Adams Park to Dr. John Park, Acton, Massachusetts, January 5 and 26, 1800 in Louisa Adams Park "Diary" Ms, original copied by Dr. John Park, 1848; "American Women's Diaries: New England," microfilm of original in American Antiquarian Society Library, Worcester, Massachusetts, 90, 93. Louisa Adams Park did die in 1813, thirteen years after this letter.

19. Jan Lewis and Kenneth A. Lockridge, " 'Sally Has Been Sick': Pregnancy and Family Limitation Among Virginia Gentry Women, 1780–1830," *Journal of Social History* 22, 1 (Fall, 1988), 11–12.

20. Drinker, "Diary," June 14 and 17, 1797. During this first labor at the age of twenty-one, Molly Drinker Rhoads evidently acquired an opening between the rectum and vagina that caused an almost constant dribbling of feces. She was referred to by her mother as having "disordered bowels." Such an ailment easily could be corrected by twentieth-century surgery, but this young eighteenth-century woman was forced to spend the rest of her life as an invalid. Years after this labor, her mother recorded that Molly was not fit to be in society. This matter is discussed in Cecil K. Drinker, M.D., *Not So Long Ago, A Chronicle of Medicine and Doctors in Colonial Philadelphia* (New York, 1973).

21. Betsy Copping Corner, *William Shippen, Jr., Pioneer in American Medical Education* with William Shippen's *Student Diary* and 1761 *Dissertation* (Philadelphia, 1951); Richard W. and Dorothy C. Wertz, *Lying-In: A History of Childbirth in America* (New Haven, Conn., 1977; expanded edition, 1989), 34–47.

22. Dr. Samuel Powel Griffitts, *Domestic Medicine, or a Treatise on the Prevention and Cure of Diseases by Regimen and Simple Medicines. Revised and Adapted to the Diseases and Climate of the United States of America* (Philadelphia, 1795), 538.

23. Ulrich, *A Midwife's Tale,* 177–179, 258–259.

24. Ibid., 171.

25. Drinker, "Diary," June 15, 1797; October 28, 1781; October 24, 1799; April 7 and 8, 1795.

26. Louisa Adams Park to Dr. John Park, Salisbury, Massachusetts, June 16, 1800, in Park, "Diary," 105–106.

27. *The Maternal Physician: A Treatise on the Nurture and Management of Infants from Birth until Two Years Old, Being the Result of Sixteen Years Experience in the Nursery, By an American Matron* (New York, 1811); Dr. William Buchan, *Domestic Medicine or the Family Physician: Being an Attempt to Render the Medical Art More Generally Useful . . . Chiefly Calculated to Recommend a Proper attention to Regimen and Simple Medicines* (Edinburgh, 1769); I am indebted to Marilyn S. Blackwell for pointing out the identity of the maternal physician in "The Republican Vision of Mary Palmer Tyler," *Journal of the Early Republic,* 12 (Spring 1992): 11–35.

28. Ross W. Beales, Jr., "Nursing and Weaning in an Eighteenth-Century New England Household," in Peter Benes, ed., *Families and Children: The Dublin Seminar for New England Folklife, Annual Proceedings, 1985* (Boston, 1987), 60; Ulrich, *A Midwife's Tale,* 196.

29. Drinker, "Diary," October 28, 1781.

30. Ibid., October 23, 1799.

31. "Manigault Family Tree," Ms. located at Joseph Manigault House in Charleston, South Carolina.

32. Ramsay, *Memoirs,* 29.

33. Jack Greene, ed., *The Diary of Colonel Landon Carter of Sabine Hall, 1752–1778* (Charlottesville, Va., 1965) October 14, 1770, 511, in Karin Calvert, "The Inventions and Reinvention of Childhood in America: 1600 to 1900," Department of American Civilization, University of Pennsylvania, 143; Lewis and Lockridge, "Sally Has Been Sick," 10.

34. *The Maternal Physician.*

35. Klepp, *Philadelphia in Transition,* 178; William P. Dewees, M.D., *Treatise on the Physical and Medical Treatment of Children* (Philadelphia, 1825), 48.

36. *The Maternal Physician,* 96.
37. Karin Calvert, *Children in the House: The Material Culture of Early Childhood, 1600–1900* (Boston, 1992), 33–36.
38. Drinker, "Diary," December 3, 1802; October 24, 1800.
39. Laurel Thatcher Ulrich, *Goodwives: Image and Reality in the Lives of Women in Northern New England, 1650–1750* (New York, 1980), 142–144; Beales, "Nursing and Weaning," 58–59.
40. *The Maternal Physician,* Chapter III, Section 1.
41. Drinker, "Diary," July 2, 1765; November 21, 1798; Fisher, "Diary," July 15 through August 15, September 9, 1778; October 9, 1779; June 14, 1789.
42. *The Maternal Physician,* 118, 120–121.
43. Dewees, *Treatise,* 187–188, 304–312.
44. *The Maternal Physician,* 158.
45. Crispus, "On the Education of Children," *The Panoplist, and Missionary Magazine,* 10 (September 1814): 393–403, in Philip J. Greven, Jr., *Child-Rearing Concepts, 1628–1861* (Itasca, Ill., 1973), 99, 111.
46. Larkin, *Reshaping of American Life,* 159–161.
47. Dewees, *Treatise,* 237.
48. Calvert, "Inventions and Reinventions," 155, 157.
49. Drinker, "Diary," September 19 and 23, 1799.
50. Margaret Izard Manigault to Gabriel Manigault, Charleston, South Carolina, December 7, 1792, Manigault Family Papers.
51. Drinker, "Diary," February 20, 1779.
52. Dewees, *Treatise,* 242.
53. Daniel Drake to his children, Louisville, Kentucky, December 31, 1847, in Mansfield, *Memoirs,* 18.
54. Larkin, *Reshaping of Everyday Life,* 184–188.
55. *Meet Your Neighbors: New England Portraits, Painters, & Society, 1790–1850* (Old Sturbridge Village, Mass., 1992), 49, 55, 58, 60, 98–99, 113, 121.
56. Calvert, "Inventions and Reinventions," 213–215.
57. Mary Ryan points out the distinction made by C. Wright Mills in *White Collar: The American Middle Classes* (New York, 1951) in *Cradle of the Middle Class: The Family in Oneida County, New York* (Cambridge, 1981), 14.
58. Dewees, *Treatise,* 107–110.
59. Louisa Jane Trumbell, "L.J. Trumbell's Book," AMs, November 7, December 5, 6, and 12, 1829; September 8, 1830; American Antiquarian Society Library, Worcester, Massachusetts.
60. William Hoppin, "Diary" in the back of "B. & T.C. Hoppin Account Book, 1813–1817," AMs, January 1 and 8, March 9, 10, and 31, 1821; American Antiquarian Society Library, Worcester, Massachusetts.

61. Daniel Drake to Margaret Austin Cross Drake, Louisville, Kentucky, January 7, 1848 in Daniel Drake, M.D., edited by Emmet Field Horine, M.D., *Pioneer Life in Kentucky, 1785–1800* (New York, 1948), 109.
62. Larkin, *Reshaping of American Life,* 170–175.
63. Cited in Richard Harrison Shryock, *Medicine and Society in America, 1660–1860* (New York, 1960), 88–89.
64. Dewees, *Treatise,* 206.
65. Philadelphia figures for 1795 to 1800 were obtained from *An Account of Baptisms and Burials in the United Churches of Christ's Church and St. Peter's* (Philadelphia, 1795 through 1800), the only churches which recorded deaths according to age. Those from 1807 to 1827 were obtained from Gouverneur Emerson, M.D., "Medical Statistics: being a Series of Tables, showing Mortality in Philadelphia and its immediate Causes, during a Period of twenty years," *The American Journal of the Medical Sciences* vol. 1 (Philadelphia, 1827). Various urban Boards of Health published mortality statistics in the nineteenth century, which were compared in *The Eclectic Repertory and Analytical Review, Medical and Philosophical* vols. 1–11 (Philadelphia, 1811 through 1821), and *The Philadelphia Journal of the Medical and Physical Sciences* vols. 1–7 (Philadelphia, 1820 through 1827), which became the *American Journal* in 1827.
66. Ibid.
67. Klepp, *Philadelphia in Transition,* 247–249, 260–264.
68. Susan Klepp has argued that as upper- and middle-class mothers ceased to breast-feed their children for longer intervals in the nineteenth century due to their desire to achieve respectability, risk for children undergoing weaning actually was increased, *Philadelphia in Transition,* 260.
69. William Currie, *An Historical Account of the Climates and Diseases of the United States of America; and of the Remedies and Methods of Treatment, which have been found most Useful and Efficacious, Particularly in those Diseases which depend upon Climate and Situation. Collected Principally from Personal Observation, and the Communications of Physicians of Talents and Experience, residing in the Several States* (Philadelphia, 1792), 133. Dr. Currie's use of laudanum (liquid opium) to quiet digestive action, and regimen to strengthen the child, was not unlike the treatment for diarrhea followed by many twentieth-century pediatricians.
70. Emerson, "Medical Statistics," 133, 138. See also Gary B. Nash, *Forging Freedom: The Formation of Philadelphia's Black Community, 1720–1840* (Cambridge, Mass., 1988), 213–214.
71. Drinker, "Diary," August 16–20, 1765; August 4 and 5, 1797; August 14, 1772; June 11 and 12, 1799.
72. Currie, *An Historical Account,* 180, 186.

73. Drinker, "Diary," March 17, 1784.
74. Fisher, "Diary," January 23, 1785.
75. Buchan, *Domestic Medicine,* 201.
76. Mortality records from *Eclectic Repertory* and *Philadelphia Journal*; Daniel Drake, "Medical Topography," *Eclectic Repertory* 6, 2 (April, 1816), 140.
77. Mary Wistar, "Religious Diary for her Children," AMs, July 24, 1817; Historical Society of Pennsylvania, Philadelphia.
78. Drinker, "Diary," May 12, 1794; February 25 and March 1, 1801; April 22, 26 and May 3, 1802; Fisher, "Diary," January 12, 18 and February 4, 1794; Martha Ballard, "Diary," August 11, 1787, in Ulrich, *A Midwife's Tale,* 43.
79. Records from *Eclectic Repertory* and *Philadelphia Journal.*
80. Records from *Eclectic Repertory* and *Philadelphia Journal;* Daniel Drake, "Medical Topography," 137; Matthew Carey, *A Short Account of the Malignant Fever, Lately Prevalent in Philadelphia* (Philadelphia, 1794), Appendix; Samuel Jackson, M.D., "An Account of the Yellow or Malignant Fever, which appeared in the City of Philadelphia, in the Summer and Autumn of 1820, with some Observations on that disease," *Philadelphia Journal* 1 (1820), 313.
81. Currie, *An Historical Account,* 161; Drinker, "Diary," September 3 through October 19, 1783; William Harris, M.D., "Observations on the Cause, Character, and Treatment of the Intermittent Fever, as it appeared in the neighborhood of the Schuylkill, in the Autumns of 1820 and 1821," *Philadelphia Journal* 3, 6 (1821), 355; Drake, "Medical Topography," 138.
82. Emerson, "Medical Statistics," 144.
83. George W. Corner, *The Autobiography of Benjamin Rush, His "Travels through Life" together with his Commonplace Book* (Princeton, N.J., 1948), 80; Shryock, *Medicine and Society in America,* 100. Elizabeth Drinker was reluctant to inoculate her first-born, Sally, in the 1760s, but by the 1790s her grandchildren were rather routinely inoculated between their third and sixth month. After Philadelphia physicians began to recommend vaccination early in the nineteenth century, she urged her children to adopt the new practice. Drinker, "Diary," October 24, 1759; December 2, 1762; February 1 through March 1, 1763; December 16, 1765 through March 27, 1766; April 18, 1793; December 5, 1795; March 19, 1796; November 19, 1797; February 16 and October 31, 1799; April 3, 14, and 20, 1803; March 23, 31, and April 2, 1805.
84. Emerson, "Medical Statistics," 123; Drake, "Medical Topography," 138; records, *Eclectic Repertory* and *Philadelphia Journal.*
85. Benjamin Rush, *An Account of the Bilious Remitting Yellow Fever as it appeared in the City of Philadelphia, 1793* (Philadelphia, 1794), 204.

86. Melvin Yazawa, *From Colonies to Commonwealth: Familial Ideology and the Beginnings of the American Republic* (Baltimore, 1985), 144–153, 158–165. Yazawa's discussion is based on Benjamin Rush, "Medicine Among the Indians in North America," in Dagobert D. Runes, ed., *The Selected Writings of Benjamin Rush* (New York, 1947), and "Introductory Lecture on the Certainty of Medicine," Ms, Historical Society of Pennsylvania, Philadelphia, Lectures of Rush, Yi2/7400/F5.

87. Donald J. D'Elia, "Dr. Benjamin Rush and the American Medical Revolution," *Proceedings of the American Philosophical Society* 110, 4 (August 23, 1966): 227–234.

88. Rush, "Introductory Lecture," in Lectures, 26–27, in Yazawa, *From Colonies to Commonwealth*, 148.

89. Dr. Samuel Powel Griffitts, *Domestic Medicine, or a Treatise on the Prevention and Cure of Diseases by Regimen and Simple Medicines. Revised and Adapted to the Diseases and Climate of the United States of America* (Philadelphia, 1795), preface.

90. Ibid., preface, 156, 159, 416, 492.

91. For example, in 1796 Charles Caldwell, a Rush student who later founded two medical colleges in Kentucky, argued that Hydrocephalus Internus (infant water on the brain), Cynanche Trachealis (diphtheria or hives), and Diarrhoea Infantum (infant diarrhea) were essentially the same disease. Each was a manifestation of the same "febrile state" in a different part of the body, and each should be treated with copious evacuations: bloodletting, purgatives "of considerable activity," antimonials to induce perspiration and a vomit, diuretics to cause the flow of urine, and sialogogues to produce salivation. *An attempt to Establish the Original Sameness of three Phenomena of Fever, Principally Confined to Infants and Children* (Philadelphia, 1796), 10. In 1798 Henry Disbourgh of New Jersey wrote his dissertation on cholera morbus. Arguing that the condition was caused by morbid excitement of the stomach and bowels, he contended that it should be treated with bleeding and purging. Although he thought that gentle laxatives were probably safer for very young children, he reported that calomel was "claiming the pre-eminence over all other evacuants in this disease," and probably was "preferable to most other cathartics." *Inaugural Dissertation on Cholera Infantum* (Philadelphia, 1798), 23, 26.

92. Arthur H. Shaffer, *To Be an American: David Ramsay and the Making of the American Consciousness* (Columbia, S.C., 1991), 226–227.

93. Mansfield, *Memoirs*, 66–70, 94, 119–120.

94. Martha Laurens Ramsay, "Diary," August 26, 1796, in David Ramsay, *Memoirs*, 193–194.

95. Drinker, "Diary," April 16, 1796; March 26 and 27, 1802. Henry Drinker, a life-long patient of Benjamin Rush, was bled routinely every

spring. His wife, Elizabeth, however, preferred the advice of Dr. Adam Kuhn for treating the illnesses of herself, her children, and her grand-children. The entire Drinker family was aware that Rush's innovations in medical practice were controversial. Both Elizabeth and her son William were avid readers of "Peter Porcupine" and followed the conservative Englishman William Cobbett's attacks on Rush's political and medical views and the Republican physician's suit for libel in retaliation. When the case came to trial in late 1799, William attended the daily sessions and reported the details to his fascinated mother. In 1805, when Henry's treatment by Drs. Rush and Griffitts had frightening effects, Henry's brother, Daniel Drinker, received an anonymous letter warning him against the practices of the two physicians. Drinker, "Diary," October 6, 1797; December 14, 15, and 17, 1799; February 23, March 3 and 5, 1805.

96. Drinker, "Diary," August 31, September 3, and October 15, 1797; January 5, 1798; November 17, 1807.
97. Ballard, "Diary," March 5, 1801, in Ulrich, *A Midwife's Tale*, 257–258.
98. Park, "Diary," April 3–10, May, 1801.
99. Review of "The Mercurial Disease. An Inquiry into the history and nature of the disease produced in the human constitution by the Use of Mercury, with observations on its connexions with the Lues Venerea," by Andrew Mathias, Surgeon Extraordinary to the Queen, etc., etc., from the *London Monthly Review* (February, 1811) and "An Inaugural Dissertation on Mercury," in *Eclectic Repertory* 3 (1813), 459, 242–244.
100. Shryock, *Medicine and Society in America*, 125–127.
101. James Mease, M.D., *The Picture of Philadelphia, Giving an Account of its Origin, Increase, and Improvements in Arts, Sciences, Manufactures, Commerce and Revenue with a Compendious View of its Societies, Literary, Benevolent, Patriotic, and Religious* (Philadelphia, 1811), 46.
102. Nathaniel Chapman, M.D., "Prospectus," and "Thoughts on the Pathology and Treatment of Cynanche Trachealis, or Croup," *The Philadelphia Journal of the Medical and Physical Sciences* 1 (1820), viii–ix, 303–304, 311.
103. For example, John Eberle's *Treatise on the Disease and Physical Education of Children* (Cincinnati, Ohio, 1833) closely followed the advice of Dr. Dewees, but recommended even more strenuous bleeding and purging.
104. Dewees, *Treatise*, Part II, iv–vi, 264, 395.

Chapter 4

1. Nathan O. Hatch, *The Democratization of American Christianity* (New Haven, Conn., 1989), 5–11.

2. Patricia U. Bonomi, *Under the Cope of Heaven: Religion, Society, and Politics in Colonial America* (New York, 1986), 115–119.
3. Ibid., 118–119.
4. Hatch, *Democratization of American Christianity*, 9–10, 14, 40–45; for a discussion of Francis Hutcheson's concept of the moral sense, see chapter 1. Jon Butler has also stressed the melding of eclectic religious traditions and "fervently spiritual atmosphere" of the early republic, *Awash in a Sea of Faith: Christianizing the American People* (Cambridge, Mass., 1990), 236.
5. Robert Coles, *The Spiritual Life of Children* (Boston, 1990), 7, 100, 104; James W. Fowler has utilized stages of development outlined by Erik Erikson to map stages of faith from early childhood through adulthood, *Stages of Faith: The Psychology of Human Development and the Quest for Meaning* (San Francisco, 1981).
6. David D. Hall, *Worlds of Wonder, Days of Judgment: Popular Religious Belief in Early New England* (Cambridge, Mass., 1989), 36–38.
7. Daniel Drake to Charles Daniel Drake, Louisville, Kentucky, December 17, 1847; Daniel Drake to Margaret Austin Cross Drake, Louisville, Kentucky, January 7, 1848, in *Pioneer Life in Kentucky 1785–1800* (New York, 1948), 29–30, 111–114.
8. Daniel Drake to Charles Daniel Drake, Louisville, Kentucky, December 17, 1847; Daniel Drake to Mrs. [Harriet Drake] James Parker Campbell, Louisville, Kentucky, January 14, 15, 16, 17, and 18, 1848; in *Pioneer Life in Kentucky*, 27–28, 179, 193–194, 203–205.
9. Daniel Drake to Mrs. [Harriet Drake] James Parker Campbell, Louisville, Kentucky, January 17 and 18, 1848; Daniel Drake to Miss Belle Graham, Louisville, Kentucky, January 10 and 12, 1848; in *Pioneer Life in Kentucky*, 198, 121–124, 133, 136–137.
10. W.P. Strickland, *Autobiography of Peter Cartwright, the Backwoods Preacher* (New York, 1857), 17, 23–24, 27, 30, 34–38, 58–63.
11. Hatch, *Democratization of American Christianity*, 193.
12. J.B. Orendorff, "Pioneers of Blooming and Randolph Groves," n.d., Ts, McLean County Historical Society, Bloomington, Illinois.
13. Bonomi, *Under the Cope of Heaven*, 115.
14. Orendorff, "Pioneers of Blooming and Randolph Groves."
15. Paper delivered by Professor Calvin Stowe to the Semi-Colon Club, Cincinnati, Ohio, 1835 in Milton Rugoff, *The Beechers: An American Family in the Nineteenth Century* (New York, 1981), 222–223. Harriet Beecher Stowe's exploration of varieties of New England religious life in the 1790s, *Oldtown Folks* (Boston, 1869), in which the child protagonist experienced similar visions, was based on the recollections of Calvin Stowe.
16. Lucy Larcom, *A New England Girlhood Outlined from Memory* (Boston, 1986, first published in 1889), 8–9, 45–47, 49–51. These

descriptions of childhood experience by Calvin Stowe and Lucy Larcom would be understood by James W. Fowler as representative of the first stage of faith, "Intuitive-Projective Faith," (ages two to six or seven years), in which the child utilizes magical thinking to organize sensory experience into meaning units, forming fragments of stories and images given by the culture into his or her own clusters of association. *Stages of Faith,* 123–129.

17. Allan Kulikoff, *Tobacco and Slaves: The Development of Southern Cultures in the Chesapeake, 1680–1800* (Chapel Hill, N.C., 1986), 346–351; Lawrence W. Levine, *Black Culture and Black Consciousness: Afro-American Thought from Slavery to Freedom* (New York, 1977), 7, 37, 39, 63, 80.

18. Levine, *Black Culture and Black Consciousness,* 7–8, 32, 36–37, 45, 78, 93.

19. Hatch, *Democratization of American Christianity,* 102.

20. Dee E. Andrews, "Religion and Social Change: The Rise of the Methodists," in *Shaping a National Culture: The Philadelphia Experience, 1750–1800,* edited by Catherine E. Hutchins (Winterthur, Del., 1994), 151–152; Gary B. Nash, *Forging Freedom: The Formation of Philadelphia's Black Community, 1720–1840* (Cambridge, Mass., 1988), 95–99, 109–133.

21. Bonomi, *Under the Cope of Heaven,* 116–117.

22. Edwin Wilbur Rice, *The Sunday-School Movement, 1780–1917, and American Sunday-School Union* (Philadelphia, 1917), 22.

23. Benjamin Rush, *A Plan for the Establishment of Public Schools and the Diffusion of Knowledge in Pennsylvania; to Which Are Added, Thoughts upon the Mode of Education, Proper in a Republic* (Philadelphia, 1786). For a discussion of Rush's education goals, see chapter 2.

24. Benjamin Rush to Richard Price, 25 May, 1786; "To the Ministers of the Gospel of All Denominations: An Address . . . , June 21, 1788; in David Freeman Hawke, *Benjamin Rush, Revolutionary Gadfly* (New York, 1971), 341, 352–353, 359.

25. Minutes of the Board of Visitors, First Day Society, Ms 1:1791–1835, December 19, 1790, and "Constitution," Presbyterian Historical Society, Philadelphia.

26. First Day Society, "Constitution," Ms, and Minutes, October 11, 1791 in American Sunday School Union, *A Century of the First Day or Sunday School Society, A Sketch of the Beginning of Sunday Schools in Philadelphia* (Philadelphia, 1891).

27. George W. Corner, ed., *The Autobiography of Benjamin Rush, His "Travels through Life" together with his Commonplace Book for 1789–1813* (Princeton, N.J., 1948), 216.

28. First Day Society Minutes, "Rules," February 1, 1791.

29. First Day Society Minutes, "Rules," February 1, 1791. In 1792, after Benjamin Rush left the rotating board and was replaced by printers Charles Cist, William Young, and Thomas Dobson, books ordered for the schools taught "natural religion," for example, Dr. Joannes Florentius Martinet, *Cathechism of Nature: for the Use of Children* (Philadelphia, 1791), George Riley, *Beauties of Creation or, A New Moral System of Natural History* (Philadelphia, 1796), and *The Oeconomy of Human Life* (Philadelphia, 1795). Reward premiums were "enlightened" children's literature: Anna Laetitia Aikin Barbauld, *Lessons for Children* (Philadelphia, 1788) and Thomas Day, *History of Sandford and Merton* (Philadelphia, 1788). In 1794 the rule limiting textbooks to the Bible was simply crossed out, although it was reinstated in 1801. First Day Society Minutes.

30. First Day Society Minutes, January 2, 1795; April 5, 1799; "Handbill," December 1799.

31. First Day Society Minutes, July 5, 1805; February 2, March 3, June 3, 1808; "Special Report to Society Members," July 19, 1810.

32. The Rev. Robert May, Minutes of the First Sabbath School in Philadelphia, Ms, October, 1811 to January, 1812; October 20, 1811; Presbyterian Historical Society, Philadelphia.

33. May, Minutes, November 10, 1811.

34. May, Minutes, November 24, December 13, 1811.

35. May, Minutes, January 19, 1812.

36. Rush, *Commonplace Book,* 310.

37. May, Minutes, "Roll."

38. Thomas James Shepherd, *History of the First Presbyterian Church, Northern Liberties, Philadelphia* (Philadelphia, 1882), 36, 41, 57.

39. The conflict caused by Patterson's revival among Philadelphia Presbyterians has been analyzed by Gordon Link in "The Politics of Religious Institutions in the Age of Jackson, The Presbyterian Schism of 1838, and the Crisis of Evangelical Liberalism" (Ph.D. dissertation, University of California, Berkeley, 1977), 69–70, 74. *The First Report of the Philadelphia Sunday and Adult School Union* (Philadelphia, 1818), 11, 13.

40. *First Report,* PSASU, 11, 13, 22–24.

41. Rice, *The Sunday School Movement,* 97; *First Report,* PSASU, 5, 11–24.

42. *The Third Report of the Philadelphia Sunday and Adult School Union* (Philadelphia, 1820), 46, 9, 4.

43. First Day Society Minutes, June 20 and 25, July 25, 1815; June 7, 1816; January 2, 1818; April 2 and October 1, 1819; *Third Report,* PSASU, 9.

44. Lynne Templeton Brickley, "Sarah Pierce's Litchfield Academy" in *To Ornament Their Minds: Sarah Pierce's Litchfield Female Academy, 1792–1833* (Litchfield, Conn., 1993), 20, 23, 28–29; Maryann Bacon, "Journal written in the 15 year of her age, 1802," June 12 and 27; Lucy

Sheldon, "Commonplace Book," 1802–1811; "Two Cousins, a play by Miss Sarah Pierce, n.d.; Sarah Beekman, "Journal," 1811; AMs, Litchfield Historical Society, Litchfield, Conn.; Catherine Van Schaack, "Journal," 1809, AMs, New York Historical Society, New York.

45. Glee Krueger, "Paper and Silk: The Ornamental Arts of the Litchfield Female Academy, 1792–1833" in *To Ornament their Minds*, 82–97; Stanley Elkins and Eric McKitrick, *The Age of Federalism: The Early American Republic, 1788–1800* (New York, 1993), 626–628; Maryann Bacon, "Journal;" Lucy Sheldon, "Commonplace Book;" Catherine Van Schaak, "Journal," summer, 1809.

46. Joan D. Hedrick, *Harriet Beecher Stowe, a life* (New York, 1994), 24–25; Brickley, "Sarah Pierce's Litchfield Female Academy," 58; Caroline M. Broadman, "Journal Book," 1815, Ts, 9, Litchfield Historical Society, Litchfield, Conn.

47. Broadman, "Journal Book," 13, 22, 38.

48. Norman Fiering, *Jonathan Edwards's Moral Thought and Its British Context* (Chapel Hill, N.C., 1981), 201, 207–210; Jonathan Edwards, "A Faithful Narrative of the Surprising Work of God," in *Basic Writings* (New York, 1966), 97–105.

49. Rugoff, *The Beechers*, 10–11, 36–38.

50. Rugoff, *The Beechers*, 4–5, 410.

51. Rugoff, *The Beechers*, 69–71. Harriet Beecher Stowe recognized the influence of a democratic society on her father's theology in the character of the Rev. Avery delineated in "Our Minister in Cloudland," (Litchfield), *Oldtown Folks*, in *Stowe, Three Novels* (New York, 1982), 1308–1323.

52. "Internal Regulations for the Sunday Schools," PSASU, reprinted in each annual report, 1818–1832. A historian such as Paul Boyer, who views urban Sunday schools as means of "social control," emphasizes this effort to instill orderly habits. *Urban Masses and Moral Order in America, 1820–1920* (Cambridge, Mass., 1976).

53. A thorough and judicious discussion of nineteenth-century Sunday schools can be found in Anne M. Boylan, *Sunday School: The Formation of an American Institution, 1790–1880* (Yale, 1988). Because of the post-Revolutionary focus on the plasticity of childhood, Boylan argues that "Children . . . were easier to reach with the message of evangelical Christianity and offered greater chances for success," 15–16, 138.

54. J.A. James, *The Sunday School Teacher's Guide* (Philadelphia, The Sunday and Adult School Union, n.d.), 17.

55. "Internal Regulations for the Sunday Schools."

56. Philadelphia Sunday and Adult School Union, *Fourth Annual Report* (Philadelphia, 1821), 81, 14–15.

57. *The Second Report of the Philadelphia Sunday and Adult School Union* (Philadelphia, 1819), 57, 60. In the 1790s, during the crisis of British

reaction to the French Revolution, the focus of British Sunday schools, like that of the entire British reform impulse, was distorted by the pressure of external events. Literary ladies like Sarah Trimmer and Hannah More, both firm supporters and flatterers of the establishment, were placed in the ironic position of having to defend their Sunday school experiments from conservative attack. Both went to great lengths to insist their educational projects were not fomenting sedition among the lower orders, and both devoted prodigious energy to producing literature for Sunday schools that was deliberately counterrevolutionary. Ford K. Brown, *Fathers of the Victorians, the Age of Wilberforce* (Cambridge, 1961), 155–233.

58. Leigh Richmond, *Little Jane, the Young Cottager* (Philadelphia: The Sunday and Adult School Union, 1822), 8.

59. Leigh Richmond, *The Dairyman's Daughter* (Philadelphia: The Sunday and Adult School Union, 1819), 11, 22–23.

60. Bills of Mortality published by various urban Boards of Health in *The Eclectic Repertory and Analytical Review,* vols. I–XI (Philadelphia, 1811–1821).

61. William P. Dewees, M.D., *Treatise on the Physical and Medical Treatment of Children* (Philadelphia, 1825).

62. The Rev. Basil Wood, *A Memoir of Bowyer Smith, a Pious Child* (Philadelphia: The Sunday and Adult School Union, 1820), 28.

63. *A Pleasing Account of George Crosby* (Philadelphia: The Sunday and Adult School Union, 1823), preface.

64. Coles, *The Spiritual Life of Children,* 100–101. According to James W. Fowler, in the first stage of faith, the fantasy life of the child can be exploited through images that create "fear, rigidity, and the brutalization of souls." Images of sin, hell, and the devil may bring a conversion experience by age seven or eight, but also may lead to "precocious identity formation," as the child takes on an inappropriate adult faith identity. By the age of nine or ten, however, the child may enter a second stage of faith, "Mythic–Literal Faith," in which he or she is able to sort out real from make believe and generate stories. At this age, in which the child constructs a linear, orderly world, story can be utilized by the child to give coherence and meaning to his or her real experience. *Stages of Faith,* 132–149.

65. Louisa Jane Trumbell, "L.J. Trumbell's Book," AMs July 9, 1832; reading list recorded 1833, February 7–10, 1833; American Antiquarian Society, Worcester, Massachusetts.

66. James Riker, Jr., "Journal Commencing Dec. 11th, 1836. To which is prefixed a summary of events from May 1822 to the above date. Designed for the private use of James Riker, Jr.," AMs copied by the author May 19, 1846; New York Historical Society, New York. Accord-

ing to James W. Fowler, a third stage of faith, "Synthetic-Conventional Faith," may emerge with adolescence, as the individual seeks a supreme being who knows, accepts, and confirms the self. In this stage, expectations and values of others are internalized, as the individual finds comfort in accepting community norms. *Stages of Faith,* 149–173.

67. Mary Lorrain Peters, "Diary," AMs, March 19, 20, and 26, May 15, 22, and 29, 1837; November 11, December 3 and 16, 1838; January 13, 1839; New York Historical Society, New York.

68. Philadelphia Sunday and Adult School Union, *Seventh Annual Report,* (Philadelphia, 1824), 90, "Constitution."

69. The American Sunday School Union, *First Annual Report* (Philadelphia, 1825), 32–33.

70. Bonomi, *Under the Cope of Heaven,* 217–222; Henry F. May, *Ideas, Faiths, and Feelings: Essays on American Intellectual and Religious History, 1952–1982* (New York, 1983); J.C.D. Clark, *The Language of Liberty, 1600–1832: Political discourse and social dynamics in the Anglo-American world* (Cambridge, 1994).

71. Committee of Publications, "Minutes and Reports, 1825–1829," Ms, Presbyterian Historical Society, Philadelphia; W.F. Lloyd, *The Teacher's Manual; or Hints to a Teacher on Being Appointed to the Charge of a Sunday-School Class* (Philadelphia: The American Sunday School Union, Revised by the Committee of Publications, 1825), preface, 48, 116–117.

72. Committee of Publications, "Commonplace Book," 1826–32, Ms, Presbyterian Historical Society, Philadelphia; *Memoir of Ann Eliza Starr of Connecticut* (Philadelphia: The American Sunday School Union, Revised by the Committee of Publications, 1827).

73. Committee of Publications, "Commonplace Book"; *Early Piety* (Philadelphia: The American Sunday School Union, Revised by the Committee of Publications, 1827), preface, 64. A copy of this book and others annotated in pencil by members of the Committee of Publications can be found in the collection of children's literature in the Rare Books Room of the Free Library, Philadelphia.

74. Committee of Publications, "Commonplace Book"; *Winter Evenings' Conversations between a Father and his Children* (Philadelphia: The American Sunday School Union, Revised by the Committee of Publications, 1826).

75. *The Union Primer or First Book for Children, compiled for the American Sunday School Union and Fitted for the Use of Schools in the United States* (Philadelphia: The American Sunday School Union, Revised by the Committee of Publications, 1826), 21, 35.

76. *Election Day* (Philadelphia: The American Sunday School Union, written for the Committee of Publications, 1827), 30, 45, 97.

77. Anna Reed, *Life of George Washington* (Philadelphia: The American Sunday School Union, Written for and revised by the Committee of Publications, 1829), 104, 21, 136, 208–209.
78. Rugoff, *The Beechers*, 75, 44–52.
79. Kathryn Kish Sklar, *Catherine Beecher: A Study in American Domesticity* (New Haven, 1973), 28–40. James W. Fowler describes a fourth stage of faith, "Individuative-Reflective Faith," reached by some in young adulthood, in which the individual becomes able to view inherited assumptions and values with critical awareness and to relocate authority within the self. *Stages of Faith,* 179–182.
80. Rugoff, *The Beechers*, 58–61; Sklar, *Catherine Beecher*, 78, 80–88. For a thorough discussion of eighteenth-century precedents, see Chapter 1.
81. Catherine Beecher, *A Treatise on Domestic Economy* (New York, 1977; first published Boston, 1841), 2–4, 6, 9, 14.
82. Beecher, *Treatise*, 17, 27–28, 39–40, 70, 124–125, 148, 153, 214–223. Although Richard L. Bushman in *The Refinement of America* (New York, 1992) proposes a tension between gentility, which he sees based on courtly antecedents, and work, I would once again point out the Whig antecedents of American genteel values, which allowed Americans to reconcile not only republican ideology but also a bourgeois emphasis on work with their passion for refinement.
83. "Horace Bushnell," in Allen Johnson, ed., *Dictionary of American Biography* vol. 3 (New York, 1929), 350–351, 354.
84. Horace Bushnell, *Views of Christian Nurture* (Hartford, Conn., 1847), 6, 8, 10, 13, 15.
85. Bushnell, *Christian Nurture*, 21–11, 27, 52–53, 209. In the 1850s this kind of thinking would make possible the plans of an original thinker like Charles Loring Brace, who founded the Children's Aid Society, to remove children of the urban poor to rural homes in the country and then the West.
86. Rugoff, *The Beechers*, 95, 98, 102, 105–106, 108–111, 215; Hedrick, *Harriet Beecher Stowe*, 26–27, 155–156. James W. Fowler posits a fifth stage of faith, "Conjunctive Faith," reached by some in mid-life, in which an individual is able to view many sides of an issue simultaneously, relinquishing ideological systems and clear boundaries of identity, and reconciling the conscious with the unconscious, in order to be able to encounter other traditions and differing points of view. *Stages of Faith,* 183–198.
87. Hedrick, 186–193. The Anglo-American "romantic" view of the child is perhaps best expressed in William Wordsworth's "Ode on Intimations of Immorality from Recollections of Early Childhood," George K. Anderson, Homer A. Watt, and George B. Woods, eds., *The Literature of England* vol. 2 (New York, 1948), 160–162. Harriet Beecher Stowe,

Uncle Tom's Cabin, or Life Among the Lowly (New York, 1986; first published, 1852), 409–411; *The Minister's Wooing* (New York, 1982; first published, 1857); *Oldtown Folks* (New York, 1982; first published, 1869); and *Poganuc People* (Hartford, Conn., 1987; first published, 1878).

Chapter 5

1. A rich literature has explored the history of common schools, especially in Massachusetts. "Revisionist" historians of the 1960s and 1970s, who studied urban issues and stressed the concept of "social control," linked the emergence of public school systems to industrial manufacturing, for example, Michael B. Katz, *The Irony of Early School Reform: Educational Innovation in Mid-Nineteenth Century Massachusetts* (Cambridge, Mass., 1968); Stanley K. Schultz, *The Culture Factory: Boston Public Schools, 1789–1860* (New York, 1973). Carl F. Kaestle, however, has argued that, (1) beginning about 1750, school enrollment increased in rural areas before the establishment of public school systems, and (2) innovation in public schools leading to centralized, bureaucratized state systems occurred in commercial, rather than manufacturing centers. Carl F. Kaestle, *The Evolution of an Urban School System: New York City, 1750–1850* (Cambridge, Mass., 1980); ed., *Joseph Lancaster and the Monitorial School Movement* (New York, 1973); with Maris A. Vinovskis, *Education and Social Change in Nineteenth-century Massachusetts* (Cambridge, Mass., 1980); *Pillars of the Republic: Common Schools and American Society, 1780–1860* (New York, 1983).

2. Christopher Clark, *The Roots of Rural Capitalism, Western Massachusetts, 1780–1860* (Ithaca, New York, 1990), 60, 63–64, 88–91, 115.

3. Kaestle, *Pillars of the Republic,* 10, 25, 27.

4. Nahum Jones, "Diaries," AMs, Vol. 1, April, 1779; June, August and November, 1780; February, March, and August, 1783; March, 1784; August, 1803; American Antiquarian Society, Worcester, Massachusetts.

5. Jones, "Diary," November 10, 1800; January 1 and 5, February 20, December 25, 1801.

6. Jones, "Diary," September 28, November 2, 1801; May 3 and 30, August 20, September 10, 1802. For a discussion of other careers, see Joyce Appleby, "The Cultural Underpinnings of Capitalist Development in the Early National Period," unpublished paper presented at the University of California, Los Angeles, February 27, 1995.

7. Milton Rugoff, *The Beechers: An American Family in the Nineteenth Century* (New York, 1981), 113–115.

8. Horace Greeley, *Recollections of a Busy Life* (New York, 1873; first edition, 1868), 38, 41–44, 46–47, 62.

9. Samuel B. Parris, "Journal," AMs, March 24, 27, and 29, 1817; March 9 and 15, 1818; American Antiquarian Society Library, Worcester, Massachusetts.

10. Sally Ripley, "Journal," AMs, July 15, 16, 20, 21, 24, 28, and 30, August 16, September 15, 20, 23, 29, 31, 1799; June 25, August 1, November 3, 1800; April 26, 1801; American Antiquarian Society, Worcester, Massachusetts.

11. Kathryn Kish Sklar, *Catherine Beecher: A Study in American Domesticity* (New Haven, Conn., 1973), 18; Lynne Templeton Brickley, "Sarah Pierce's Litchfield Female Academy" in *To Ornament Their Minds: Sarah Pierce's Litchfield Female Academy, 1792–1833* (Litchfield, Conn., 1993), 27; "Sarah Pierce's Litchfield Female Academy, 1792–1833," Ph.D. dissertation, Harvard University, 1985, and Emily Noyes Vanderpoel, *More Chronicles of a Pioneer School: From 1792 to 1833* (New York, 1927), 9, in Joan D. Hedrick, *Harriet Beecher Stowe, a life* (New York, 1994), 26–27; Harriet Beecher Stowe, *Oldtown Folks*, in *Stowe, Three Novels* (New York, 1982), 1299, 1301.

12. Laura Maria Wolcott, "Journal, December 6, 1826—March 7, 1827," Ts, 4–5, 41, 52, 66, 72, 76, 79, Litchfield Historical Society, Litchfield, Connecticut; Brickley, "Litchfield Female Academy," 565, in Hedrick, *Harriet Beecher Stowe*, 33.

13. John Mack Faragher, *Sugar Creek: Life on the Illinois Prairie* (New Haven, Conn., 1986), 43–50. Historians who have discussed yeoman culture in the South include Allan Kulikoff, *The Agrarian Origins of American Capitalism* (Charlottesville, Va., 1992); Rachel N. Klein, *Unification of a Slave State: The Rise of the Planter Class in the Southern Carolina Backcountry, 1760–1808* (Chapel Hill, N.C., 1990); Steven Hahn, *The Roots of Southern Populism: Yeoman Farmers and the Transformation of the Georgia Upcountry, 1850–1890* (New York, 1983).

14. Daniel Drake to Harriet Echo, December 15, 1847; Daniel Drake to Charles Daniel Drake, December 17, 1847; Daniel Drake to Mrs. Alexander Hamilton McGuffey, January 13, 1848; in Daniel Drake, M.D., *Pioneer Life in Kentucky, 1785–1800* (New York, 1948), 8, 26–27, 33–34, 36, 143–150, 160. Edward D. Mansfield, *Memoirs of the Life and Services of Daniel Drake, M.D.* (Cincinnati, Ohio, 1860), 21, 46.

15. William G. McLoughlin, *Cherokee Renascence in the New Republic* (Princeton, N.J., 1986), 8, 21–25, 27, 34–37.

16. McLoughlin, *Cherokee Renascence*, 47, 70–73. Moravian Mission Diaries, 1800–1810, Ts, translated by Dr. Carl Maelshagen, March 28, April 2, 1801; June 5 and 23, 1803; August 15, October 8, 1804; August 15, 1806; Georgia Department of Archives and History, Atlanta.

17. Moravian Mission Diaries, February 1, May 31, June 1, September 22, October 28, November 6, 1805; March 14, May 7, July 16, 1806. Daniel B. Thorp, *The Moravian Community in Colonial North Carolina: Pluralism on the Southern Frontier* (Knoxville, Tenn., 1989), 53–57. It is interesting to point out that Chulio had three wives, the first a full–blood Cherokee, the second a white woman, Clarinda Ellington, who had been captured in Tennessee in 1792 when she was eleven, and the third a black slave after Clarinda returned with her children to her Kentucky relatives in 1804. His children at the Moravian school in 1806–1807 were probably full-blood Cherokees. McLoughlin, *Cherokee Renascence*, 343–345.

18. Moravian Mission Diaries, June 20, 1805; December 25, 1806; April 19, 1807; May 5, December 26 and 27, 1808; February 21, August 20, December 26, 1809; January 7, February 10, May 20 and 31, June 15, July 2, August 13, 1810. McLoughlin, *Cherokee Renascence*, 109–111, 124–128, 141, 151, 159–163, 167, 177, 181, 300–301, 367–368, 400, 448–451. In 1835, convinced that removal was reality, Major and John Ridge, Elias Boudinot, and David Vann signed the Treaty of New Echota, ceding their homeland for five million dollars in exchange for reestablishment in lands that would become northeastern Oklahoma. Still exhibiting faith in education, they incurred the deep resentment of other Cherokee factions who endured the Trail of Tears, and in 1839 John and Major Ridge and Elias Boudinot were murdered. James W. Parins, *John Rollin Ridge: His Life and Works* (Lincoln, Neb., 1991), 4–12, 22, 25, 29–31.

19. Jeremiah Austill, "Partial Autobiography," Ts, and Margaret Ervin Austill, "Early Life," Ts, 2214–Z, Southern Historical Collection, University of North Carolina, Chapel Hill.

20. Austill, "Early Life." McLoughlin, *Cherokee Renascence*, 191–194, 203, 205.

21. Kaestle, *Pillars of the Republic,* 183–185.

22. Faragher, *Sugar Creek,* 4, 27–31, 33, 124–125.

23. Maria Dawson Paist, "Reminiscences," Ts, n.d., McLean County Historical Society, Bloomington, Illinois. Don Munson, Martin A. Wyckoff and Greg Koos, *The Illustrated History of McLean County* (Transactions of the McLean County Historical Society, VIII, 1982), 21, 58–59.

24. Eliza Clitherall, "Autobiography and Diary," 1751–1860, AMs and Ts, Vol. I, 46; Vol. II, 6–7; Vol. III, 7; Vol. VI, 31; Vol. VII, 38; Vol. VIII, 7, 33; Southern Historical Collection, University of North Carolina Library, Chapel Hill.

25. Thorp, *Moravian Community,* 17, 68, 71–73; *A Laudable Example for Others: The Moravians and their Town of Salem* (Winston-Salem, N.C., n.d.), 16–18; Dr. James Stuart, "Journal," 1814, AMs, 2,295-Z, South-

ern Historical Collection, University of North Carolina Library, Chapel Hill.

26. Schultz, *The Culture Factory*, 8–25.

27. Carl F. Kaestle, *The Evolution of an Urban School System: New York City, 1750–1850* (Cambridge, Mass., 1973), 2–12; James Pyle Wickersham, *A History of Education in Pennsylvania, Private and Public, Elementary and High from the time the Swedes settled on the Delaware to the Present Day* (Lancaster, Penn., 1886); *The Rise and Progress of the Young Ladies' Academy of Philadelphia: Containing a Number of Public Examinations and Commencements; The Charter and Bye-Laws; Likewise a Number of Orations delivered by the Young Ladies, and several by the Trustees of said Institution* (Philadelphia, 1794).

28. John C. Thomas, "Memoirs of Stephen Allen," (New York, 1927) Ts, 5, 8, 17, New York Historical Society, New York.

29. First Day Society, "Handbill," Ms., December 1799, Presbyterian Historical Society, Philadelphia.

30. Kaestle, *Evolution of an Urban School System*, 81–84; J. Thomas Scharf and Thompson Westcott, *History of Philadelphia. 1609–1884* (Philadelphia, 1884).

31. Joseph Lancaster, *Improvements in Education as it Respects the Industrious Classes of the Community* (London, 1806).

32. Sean Wilentz, *Chants Democratic: New York City & the Rise of the American Working Class, 1788–1850* (New York, 1984), 33–34.

33. Priscilla Ferguson Clement, "The Philadelphia Welfare Crisis of the 1820s," *Pennsylvania Magazine of History and Biography* 105, 2 (April, 1981): 150–154.

34. Charles Calvert Ellis, "Lancasterian Schools in Philadelphia" (Ph.D. dissertation, University of Pennsylvania, 1907), 38–39.

35. Scharf and Westcott, *History of Philadelphia*, 593–594.

36. Kaestle, *Evolution of an Urban School System*, 84–87.

37. Carl F. Kaestle, ed., *Joseph Lancaster and the Monitorial School Movement* (New York, 1973), 12, 15, 37, 40; Nita Katherine Pyburn, "The Public School System of Charleston before 1860," *The South Carolina Historical Magazine* LXI (1960): 88.

38. New Bern Academy Museum; Mary Ellen Gadski, *The History of the New Bern Academy* (New Bern, N.C., 1986), 62–63, 65.

39. Kaestle, *Evolution of an Urban School System*, 174–175; *Pillars of the Republic*, 47–48.

40. Ellis, "Lancasterian Schools," 55.

41. *The Seventh Report of the Philadelphia Sunday and Adult School Union* (Philadelphia, 1824), 68–69; Scharf and Westcott, *History of Philadelphia*, 593–594.

42. Robert B. Downs, *Heinrich Pestalozzi: Father of Modern Pedagogy* (Boston, 1975), 17, 21, 24–29, 32, 49, 67–76, 109–111, 119–121; Johann Heinrich Pestalozzi, *How Gertrude Teaches Her Children: An Attempt to Help Mothers to Teach their Own Children and An Account of the Method,* translated by Lucy E. Holland and Francis C. Turner (London, 1915); Edgar W. Knight, ed., *Reports on European Education* (New York, 1930).

43. Clark, *Roots of Rural Capitalism,* 121, 125–126, 135–138, 141–148, 180–189, 217.

44. Jonathan Messerli, *Horace Mann* (New York, 1972), 15–17, 27, 30, 62–65, 85–88, 91, 105–108, 117–118, 128, 136, 221, 236–241.

45. Ibid., 236, 248–249, 251, 264, 292–293.

46. Ibid., 309–315.

47. Anne M. Boylan, *Sunday School: The Formation of an American Institution, 1790–1880* (New Haven, Conn., 1988), 54–59.

48. Kaestle, *The Evolution of an Urban School System,* 121–125, 147–158.

49. Gary B. Nash, *Forging Freedom: The Formation of Philadelphia's Black Community, 1720–1840,* 202–210.

50. Kaestle, *Pillars of the Republic,* 172–173, 177–179; Schultz, *The Culture Factory,* 157–205.

51. Kaestle and Vinovskis, *Education and Social Change in Nineteenth-century Massachusetts,* 56–66, 246–247; Kaestle, *Pillars of the Republic,* 123–130; The Rev. John S.C. Abbott, quoted in Schultz, *The Culture Factory,* 57–59, 67–68.

52. Ralph Waldo Emerson, *Journals* [September 14, 1839] in Stephen E. Whicher, ed., *Selections from Ralph Waldo Emerson* (Boston, 1957), 136; see also Messerli, *Horace Mann,* 347–348. Kaestle and Vinovskis, *Education and Social Change in Nineteenth-century Massachusetts,* 178–181, 216–230.

53. Faragher, *Sugar Creek,* 179–187, 205, 211.

54. Helen M. Cavanaugh, *Funk of Funk's Grove* (Bloomington, Ill., 1952), 10–13, 40, 50, 82, 160.

55. *Semi-Centennial History of the Illinois State Normal University, 1857–1907* (Normal, Ill., 1907), 33, 192, 195.

56. Kaestle, *Pillars of the Republic,* 197, 202–203.

57. Laylon Wayne Jordan, "Education for Community: C.G. Memminger and the Origination of Common Schools in Ante-bellum Charleston," *South Carolina Historical Magazine* 83, 2 (April, 1982), 100–102, 109, 112–114.

58. James Monroe Adams, "Reminiscence Book," AMs, 1911, 102–103, 106, 110–112.

Chapter 6

1. Daniel Drake to Charles Daniel Drake, Louisville, Kentucky, December 17, 1847; Daniel Drake to Alexander Hamilton McGuffey, Louisville, Kentucky, December 18, 20, 21, and 30, 1847; Daniel Drake to James Parker Campbell, Louisville, Kentucky, December 31, 1847; in Daniel Drake, M.D., edited by Emmet Field Horine, M.D., *Pioneer Life in Kentucky, 1785–1800* (New York, 1948), 36–38, 45–49, 57–60, 64–67, 74–79, 86.

2. Daniel Drake to Alexander Hamilton McGuffey, Louisville, Kentucky, December 21 and 30, 1847 in Drake, *Pioneer Life,* 64, and Edward D. Mansfield, *Memoirs of the Life and Services of Daniel Drake, M.D.* (Cincinnati, 1860), 23–24.

3. Daniel Drake to Margaret Austin Cross Drake, Louisville, Kentucky, January 7, 1848 in Drake, *Pioneer Life,* 93–109.

4. "Diary kept by Elizabeth Fuller," n.d., quoted in Thomas Dublin, *Women at Work: The Transformation of Work and Community in Lowell, Massachusetts, 1826–1860* (New York, 1979), 14–15.

5. Laurel Thatcher Ulrich, *A Midwife's Tale: The Life of Martha Ballard, Based on Her Diary, 1785–1812* (New York, 1991), 76, 79, 81, 211, 221, 231; Session on "Domestic Cloth Production and the Gender Division of Labor in North America," Organization of American Historians, April 16, 1993.

6. Christopher Clark, *The Roots of Rural Capitalism: Western Massachusetts, 1780–1860* (Ithaca, New York, 1990), 73–74, 88, 90.

7. Horace Greeley, *Recollections of a Busy Life* (New York, 1873; first edition, 1868), 38–40, 48–49, 57–58.

8. Clark, *Rural Capitalism,* 97.

9. Alan Dawley, *Class and Community: The Industrial Revolution in Lynn* (Cambridge, Mass., 1976), 17–18, 20–21, 27, 29.

10. W.J. Rorabaugh, *The Craft Apprentice: From Franklin to the Machine Age in America* (New York, 1986), 4–5, 25, 29–30; Sharon Salinger, "Artisans, Journeymen, and the Transformation of Labor in Late Eighteenth-Century Philadelphia," *The William and Mary Quarterly,* 3rd ser., vol. XL. no. 1 (January, 1983), 69–74; Sean Wilentz, *Chants Democratic: New York City & the Rise of the American Working Class, 1788–1850* (New York, 1984), 33.

11. John C. Thomas, "Memoirs of Stephen Allen," Ts, November, 1825, 21–23, 28–30, 32–43; June, 1826, 37–38; New York Historical Society, New York.

12. Quoted in Rorabaugh, *The Craft Apprentice,* 41–43, 49.

13. Wilentz, *Chants Democratic,* 87–96.

14. Ibid., 30–31, 42, 45–47.

15. Ibid., 33, 51–52, 57; "Circular of the New York Typographical Society, July 13, 1811, in New York State Department of Labor, *Annual Report of*

Bureau of Labor Statistics, 1911 (Albany, 1912), 67–69, in Robert H. Bremner, ed., *Children and Youth in America: A Documentary History, Vol. I: 1600–1865* (Cambridge, Mass., 1970), 162.

16. Gary B. Nash and Jean R. Soderlund, *Freedom by Degrees: Emancipation in Pennsylvania and its Aftermath* (New York, 1991), 3, 103, 108, 174–179.

17. Elizabeth Drinker, "Diary," AMs, October 18, 19, and 28, November 2 and 7, December 6, 10, and 26, 1794; May 3 and 6, 1795; March 30 and August 6, 1796; February 11 and July 5, 1801; November 14, 1802; March 20, 1805; February 6 and 8, and September 23, 1805; Historical Society of Pennsylvania, Philadelphia.

18. Bremner, ed., *Children and Youth in America,* vol. I, 631, 633–639.

19. Female Orphan Society, "Minutes, 1814–1823," Ms., Constitution, Rules and Regulations, January 5, March 21, May 2, August 1, 1815; May 7, 1817; Receipt for children received from Almshouse, March 1, 1815; "Memorial to Legislature" (after fire in the asylum in which twenty-three children died), January 26, 1822; *The Orphan Society of Philadelphia, 1815–1940* (125th Anniversary Pamphlet), 3; Historical Society of Pennsylvania, Philadelphia.

20. Female Orphan Society, Book of Indentures, and "Minutes," March 2 and May 4, 1819; December 16 and 31, 1822; February 4 and December 23, 1823; August 3 and October 5, 1824; January 22, 1827; February 5, 1828; and March 2, 1830.

21. Letter of Smith Wilkinson to George White, May 30, 1835, in George S. White, *Memoir of Samuel Slater* (Philadelphia, 1836), 76; *Massachusetts Spy,* May 13, 20, and 27, 1818; in Bremner, *Children and Youth in America,* 145–149, 175–177.

22. Albert Gallatin, "Manufactures, April 19, 1810," *American State Papers, Finance, II* (1832), 427; *Niles' Weekly Register,* October 5, 1816, 86–87; White, *Samuel Slater,* 107–108; "An act in addition to an act, entitled "An act relating to masters and servants, and apprentices,'" 1813—ch. 2, *Public Statutes of Connecticut, Oct. 1808-May 1819,* May Session, 1813 (Hartford, 1813), 117–118; in Bremner, *Children and Youth in America,* 171, 174–175, 177–181.

23. Clark, *Roots of Rural Capitalism,* 121, 125, 146–148, 152–153, 155, 160, 166–167, 177, 180–189.

24. Dublin, *Women and Work,* 4, 26–27, 31, 43.

25. Lucy Larcom, *A New England Girlhood* (Boston, 1986; first edition, 1889), 146, 150–157, 209–211.

26. Harriet Hanson Robinson, *Loom and Spindle* (1898), 84–85; in Dublin, *Women and Work,* 25, 99.

27. Larcom, *A New England Girlhood,* 153; Brian C. Mitchell, *The Paddy Camps: The Irish of Lowell, 1821–61* (Urbana, Ill., 1988), 116; "An act

to provide for the better instruction of youth employed in manufacturing establishment," 1836—ch. 245, *Laws of Massachusetts, Jan. 1834-Apr. 1836* (Boston, 1836), 950–951, Summary of school attendance laws enacted before 1860 adapted from U.S. Bureau of Labor, *Report on Condition of Woman and Child Wage-Earners in the United States,* VI, 208–209, and *Boston Daily Times,* July 16, 1839 in Bremner, *Children and Youth in America,* 621–622, 624.

28. Rorabaugh, *The Craft Apprentice,* 61, 63.
29. David Clapp, Jr., "Diary," AMs, May 13, July 19, and December 15, 1822; May 7 and 29, July 28, 1823; American Antiquarian Society, Worcester, Massachusetts.
30. Greeley, *Recollections of a Busy Life,* 62–63; *Hints Toward Reform,* 30–33 in Bremner, *Children and Youth in America,* 625–626.
31. Rorabaugh, *The Craft Apprentice,* 89; *Mechanics Free Press,* (Philadelphia), August 21, 1830, *Boston Evening Transcript,* March 24, 1832, in Bremner, *Children and Youth in America,* 612, 614–615; Wilentz, *Chants Democratic,* 232, 249, 254, 371; Christine Stansell, *City of Women: Sex and Class in New York, 1789–1860* (Urbana, Ill., 1987), 142, 149.
32. Stansell, *City of Women,* 116–177, 50–51.
33. Joseph Tuckerman, *An Essay on the Wages Paid to Females for their Labour* (Philadelphia, 1830), 21–35; Daniel Rogers, Comp., *The New York City-Hall Recorder for the Year 1820* (New York, 1821), 137–138, 177–178; New York Society for the Reformation of Juvenile Delinquents, *Memorial to the Legislature of New York . . .* (New York, 1824), 16–18, 22–26; Boston Prison Discipline Society, *Second Annual Report, 1827* (Boston, 1827), 28–29; in Bremner, *Children and Youth in America,* 613, 314–315, 677—680.
34. Benjamin Rush, "An Enquiry into the Effects of Public Punishments upon Criminals, and upon Society, Read in the Society for Promoting Political Enquiries, Convened at the House of Benjamin Franklin, Esq. in Philadelphia, March 9th, 1787" in *Essays, Literary, Moral and Philosophical* (Philadelphia, 1806), 150–157; Michael Meranze, "Public Punishments, Reformative Incarceration, and Authority in Philadelphia, 1750–1835," Ph.D. dissertation, University of California, Berkeley, 1985, 154–158, 239–245, 461.
35. Priscilla Clement, *Welfare and the Poor in the Nineteenth-Century City: Philadelphia, 1800–1854* (Cranbury, N.J., 1985), 50–54.
36. Board of Managers, Philadelphia House of Refuge, "Minutes, 1826–1831," Ms, October 17, 1826, Historical Society of Pennsylvania, Philadelphia. Anne M. Boylan, *Sunday School: The Formation of an American Institution, 1790–1880* (New Haven, Conn., 1988), 64.

37. Board of Managers, "Minutes," October 17, 1826; "Rules and Regulations," adopted November 14, 1828. Steven L. Schlossman, *Love & the American Delinquent: The Theory and Practice of "Progressive" Juvenile Justice, 1825–1920* (Chicago, 1977), 20–25, 28–32.

38. New York Society for the Reformation of Juvenile Delinquents, *Examination of subjects who are in the House of Refuge in the City of New York* (Albany, 1825), 3, 5, 11, 15–17, in Bremner, *Children and Youth in America*, 686–687; Schlossman, *Love & the American Delinquent*, 29; Stansell, *City of Women*, 184, 244.

39. *Ex parte Crouse*, 4 Whart. 9, 11–12 (Pa. 1839) in Michael Grossberg, *Governing the Hearth: Law and the Family in Nineteenth-Century America* (Chapel Hill, N.C., 1985), 266–267; Schlossman, *Love & the American Delinquent*, 8–10; Joseph M. Hawes, *Children in Urban Society: Juvenile Delinquency in Nineteenth-century America* (New York, 1971), 59; *The Children's Rights Movement: A History of Advocacy and Protection* (New York, 1991), 17.

40. Clark, *Roots of Rural Capitalism*, 214–266, 250, 253, 261, 305; Rorabaugh, *The Craft Apprentice*, 127, 152–154; Wilentz, *Chants Democratic*, 113–118, 130, 134–135, 138–140.

41. Kerby A. Miller, *Emigrants and Exiles: Ireland and the Irish Exodus to North America* (New York, 1985), 58, 169–173, 197–198, 276, 291–292, 296; Dennis Clark, *The Irish in Philadelphia: Ten Generations of Urban Experience* (Philadelphia, 1973), 20–21; Charles Sellers, *The Market Revolution: Jacksonian America, 1815–1846* (New York, 1991), 390; Wilentz, *Chants Democratic*, 315–321.

42. Oscar Handlin, *Boston's Immigrants, 1790–1865* (Cambridge, Mass., 1941), 53–54, 56, 79–80, 94–98, 106–108, 113–115, 117–119; Clark, *The Irish in Philadelphia*, 29–32, 49–56.

43. Clark, *The Irish in Philadelphia*, 62–75; Mitchell, *The Paddy Camps*, 21–26, 30–34, 39–42, 49–5481, 85–90; Dublin, *Women and Work*, 138–140.

44. Dublin, *Women and Work*, 140–144, 178–181; Mitchell, *The Paddy Camps*, 98–99, 115–117, 126.

45. Miller, *Emigrants and Exiles*, 331–334; Handlin, *Boston's Immigrants*, 167–168, 173–174; Mitchell, *The Paddy Camps*, 126–130, 133–134; Clark, *The Irish in Philadelphia*, 95–100; Hasia R. Diner, *Erin's Daughters in America: Irish Immigrant Women in the Nineteenth Century* (Baltimore, 1983), 77, 92–94, 132–134; Lawrence A. Glasco, "The Life Cycles and Household Structure of American Ethnic Groups: Irish, Germans, and Native-born Whites in Buffalo, New York, 1855," in Tamara K. Hareven, ed., *Family and Kin in Urban Communities, 1700–1930* (New York, 1977), 136, 141–142.

46. Walter D. Kamphoefner, Wolfgang Helbich, and Ulrike Sommer, eds., Susan Carter Vogel, trans., *News from the Land of Freedom: German Immigrants Write Home* (Ithaca, N.Y., 1991), 2–3, 7–8, 12; Bruce Levine, *The Spirit of 1848: German Immigrants, Labor Conflict, and the Coming of the Civil War* (Urbana, Ill., 1992), 2–3, 15–17, 69–71, 181–182; quoted in Wilentz, *Chants Democratic*, 124, 126.

47. Wilhelm Stille to "Dear parents, brothers, and sisters," Powhatan Point, Ohio, Spring, 1834, in Kamphoefner, et. al., *News from the Land of Freedom*, 68, 20–21; quoted in Stansell, *City of Women*, 205–206.

48. Levine, *The Spirit of 1848*, 62, 83, 91–96, 98.

49. Wilhelm Stille to parents, brothers, and sisters, Powhatan Point, Ohio, February 16, 1836; October 18, 1837; Wilhelm Krumme to mother, brothers-in-law, and sisters-in-law, Traidelphia, Virginia, May 30, 1842; January 27, 1843; July 14, 1846; March 21, 1850; February 1, 1858; [probably May, 1859]; in Kamphoefner, et. al., eds., *News from the Land of Freedom*, 21, 62–65, 69–70, 78, 80, 82, 91, 93–94.

50. George W. Matsell, chief of police, to Hon. Caleb S. Woodhull, mayor of the city of New York, October 31, 1849, in New York City, Police Department, *Semi-Annual Report, May 31–October 31, 1849* (New York, 1849) in Bremner, *Children and Youth in America*, 755–756; Clement, *Welfare and the Poor in the Nineteenth-Century City*, 134–136.

51. Grossberg, *Governing the Hearth*, 13–14, 24, 29, 236–243; Schlossman, *Love & the American Delinquent*, 25–26.

52. "An Act to establish the State Reform Schools," 1847—ch. 185, Massachusetts, *Acts and Resolves*, 1847 (Boston, 1847), 405–407; Massachusetts, House, "Report of the Commissioners appointed to consider the subject of the Reform School for Girls," Doc. 85, *Documents, 1851* (Boston, 1851), 7–10; "An Act concerning the Attendance of Children at School," 1852—ch. 240, *Acts and Resolves Passed by the General Court of Massachusetts . . . 1852* (Boston, 1852), 170–171; in Bremner, *Children and Youth in America*, 697–698, 700–701, 466–468; Stanley K. Schultz, *The Culture Factory: Boston Public Schools, 1789–1860* (New York, 1973), 300–301; *Trustees of the State Industrial School for Girls at Lancaster* (Boston, 1857), 6, in Schlossman, *Love & the American Delinquent*, 34–42; Hawes, *Children in Urban Society*, 81–86.

53. "Unpublished records of the Children's Mission to the Children of the Destitute," Parents' and Children's Services of Children's Mission, Office of the Mission, Boston, in Bremner, *Children and Youth in America*, 729–732; Grossberg, *Governing the Hearth*, 271–272.

54. *The Life of Charles Loring Brace Chiefly Told in His Own Letters*, edited by his Daughter (London, 1894), 1–8, 59, 75–77, 94, 100–101, 150–155; Charles Loring Brace, *The Dangerous Classes of New York and Twenty Years Work Among Them* (New York, 1872), 78.

55. *Life of Charles Loring Brace,* 170–171; Brace, *Dangerous Classes of New York,* 225, 236.

56. "The Children's Exodus," *The Five Points Monthly* (June, 1857), 66–67; Levi Silliman Ives, "The Protection of Destitute Catholic Children," in New York Catholic Protectory, *First Annual Report, 1864* (New York, 1864), 71–71, 74, 80–81; *Second Annual Report* (New York, 1865) in Bremner, *Children and Youth in America,* 745–750; Stansell, *City of Women,* 198, 210.

Chapter 7

1. Kenneth M. Stampp, *The Peculiar Institution: Slavery in the Ante–Bellum South* (New York, 1956), 29; Rachel N. Klein, *Unification of a Slave State: The Rise of the Planter Class in the South Carolina Backcountry, 1760–1808* (Chapel Hill, N.C., 1990), 47–77, 178–202.

2. Allan Kulikoff, *The Agrarian Origins of American Capitalism* (Charlottesville, Va., 1992), 227, 231–233, 255; Steven Deyle, "The Irony of Liberty: Origins of the Domestic Slave Trade," *Journal of the Early Republic,* 12, 1 (Spring, 1992): 39–43, 50, 57–58. Discussion of capitalistic values in the South and definition of the plantation household can be found in Eugene D. Genovese, *Roll, Jordan, Roll: The World the Slaves Made* (New York, 1972) and Elizabeth Fox-Genovese, *Within the Plantation Household: Black and White Women of the Old South* (Chapel Hill, N.C., 1988). Suggestion of the relationship between white and black children can be found in Kulikoff, *Agrarian Origins,* 226. If capitalism is defined in terms of hiring labor for wages, then southern planters clearly were not capitalists, although they did increasingly view slave children as a commodity. Nevertheless, professional traders clearly were, as they sought to profit from buying and selling human beings.

3. Many historians have studied slave family life, including Allan Kulikoff, *Tobacco and Slaves: The Development of Southern Cultures in the Chesapeake, 1680–1800* (Chapel Hill, N.C., 1986); Herbert G. Gutman, *The Black Family in Slavery & Freedom, 1750–1925* (New York, 1976); John W. Blassingame, *The Slave Community: Plantation Life in the Antebellum South* (New York, 1972); Jacqueline Jones, *Labor of Love, Labor of Sorrow: Black Women, Work and the Family from Slavery to the Present* (New York, 1985); Deborah Gray White, *Arn't I A Woman? Female Slaves in the Plantation South* (New York, 1985).

4. Kulikoff, *Agrarian Origins,* 227–229; Steven Deyle, "'By farr the most profitable trade': Slave Trading in British Colonial North America," *Slavery & Abolition* 10, 2 (September, 1989): 112–113, 115; Darrett B. and Anita H. Rutman, *A Place in Time: Middlesex County, Virginia, 1650–1750* (New York, 1984), 164, 169.

5. Robert Pringle to Edward Pare, 5 May, 1744, *Letterbook of Robert Pringle,* 2: 684; *New York Gazette, or the Weekly Post-Boy,* 17 May 1756, 28 November 1768; *Pennsylvania Gazette,* 21 May 1767, 26 February 1767; *Virginia Gazette,* 2 November 1769; quoted in Deyle, "'By farr the most profitable trade,'" 113–114, 117–118.

6. Kulikoff, *Agrarian Origins,* 229; Deyle, "The Irony of Liberty," 43–49.

7. Kulikoff, *Agrarian Origins,* 238–239; *Virginia Gazette,* 18 February 1773; Thomas Jefferson to John W. Eppes, June 30, 1820 in Edwin M. Betts, ed., *Thomas Jefferson's Farm Book* (Princeton, N.J., 1953), 46; quoted in Deyle, "The Irony of Liberty," 50–51.

8. Kulikoff, *Agrarian Origins,* 239–241; Deyle, "The Irony of Liberty," 42; Klein, *Unification of a Slave State,* 178–202.

9. Kulikoff, *Agrarian Origins,* 241–245.

10. Jan Lewis, *The Pursuit of Happiness: Family and Values in Jefferson's Virginia* (Cambridge, 1983), 106–168; with Kenneth A. Lockridge, "'Sally Has Been Sick': Pregnancy and Family Limitation Among Virginia Gentry Women, 1780–1830," *Journal of Social History* 22, 1 (Fall, 1988), 11–12; Joan E. Cashin, *A Family Venture: Men and Women on the Southern Frontier* (Baltimore, 1991), 26.

11. Thomas Jefferson, *Notes of Virginia* in Adrienne Koch and William Peden, eds., *The Life and Selected Writings of Thomas Jefferson* (New York, 1944), 278; Winthrop D. Jordan, *White Over Black: American Attitudes Toward the Negro, 1550–1812* (Chapel Hill, N.C., 1968), 430–433.

12. Ellen W. Coolidge to Virginia Trist, May 3, [18]29; Ellen Wayles Coolidge Autobiographical Papers, June 15, 1828 and July 13, 1828, Ellen Wayles Coolidge Correspondence, quoted in Lewis, *Pursuit of Happiness,* 152–153.

13. Rhys Isaac, *The Transformation of Virginia, 1740–1790* (Chapel Hill, N.C., 1982), 308–310; Jordan, *White Over Black,* 347–348; Gerald W. (Michael) Mullin, *Flight and Rebellion: Slave Resistance in Eighteenth-Century Virginia* (New York, 1972), 83–123; *Africa in America: Slave Acculturation and Resistance in the American South and the British Caribbean, 1736–1800* (Urbana, Ill., 1992), 225–226, 230–231; Kulikoff, *Tobacco and Slaves,* 350.

14. Kulikoff, *Tobacco and Slaves,* 337–338, 340–341, 346–349, 358–371; Baily Cunningham, interviewed by I.M. Warren, Starkey, Va., before March 14, 1938; Levi Pollard, unknown interviewer, Richmond Va., n.d.; Mr. Beverly Jones, interviewed by William T. Lee, Gloucester Court House, Va., n.d.; Mrs. Sarah Wooden Johnson, interviewed by Susie R.C. Byrd, Petersburg, Va., n.d.; in Charles L. Perdue, Jr., Thomas E. Barden, and Robert K. Phillips, eds., *Weevils in the Wheat:*

Interviews with Virginia Ex-Slaves (Bloomington, Ind., 1976), 82, 227, 181, 164.

15. Much of this material is recalled by former slaves who were children in the 1840s and 1850s. Although memory may be distorted, it is highly likely that adults truthfully reported the work they did as children. Frank Bell, interviewed by Claude W. Anderson, Vienna, Va., n.d.; Cornelius Garner, interviewed by Emmy Wilson and Claude W. Anderson, Norfolk, Va., May 18, 1937; Robert Ellett, interviewed by Claude W. Anderson, Hampton, Va., December 25, 1937; Simon Stokes, interviewed by Lucille B. Jayne, Guinea, Va., prior to April 14, 1937; Nancy Williams, interviewed by Emmy Wilson and Claude S. Anderson, Norfolk, Va., May 18, 1937; Ellis Bennett, interviewed by Claude W. Anderson, Hampton, Va., January 7, 1937; Gabe Hunt, interviewed by William T. Lee, Rustburg, Va., n.d.; Levi Pollard, unknown interviewer, Richmond, Va., n.d.; William I. Johnson, interviewed by Milton L. Randolph, Richmond, Va., May 28, 1937; West Turner, unknown interviewer, Nansemond Co., Va., n.d.; Mrs. Katie Blackwell Johnson, unknown interviewer, Washington Co., Va., n.d.; Miss Caroline Hunter, interviewed by Thelma Dunston, Portsmouth, Va., January 8, 1937; Julia Frazier, interviewed by Claude W. Anderson, April 20, 1937; Mrs. Candis Goodwin, interviewed by Claude W. Anderson, Cape Charles, Va., n.d.; Aunt Susan Kelly, interviewed by Lucille B. Jayne, Guinea, Va., prior to April 14, 1937; in Perdue, Barden, and Phillips, eds., *Weevils in the Wheat,* 102, 26, 85, 28, 322, 29, 148, 228, 165, 288, 161, 149, 97, 107, 189.

16. George White, interviewed by William T. Lee, Lynchburg, Va., April 20, 1937; Robert Ellett; Candis Goodwin; Fannie Berry; Uncle Bacchus White, interviewed by Sue K. Gordon, Fredericksburg, Va., Fall, 1939; Annie Wallace, interviewed by Margaret Jeffries, Culpeper, Va., April 1, 1940; John Brown, interviewed by Susie R. C. Byrd, Petersburg, Va., April 2, 1937; Phillip Ward, unknown interviewer, Farmville, Va., n.d.; Priscilla Joiner, unknown interviewer, Suffolk Va., n.d.; Levi Pollard; Mrs. Hannah Johnson, interviewed by Faith Morris, Richmond, Va., n.d.; Nancy Williams; Elizabeth Sparks, interviewed by Claude W. Anderson, Mathews Court House, Va., January 13, 1937; Baily Cunningham; Mrs. Alice Marshall, interviewed by Emmy Wilson and Claude W. Anderson, Fredericksburg, Va., n.d.; Sally Ashton, interviewed by Susie R.C. Byrd, Keswick, Va., n.d.; Susie Melton, unknown interviewer, Newport News, Va., n.d.; in Perdue, Barden, and Phillips, eds., *Weevils in the Wheat,* 309, 84, 107, 45, 47, 305–306, 295, 61, 301, 175, 230, 159, 316, 277, 81, 203, 14, 212; Frederick Douglass, *My Bondage and My Freedom* (New York, 1855), 72.

17. Douglass, *My Bondage and My Freedom*, 49, 66, 75, 77, 89–91, 108, 133; William S. McFeely, *Frederick Douglass* (New York, 1991), 12–14, 19–23; Mullin, *Africa in America*, 137–139.

18. Douglass, *My Bondage and My Freedom*, 138, 145–147, 155–159, 166–172; McFeely, *Frederick Douglass*, 22, 29–30, 32, 34–36; issues of acculturation and assimilation in Chesapeake slavery have been sensitively explored by Mullin in *Flight and Rebellion*, 38, 83–123, and *Africa in America*, 232–235.

19. George Carter, interviewed by Morris Adams, Savannah Georgia, January 17, 1939, Ts, Federal Writers Project, 1490–1504, Southern Historical Collection, University of North Carolina Library, Chapel Hill. Interviewers of ex-slaves in the Federal Writers Project in the 1930s attempted to preserve dialect with various spellings. Although these dialects were filtered through the consciousness of the particular interviewer, I have chosen to quote them as written, in order to accurately reflect the primary source.

20. Josephine Smith, interviewed by Mary A. Hicks, Raleigh, N.C., n.d. in Belinda Hurmence, ed., *My Folks Don't Want Me To Talk About Slavery* (Winston-Salem, N.C., 1984), 32.

21. Steven Deyle estimates that $1,000 in 1850 would be around $17,000 today.

22. Thomas Hall, interviewed by T. Pat Matthews, Raleigh, N.C., n.d.; in Hurmence, ed., *My Folks Don't Want Me To Talk About Slavery*, 51–52; Robert Williams, interviewed by William T. Lee, Lynchburg, Va., May 8, 1937; Mrs. Katie Blackwell Johnson; West Turner, interviewed by Faith Morris and Susie R. C. Byrd, Richmond, Va., n.d.; in Perdue, Barden, and Phillips, eds., *Weevils in the Wheat*, 325–326, 161, 291, 237; Allan Kulikoff estimates that young enslaved women in Prince George's County, Maryland, from 1720–1759, began bearing children between the ages of sixteen and nineteen. This age may have dropped slightly in the ante-bellum period. *Tobacco and Slaves*, 375.

23. Charles Ball, *Fifty Years in Chains, or, the Life of an American Slave* (New York, 1859), 10–11.

24. Charles Grandy, interviewed by David Hoggard, Norfolk, Virginia, February 26, 1937; Virginia Hayes Shepherd, interviewed by Emmy Wilson and Claude W. Anderson, Norfolk, Virginia, May 18, 1937; in Perdue, Barden, and Phillips, eds., *Weevils in the Wheat*, 114–115, 258.

25. Mandy Long Roberson, interviewed by Coalee Dunnagan, Yadkinville, N.C., April 6, 1939, revised by Claude V. Dunnagan, Ts, Federal Writers Project, 4770–4776, Southern Historical Collection, University of North Carolina Library, Chapel Hill.

26. Amos Abner Cotton, interviewed by Robert Dotson Glenn, Raleigh, N.C., January 11, 1939, Ts, Federal Writers Project, 8258–8271,

Southern Historical Collection, University of North Carolina Library, Chapel Hill.

27. Baily Cunningham; Rev. Ishrael Massie, interviewed by Susie R.C. Byrd, Petersburg, Va., April 23, 1937; Nancy Williams; in Perdue, Barden, and Phillips, eds., *Weevils in the Wheat,* 82, 211, 319.

28. Bailey Cunningham; Robert Williams, interviewed by William T. Lee, Lynchburg, Va., May 8, 1937 in Perdue, Barden, and Phillips, eds., *Weevils in the Wheat,* 82, 323.

29. W.L. Bost, interviewed by Marjorie Jones, Asheville, N.C., September 27, 1937 in Hurmence, ed., *My Folks Don't Want Me To Talk About Slavery,* 92–93.

30. Fannie Berry; Allen Wilson, interviewed by Susie R.C. Byrd, Petersburg, Va., July 16, 1937; Elizabeth Sparks; Mrs. Louise Jones, interviewed by Susie R.C. Byrd, Petersburg, Va., February 12, 1937; in Perdue, Barden, and Phillips, eds., *Weevils in the Wheat,* 42, 328, 274–275, 185–186.

31. Peter H. Wood, *Black Majority: Negroes in Colonial South Carolina from 1670 through the Stono Rebellion* (New York, 1974), 164–165, 340; Daniel C. Littlefield, *Rice and Slaves: Ethnicity and the Slave Trade in Colonial South Carolina* (Urbana, Ill., 1981), 20–21, 112–114; Margaret Washington Creel, *"A Peculiar People": Slave Religion and Community-Culture Among the Gullahs* (New York, 1988), 16–19, 37; Charles Joyner, *Down by the Riverside: A South Carolina Slave Community* (Urbana, Ill., 1984), 14–15, 203–209, 222–224.

32. Joyner, *Down by the Riverside,* 208; Catherine Clinton, "Appendix A: Comparison of Southern Sample Group (750 members of the planter elite born between 1765 and 1815) and Northern Sample Group (100 members of the Hudson Valley Dutch planter elite born between 1765 and 1815)," in *The Plantation Mistress: Woman's World in the Old South* (New York, 1982), 233–235.

33. According to the census of 1850, white childbirth deaths as a percentage of white women's deaths were 5.4 in Florida, 5.0 in Georgia, 4.9 in Texas, 3.8 in North Carolina, and 3.8 in South Carolina. The only other state with a percentage over 3.5 was Maine with 4.8. *U.S. Federal Census, Mortality Statistics of the Seventh Census of the United States, 1850,* ed. J.D.B. DeBow (Washington, D.C., 1855), Table III, Appendix One in Sally G. McMillen, *Motherhood in the Old South* (Baton Rouge, 1990).

34. McMillen, *Motherhood in the Old South,* 24–56, 176–179.

35. Thomas Chaplin, "Diary," September 26, 1845, November 5, 1850; in Theodore Rosengarten, ed., *Tombee: Portrait of a Cotton Planter,* 168–169, 369, 507–508; Frances Anne Kemble to Elizabeth Dwight Sedgwick, Butler Island, Ga., January, 1839; St. Simon's Island, Ga., February

28–March 2, March 4, 5, and 8, 1839; in John A. Scott, ed., *Journal of a Residence on a Georgian Plantation in 1838–1839* (Athens, Ga., 1984; first edition London, 1863), 77, 95–96, 229–230, 240, 245–246, 255–256.

36. Eliza Burgwin Clitherall, "Autobiography and Diary," 19 vols., AMs and Ts, vol. 5, 17–18, 20–21, 37; vol. 6, 5, 18–21; Southern Historical Collection, University of North Carolina Library, Chapel Hill; Chaplin, "Diary," October 18, 21, and 24, November 7, 1845; May 29, 1846; September 27, 1848; August 14, 15, and 17, 1851; in Rosengarten, ed., *Tombee*, 373, 376, 417, 446, 539. Mortality statistics of the U.S. Census of 1850 include enslaved as well as white children. Sally G. McMillen found that letters and diaries of privileged white mothers rarely mentioned croup; nevertheless, it prevailed among enslaved children. Children under the age of five accounted for 38.31 percent of all deaths in 1850 and 42.95 percent in 1860. Although this is a higher child mortality rate than that of children under the age of ten accounting for about 40 percent of all deaths in the 1820s previously discussed, the national statistics include the very high rates of infant and child mortality among Irish and German immigrants and in northwestern states such as Illinois, Iowa, Michigan, Wisconsin, or California. *U.S. Federal Census, Mortality Statistics, 1850,* Joseph C.G. Kennedy, *Preliminary Report on the Eighth Census* (Washington, D.C., 1862), Tables V, VI, and VII, Appendix One in McMillen, *Motherhood in the Old South,* see also 135–164.

37. Chaplin, "Diary," July 14 and August 25, 1846; in Rosengarten, ed., *Tombee*, 419–420, 183–184; Sam Polite, interviewed by Chlotilde R. Martin, Beaufort County, S.C., n.d.; Savilla Burrell, interviewed by W.W. Dixon, Winnsboro, S.C., n.d.; in Belinda Hurmence, ed., *Before Freedom: When I Just Can Remember* (Winston-Salem, N.C., 1989), 69, 79, 135.

38. James Henry Hammond, "Diary," March 7, July 3, September 5 and 21, November 2, 1841; in Carol Bleser, ed., *Secret and Sacred: The Diaries of James Henry Hammond, a Southern Slaveholder* (New York, 1988), 63, 73, 75, 80–81; Drew Gilpin Faust, *James Henry Hammond and the Old South: A Design for Mastery* (Baton Rouge, 1982), 76–82.

39. Chaplin, "Diary," June 19, 1850; January 13 and 24, February 10, March 30, 1852; May 17, 1855; in Rosengarten, ed., *Tombee*, 501, 556–557, 561, 566, 635–636.

40. Michael Tadman, *Speculators and Slaves: Masters, Traders, and Slaves in the Old South* (Madison, Wis., 1989), 12; Chaplin, "Diary," October 12, 1847; May 8 and 9, 1848; in Rosengarten, ed., *Tombee*, 100–111, 429, 433; Peter Clifton, interviewed by W.W. Dixon, Winnsboro, S.C., n.d.; Sylvia Cannon, interviewed by Annie Ruth Davis, Florence S.C.,

October, 1937; Rebecca Jane Grant, interviewed by Phoebe Faucette, Lena, S.C., n.d.; in Hurmence, ed., *Before Freedom,* 57–59, 110, 123–124; Kemble to Elizabeth Dwight Sedgwick, St. Simon's Island, April 5–7, 1839; in Scott, ed., *Journal,* 315. Herbert Gutman and Deborah Gray White both have argued that bearing large numbers of children offered female slaves some measure of security on plantations as child-bearing women (and their husbands), who increased the master's wealth, may have been less likely to be sold. Herbert G. Gutman, *The Black Family in Slavery and Freedom, 1750–1925* (New York, 1976), 75–76; Deborah Gray White, "Female Slaves: Sex Roles and Status in the Antebellum Plantation South" in Ellen Carol DuBois and Vicki L. Ruiz, *Unequal Sisters* (New York, 1990), 28–29.

41. Joyner, *Down by the Riverside,* 2, 19, 120–126; Kemble to Elizabeth Dwight Sedgwick, Butler Island, Ga., January, 1839; in Scott, ed., *Journal,* 67–68; Zack Herndon, interviewed by Caldwell Sims, Gaffney, S.C., May 1937; George Briggs, interviewed by Caldwell Sims, Union, S.C., June 1937; Isiah Jefferies, interviewed by Caldwell Sims, Gaffney, S.C., August 1937; in Hurmence, ed., *Before Freedom,* 50–51, 94, 114.

42. James L. Michie, *Richmond Hill Plantation, 1810–1868: The Discovery of Antebellum Life on a Waccamaw Rice Plantation* (Spartenburg, S.C., 1990), 125–132; Joyner, *Down by the Riverside,* 90–100; Hester Hunter, interviewed by Annie Ruth Davis, Marion, S.C., May 1937; Robert Toatley, interviewed by W.W. Dixon, near White Oak, S.C., n.d.; Savilla Burrell; in Hurmence, ed., *Before Freedom,* 17–18, 119–120; 134.

43. Joyner, *Down by the Riverside,* 108–111; Ben Horry; Zack Herndon; in Hurmence, ed., *Before Freedom,* 22–23, 53.

44. Chaplin, "Diary," September 27, 1845; May 15, 1851; in Rosengarten, ed., *Tombee,* 370, 532; Rebecca Jane Grant, in Hurmence, ed., *Before Freedom,* 57; Kemble to Elizabeth Dwight Sedgwick, Butler Island, January, 1839; in Scott, ed., *Journal,* 93.

45. Joyner, *Down by the Riverside,* 43–45; Prince Smith, interviewed by Augustus Ladson, Wardmalaw Island, S.C., n.d.; Peter Clifton; Adeline Jackson; Alexander Scaife, interviewed by Caldwell Sims, Pacolet, S.C., n.d.; Zack Herndon; Rebecca Jane Grant; Adeline Johnson, interviewed by W.W. Dixon, Winnsboro, S.C., n.d.; in Hurmence, ed., *Before Freedom,* 91, 111, 36, 47, 52, 60, 56.

46. Joyner, *Down by the Riverside,* 126, 172–183.

47. Ibid., 183–189.

48. Ibid., 141; Creel, *"A Peculiar People,"* 92–93, 133, 148–161, 216–217, 230–233.

49. *The Dutiful Servant; or the Conversion of Black Will and the Reformation of the Neighborhood* (Philadelphia: The Sunday and Adult School

Union, 1822); Creel, *"A Peculiar People,"* 235–237; Rebecca Jane Grant, in Hurmence, ed., *Before Freedom,* 61.

50. Creel, *"A Peculiar People,"* 286–289, 293–294, 297–299.

51. Joyner, *Down by the Riverside,* 142, 150–153; Amos Long, interviewed by Bernice Kelly Harris, Seaboard, N.C., February 22, 1939; Lettice J'yner, interviewed by Bernice Kelly Harris, Seaboard, N.C., May 3, 1939; Ma (Liza) Williams, interviewed by Virginia Thorpe, Savannah, Ga., January 13, 1939; Ts, Federal Writers Project 3709, 5990–5995, 5488A–5503, 3340–3348; Southern Historical Collection, University of North Carolina Library, Chapel Hill.

52. Joyner, *Down by the Riverside,* 142, 146–147; Lettice J'yner; Ma (Liza) Williams; Benjamin Johnson, interviewed by Geneva Tonsell, Atlanta, Ga., September 1939; Ts, Federal Writers Project, 3709, 3361–3374; Southern Historical Collection, University of North Carolina Library, Chapel Hill.

53. Savilla Burrell; Sylvia Cannon; in Hurmence, ed., *Before Freedom,* 134, 124.

54. James Henry Hammond to Harry Hammond, February 19, 1856, James Henry Hammond Papers, South Caroliniana Library, University of South Carolina, Columbia; in Bleser, ed., *Secret and Sacred,* 19.

55. George C. Rogers, Jr., *Charleston in the Age of the Pinckneys,* (Columbia, S.C., 1980), 144; free persons were about 3 percent of the South Carolina's black population in 1800, but 2 percent by 1860, Klein, *Unification of a Slave State,* 273, Michael P. Johnson and James L. Roark, eds., *No Chariot Let Down: Charleston's Free People of Color on the Eve of the Civil War* (New York, 1984), 6.

56. "Hager, her own book" and accounts, March 8, July 30, 1816; June 6, November 6, 1818; February 6, 1819; January 6, June 6, 1821; July 6, December 6, 1824; April 6, July 6, October 6, 1825; May 29, 1826; October 15, 1828; AMs, Vanderhorst Family Papers, 12–195, Folders 27, 28, and 29, South Carolina Historical Society, Charleston.

57. Kulikoff, *Agrarian Origins,* 258–260; Ann Patton Malone, *Sweet Chariot: Slave Family and Household Structure in Nineteenth-Century Louisiana* (Chapel Hill, N.C., 1992), 20–23.

58. Amelia Thompson Watts, "A Summer on a Louisiana Cotton Plantation in 1832," in Louise Taylor Pharr, "Book," 1955, Ts., #3132, 94, Southern Historical Collection, University of North Carolina Library, Chapel Hill; James Foster and Family Papers, U-117, #1705, Louisiana and Lower Mississippi Valley Collection, Louisiana State University, Baton Rouge; Malone, *Sweet Chariot,* 28–31.

59. Malone, 28–39, 57, 139–146, 150–157.

60. Cashin, *A Family Venture,* 32–35, 79–83, 99–102, 113–118.

61. Charlotte Beatty, "Diary," vol. 2, February 2, 4, 17, 19, 23; April 25; May 10 and 11; August 3; October 12, 17, 18, 27, and 29, 1843; AMs,

Beatty, Taylor Papers #54, Series 3, #3, Southern Historical Society, University of North Carolina Library, Chapel Hill; Eliza L. Magruder, "Diary," January 19, 22, 23, 24, and 31; February 3, 9, 11, 17, 20; March 15 and 16, 1846; microfilm, Historic New Orleans Collection, New Orleans, La.

62. Nicholas A. Destrehan, "Memoirs" in "Letter Book," September 4, 1850, AMs, Mss 129, Historic New Orleans Collection, New Orleans, La.; Mary Susan Ker, "Journal," March 25, 26, and 30; April 5, 11, 15, 17, 18, and 29; May 3, 4, 7, and 10; June 21, 1850; AMs, John Ker and Family Papers #3539, Louisiana and Lower Mississippi Valley Collection, Louisiana State University, Baton Rouge, La.

63. Ker, "Journal," June 21, 1850; March 16, 1851; "Anonymous Diary," June 3, 9, and 10; July 21, November 12, December 11, 1835; January 12, February 27, 1837; Ts, M-19e #533; Edward Turner, Franklin Place, to Fanny, Natchez, November 31, 1840, AMs, Edward Turner and Family Papers, S-120 #1403, Louisiana and Lower Mississippi Valley Collection, Louisiana State University, Baton Rouge, La.

64. Georgia Baker, John Crawford, Martin Jackson, Elmo Steele, Mary Reynolds, Jack Maddox, Calvin Moye, Katie Rowe in James Mellon, ed., *Bullwhip Days, The Slaves Remember: An Oral History,* 3, 305, 225, 280, 16, 120–121, 161, 28–29.

65. Rose Williams, Rachel Cruze, Mollie Dawson, Cato Carter, in Mellon, *Bullwhip Days,* 129–130, 208, 423, 273.

66. Kulikoff, *Agrarian Origins,* 262; Calvin Moye, Thomas Cole, Mary Reynolds in Mellon, ed., *Bullwhip Days,* 163–164, 55–56, 16–18; Julia (Aunt Sally) Brown, interviewed by Geneva Tonsill, Atlanta, Ga., July 25, 1939; Ts, Federal Writers Project 3709, 3439–3451, Southern Historical Collection, University of North Carolina Library, Chapel Hill.

67. Thomas Cole, John Crawford, Charlie Davenport, Ellen Betts, Neal Upson, Jacob Manson, Calvin Moye, in Mellon, ed., *Bullwhip Days,* 55, 309, 371, 381, 358, 220, 164–165.

68. Thomas Cole, Charlie Davenport, Rosa Maddox, Katie Sutton, Mollie Dawson, Jack Maddox, George Fleming, in Mellon, ed., *Bullwhip Days,* 58, 374, 164–165, 39, 427–428, 119, 255.

69. Robert Farmer, Thomas Cole, Rachel Cruze, William Colbert, William Moore, Mollie Dawson, John Crawford, Lulu Wilson, in Mellon, *Bullwhip Days,* 239, 59–60, 210–211, 418–420, 332, 309, 324; Henrietta King, unknown interviewer, West Point, Va., n.d.; William Lee, interviewed by Susie R.C. Byrd, Richmond, Va., n.d.; in Perdue, Barden, and Phillips, *Weevils in the Wheat,* 191, 194; Fannie Griffin, Sylvia Cannon, in Hurmence, ed., *Before Freedom,* 83, 127.

70. Stephanie McCurry, *Master of Small Worlds: Yeoman Households, Gender Relations, and the Political Culture of the Antebellum South*

Carolina Low Country (New York, 1995), 24–30, 56–59, 82–91; Steven Hahn, *The Roots of Southern Populism: Yeoman Farmers and the Transformation of the Georgia Upcountry, 1850–1890* (New York, 1983), Chapters 1 and 2; Kulikoff, *The Agrarian Origins of American Capitalism,* Chapters 1 and 2.

71. James Monroe Adams, "Reminiscence Book," 1911; 88–002, 2131–13; 21, 100, 102–103, 105–107, 115–117; AMs, Georgia Department of Archives & History, Atlanta, Ga.

72. Elmina Foster Wilson, "Reminiscences," 1827–1917, 1–2, 4–6, 8, 14–16; Ts, Southern Historical Collection, University of North Carolina Library, Chapel Hill.

73. Charles C. Bolton, *Poor Whites of the Antebellum South: Tenants and Laborers in Central North Carolina and Northeast Mississippi* (Durham, N.C., 1994), 5–9, 14–17, 31–50, 54–55.

74. Rev. Charles C. Pinckney, in *Sixty-sixth Anniversary of the Charleston Orphan House,* 24–25, quoted in Barbara L. Bellows, *Benevolence Among Slaveholders: Assisting the Poor in Charleston, 1670–1860* (Baton Rouge, La., 1993), 139, see also 120–157; Alan Keith-Lucas, *A Legacy of Caring: The Charleston Orphan House, 1790–1990* (Charleston, S.C., 1991), 1–19.

75. Bellows, *Benevolence Among Slaveholders,* 22, 32–35.

76. Caroline Howard Gilman, Charleston, to A.M. White, January 15, 1833; to Louisa, December 17, 1833; to Harriet Fay, Boston, October 27, 1835, folder 2, #29, #31, and #32, AMs; "Autobiography," 7–8, Ts; South Carolina Historical Society, Charleston.

77. Edgar W. Knight, "The Academy Movement in the South, Part III," *The High School Journal* 3, 1 (January, 1920): 6–11; Layton Wayne Jordan, "Education for Community: G.G. Memminger and the Origination of Common Schools in Ante-bellum Charleston," *South Carolina Historical Magazine* 83, 2 (April, 1982): 99–115; Bellows, *Benevolence Among Slaveholders,* 157–159.

78. *The Southern Reader or Child's Second Reading Book* (Charleston, S.C., 1841), 5, 63, 69, 84–87, 140–142, 155–157.

Epilogue

1. Charles Loring Brace, *The Dangerous Classes of New York and Twenty Years Work Among Them* (New York, 1872), 46.

2. Barbara M. Cross, ed., *The Autobiography of Lyman Beecher* (Cambridge, Mass., 1961), vol. 1, 10; Joan D. Hedrick, *Harriet Beecher Stowe, a life* (New York, 1994), 12–13, 18–19, 26–27, 31, 50–57.

3. Hedrick, *Harriet Beecher Stowe,* 67–70, 98–99, 111, 117, 154–156, 174–175, 191.

4. Harriet Beecher Stowe to Eliza Cabot Follen, December 16, 1852, Dr. Williams Library, London, quoted in Hedrick, *Harriet Beecher Stowe,* 192–193, see also 141–142, 189–191.

5. Hedrick, *Harriet Beecher Stowe,* 208–216; Harriet Beecher Stowe, *Uncle Tom's Cabin, or Life Among the Lowly* (New York, 1981; first published 1852).

Bibliographical Essay

This project began many years ago as my Ph.D. dissertation, "Attitudes toward and Practices of Child-rearing: Philadelphia, 1790 to 1830" (University of California, Berkeley, 1977), in which I argued that the seminal work for eighteenth-century child-rearing concepts was John Locke's *Some Thoughts Concerning Education* (London, 1693). Years later I discovered that Locke's approach was popularized and applied to the education of girls by Joseph Addison in *The Spectator* papers (London, 1711–1712). Francis Hutcheson added concepts of the Scottish Enlightenment in *Inquiry Into the Original of Our Ideas of Beauty and Virtue* (1725). Jean-Jacques Rousseau's child-rearing manual, *Emile, or On Education* (1762), was also a book that Americans read, even though many of them somewhat disapproved of it.

British physicians who expanded Locke's medical advice include William Cadogan, *Essay upon Nursing and the Management of Children From Their Birth to Three Years of Age, by a Physician, in a Letter to One of the Governors of the Foundling Hospital* (1747), and William Buchan, *Domestic Medicine, or the Family Physician: Being an Attempt to Render the Medical Art More Generally Useful . . . Chiefly Calculated to Recommend a Proper Attention to Regimen and Simple Medicines* (Edinburgh, 1769). Similar works reprinted in America were Alexander Hamilton's *Treatise on the Management of Female Complaints and of Children in Early Infancy* (New York, 1792); Hugh Smith's *Letters to Married Women on Nursing and Management of Their Children* (Philadelphia, 1793); and Michael Underwood's *Treatise on the Diseases of Children with General Directions for the Management of Infants from Their Birth* (Philadelphia, 1793).

When American physicians offered advice on infant and child management, they tended to republish Buchan's *Domestic Medicine* adapted to the American environment with their own footnotes—for example, Dr. Samuel Powel Griffitts, *Domestic Medicine: or a Treatise on the Prevention and Cure of Diseases, by Regimen and Simple Medicines, Revised and Adapted to the*

Diseases and Climate of the United States of America (Philadelphia, 1795); and Dr. Isaac Cathrall, *Domestic Medicine or a Treatise on the Prevention and Cure of Diseases by Regimen and Simple Medicines Adapted to the Climate and Diseases of America* (Philadelphia, 1797). An original work by Dr. William Currie, *Historical Account of the Climates and Diseases of the United States of America; and of the Remedies and Methods of Treatment, Which Have Been Found Most Useful and Efficacious, Particularly in Those Diseases Which Depend Upon Climate and Situation* (Philadelphia, 1792) contains a valuable account of the diseases he encountered and treated.

While Locke's medical advice was popularized and expanded by physicians, printers elaborated on his educational plan. John Newbery created a new genre of children's literature with his *Little Pretty Pocket-book* (London, 1744). Samuel Richardson disseminated concepts of the anti-patriarchal family in *Pamela or Virtue Rewarded* (London, 1740) and *Clarissa, Or the History of a Young Lady* (London, 1747). An American adaptation blending the format of the Newbery books with religious content is *The History of Little King Pippin with an Account of the Melancholy Death of Four Naughty Boys Who Were Devoured by Wild Bears and the Wonderful Delivery of Master Harry Harmless by a Little White Horse* (Philadelphia, 1786). British children's literature popular in America after the Revolution included Anna Laetitia Aikin Barbauld's *Lessons for Children* (Philadelphia, 1788) and Thomas Day's *History of Sandford and Merton: A Work Intended for the Use of Children* (Philadelphia, 1788). Barbauld's lessons were blended with religious content in such books as *The New England Primer, Much Improved; Containing a Variety of Easy Lessons for Attaining the True Reading of English* (Philadelphia, 1792) or the Quaker schoolmaster John Ely's *The Child's Instructor: Consisting of Easy Lessons for Children on Subjects which Are Familiar to them, in Language Adapted to their Capacities* (Philadelphia, 1793).

American printers produced for children factual books on the new republic such as *Introduction to the History of America* (Philadelphia, 1787) or *A General Description of the Thirteen States of America, Containing Their Situations, Boundaries, Soil and Produce, Rivers, Capitals, Constitutions, Religious Tests, and Numbers of Inhabitants* (Reading, 1788). Biographies of President Washington were immensely popular, one of which, *The Life of General Washington, Commander in Chief of the American Army During the Late War, and Present President of the United States* (Philadelphia, 1794), was accompanied by *The Life of Judas Iscariot Who Betrayed His Lord and Master* (Philadelphia, 1794). In the 1790s children were instructed with books teaching "natural religion": Dr. Joannes Florentius Martinet, *Catechism of Nature: For the Use of Children* (Philadelphia, 1791) or George Riley, *Beauties of Creation or, A New Moral System of Natural History: Displayed in the Most Singular, Curious, and Beautiful Quadrupeds, Birds, Insects, Trees and Flowers, Designed to Inspire Youth with Humanity Towards the Brute Creation, and to*

Bring Them Early Acquainted with the Wonderful Works of the Divine Creator (Philadelphia, 1796). By the end of the decade, however, printers offered evangelical works such the eight volumes of *Cheap Repository Tracts, Entertaining, Moral and Religious* (New York, n.d.) by the English author Hannah More.

In post-Revolutionary decades Americans proposed their own educational theories and child-rearing advice. Enos Hitchcock addressed to Martha Washington his *Memoirs of the Bloomsgrove Family. In a Series of Letters to a respectable Citizen of Philadelphia. Containing Sentiments on a Mode of Domestic Education, Suited to the present State of Society, Government, and Manners in the United States of America: and on the Dignity and Importance of the Female Character interspersed with a Variety of Interesting Anecdotes* (Boston, 1790). Charles Willson Peale described his effort to provide visual embodiments of republican ideals in "Memoirs of Charles Willson Peale from his Original MS. with notes by Horace Wells Sellers," which is in the American Philosophical Society Library. Peale's work is beautifully illustrated in *Charles Willson Peale and His World* (New York, 1982). Noah Webster sought a common language through *A Grammatical Institute of the English Language, comprising An easy, concise, and systematic Method of Education, Designed for the Use of English Schools in America* (Hartford, Conn., 1783). And Benjamin Rush explored the interconnection between republican principles and methods of child-rearing in *A Plan for the Establishment of Public Schools and the Diffusion of Knowledge in Pennsylvania; to which Are Added, Thoughts upon the Mode of Education, Proper in a Republic* (Philadelphia, 1786) and *Thoughts upon Female Education, Accommodated to the Present State of Society, Manners, and Government in the United States of America,* both reprinted in Frederick Rudolph, ed., *Essays on Education in the Early Republic* (Cambridge, Mass, 1965).

A rich historical literature deals with the experience of colonial children and their parents. Secondary sources that I have found valuable include the following: David Hackett Fischer, *Albion's Seed: Four British Folkways in America* (New York, 1989); Edmund S. Morgan, *The Puritan Family: Religion and Domestic Relations in Seventeenth-Century New England* (New York, 1944); John Demos, *A Little Commonwealth: Family Life in Plymouth Colony* (New York, 1970); Philip J. Greven Jr., *Four Generations: Population, Land, and Family in Colonial Andover, Massachusetts* (Ithaca, N.Y., 1970), *Child-rearing Concepts, 1628–1861* (Itasca, Ill., 1973), and *The Protestant Temperament: Patterns of Child-Rearing, Religious Experience, and the Self in Early America* (New York, 1977); Allan Kulikoff, *Tobacco and Slaves: The Development of Southern Cultures in the Chesapeake, 1680–1800* (Chapel Hill, N.C., 1986); Daniel Blake Smith, *Inside the Great House: Planter Family Life in Eighteenth-Century Chesapeake Society* (Ithaca, N.Y., 1980); Jan Lewis, *The Pursuit of Happiness: Family and Values in Jefferson's*

Virginia (Cambridge, 1983); J. William Frost, *The Quaker Family in Colonial America* (New York, 1973); and Barry Levy, *Quakers and the American Family: British Settlement in the Delaware Valley* (New York, 1988).

Richard L. Bushman traces the diffusion of "gentility" in *The Refinement of America: Persons, Houses, Cities* (New York, 1992). Religion in early American life has been discussed by Patricia U. Bonomi in *Under the Cope of Heaven: Religion, Society, and Politics in Colonial America* (New York, 1986) and "Religious Dissent and the Case for American Exceptionalism," in Ronald Hoffman and Peter J. Albert, eds., *Religion in a Revolutionary Age* (Charlottesville, Va., 1994): 31–51; by Jon Butler in *Awash in a Sea of Faith: Christianizing the American People* (Cambridge, Mass., 1990); by Norman Fiering in *Jonathan Edwards's Moral Thought and Its British Context* (Chapel Hill, N.C., 1981); by Nathan O. Hatch in *The Democratization of American Christianity* (New Haven, Conn., 1989); and by Henry F. May in *The Enlightenment in America* (New York, 1976) and *The Divided Heart: Essays on Protestantism and the Enlightenment in America* (New York, 1991).

My interpretation of the American Revolution relies heavily on sources such as Jay Fligelman, *Prodigals & Pilgrims: The American revolution against patriarchal authority, 1750–1800* (Cambridge, 1982); J.G.A. Pocock, *The Machiavellian Moment: Florentine Political Thought and the Atlantic Republican Tradition* (Princeton, N.J., 1975); Garry Wills, *Inventing America: Jefferson's Declaration of Independence* (New York, 1978); Gordon Wood, *The Creation of the American Republic, 1776–1787* (Chapel Hill, N.C., 1969) and *The Radicalism of the American Revolution* (New York, 1992); and J.C.D. Clark, *The Language of Liberty, 1660–1832: Political discourse and social dynamics in the Anglo-American world* (Cambridge, 1994).

As I sought to understand not only child-rearing but childhood—the actual experience of children themselves—I turned to letters and diaries in several repositories around the nation. The best account of the health of an early American family has been left by Elizabeth Drinker of Philadelphia. Her "Diary," covering the years 1759 to 1807, is in the Historical Society of Pennsylvania and has been edited by Elaine Forman Crane, *The Diary of Elizabeth Drinker* 3 vols. (Boston, 1990). Manuscripts in that archive include Sarah Logan Fisher, "Diary, 1776–1795," Rebecca Guest, "Diary, 1800–1810," and Mary Wistar, "Religious Diary for her Children, 1817–1818." Nancy Shippen Livingston's journal has been edited by Ethel Armes, *Nancy Shippen, Her Journal Book* (Philadelphia, 1935).

The American Antiquarian Society Library in Worcester, Massachusetts, has an excellent collection of women's diaries, available on microfilm as "American Women's Diaries: New England" and including the letters and "Diary, 1800–1801" of Louisa Adams Park. The AAS is one of few archives in which sources written by children have been catalogued separately, including Louisa Jane Trumbell's "L.J. Trumbell's Book," William Hoppin's

"Diary," Sally Ripley's "Journal," and David Clapp's "Diary." Manuscript letters of Margaret Izard Manigault can be found in the Manigault Family Papers at the South Caroliniana Library in Columbia, South Carolina. *Memoirs of the Life of Martha Laurens Ramsay* (Philadelphia, 1811) was complied by her husband, David Ramsay, M.D. And material on Abigail Adams can be found in L.H. Butterfield, et. al., eds., *The Adams Family Correspondence* 4 vols. (Cambridge, Mass., 1963–1973), and Edith B. Gelles, *Portia: The World of Abigail Adams* (Bloomington, Ind., 1992).

Mary Palmer Tyler published her child-rearing advice as *The Maternal Physician: A Treatise on the Nurture and Management of Infants from Birth until Two Years Old, Being the Result of Sixteen Years Experience in the Nursery, By an American Matron* (New York, 1811). Material about her life is available in Helen Tyler Brown and Frederick Tupper, eds., *Grandmother Tyler's Book: The Recollections of Mary Palmer Tyler (Mrs. Royall Tyler) 1775–1866*; correspondence in the Vermont Historical Society, Montpelier, and in Marilyn S. Blackwell, "The Republican Vision of Mary Palmer Tyler," *Journal of the Early Republic* 12 (Spring, 1992): 11–35, as well as "Love and Duty: Mary Palmer Tyler and Republican Childrearing" (M.A. thesis, University of Vermont, 1990).

Although secondary sources on the evolution of the maternal role in the early republic abound, I find particularly valuable the work of Linda K. Kerber, *Women of the Republic: Intellect & Ideology in Revolutionary America* (Chapel Hill, N.C., 1980); Jan Lewis, "The Republican Wife: Virtue and Seduction in the Early Republic," *The William and Mary Quarterly* 3rd ser., 44, 4 (October, 1987); and Nancy F. Cott, *The Bonds of Womanhood: "Woman's Sphere" in New England, 1780–1835* (New Haven, Conn., 1977). Laurel Thatcher Ulrich's *A Midwife's Tale: The Life of Martha Ballard, Based on her Diary, 1785–1812* (New York, 1990) is a valuable source on ordinary rural Americans, as is Jack Larkin's *The Reshaping of Everyday Life, 1790–1840* (New York, 1988) and Robert V. Wells' *Revolutions in Americans' Lives: A Demographic Perspective on the History of Americans, Their Families, and Their Society* (Westport, Conn., 1982). Information on material culture is contained in Karin Calvert, *Children in the House: The Material Culture of Early Childhood, 1600–1900* (Boston, 1992) and in articles in Robert Blair St. George, ed., *Material Life in America, 1600–1860* (Boston, 1988).

I came to understand the impact of Dr. Benjamin Rush's "American Revolution" in medicine through his own words in sources such as *An Account of the Bilious Remitting Yellow Fever as It Appeared in the City of Philadelphia, 1793* (Philadelphia, 1794); L.H. Butterfield, ed., *Letters of Benjamin Rush, Volume II: 1793–1813* (Princeton, N.J., 1951); George W. Corner, ed., *The Autobiography of Benjamin Rush, His "Travels Through Life" Together with His Commonplace Book for 1789–1813* (Princeton, N.J., 1948); Benjamin Rush, *Essays, Literary, Moral and Philosophical* (Philadelphia, 1806); and

Dagobert D. Runes, ed., *The Selected Writings of Benjamin Rush* (New York, 1947). Rush's treatment of yellow fever in 1793 was criticized by Dr. William Currie in *An Impartial Review of That Part of Dr. Rush's Late Publication Entitled An Account of the Bilious Yellow Fever as It Appeared in the City of Philadelphia, 1793* (Philadelphia, 1794) and by Dr. Isaac Cathrall in *A Medical Sketch of the Synochus Maligna or Malignant Yellow Fever, as It Appeared in the City of Philadelphia* (Philadelphia, 1796). Helpful secondary sources are Richard Harrison Shryock, *The Development of Modern Medicine, An Interpretation of the Social and Scientific Factors Involved* (London, 1948) and *Medicine and Society in America, 1660–1860* (New York, 1960); Donald J. D'Elia, "Dr. Benjamin Rush and the American Medical Revolution," *Proceedings of the American Philosophical Society* 110, 4 (August 23, 1966): 227–234; and Melvin Yazawa, *From Colonies to Commonwealth: Familial Ideology and the Beginnings of the American Republic* (Baltimore, 1985).

To ascertain the influence of Rush's therapy on the treatment of children, I read dissertations written by his students at the University of Pennsylvania medical school—for example, Charles Caldwell, *An Attempt to Establish the Original Sameness of Three Phenomena of Fever, Principally Confined to Infants and Children* (Philadelphia, 1796); Robert G.W. Davidson, *An Inaugural Dissertation of the Suffocatio Stridula or Croup* (Philadelphia, 1794); and Henry Disbourgh, *Inaugural Dissertation on Cholera Infantum* (Philadelphia, 1798). Bills of mortality and entries on medical practice can be found in early professional journals such as *The Eclectic Repertory and Analytical Review, Medical and Philosophical* vols. 1–11 (Philadelphia, 1811 through 1821) and *The Philadelphia Journal of the Medical and Physical Sciences* vols. 1–7 (Philadelphia, 1820 through 1827), which became the *American Journal of the Medical Sciences* in 1828. Susan E. Klepp analyzes fertility and mortality in *Philadelphia in Transition: A Demographic History of the City and Its Occupational Groups, 1720–1830* (New York, 1989).

Students of Rush who proclaimed his "American Revolution in medicine" include James Mease, M.D., *The Picture of Philadelphia, Giving an Account of its Origin, Increase, and Improvements in Arts, Sciences, Manufactures, Commerce and Revenue with a Compendious View of its Societies, Literary, Benevolent, Patriotic, and Religious* (Philadelphia, 1811); Nathaniel Chapman, M.D., author of "Thoughts on the Pathology and Treatment of Cynanche Trachealis, or Croup," and editor of *The Philadelphia Journal of the Medical and Physical Sciences* 1 (1820), which became *The American Journal of the Medical Sciences* in 1828; and William Potts Dewees, M.D., *Treatise of the Physical and Medical Treatment of Children* (Philadelphia, 1825), whose advice was transmitted to western states by John Eberle, M.D., in *Treatise on the Diseases and Physical Education of Children* (Cincinnati, 1833).

Twentieth-century authors who discuss the religious experience of children are Robert Coles, *The Spiritual Life of Children* (Boston, 1990) and

James W. Fowler, *Stages of Faith: The Psychology of Human Development and the Quest for Meaning* (San Francisco, 1981). I found the typescript description of a Peter Cartwright camp meeting in the McLean County Historical Society in Bloomington, Illinois. Primary sources on the Sunday school movement are in the Presbyterian Historical Society in Philadelphia, including "Minutes of the Board of Visitors, First Day Society, 1791–1835" and "Minutes of the First Sabbath School in Philadelphia, October, 1811 to January, 1812," kept by the Rev. Robert May. Annual reports of the Philadelphia Sunday and Adult School Union and American Sunday School Union, and the latter's Committee of Publications' "Minutes" and "Commonplace Book, 1826–32," are also in that archive.

The collection of Sunday School Union literature at Philadelphia's Free Library contains numerous tracts, such as *Poor Sarah, or Religion Exemplified in the Life of an Indian Woman* (Philadelphia, 1822); *Memoir of Margaret Ann Crutchfield, the First Convert from the Cherokee Nation, at the Missionary Settlement of the United Brethren, Called Spring Place* (Philadelphia, 1822); *The Dutiful Servant; or the Conversion of Black Will and the Reformation of the Neighborhood* (Philadelphia, 1822); Leigh Richmond's *Little Jane, the Young Cottager* (Philadelphia, 1822) and *The Dairyman's Daughter* (Philadelphia, 1819); and The Rev. Basil Wood's *A Memoir of Bowyer Smith, A Pious Child* (Philadelphia, 1820); as well as teachers' manuals by J.A. James, *The Sunday School Teacher's Guide* (Philadelphia, n.d.) and W.F. Lloyd, *The Teacher's Manual; or Hints to a Teacher on Being Appointed to the Charge of a Sunday-School Class* (Philadelphia, 1825). London Sunday School Union books displaying penciled annotations by members of the American Sunday School Union Committee of Publications are *Early Piety* (Philadelphia, 1827) and *Winter Evenings' Conversations between a Father and his Children* (Philadelphia, 1826). *The Union Primer or First Book for Children, Compiled for the American Sunday School Union and Fitted for the Use of Schools in the United States* (Philadelphia, 1826); *Election Day* (Philadelphia, 1826); and Anna Reed, *Life of George Washington* (Philadelphia, 1829) are also in that collection. Secondary sources on the Sunday schools are Edwin Wilbur Rice, *The Sunday School Movement, 1780–1917, and the American Sunday School Union* (Philadelphia, 1917), and the recent work by Anne M. Boylan, *Sunday School: The Formation of an American Institution, 1790–1880* (New Haven, Conn., 1988).

Members of the Beecher family, so instrumental in the evolution of nineteenth-century American culture, should be encountered through their own words: *The Autobiography of Lyman Beecher* 2 vols. (Cambridge, Mass., 1961); Catherine Beecher, *A Treatise on Domestic Economy* (Boston, 1841); and novels by Harriet Beecher Stowe, *Uncle Tom's Cabin, or Life Among the Lowly* (1852) and *The Minister's Wooing* (1857); *Oldtown Folks* (1869); and *Poganuc People* (1878), which describe her New England childhood. Horace

Bushnell published *Views of Christian Nurture* (Hartford, Conn.) in 1847. Secondary works include Milton Rugoff, *The Beechers: An American Family in the Nineteenth Century* (New York, 1981); Kathryn Kish Sklar, *Catherine Beecher: A Study in American Domesticity* (New York, 1977); Joan D. Hedrick, *Harriet Beecher Stowe, a life* (New York, 1994); and the introduction to *Oldtown Folks* by Henry F. May, reprinted in *The Divided Heart: Essays on Protestantism and the Enlightenment in America* (New York, 1991).

I discovered Sarah Pierce's Litchfield Female Academy when I read Catherine Van Schaak's manuscript "Journal, 1809" at the New York Historical Society. Additional manuscript sources in that archive are James Riker Jr., "Journal . . ." and Mary Lorrain Peters, "Diary." The Litchfield Historical Society in Connecticut holds journals and commonplace books required from Sarah Pierce's students as well as ornamental arts they produced. Emily Noyes Vanderpoel collected some of this material in *More Chronicles of a Pioneer School: From 1792 to 1833* (New York, 1927), and Lynne Templeton Brickley has written "Sarah Pierce's Litchfield Female Academy, 1792 to 1833" (Ph.D. dissertation, Harvard University, 1985) and "Sarah Pierce's Litchfield Academy," in *To Ornament Their Minds: Sarah Pierce's Litchfield Female Academy, 1792–1833* (Litchfield, Conn., 1993).

A rich literature has explored the history of education in the United States. Secondary works on public schools that I found useful were Carl F. Kaestle, *Pillars of the Republic: Common Schools and American Society, 1780–1860* (New York, 1983), *The Evolution of an Urban School System: New York City, 1750–1850* (Cambridge, Mass., 1980), and, with Maris A. Vinovskis, *Education and Social Change in Nineteenth-Century Massachusetts* (Cambridge, Mass., 1980). Stanley K. Schultz has written *The Culture Factory: Boston Public Schools, 1789–1860* (New York, 1973), and Jonathan Messerli the biography *Horace Mann* (New York, 1972). The influence of Pestalozzi has been described by Robert B. Downs in *Heinrich Pestalozzi: Father of Modern Pedagogy* (Boston, 1975), although the educator's methods are best described in his own words: *How Gertrude Teaches Her Children: An Attempt to Help Mothers to Teach their Own Children and An Account of the Method*, translated by Lucy E. Holland and Francis C. Turner (London, 1915). Edgar W. Knight has edited American *Reports on European Education* (New York, 1930).

Joseph Lancaster's monitorial method should also be understood by reading his own work, *Improvements in Education as it Respects the Industrious Classes of the Community* (London, 1806). Older but still valuable works are those of Charles Calvert Ellis, "Lancaster Schools in Philadelphia" (Ph.D. dissertation, University of Pennsylvania, 1907), and James Pyle Wickersham, *A History of Education in Pennsylvania, Private and Public, Elementary and High from the time The Swedes settled on the Delaware to the Present Day*

(Lancaster, Penn., 1886). Priscilla Ferguson Clement analyzes economic context in "The Philadelphia Welfare Crisis of the 1820s," *Pennsylvania Magazine of History and Biography* 105, 2 (April, 1981) and *Welfare and the Poor in the Nineteenth-Century City: Philadelphia, 1800–1854* (Cranbury, N.J., 1985). Carl F. Kaestle provides an overview in *Joseph Lancaster and the Monitorial School Movement* (New York, 1973).

A translated typescript of the "Moravian Mission Diaries" is in the Georgia Department of Archives and History in Atlanta. William G. McLoughlin has analyzed Cherokee cultural change in *Cherokee Renascence in the New Republic* (Princeton, N.J., 1986). The living museum at the site of the Moravian community in Salem, North Carolina, illustrates that group's artifacts and unique lifestyle, as does *A Laudable Example for Others: The Moravians and their Town of Salem* (Winston-Salem, N.C., n.d.). Daniel B. Thorp provides a scholarly work, *The Moravian Community in Colonial North Carolina: Pluralism on the Southern Frontier* (Knoxville, Tenn., 1989).

A first-rate collection of historical works is beginning to fill in the contours of cultural and economic patterns of yeoman households, North and South. Allan Kulikoff provides an overview in *The Agrarian Origins of American Capitalism* (Charlottesville, Va., 1992). Christopher Clark delineates the process of economic transformation in the rural Northeast in *The Roots of Rural Capitalism, Western Massachusetts, 1780–1860* (Ithaca, New York, 1990), and John Mack Faragher describes later development in the Midwest in *Sugar Creek: Life on the Illinois Prairie* (New Haven, Conn., 1986). South Carolina has been studied by Rachel N. Klein, *Unification of a Slave State: The Rise of the Planter Class in the Southern Carolina Backcountry, 1760–1808* (Chapel Hill, N.C., 1990), and Stephanie McCurry, *Masters of Small Worlds: Yeoman Households, Gender Relations, and the Political Culture of the Antebellum South Carolina Low Country* (New York, 1995). Charles C. Bolton analyzes the position of landless Southern whites in *Poor Whites of the Antebellum South: Tenants and Laborers in Central North Carolina and Northeast Mississippi* (Durham, N.C., 1994), while Stephen Hahn argues that yeomen households in the South were not transformed by market forces until after the Civil War in *The Roots of Southern Populism: Yeoman Farmers and the Transformation of the Georgia Upcountry, 1850–1890* (New York, 1983).

Diaries and autobiographies trace the contributions of children to household strategies and economic change. The "Diaries" of Nahum Jones, "Journal" of Samuel Parris, and "Diary" of David Clapp are in the American Antiquarian Society Library. Daniel Drake's letters to his children are reprinted in Emmet Field Horine, M.D., ed., *Pioneer Life in Kentucky, 1785–1800* (New York, 1948); Horace Greeley's childhood is described in *Recollections of a Busy Life* (New York, 1868); and Stephen Allen's experience is related in John C. Thomas, "Memoirs of Stephen Allen," a typescript in the New York Historical Society.

Historical literature analyzing the penetration of the trades by capitalism and early stages of industrialization includes Sharon Salinger, "Artisans, Journeymen, and the Transformation of Labor in Late Eighteenth-Century Philadelphia," *The William and Mary Quarterly*, 3rd ser., vol. 40, no. 1 (January, 1983); Sean Wilentz, *Chants Democratic: New York City & the Rise of the American Working Class, 1788–1850* (New York, 1984); and Christine Stansell, *City of Women: Sex and Class in New York, 1789–1860* (Urbana, Ill., 1987). Alan Dawley analyzes change in shoemaking in *Class and Community: The Industrial Revolution in Lynn* (Cambridge, Mass., 1976). W.J. Rorabaugh describes changing patterns of apprenticeship in *The Craft Apprentice: From Franklin to the Machine Age in America* (New York, 1986), and Gary B. Nash and Jean R. Soderlund discuss the indenture of black children in *Freedom by Degrees: Emancipation in Pennsylvania and its Aftermath* (New York, 1991). Thomas Dublin analyzes shifts in the work force in the Lowell mills in *Women and Work: The Transformation of Work and Community in Lowell, Massachusetts, 1826–1860* (New York, 1979), and Lucy Larcom in *A New England Girlhood* (Boston, 1889) and Harriet Hanson Robinson in *Loom and Spindle* (Boston, 1898) describe work they did as children. Primary materials dealing with children's work are contained in Robert Bremner, ed., *Children and Youth in America: A Documentary History* 3 vols. (Cambridge, Mass., 1970). The most recent interpretation of early nineteenth-century economic change is Charles Sellers, *The Market Revolution: Jacksonian America, 1815–1846* (New York, 1991), supplemented by Melvyn Stokes and Stephen Conway, eds., *The Market Revolution in America: Social Political, and Religious Expressions, 1800–1880* (Charlottesville, Va., 1996).

I encountered the "Minutes" and "Book of Indentures" kept by Philadelphia's Female Orphan Society, as well as the "Minutes" of the Board of Managers of the Philadelphia House of Refuge, at the Historical Society of Pennsylvania. Michael Meranze's Ph.D. dissertation, "Public Punishments, Reformative Incarceration, and Authority in Philadelphia, 1750–1835" (University of California, Berkeley, 1985) will soon be incorporated into a book. Juvenile delinquency has been discussed by Joseph M. Hawes, *Children in Urban Society: Juvenile Delinquency in Nineteenth-century America* (New York, 1971), and Steven L. Schlossman, *Love & the American Delinquent: The Theory and Practice of "Progressive" Juvenile Justice, 1825–1920* (Chicago, 1977). Michael Grossberg analyzes legal change affecting children in *Governing the Hearth: Law and the Family in Nineteenth-Century America* (Chapel Hill, N.C., 1985), and Joseph M. Hawes covers *The Children's Rights Movement: A History of Advocacy and Protection* (New York, 1991). Charles Loring Brace, founder of the Children's Aid Society, should be encountered in his own work, *The Dangerous Classes of New York and Twenty Years Work Among Them* (New York, 1872), supplemented by *The Life of Charles Loring Brace*, edited by his daughter (London, 1894).

Secondary sources on Irish immigration include the following: Kerby A. Miller, *Emigrants and Exiles: Ireland and the Irish Exodus to North America* (New York, 1985); Dennis Clark, *The Irish in Philadelphia: Ten Generations of Urban Experience* (Philadelphia, 1973); Oscar Handlin, *Boston's Immigrants, 1790–1865* (Cambridge, Mass., 1941); Brian C. Mitchell, *The Paddy Camps: The Irish of Lowell, 1821–61* (Urbana, Ill., 1988); and Hasia R. Diner, *Erin's Daughters in America: Irish Immigrant Women in the Nineteenth Century* (Baltimore, 1983). Letters written by German immigrants have been edited by Walter D. Kamphoefner, Wolfgang Helbich, and Ulrike Sommer, and translated by Susan Carter Vogel in *News from the Land of Freedom: German Immigrants Write Home* (Ithaca, N.Y., 1991). Another useful work is Bruce Levine, *The Spirit of 1848: German Immigrants, Labor Conflict, and the Coming of the Civil War* (Urbana, Ill., 1992).

A rich secondary literature explores the experience of slavery. Works I have consulted include the following: John W. Blassingame, *The Slave Community: Plantation Life in the Antebellum South* (New York, 1972); Elizabeth Fox-Genovese, *Within the Plantation Household: Black and White Women of the Old South* (Chapel Hill, N.C., 1988); Eugene D. Genovese, *Roll, Jordan Roll: The World the Slaves Made* (New York, 1972); Herbert G. Gutman, *The Black Family in Slavery & Freedom, 1750–1925* (New York, 1976); Jacqueline Jones, *Labor of Love, Labor of Sorrow: Black Women, Work and the Family from Slavery to the Present* (New York, 1985); Allan Kulikoff, *Tobacco and Slaves: The Development of Southern Cultures in the Chesapeake, 1680–1800* (Chapel Hill, N.C., 1986); Ann Patton Malone, *Sweet Chariot: Slave Family & Household Structure in Nineteenth-Century Louisiana* (Chapel Hill, N.C., 1992); Kenneth M. Stampp, *The Peculiar Institution: Slavery in the Ante-Bellum South* (New York, 1956); and Deborah Gray White, *Arn't I A Woman? Female Slaves in the Plantation South* (New York, 1985). I have relied upon the discussion of the domestic slave trade by Steven Deyle in "The Irony of Liberty: Origins of the Domestic Slave Trade," *Journal of the Early Republic*, 12, 1 (Spring, 1992) and " 'By farr the most profitable trade': Slave Trading in British Colonial North America," *Slavery & Abolition* 10, 2 (September, 1989); and by Allan Kulikoff in "Uprooted Peoples: The Political Economy of Slave Migration, 1780–1840" in *The Agrarian Origins of American Capitalism* (Charlottesville, Va., 1992). Michael Tadman has provided *Speculators and Slaves: Masters, Traders, and Slaves in the Old South* (Madison, Wis., 1989).

Insightful studies discussing slavery in the Chesapeake region are those of Rhys Isaac, *The Transformation of Virginia, 1740–1790* (Chapel Hill, N.C., 1982); Winthrop D. Jordan, *White Over Black: American Attitudes Toward the Negro, 1550–1812* (Chapel Hill, 1968); and Gerald W. (Michael) Mullin, *Flight and Rebellion: Slave Resistance in Eighteenth-Century Virginia* (New York, 1972) and *Africa in America: Slave Acculturation and Resistance in the American South and the British Caribbean, 1736–1800* (Urbana, Ill., 1992).

Frederick Douglass is best encountered through his eloquent autobiography, *My Bondage and My Freedom* (New York, 1855), supplemented by William S. McFeely, *Frederick Douglass* (New York, 1991).

Low Country slavery is described by Charles Joyner, *Down by the Riverside: A South Carolina Slave Community* (Urbana, Ill., 1984); Margaret Washington Creel, *"A Peculiar People": Slave Religion and Community-Culture Among the Gullahs* (New York, 1988); Daniel C. Littlefield, *Rice and Slaves: Ethnicity and the Slave Trade in Colonial South Carolina* (Urbana, Ill., 1981); and Peter N. Wood, *Black Majority: Negroes in Colonial South Carolina from 1670 through the Stono Rebellion* (New York, 1974). The world of Low Country planters is revealed in the "Diary" of Thomas Chaplin, edited by Theodore Rosengarten, *Tombee: Portrait of a Cotton Planter* (New York, 1986); the "Diaries" of James Henry Hammond, edited by Carol Bleser, *Secret and Sacred: The Diaries of James Henry Hammond, a Southern Slaveholder* (New York, 1988), supplemented by Drew Gilpin Faust, *James Henry Hammond and the Old South: A Design for Mastery* (Baton Rouge, La., 1982); the letters of Fanny Kemble edited by John A. Scott, *Journal of a Residence on a Georgian Plantation in 1838–1839* (Athens, Ga., 1984); and the archaeological work of James L. Michie, *Richmond Hill Plantation, 1810–1868: The Discovery of Antebellum Life on a Waccamaw Rice Plantation* (Spartenburg, S.C., 1990). Sally McMillen discusses health and mortality in *Motherhood in the Old South* (Baton Rouge, La., 1990), and Joan E. Cashin explores family change through migration to the Southwest in *A Family Venture: Men and Women on the Southern Frontier* (Baltimore, 1991).

Manuscript letters and diaries of planter families are in the Southern Historical Collection, University of North Carolina Library, Chapel Hill. Typescript interviews with ex-slaves conducted through the Federal Writers Project in the 1930s can also be found in that archive. The use of interviews in the 1930s to re-create the experience of antebellum slavery raises many issues—faulty memory, tendency for the ex-slave to conceal or embellish when confronted with a white interviewer, and racism embedded in some descriptions. Yet material recording the voices of the enslaved is very rare. Individuals alive in the 1930s were children in the 1840s and 1850s, and their interviews contain fresh and vivid descriptions of childhood. The interviews are supplemented with nineteenth-century autobiographies of slaves. In order to reflect the primary source accurately, I decided not to change efforts to preserve dialect through various spellings. Accounts by ex-slaves have been edited and published by Charles L. Perdue, Jr., Thomas E. Barden, and Robert K. Phillips, *Weevils in the Wheat: Interviews with Virginia Ex-Slaves* (Bloomington, Ind., 1976); Belinda Hurmence, *My Folks Don't Want Me to Talk About Slavery* (Winston-Salem, N.C., 1984) and *Before Freedom: When I Just Can Remember* (Winston-Salem, N.C., 1989); and James Mellon, *Bullwhip Days, The Slaves Remember: An Oral History* (New York, 1988).

"Hager, her own book," the story of the mulatto children Eliza and Peter, is in the Vanderhorst Family Papers at the South Carolina Historical Society in Charleston. Michael P. Johnson and James L. Roark have edited and published materials produced by that city's mulatto community in *No Chariot Let Down: Charleston's Free People of Color on the Eve of the Civil War* (New York, 1984). Papers of Caroline Howard Gilman are also in the South Carolina Historical Society. Benevolent activity in Charleston is described by Barbara L. Bellows, *Benevolence Among Slaveholders: Assisting the Poor in Charleston, 1670–1860* (Baton Rouge, La., 1993), and Alan Keith-Lucas, *A Legacy of Caring: The Charleston Orphan House* (Charleston, S.C., 1991). Layton Wayne Jordan discusses that city's public school system in "Education for Community: G.G. Memminger and the Origination of Common Schools in Ante-bellum Charleston," *South Carolina Historical Magazine* 83, 1 (April, 1982).

As I searched for voices of antebellum children throughout the South, I found their diaries or journals were few and far between. Nicholas A. Destrehan's "Memoirs" in his "Letter Book" are in the Historic New Orleans Collection. Mary Susan Ker's "Journal" is in the Ker Family Papers in the Louisiana and Lower Mississippi Valley Collection at Louisiana State University in Baton Rouge. Eliza L. Magruder's "Diary" and the typescript of the "Anonymous Diary" by a northern governess are in the collection at LSU. I found the "Reminiscence Book" of James Monroe Adams at the Georgia Department of Archives & History in Atlanta, and Elmina Foster Wilson's "Reminiscences" in the Southern Historical Collection at Chapel Hill. Yet the sleuthing continues. Our task will be to collect and catalog these voices of children and adults who recorded their childhood years, in order to fully comprehend the important role played by children in the ongoing story of American life.

Index

The Author

Jacqueline S. Reinier has been a professor of history for over two decades and is currently at California State University, Sacramento. She holds a B.A. from the University of Virginia and an M.A. and a Ph.D. from the University of California, Berkeley. She is the author of several aricles on women's history and the history of the family.